THE 'NEW' PUBLIC BENEFIT REQUIREMENT: MAKING SENSE OF CHARITY LAW?

This book examines the 'public benefit requirement', which provides that a charity's purposes must be for the public benefit. This requirement was given statutory force by the Charities Act 2006, which also provided that 'public benefit' is to be construed in accordance with existing case law and not presumed. The author examines guidance published by the Charity Commission in 2008 and 2013 and measures its accuracy against principles extrapolated from case law, with a focus on fee-charging charities, and independent schools in particular. She also considers the implementation of the Charity Commission's public benefit assessments of independent schools during 2008–10. The book offers a comparative study of the law relating to public benefit in Scotland and presents an analysis of the decision of the Upper Tribunal (Tax and Chancery) in proceedings brought by the Independent Schools Council and Attorney General in 2011. It also considers subsequent reviews of the 2006 Act by Lord Hodgson and the Public Administration Select Committee and the Government's response to those reviews in September 2013.

The fact that the law automatically bestows certain privileges on charities, including tax exemptions, means that the charitable status of fee-paying schools has proved particularly contentious and was described by Lord Campbell-Savours as making 'an absolute nonsense' of charity law. Here, the author asks whether the public benefit requirement, as enacted and interpreted, has succeeded in bringing any sense to our law of charity in recent years.

The 'New' Public Benefit Requirement

Making Sense of Charity Law?

Mary Synge

· HART ·
PUBLISHING
OXFORD AND PORTLAND, OREGON
2017

Hart Publishing
An imprint of Bloomsbury Publishing Plc

Hart Publishing Ltd
Kemp House
Chawley Park
Cumnor Hill
Oxford OX2 9PH
UK

Bloomsbury Publishing Plc
50 Bedford Square
London
WC1B 3DP
UK

www.hartpub.co.uk
www.bloomsbury.com

Published in North America (US and Canada) by
Hart Publishing
c/o International Specialized Book Services
920 NE 58th Avenue, Suite 300
Portland, OR 97213-3786
USA

www.isbs.com

First published in hardback, 2015
Paperback edition, 2017

British Library Cataloguing-in-Publication Data
A catalogue record for this book is available from the British Library.

ISBN: PB: 978-1-50991-773-0
HB: 978-1-84946-593-9

Typeset by Compuscript Ltd, Shannon
Printed and bound in Great Britain by
Lightning Source UK Ltd

For Mum and Dad

FOREWORD

I am happy to hail this important fresh extended study of the new public benefit requirement introduced by the Charities Act 2006 and now absorbed into the consolidating Charities Act 2011.

Mary Synge had already written in 2012 an illuminating Note in the *Modern Law Review* which had caught my eye and its perceptive argumentation recommended itself to me and was clearly a herald of a more portentous work. This was her preliminary offering in the inquest on the Independent Schools Council case in the Upper Tribunal (Tax and Chancery) to which Professor Peter Luxton has to date been the most substantial contributor. The contents of the present monograph represent the outcome of a skilful and detailed analysis of what, *omnium consensu*, is a pretty sorry tale. It therefore bears careful comparison with the theoretical structure of Jonathan Garton's textbook, *Public Benefit in Charity Law* (Oxford University Press, 2013) and Matthew Harding's very recent thoughtfully philosophical *Charity Law and the Liberal State* (Cambridge University Press, 2014). It alludes critically to the decisions of the Upper Tribunal concerning poverty and the charging of fees and effectively assails the relevance of fee-charging and of the relief of poverty in the law of charities and the social benefit stance taken by the Charity Commission. The compromised Preston Down Trust case is mentioned but, perhaps understandably, left to be further dealt with in a later study.

The work evidences a pleasing structure and attention to principle. There is a useful comparison with the Scottish experience and outline of the developments in other jurisdictions, and an important update on developments at policymaking level. But at the very heart of this study is the juxtaposition of a proper legal narrative on the one hand and the cursory impressionistic analysis vouchsafed by the then Policy Division of the Charity Commission in its compilation of the 2008 guidance and its superseded document 'Public Character of Charity' on the other. As such it provides a salutary order and discipline to unravelling the tangled conclusions of the ISC case in chapter eight and the continuation of the debate on the fitness for purpose of the new public benefit requirement and of the bodies charged to supervise this muddled and ill-starred concept and its unprincipled interpretation. The analysis contained in chapters two to six is rigorous, reflective and searching. It exposes with insight substantial flaws in the original conception of the requirement and in the execution by the Commission of the mandate consigned to it, perhaps unfairly, by Parliament. Dr Synge does not shrink from classifying the Commission's analysis as poor and inadequate, making good her case by specific scholarly and punctilious reference to the case law.

For all that, the augurs for the future are not particularly promising, to judge by the hedging, qualified responses from the Coalition Government to the self-denying ruminations of Lord Hodgson's Review and the wider ranging and more severe criticisms deployed in the PASC Report, all of which are given appropriate coverage in chapter nine under the heading 'More Recent Developments'. The General Election in May 2015 is a further generator of uncertainty. The outcome of the work of the Law Commission is likewise uncertain.

The interstices of the paraded reasoning of the Commission are set out with accuracy and acuity in this impressive book. The criticisms directed by the author at that reasoning are perceptive and soundly backed by authority. They merit in turn, I venture to suggest, anxious and careful reading, and, where in point and appropriate, adoption or at the very least consideration, by charity law textbook or article writers, by solicitors making submissions to the Charity Commission or by counsel advising clients or arguing thereafter before the Upper Tribunal and higher.

Hubert Picarda QC
Top Floor North
9 Old Square
Lincoln's Inn
29 December 2014

ACKNOWLEDGEMENTS

This book began its life as a PhD thesis (University of Bristol, 2012) and, for that reason I should like to acknowledge, with thanks, the contributions of my supervisors, Professor Roger Kerridge and Dr Gwen Seabourne. I should also like to thank the examiners, Professor Peter Luxton and Professor Simon Baughen, whose comments persuaded me that I should endeavour to publish my work. All mistakes are mine, nonetheless.

I am also greatly honoured that this book carries a foreword by Hubert Picarda QC, widely recognised as the leading charity lawyer in the jurisdiction, and I wish to thank him for undertaking this task.

CONTENTS

Charity law is being made an absolute nonsense of by this provision in our law… Why cannot we deal with it by putting it in a Finance Bill, bringing it before Parliament and letting Parliament decide on these matters? … why cannot this matter be taken out of this whole sector, thus bringing the law back into repute? … For once, let us sort it out.

Lord Campbell-Savours

[T]he question for us is whether we have the spine to confront an unfairness and whether we dare to cut any track towards more equality and greater diversity and opportunity. You cannot do that unless you confront the taxation advantage of charities for educational purposes in public schools.

Lord Wedderburn

House of Lords
9 February 2005

1

Introduction

It has been an interesting decade for charity law.

A major piece of legislative reform was introduced in 2004 and then lambasted in 2013 as 'critically flawed' and 'an administrative and financial disaster' by the Public Administration Select Committee.[1] A newly formed Charity Commission (the Commission) came into existence in 2008 and was then castigated as 'not fit for purpose' in 2014 by the Chair of the Public Accounts Committee.[2] Guidance on the public benefit requirement was published by the Commission in 2008 and then completely replaced in 2013 after the Upper Tribunal (Tax and Chancery) (the Tribunal) subjected it to criticism and called it 'wrong' in places.[3] The Tribunal, for its part, had the opportunity to bring clarity and order to the disarray which had marked the early part of the new millennium, but instead delivered a judgment which has been widely criticised for its unfathomability and lack of a sound legal base.[4] And, although not normally a high profile subject, charity law aroused strong public opinion and found itself in the headlines: 'Private schools are victims of 'medieval' attack',[5] 'Private schools win £100m charity tax relief case'[6] and 'Churches battle "anti-Christian" charity chiefs',[7] to name but a few.

The reform in question was the new statutory definition of charity in the Charities Act 2006 (the 2006 Act), which required a charitable institution's purposes to be 'for the public benefit'.[8] Whilst not a new requirement in itself, its statutory

[1] *The role of the Charity Commission and 'public benefit': Post-legislative Scrutiny of the Charities Act 2006*, Third Report of Session 2013–14 (TSO, June 2013) paras 92 and 86 respectively.

[2] Margaret Hodge MP (Statement, 5 February 2014): www.parliament.uk/business/committees/committees-a-z/commons-select/public-accounts-committee/news/publication-of-report-tax-reliefs-on-charitable-donations.

[3] *R (Independent Schools Council) v Charity Commission* [2011] UKUT 421 (TCC), [2012] Ch 214 [235].

[4] eg, P Luxton, 'Opening Pandora's Box: The Upper Tribunal's Decision on Public Benefit and Independent Schools' (2012–13) 15 *Charity Law & Practice Review* 27; M Synge, '*Independent Schools Council v Charity Commission*' (2012) 75 *MLR* 624; and see ch 8.

[5] *The Telegraph*, 5 October 2009.

[6] *The Guardian*, 14 October 2011. For a review of the media coverage in respect of independent schools, see 'The Public Benefit Issue: A Media Analysis 2008–2012', Independent Schools Council bulletin (undated): www.isc.co.uk/Resources/Independent%20Schools%20Council/Research%20Archive/Bulletin%20Articles/2012/Bulletin29_Media_analysis.pdf.

[7] *The Sunday Times*, 29 July 2012.

[8] 2006 Act, s 2(1)(b).

enactment gave it a prominence which placed it centre stage and provoked widespread debate about its meaning.[9] Few concerned with charity law and the charity sector will be unfamiliar with the developments described in the chapters which follow, but for those who might have lacked sufficient time to question closely their legitimacy or justification in legal terms, it is hoped that this book will be both helpful and thought-provoking. The sympathy which must be felt for charity trustees, who have been bombarded with copious publications from the Commission and two lengthy Tribunal judgments, might also be extended to law lecturers and legal practitioners who must now find a way to articulate and advise upon the public benefit requirement in a way that makes sense. Particularly in the realms of fee-charging charities and religion, this requirement has proved to be something of a hot potato, politically divisive and far-reaching in its impact, yet strangely elusive in definition.

Perhaps we should not be surprised by either the criticisms or the confusion of recent years. The Joint Committee, which was appointed by the House of Lords and the House of Commons to report on the Charities Bill (which later became the 2006 Act), was clearly confused about the very reasons behind the Bill.[10] Reasonably clear was the intention that high-fee charging charities should qualify for charitable status only if they widened access to their services to people who were unable to afford the fees they charged, but rather less clear was, first, whether this represented any change in the law and, second, whether existing charities, most notably perhaps independent schools and private hospitals, were at risk of losing their charitable status. Conflicting messages were coming from the Home Office and the Commission as to what difference the legislation would make,[11] the Government having taken issue with the Commission's suggestion that it would probably not affect independent schools very much. Although the publication of a Concordat went some way towards reconciling these messages on a general level,[12] the lack of clarity which surrounded both the criteria for judging public benefit and the consequences of a charity losing its charitable status was never rectified and the scope for confusion persisted.[13] There was also serious concern over the capacity of the Commission to perform its intended role and about the prospect of incompatibility between the separate jurisdictions of the United Kingdom.[14]

[9] It is only in the sense of this statutory incarnation that the public benefit requirement should properly be considered 'new'.

[10] Joint Committee on the Draft Charities Bill, *The Draft Charities Bill* (2003–04, HL 167-I, HC 660-I) paras 14–22.

[11] Specifically, what difference the purported removal of an alleged presumption of public benefit would make (see text to nn 57–59 below), a dispute which the Joint Committee described as 'nothing short of farcical' (ibid, para 76).

[12] A joint letter from Fiona Mactaggart MP and Geraldine Peacock, Chair of the Charity Commissioners, an extract of which is reproduced in the Report (n 10) para 78.

[13] The non-exclusive criteria for judging public benefit which had been set out in the Concordat never found their way onto the face of the Bill and the Commission (as opposed to the Home Office) was charged with publishing guidance on public benefit, as discussed at various points in this book.

[14] Matters of charity law having been devolved in Scotland and Northern Ireland.

At the same time, questions of law became confused with questions of policy. In the public domain, it was easy to understand attention being diverted to whether independent schools *should* be charitable, rather than whether they *were* charitable as a matter of law, especially since the latter question depended on a technical definition of charity that had been developed by the courts over several centuries and because the automatic legal entitlement of charities to significant tax privileges meant that the impact on the public purse was significant.[15] One might well sympathise with a view that fee-charging schools should only qualify for charitable status, and therefore the tax privileges that go with it, if they offer people who cannot afford their fees adequate opportunities to benefit from the services and activities they provide. Such a view might be morally or politically legitimate, but it is also necessary to ask whether it has a sound basis in law or whether it is, in fact, contrary to law and in need of legislative reform to validate it: that is the question addressed here. It is important to emphasise that the issue is not whether or not one favours independent schools, or private hospitals or religious organisations, or even whether one believes that they should enjoy tax advantages or not: the issue is whether or not they are charitable as a matter of law.

Confusion about the interface between law and policy was not limited to the minds of the general public, however. Indeed, the following chapters will raise questions about law-making processes and the integrity of the law on a much deeper level. Lawyers are familiar with the separation of powers being a fundamental part of the Rule of Law, requiring clearly marked boundaries between the legislative, judicial and executive functions of government.[16] On the face of it, the Legislature legitimately passed an Act of Parliament which expressly preserved case law previously developed by the Judiciary, and the Executive (in the form of the Commission) was charged with applying that law in deciding whether or not to add an institution to the Register of Charities (the Register) or to remove one already registered. The Judiciary was also presented with an opportunity to 'check'[17] the Executive in the judicial review proceedings which challenged the Commission's interpretation of the law.[18] In the detail, however, it will be seen that the boundaries may have been blurred amid signs of a rather less conservative approach, as the Commission's role of explaining and applying the public benefit requirement arguably metamorphosed into one of also defining the term itself. At the same time, it seemed that the normal process of expounding the law by reference to legal precedent and legal principle was being replaced by a nod in the direction of concepts which had rather less rigour and formality: changing 'social and economic circumstances', for example, and the need for organisations to 'earn'

[15] Considered below.

[16] This is something of a simplification of a highly complex subject, but it is adequate for our purposes.

[17] The Rule of Law is safeguarded by a system of 'checks and balances' which operates between the three separate branches of State and is designed to ensure that no one branch exceeds its powers.

[18] *ISC* (n 3) (see ch 8).

charitable status and for the acquisition of that privileged status to be endorsed by public opinion.[19]

But first things first. It may be helpful to say a little about charitable status and then to set out a brief summary of the recent developments which have prompted the analysis in this book and to explain how these will be dealt with during the next nine chapters. Much of the book's content relates to the public benefit requirement and charity law in general terms, but there is a focus on fee-charging charities and independent schools in particular. The author makes no apology for this. Institutions with purposes for the advancement of religion can also be singled out as having been prejudiced by the Commission's interpretation of the law, but the issues are quite different and worthy of dedicated study on another occasion, although they will be touched upon in these pages where appropriate. The debate surrounding the status and fiscal treatment of fee-charging independent schools, however, raised important questions about social deprivation and advantage and about fiscal policy. Described as 'the only potentially partisan issue in the Bill',[20] this debate was particularly heated during the legislative journey of the 2006 Act and the impact of developments on fee-charging charities since its enactment is also particularly striking. Anyone would be forgiven for believing that the charitable status of independent schools (and other charities which charge fees) is partly dependent on their trustees widening access to those unable to afford their fees, although he or she might also be unsure whether this has always been the case or whether it was a new requirement brought in by the 2006 Act. It is hoped that this book will encourage the reader to question whether or not, as a matter of law, that belief is even well founded.

Charitable Status

Charitable status is highly prized but not easily explained. It does not depend on constitutional structure, nor is it the case that not-for-profit organisations or 'public-spirited' purposes are necessarily charitable. Charities have no distinct legal form but include trusts, companies, unincorporated associations and charitable incorporated organisations,[21] and charitable status is determined according to a legal, or 'technical', definition which is applied to the institution's purposes (as opposed to its activities). As a result, there is often a mismatch between what a layman might think of as charitable and what *is* charitable in law: one survey revealed that only seven per cent of respondents realised that Eton School was charitable, for example.[22] And although a lawyer recognises that religion and

[19] The idea of charitable status being 'a privilege, not a right' is questioned later in the text, along with the relevance of changing social and economic circumstances.

[20] HL Deb 20 January 2005, vol 668, col 906 (Lord Phillips).

[21] Charitable incorporated associations were introduced by the 2006 Act, although the first such entities were not registered until January 2013.

[22] And 73% thought that it was not: *Report of Findings of a Survey of Public Trust and Confidence in Charities* (Opinion Leader Research (for the Charity Commission) November 2005) 16, 17.

charity have long been closely associated, a layman might be surprised to learn that the law readily accepts religious organisations as charitable. Such mismatches between popular perceptions of charity and the legal position might arise from a belief that charity is necessarily associated with relieving poverty, for example, or that charities should be staffed by volunteers, or that they should not be in receipt of state funding. But whilst disparity between the legal and public understanding of charity might be marked, and whilst it might provide a legitimate impetus for legislative reform, it should not be allowed to displace proper legal analysis, precedent or legal doctrine.

The charity 'brand' brings with it public respect and confidence, the volunteering of time and money and also certain legal privileges. A trust which is expressed to endure indefinitely, or which is uncertain in its terms, for example, will be void if it is a private trust, but not if it is a charitable, or 'public', trust.[23] More significant, however, are the tax privileges which are automatically conferred on charities, subject to their being registered (if required to be registered) and the managers being 'fit and proper persons'.[24] Thus, at a basic level,[25] a charity is not subject to income or corporation tax,[26] for example, nor capital gains tax,[27] and the substantial relief from business rates of 80 per cent or more can be particularly valuable.[28] There are also reductions in inheritance tax where testators leave a qualifying legacy to charity[29] and a limited number of VAT reliefs,[30] although the inability of most charities to recover VAT remains a contested issue. The availability of tax advantages is not a factor which can legitimately be taken into account in determining charitable status, but it does mean that whether or not an institution is charitable is of substantially more than academic or linguistic interest.[31]

[23] It must be clear that certain property was intended to be given for charitable purposes, but any uncertainty in the exact nature of those purposes can be overcome by the court making an order for the direction of a scheme under its inherent jurisdiction. See, eg, P Pettit, *Equity and the Law of Trusts*, 12th edn (Oxford, Oxford University Press, 2012) 330 ff.

[24] Finance Act 2010, s 30, sch 6 (subject also to a jurisdiction condition). For comment on problems arising with these new provisions, see J Smith, 'Notes on the Finance Acts: Section 30 of and Schedule 6 to the Finance Act 2010: Charity Re-defined' [2010] *British Tax Review* 415.

[25] The summary here is necessarily simplistic. For a fuller discussion of the tax position, see H Picarda, *The Law and Practice Relating to Charities*, 4th edn (Haywards Heath, Bloomsbury Professional, 2010) and First Supplement (Haywards Heath, Bloomsbury Professional, 2014) chs 55–57.

[26] Save in respect of trading activities outside its primary purposes: Income Tax Act 2007, ss 521–36; Corporation Tax Act 2010, ss 466–93.

[27] Taxation of Chargeable Gains Act 1992, s 256.

[28] Local Government Finance Act 1988, ss 43, 47. In the case of independent schools, it was noted that over 70% of the tax benefits were attributable to business rates relief: HL Deb 28 June 2005, vol 673, col 154.

[29] Finance Act 2012, sch 33. Charitable legacies are not included in a valuation of the estate for inheritance tax purposes and lifetime donations to charity are also tax-efficient.

[30] See Value Added Tax Act 1994, as amended (eg, VAT cost-sharing exemption provisions in group 16, sch 9, introduced by s 197 Finance Act 2012).

[31] The impact of tax advantages has led many to question whether this is or should be a factor, but the legal authority for such a proposition is scarce (see text to nn 109–33, ch 2).

The automatic grant of fiscal privileges was noted to be 'clearly the most controversial' issue in the Joint Committee's deliberations on the draft legislation,[32] and it is this which, undoubtedly, has given rise to much of the opposition to the charitable status of fee-charging charities, at least in respect of independent schools. In the course of a debate in the House of Lords in 2005, the value of these privileges to the independent schools sector was noted to be £100m, although this was contrasted with more than £300m in fee reductions, grants and other charitable activities provided by the sector and £200m suffered in irrecoverable VAT. At the same time, the saving to the public purse, by reason of independent school pupils not taking up places in the state education system, was put at £2bn.[33]

It is more than a question of figures, however, and the legal and political debate surrounding the public benefit requirement has not been conducted in the fiscal arena, but in the name of charity regulation. Even if it had been put beyond doubt that the independent schools sector contributes more to the economy than it receives in fiscal benefits, it is likely that the debate as to whether independent schools should receive any or all of those benefits, and whether they should be entitled to call themselves charities, would still have taken place and recent developments have done little to silence the debate. Opposition to the sector is not new: political challenges in the past have included proposals for the outright abolition of independent schools or the imposition of VAT on their fees, as well as the removal of their charitable status.[34] To the extent that the developments described and analysed in the forthcoming chapters portray a sector under attack, however, it is suggested that this reveals a political desire to focus attention on, and to increase, the benefits which independent schools provide to society over and above the immediate benefit of providing an education to their fee-paying pupils, rather more than a drive to secure their abolition or even the blanket removal of their charitable status or fiscal privileges.[35]

It may seem rather obvious that entitlement to tax privileges could more helpfully be dealt with separately in fiscal legislation. This book owes its title to the words of Lord Campbell-Savours, who, during the passage of the Charities Bill, complained that attempts to address questions of tax, and the automatic conferral of tax privileges, in the name of charity law was making 'an absolute nonsense' of charity law and risked bringing the law into disrepute.[36] Not the first or the

[32] HL Deb 9 February 2005, vol 669, col GC69 (Lord Campbell-Savours). For our purposes, references to the automatic conferral of tax privileges on charities should be understood to be subject to the conditions noted above (n 24).

[33] HL Deb (n 28) col 155 (Lord Brooke).

[34] D Morris, *Schools: An Education in Charity Law* (Aldershot, Dartmouth Publishing, 1996) 24–29; I Williams, *The Alms Trade* (London, Unwin Hyman, 1989) 57–85. Both authors provide a historical account of various political challenges to independent schools.

[35] At least in the short term. It is possible that the abolition of independent schools, or the removal of their tax privileges, might have been part of the medium or long-term strategy.

[36] HL Deb (n 32) col GC69 (Lord Campbell-Savours) (see p xiii).

last to be acutely aware of the tensions created by failing to separate questions of charitable status from the automatic tax privileges which accompany it, however, his plea 'for once, let us sort it out' went unheeded.[37]

The Dawn of the Charities Act 2006

In 2001, the Labour Government initiated a review of the legal and regulatory framework for the charitable and wider not-for-profit sector. This was conducted by the Strategy Unit, a part of the Cabinet Office which was established in 2002 by former Prime Minister, Tony Blair, to provide advice and analysis on matters of strategy and government policy.[38] The Strategy Unit published its conclusions and recommendations for reform in a consultation paper (Strategy Unit Report) in September 2002.[39]

This was by no means the first initiative in reforming charity law, but it laid the foundation for the 2006 Act, not least in its recommendation of the enactment of a statutory definition of charity, something which had long been debated but never adopted.[40] It was proposed that the legislation should set out broad headings of charitable purpose in modern language and impose an obligation to provide public benefit, but also that 'public benefit' should not be defined in the statute. Such a definition was considered to be inadvisable on the grounds that it would be difficult to achieve, would lose the benefits of flexibility which case law offered and increase the risk of political interference.[41]

The intention was that the level of each charity's provision of public benefit should be assessed on a case-by-case basis and that, where it was considered insufficient, a charity should be encouraged to improve its provision, rather than lose its charitable status (although that was not ruled out).[42] It is evident from the Strategy Unit Report that its authors believed the law to stipulate that any fees charged by charities were required to be reasonable and that high-fee charging schools were obliged to 'make significant provision for those who cannot pay

[37] ibid; Lord Wedderburn was also direct (ibid, col GC68 (see p xiii)).

[38] Signalling that the third sector was significant for all arms of government and not just the Home Office: G Morgan, 'Public Benefit and Charitable Status: Assessing a 20-year Process of Reforming the Primary Legal Framework for Voluntary Activity in the UK' (2012) 3 *Voluntary Sector Review* 67, 68; the Strategy Unit Report also noting that many of the issues covered affected all UK jurisdictions and not just England and Wales (n 39 below) 10).

[39] *Private Action, Public Benefit: A Review of Charities and the Wider Not-For-Profit Sector* (Cabinet Office, September 2002) (Strategy Unit Report).

[40] See, eg, *Report of the Committee on the Law and Practice Relating to Charitable Trusts* (Cmd 8710, 1952) (Nathan Report); National Council of Social Service, *Charity Law and Voluntary Organisations* (1976) (Goodman Report); Home Office, *Charities: A Framework for the Future* (Cm 694, 1989); and *Report of the Commission on the Future of the Voluntary Sector: Meeting the Challenge of Change, Voluntary Action into the 21st Century* (1996) (Deakin Report).

[41] Strategy Unit Report (n 39) paras 4.18, 4.21.

[42] The preference was for the institution's provision of public benefit to be developed 'rather than immediately losing charitable status': ibid, para 4.30. Although removal of charitable status was countenanced, the consequences of removal were never addressed in the Report.

full fees'.[43] This appeared to have been based on a publication by the Commission in 2001,[44] which had set out the Commission's interpretation of the legal criteria for charitable status, but without any consideration of whether these criteria had been accurately represented.[45] Nonetheless, the Strategy Unit considered the law on charitable status to be 'outdated and unclear' and proposed that there should be a stronger emphasis on the delivery of public benefit, particularly in relation to charities which charge high fees.[46] This was to be backed up by putting a 'systematic programme' in place, in order to check that charities were complying with these obligations.[47]

The Government accepted the majority of the Strategy Unit's recommendations and a draft Charities Bill was published in May 2004. A significant part of the Bill's long progress[48] was taken up with debate on public benefit and the potential impact of the legislation on fee-charging charities, in particular independent schools and private hospitals.[49] Introducing the Bill, Baroness Scotland explained that the purpose was 'to create a modern legislative framework' for the charitable sector and not to 'single out independent schools in any way'.[50] In fact, the Bill was criticised both for failing to remove *and* failing to protect the schools' charitable status,[51] and ambiguity about its intention and its effect continued long after it had become law.

The resulting 2006 Act failed to reflect entirely the Strategy Unit's intentions and some of the more strenuously argued amendments to the Bill. Although public benefit can be described as central to its new definition of charity, the statute provided that a charity's *purposes* should *be* for the public benefit and not that a charity should *provide* public benefit. The difference may appear pedantic but, as will be seen in the chapters to follow, that is far from the case. The term 'public benefit' was neither defined nor given defining characteristics in a way which would have reflected the criteria that the Commission had been applying to date. Attempts had been made during the legislative process to amend the Bill so that the term should be defined or applied, at least in part, by reference to the impact of

43 Strategy Unit Report (n 39) para 4.26.

44 *The Public Character of Charity* (Commission, February 2001); Strategy Unit Report (n 39) para 4.7.

45 It is suggested that they were not (see chs 3 and 5).

46 Strategy Unit Report (n 39) 8 and paras 4.15–4.30.

47 ibid, para 4.18.

48 The Bill was examined by a Joint Committee, which heard witnesses and received written representations, and then introduced in the House of Lords (and reintroduced following the General Election in 2005), where it also completed its passage and received Royal Assent on 8 November 2006.

49 Other major issues included the impact on religious organisations and the independence of the Commission.

50 HL Deb (n 20) cols 883, 885 (Baroness Scotland).

51 ibid.

any fees charged, but those attempts had failed.[52] Rather, the statute provided that the term should have the meaning given to it in centuries of case law.[53] By tying the definition of public benefit to a body of case law which had frequently been criticised for its complexity and 'illogicalities',[54] however, Parliament may have avoided the shortcomings of a rigid definition, but any intention to bring order and clarity to the law of charitable status, or indeed to reform it, was in danger of falling at the first hurdle.[55] Essentially, charitable status, with its full and automatic privileges, was to be determined by the Commission on the basis of a legal term which lacked any clear or easy definition. This was an unenviable, if not impossible, task for a poorly equipped public body.[56]

The 2006 Act also provided that it should not be presumed that any particular purpose was for the public benefit.[57] The rationale for this appears to have been to ensure a level playing field for all potentially charitable organisations, it having been a commonly held view (possibly still held by some) that certain purposes, including the advancement of education, had previously been presumed to be for the public benefit and that this provision, therefore, would remove that presumption and require educational institutions to demonstrate the benefit that they provided to the public.[58] The significance of this argument may be greatest in the realm of religious charities, where it was also employed by the Commission to cast doubt upon long established legal authority, but its impact on the advancement of education will also be considered. It will be suggested that the better view is that no such presumption ever existed and, therefore, that this provision effected no change in the law at all.[59]

Although the new statute appeared to preserve the old law, interpretations of the term 'public benefit' varied considerably, most particularly in relation to fee-charging charities. In the case of independent schools, for example, was it the case that they had always been subject to a legal duty to demonstrate that they were delivering public benefit, or was this a new obligation somehow introduced by the 2006 Act? And was this a duty which pertained to establishing the charitable status of the institution, or was it an operational duty to be performed

[52] An amendment which would make it necessary to 'consider the effect on public benefit of the charging policy of any charity', for example, was rejected by 139 votes to 60 (HL Deb 12 October 2005, vol 674, cols 310–20).

[53] 2006 Act, s 3(3).

[54] *Oppenheim v Tobacco Securities Trust Co Ltd* [1951] AC 297, 306 (Lord Simonds).

[55] Which was evident to some: 'for this Bill to go through with [the public benefit guidance clause] unamended would lead at best to confusion and at worse to no change at all in the law regarding public benefit' (HL Deb (n 32) col GC112 (Lord Phillips)).

[56] Although there has been much criticism of the Commission's performance of this task (by the author and others), one should also take account of the financial and staffing resources available to the Commission (see text to nn 110–12 below and ch 10, n 33).

[57] 2006 Act, s 4(3).

[58] The purposes of relieving poverty and advancing religion are also considered by some to have been presumed to be for the public benefit.

[59] The no-presumption provision is considered in ch 2, part II.

by the trustees in carrying out the institution's purposes? In either case, was any such requirement satisfied by simply educating the school's pupils, or did it necessitate offering means-tested bursaries to pupils who could not afford the fees? Or could it be satisfied by widening access in other ways, perhaps by a school sharing its facilities or staff with state schools in its locality? These were important questions which were not given the attention they deserved. At the same time, the use of the term 'public benefit' to refer to a charity's provision for people beyond its immediate class of beneficiaries, in particular for those unable to afford any fees charged, became widespread. And yet analysis of the legal authorities will show that such an interpretation was entirely new and lacked any clear foundation in case law. The term 'social benefit' might have been more accurate and, where appropriate, will be used in the following chapters to refer to such facilitated (financial) access and other opportunities for those unable to afford a charity's fees.[60]

In fact, the debate was focused neither on the justification for fiscal privileges, nor the proper performance of trustees' duties, but on charitable status itself. Essentially, doubts had been cast over the correctness, or continued correctness, of independent schools being recognised as charities, doubts which necessitated a careful interpretation of the term 'public benefit' in case law and also the provisions of the 2006 Act, if they were to be resolved. Chapter two examines both and explains how charitable status was, and should be, determined as a matter of law. It also considers in what circumstances an organisation's charitable status might come to an end, principally because the risk of charitable status being lost assumed a new significance in the Commission's interpretation, even though it had featured rarely in case law.

The 2006 Act was subsequently consolidated in the Charities Act 2011 (the 2011 Act), which was passed in December 2011 and came into force on 14 March 2012.[61] Statutory references hereinafter appearing are to the 2011 Act, unless the context requires otherwise.[62]

The Charity Commission

The Commission is a non-ministerial government department and body corporate, which was established by the 2006 Act.[63] Its status and independence were

[60] See ch 4. 'Facilitated access' is a term commonly used to refer to means-tested bursaries (and often other financial assistance such as scholarships and discounts). 'Widened access' might appear preferable to 'social benefit', but its usage is commonly restricted to independent schools, whereas 'social benefit' has a wider relevance. (The term 'social benefit' is also used to describe the (repealed) right of trustees under the Law of Property Act 1925, s 28: C Jessel, 'Public Benefit Gifts by Trustees of Land' (1998) 72 *Conveyancer and Property Lawyer* 246.)

[61] Consolidating (principally) the Recreational Charities Act 1958, the Charities Act 1993 and much of the 2006 Act (but not Part 3 of that Act, dealing with public charitable collections).

[62] In which case the appropriate reference is given in addition.

[63] The Commission replaced the Charity Commissioners, individuals appointed by the Secretary of State to hold an office originally created by the Charitable Trusts Act 1853 (although the term 'Charity Commission' was in use prior to the 2006 Act, hence the publication of documents in the name of the Commission, such as *The Public Character of Charity* (n 44)).

much debated during the passage of the Bill[64] and continued to be of concern to some who questioned the Commission's adherence to the law and its statutory remit following the 2006 Act.[65] It is accountable to Parliament, through submission of an annual report and accounts,[66] and to the court which may overturn its decisions,[67] but it is required to be free from ministerial influence or control over the exercise of its functions.[68]

The Commission was assigned both regulatory and advisory functions and is required to observe and apply the law, but it was not given specific law-making powers.[69] In particular, it is charged with determining charitable status on applications for registration and with maintaining a public register of charities.[70] The 2006 Act also required the Commission to publish guidance on the public benefit requirement, in order to 'promote awareness and understanding' of its operation.[71] The Commission duly did so during 2008, issuing extensive general guidance[72] and supplemental guidance which related specifically to individual sectors, including charities for the advancement of education,[73] and to fee-charging charities.[74] None of these publications had force of law, but were intended to be 'a guide' to, and 'summary of', the law relating to public benefit and the Commission's interpretation and application of that law.[75] It also published its own legal analysis of the law underpinning the guidance.[76] Trustees of charities are obliged by statute to

[64] Lord Hodgson insisted that it was 'quite wrong', for example, that the Commission should be a non-ministerial government department (HL Deb 10 February 2005, vol 669, col GC127) and Lord Swinfen believed that the status made the Commission 'vulnerable to back-door interference' (HL Deb 7 June 2005, vol 672, col 813).

[65] See, eg, P Luxton, 'Making Law? Parliament v The Charity Commission' (Politeia, 2009), who suggested that the Commission was simply carrying out the Government's agenda. To what extent independence has been achieved may merit scrutiny, but it is beyond the scope of this work.

[66] It is also subject to the scrutiny of the National Audit Office (which reported on its regulatory effectiveness in December 2013: *The Regulatory Effectiveness of the Charity Commission* (HC 20013–14, 813) 21); see also the Reports noted at nn 1 and 103 (considered further in ch 9).

[67] Appeal against the Commission's decisions lies to the First-tier Tribunal (Charity), then to the Upper Tribunal (Tax and Chancery) and thereafter to the Court of Appeal.

[68] 2011 Act, s 13(4) (although the members of the Commission are appointed by the appropriate government minister, after a public appointments process).

[69] The dual regulatory and advisory role has often been criticised for creating conflicts of interest to the prejudice of charities.

[70] 2011 Act, s 15(1), (4).

[71] 2006 Act, s 4 (as part of its 'public benefit objective').

[72] *Charities and Public Benefit* (Commission, January 2008).

[73] *The Advancement of Education for the Public Benefit* (Commission, December 2008). The Commission also published guidance relating to the charitable or non-charitable nature of research conducted by universities and other higher education organisations (*Research by Higher Education Institutions*, June 2009), but the focus on fee-charging educational charities in this work is limited to independent schools. (Other publications addressed charities for the relief of poverty and the advancement of religion.)

[74] *Public Benefit and Fee-charging* (Commission, December 2008).

[75] *Charities and Public Benefit* (n 72) D2 and C4.

[76] The relevant analyses being *Analysis of the law underpinning Charities and Public Benefit* and *Analysis of the law underpinning Public Benefit and Fee Charging* (Commission, December 2008). The second publication, with the exception of one footnote, was an extract of the first (and used the same paragraph numbering). References to the 'Analysis', therefore, are to either publication.

'have regard to any such guidance when exercising any powers or duties to which the guidance is relevant'.[77]

During the consultation process prior to publication of its guidance in 2008, the Commission dismissed 'significant challenges' to the legal basis of its draft documents, remaining satisfied that both its guidance and legal understanding were correct.[78] And, notwithstanding the difficulties in extrapolating legal principles from centuries of case law, the Commission also rejected calls for the guidance to be written by a panel of experts on charity law.[79] In fact, the 2008 guidance was written by its own Policy Division, whose members are responsible for proposing and developing the Commission's policies and strategies.[80]

As mentioned above, the guidance published in 2008 was later subjected to legal challenge and replaced in 2013. Although the structure and content were altered in the revised publications, fundamental aspects of the original guidance remained and an appreciation of the original version is crucial to an understanding of how the public benefit requirement has developed, both as a matter of law and in practice. Chapter three examines the 'key principles' set out in the 2008 guidance, which the Commission maintained were 'distilled … from the relevant case-law',[81] and compares them to the principles expounded in the preceding chapter, concluding that the Commission's legal interpretation was flawed. It also comments on the quality and accuracy of the Commission's guidance and legal analysis, noting in particular the Commission's focus on a charity's activities, as opposed to its purposes, and its explanation of the consequences which it said would flow from a failure to meet the public benefit requirement. (Relevant changes made in the 2013 guidance are noted where appropriate, but addressed more directly in chapter nine.)

The Significance of Poverty and Fee-Charging

Two of the principles put forward by the Commission in 2008 proved to be particularly contentious. These were: (i) that a charity must ensure that people in poverty are not excluded from the opportunity to benefit; and (ii) in the case of fee-charging charities, that opportunities should not be unreasonably restricted by the fees charged. Although these principles were subjected to criticism by the

[77] 2011 Act, s 17(5).

[78] Including challenges from the Charity Law Association and the Independent Schools Council: *Public Benefit and Fee-charging: Summary of consultation responses* (Commission, undated) 3.

[79] Proposed by the Independent Schools Council, for example, in its response to the draft guidance, 6 June 2007. Lord Phillips had also suggested that the Attorney-General might obtain an independent legal opinion, as he warned that the Bill would not achieve the legal effect intended (HL Deb (n 28) col 171).

[80] The guidance (and *The Public Character of Charity* (n 44)) was 'written by staff in the Policy Division, with input/assistance from legal and signed off at board level'. (This information was obtained in a response to a request for information made by the author, 11 August 2010.)

[81] Foreword to *Charities and Public Benefit* (n 72).

Tribunal and given far less prominence in the 2013 guidance,[82] the essence of them remains: it is still the case that fee-charging charities are said to be required by law to provide opportunities to the poor, although whether this is a matter of trustees' duties or potentially a condition of charitable status, or both, is less clear. Whether consideration of poverty is an essential ingredient in charity *has* proved contentious at times, but the Commission's interpretation appears to be fundamentally flawed: case law, which properly informs the interpretation of public benefit,[83] contained no obligation for charity trustees to consider the financial means of intended beneficiaries, or to accommodate the needs of potential beneficiaries who are unable to afford any fees charged. Nor did that law make charitable status conditional upon the existence or performance of any such obligation.

Chapter four offers an analysis of the law regarding poverty and the charging of fees and this can be contrasted with chapter five, where the Commission's legal interpretation in the 2008 guidance is considered (the 2013 guidance, again, principally being noted in chapter nine).

The Schools

The long anticipated Charities Bill, and the lively debates which accompanied its journey through Parliament, meant that the issue of independent schools widening their access and offering financial and other assistance to non-pupils featured prominently in the sector and general press. It was also acknowledged, during the legislative process, that many independent schools already offered such forms of social benefit and that the level of provision had increased as charities had seen 'what was coming on the wind',[84] but the momentum for legislative action was undiminished. Concerns remained that such practice among independent schools was not sufficiently widespread, and/or that it was insufficient in some cases, and also that no sanctions had been imposed in cases where provision could be seen as 'inadequate'.

'Public benefit' became the new catchwords in school governors' annual reports and summaries[85] and there was a visible shift in emphasis in the type of financial assistance offered by independent schools, so that scholarships awarded on merit and regardless of means came to be replaced by bursaries or scholarships which were means-tested and/or capped. Thus, a benchmarking survey of independent schools recorded a 59 per cent increase in the level of concessions during the

[82] eg, there is no longer a separate publication in respect of fee-charging charities, but rather a short annex in one of the general publications (see ch 9).

[83] 2011 Act, s 4(3); so ignoring for the moment the Tribunal's judgment in 2011 (*ISC* (n 3)).

[84] HL Deb (n 32) col GC118 (Baroness Scotland).

[85] Summary Information Returns, previously part of the Annual Return for larger charities (but discontinued in early 2014).

six-year period to 2006.[86] It also noted a slight reduction in the number of pupils receiving assistance and suggested that this indicated a greater 'targeting' of financial aid to those most in need of it.[87]

Some schools, of course, are richly endowed with extensive funds which are restricted for the purpose of providing assistance with fees, but most are not.[88] In the absence of such dedicated funds, a school must raise funds by other means if it is going to offer bursaries, namely by seeking donations and legacies, trading and/or by increasing the fees charged to existing pupils.[89] Opportunities for widening access and participation also differ between schools across the sector: a small rural preparatory school, for example, is likely to have fewer opportunities to share its staff with neighbouring schools than a large city school. It was evident that the less wealthy schools were most likely to struggle with any test of charitable status which depended on providing social benefit.

Between October 2008 and July 2009, the Commission conducted its first round of public benefit assessments, examining 12 registered charities, including five independent schools. The process was intended to be part of a long-term review of existing charities, a project which it had already outlined in October 2001,[90] and which now had the added support of a recommendation from the Strategy Unit and acceptance of that recommendation by the Government.[91] Nonetheless, provision for such a 'systematic programme'[92] had not been incorporated in the 2006 Act and this omission left the legal basis for reviewing the status of existing charities unclear.[93] The project was later cut short, in August 2010, although this was attributed to a lack of resources rather than any doubt over its rationale or legality. No other schools had been assessed since the first round.

In respect of each school assessed as part of this programme, the Commission listed (at length) the benefits offered, together with details of the means-tested and non-means tested financial assistance given or made available. The Commission

[86] Horwath Clark Whitehill, *Benchmarking Financial Performance in Independent Schools* (2007) 8.

[87] ibid. (The survey also noted that fee concessions were also used to attract and retain pupils and not solely as a means of delivering social benefit.)

[88] Caritas Data, *Independent Schools Financial Yearbook* (2009/10) (Caritas Data, 2009) 2.26–2.35; of course, schools may also utilise unrestricted funds for widening access. By way of illustration, Eton College reported income of £4,900,000 available for scholarships and bursaries in the year 2012/2013, whilst Highfield Priory (one of the schools which initially 'failed' the Commission's public benefit assessment (see ch 6)) reported fundraising of almost £11,000 for the same period.

[89] More than 91% fee remissions were granted out of schools' own resources ('inevitably' meaning higher fees) during the 2007/08 academic year, increased from 84.7% a decade earlier, but down from 93.25% a year earlier, possibly suggesting that 'some sort of ceiling might have been reached': Horwath Clark Whitehill, *Benchmarking Financial Performance in Independent Schools* (2009) 12.

[90] *The Review of the Register of Charities* (Commission, October 2001).

[91] *Charities and Not-for-Profits: A Modern Legal Framework, The Government's Response to 'Private Action, Public Benefit'* (Home Office, July 2003) para 3.25.

[92] See text to n 47.

[93] See ch 3, part IV; its purpose and merits, in legal terms, are also questioned (see ch 2, part III, Rule 3).

had indicated that it would take into account the size and resources of each school, but its published reports failed to explain how this had been done and the Commission's refusal to indicate what level of financial assistance and other benefits it considered appropriate in each case meant that the actual significance of a school's size and resources was far from clear.

Two of the schools 'failed' the Commission's application of the public benefit requirement, attracting damaging publicity in the national press. In its published findings, the Commission suggested that the schools' governors were in breach of trust and also cast doubt upon the schools' charitable status. Unable to appeal against these findings because they did not constitute 'decisions' within the jurisdiction of the newly formed Charity Tribunal,[94] the two schools had little choice but to respond to the Commission's invitations to draw up plans which indicated an intention to increase the level of social benefit on offer. This they did and the schools' charitable status was affirmed as a result.

Chapter six considers this assessment process and the reports published in respect of the five schools. It draws attention to some of the inconsistencies in the Commission's approach, both as between individual assessments and more broadly, and considers what conclusions can be drawn from the programme.

Charity Law in Scotland

The supervision and regulation of charities had been devolved to the Scottish Parliament by the Scotland Act 1998 and so, while the Charities Bill was making its way through the parliamentary process in Westminster, a similar (but not identical) Bill was being debated north of the border. It was clearly the intention of the UK Government that the legislation in each jurisdiction should be 'fully compatible'[95] and the two regulators resolved to reach a 'common position' on matters of public benefit 'wherever possible'.[96]

Consistency in the law, however, was not achieved and so charities which operated both north and south of the border emerged with two regulators applying two distinct tests of charitable status. The Charities and Trustee Investment (Scotland) Act 2005 introduced a 'charity test', which expressly focuses on a charity's activities and the delivery of social benefit (although the term 'public benefit' is used). The Scottish regulator was given considerable discretion in its interpretation and application of 'public benefit', the definition of which is not tied to case law in the Scottish Act, and the legislation makes clear on the face of it that 'unduly restrictive' fees or charges might result in depriving an organisation of charitable status. Tax reliefs associated with charitable status were not devolved, however,

[94] 2006 Act, sch 4; 2011 Act, sch 6.

[95] HL Deb (n 20) col 884 (Baroness Scotland).

[96] *Memorandum of Understanding* (Office of the Scottish Charity Regulator/Commission, May 2007) Annex 3.2.

and constitute a reserved matter for the Parliament in Westminster, meaning that the definition of charity in England and Wales continues to be relevant to Scottish charities for tax purposes.

Chapter seven compares and contrasts the tests of charitable status north and south of the border and identifies some of the discrepancies between the two jurisdictions. It also examines the public benefit assessments of independent schools in Scotland, which the Scottish regulator has undertaken as part of its statutory obligation to review each entry on the Scottish Register from time to time, and makes a comparison with the Commission's approach described in chapter six.[97]

The Legal Challenge

Seven months after the reports on the two 'failed' schools were published, the Independent Schools Council (the ISC), an umbrella organisation for independent schools, sought judicial review and an order to quash parts of the Commission's guidance on public benefit.[98] The Attorney-General also submitted a Reference, seeking clarification as to whether the public benefit requirement was met in a series of hypothetical scenarios involving schools of various descriptions.[99] The Commission argued that the ISC's application should be rejected on the grounds of delay and/or because it had been rendered otiose by the Attorney-General's application, but the argument was dismissed and both applications were transferred to the Tribunal,[100] where they were heard during May 2011.[101]

If the public benefit requirement had failed to make much sense of charity law in the hands of the Commission, it fared little better in the hands of the Tribunal, which gave its judgment in October 2011. This appeared to confirm the view that the trustees of an independent school have a legal duty to provide opportunities to benefit for those unable to afford the fees charged, although the manner and extent of such provision was described as a matter for the trustees' discretion and not for the Commission. Although not without ambiguity, the Tribunal also appeared to reduce (but not remove) the risk of a school losing its charitable status. Following the parties' failure to agree a revised form of guidance, the Tribunal released a further decision, in December 2011, identifying those parts of the Commission's guidance which it said would be quashed if the Commission did not withdraw them first.[102] The Commission duly withdrew those affected parts of the guidance and neither party appealed either decision.

[97] A much briefer glance at Northern Ireland (in ch 9) will highlight the fragmented landscape of charitable status across the UK.

[98] *ISC* (n 3).

[99] In a Reference submitted pursuant to the Charities Act 1993, s 2A(4)(b), as amended (now 2011 Act, s 326).

[100] *R (Independent Schools Council) v Charity Commission* [2010] EWHC 2604 (admin), [2011] ACD 2. (This hearing took place on 7 October 2010.)

[101] *ISC* (n 3).

[102] *Independent Schools Council v Charity Commission* TCC-JR/03/2010, available at: www.bailii.org/uk/cases/UKUT/TCC/2011/B27.html.

Chapter eight offers an analysis of the judgment in this case and questions its legitimacy.

Later Developments

A review of the operation of the 2006 Act was commenced by Lord Hodgson in January 2012 and the resulting conclusions and recommendations were published six months later.[103] This review included consideration of the obligations which attach, or should attach, to charitable status (including an examination of the public benefit issue) and the nature and extent of regulation of the charitable sector. It recommended no legislative reform of either the definition of charity or the public benefit requirement. The 2006 Act was subjected to rather fiercer criticism by the Public Administration Select Committee in 2013, which disagreed with Lord Hodgson in a number of respects, most particularly by calling for legislative reform of the public benefit requirement (including the removal of the no-presumption provision).[104] The Government preferred Lord Hodgson's approach and the status quo, at least for the time being.[105] All the signs were that any charity law reform still to come would not include reform of the public benefit requirement, but a recent proposal by the Labour Party raises the possibility that the issues addressed in this book might not rest undisturbed for long.[106]

Although revised guidance was initially intended to be published in March 2012, it was another 18 months before it appeared. The Commission chose to replace the entire 2008 guidance and substitute new guidance in an altered format, but the key principles were barely altered.[107] One of the most striking differences was that guidance for fee-charging charities was no longer contained in a separate publication but tucked away in a brief annex which, together with the revised legal analysis, relied heavily on the Tribunal's decision in *ISC*[108] and did little to improve the assistance given to charity trustees and others.

The Commission has suffered harsh and repeated criticism and this book is inevitably critical. It seems only fair, therefore, to note both the extensive range of responsibilities assigned to it by the 2006 Act[109] and the continuing reductions in the Commission's resources which may have impacted on its performance. Initially established with a budget of £32.6m in 2007/2008,[110] repeated public spending

[103] *Trusted and Independent: Giving charity back to charities* (TSO, July 2012).

[104] *Post-legislative Scrutiny* (n 1); see nn 57, 59 above.

[105] *Government Responses* (Cm 8700, 2013).

[106] Tristram Hunt MP, Shadow Education Secretary, writing in *The Guardian*, 24 November 2014 (proposing the introduction of a School Partnership Standard which requires all private schools to form 'genuine and accountable partnerships with state schools' in order to retain business rates relief).

[107] The publications noted at nn 72, 74 and 76 above were replaced; the sector-specific guidance (n 73) remains available, but is noted to be awaiting replacement.

[108] *ISC* (n 3).

[109] Its 'objectives', 'functions' and 'duties' are now set out in the 2011 Act, ss 14–16; see also text to nn 44–47, ch 9.

[110] National Audit Office Report (n 66) 1.12.

cuts reduced this to £22.7m in 2013/2014[111] and this is due to fall to £20.2m in 2015/16.[112] With such depletion in its resources, the prospects of it carrying out any further public benefit assessments or of enforcing reported failures to meet the public benefit requirement are surely weak.

Chapter nine considers the impact of these developments coming after the Tribunal's decision in *ISC*,[113] and also takes a very brief glance at charity law reforms in other jurisdictions. Chapter ten concludes by taking an overview of the events described in preceding chapters and asks, in light of those developments, to what extent the public benefit requirement has helped to make sense of charity law.

The content of this book reflects the position as at 30 November 2014.

[111] ibid.

[112] Following the December 2013 Spending Review: www.thirdsector.co.uk/charity-commission-budget-cut-further-450000-two-years/finance/article/1224717; note, however, that a further £9m, over 3 years and specifically for improving its identification of abuse and mismanagement (rather than addressing questions of public benefit), was announced in October 2014: www.thirdsector.co.uk/david-cameron-announces-9m-new-funding-charity-commission-three-years/governance/article/1318316.

[113] *ISC* (n 3).

2

Charitable Status and Public Benefit: The Law

'[C]harity' means an institution which is established for ... a purpose which ... is for the public benefit.

2006 Act[1]

I. Introduction

The 2006 Act broke new ground by providing a statutory basis for defining charity,[2] but, so far as public benefit and charitable status are concerned, made no material change to the law which had applied previously.[3] A study of the case law shows how charitable status was a matter of law, determined by a number of legal rules and principles which often, but not always, were framed in the language of 'public benefit'. This chapter (and chapter four) identifies those principles and hence the author's interpretation of 'public benefit' and the legal test of charitable status. To the extent that this differs from the interpretation given by the Tribunal in 2011 (when the Commission's interpretation was challenged),[4] one can either prefer the Tribunal's interpretation as an accurate statement of the law or, if that is not the case, question whether that decision has effected a change in the law.[5]

II. The 2006 Act

The 2006 Act defined 'charity' as an institution which is established for 'charitable purposes' and which 'falls to be subject to the control of the High Court in

[1] 2006 Act, ss 1, 2; 2011 Act, ss 1, 2.

[2] *cf* Charities Act 1993, s 96(1) (which, for the purposes of 'general interpretation', provided only that 'charity' should be construed to mean an institution with charitable purposes (according to case law)).

[3] An argument that the law was changed by the removal of a presumption of public benefit is also addressed in part II below.

[4] *R (Independent Schools Council) v Charity Commission* [2011] UKUT 421 (TCC), [2012] Ch 214 (see ch 8).

[5] See chs 8 and 10.

the exercise of its jurisdiction with respect to charities'.[6] An 'institution' may be incorporated or unincorporated[7] and the jurisdictional requirement is not solely territorial, but also requires that the court's jurisdiction has not been ousted by statute.[8] The word 'established' may have an element of ambiguity, since it can be interpreted as referring only to the point of creation or as a descriptive term of an organisation's ongoing status and character, but it is clear that the courts have adopted the former interpretation.[9]

'Charitable purposes' are purposes of the institution which satisfy two tests.[10] First, they must fall within the purposes listed in the statute.[11] This statutory list sets out specifically named purposes, which broadly codify those already recognised as charitable, but with some modifications which have the effect of *broadening* the scope of charity, for example, by adding the 'prevention of poverty' and 'advancement of amateur sport'.[12] It also preserves the common law process of recognising new purposes which are analogous to existing purposes.[13] Second, the purposes must be 'for the public benefit' and 'public benefit' is ascribed the meaning which it bore in underlying case law prior to the Act.[14] Before examining that case law in order to understand the meaning of the term, however, it may be helpful to consider at this stage one other important provision of the 2006 Act, which has given rise to much of the difficulty surrounding the public benefit requirement.

The 'No-Presumption Provision'

This is the statutory provision that 'it is not to be presumed that a purpose of a particular description is for the public benefit'.[15] The Commission and others

[6] 2006 Act, s 1; 2011 Act, s 1. The courts have an extensive inherent jurisdiction in relation to charitable trusts.

[7] 2006 Act, s 78(5); 2011 Act, s 9. Thus, a charity might be a trust or unincorporated association, a company limited by guarantee or incorporated by Royal Charter, or a charitable incorporated organisation.

[8] *Construction Industry Training Board v AG* [1973] Ch 173 (CA).

[9] eg, *IRC v Yorkshire Agricultural Society* [1928] 1 KB 611 (CA) 629 ('I am not prepared to say that there is much difference between established and formed' (Atkin LJ)). The Tribunal's view also was that it referred to what the charity was 'set up to do': *ISC* (n 4) [188].

[10] 2006 Act, s 2(1); 2011 Act, s 2(1).

[11] 2006 Act, s 2(2); 2011 Act, s 3.

[12] 2006 Act, s 2(2)(a), (g); 2011 Act, s 3(1)(a), (g). The express provision that 'religion' shall include religions with a belief in more than one god or not involve belief in a god at all also tends to widen (not restrict) the scope of charitable purposes (2011 Act, s 3(2)(a)). Sir John Mummery calls the list 'longer but not an improvement' over the four heads of charity which previously governed the recognition of charitable purposes: '*The Commissioners for Special Purposes of Income Tax v Pemsel*' (2013–14) 16 *Charity Law & Practice Review* 1, 18.

[13] 2006 Act, s 2(2)(m); 2011 Act, s 3(1)(m)(ii); see too text to nn 163–67 below.

[14] 2006 Act, s 3(3); 2011 Act, s 4(3).

[15] 2006 Act, s 3(2); 2011 Act, s 4(2). The provision appears to apply equally to a purpose appearing on the statutory list and a purpose appearing in the will, deed or other governing document; *cf* P Luxton, 'Making Law? Parliament v The Charity Commission' (Politeia, 2009) 9; see also *ISC* (n 4) [84].

have argued that this provision brought about a fundamental change in the law by removing a presumption which had previously existed and which had meant that certain purposes were presumed to be for the public benefit. These purposes were the relief of poverty, advancement of education and advancement of religion, the first three heads of the four heads of charity expounded by Lord Macnaghten in *Special Commissioners of Income Tax v Pemsel.*[16] Serious consequences were said to flow from this alleged change in the law. First, institutions having those purposes would now be required to prove that they were for the public benefit and, second, decisions in previous cases were no longer reliable, at least to the extent that they turned upon the basis of such a presumption.

The first consequence was evident throughout the Commission's interpretation of public benefit and troublesome in its approach to independent schools, where it seemed that the public benefit requirement was to be satisfied, not so much by demonstrating that education was beneficial, but by demonstrating that the schools' activities were beneficial to people on relatively low incomes, both within and outside the school.[17]

The second consequence was not prominent in the area of education, although it might have been,[18] but was most pronounced in the context of religion, where the Commission cast doubt upon centuries of case law. Following the 2006 Act, certain charities which had previously been excepted from the need to register,[19] including churches and chapels of some Christian denominations, were required to apply for registration. One such application was made by the Preston Down Trust, a Gospel Hall trust of the Plymouth Brethren Christian Church, whose charitable status rested on abundant legal precedent which regarded the advancement of religion as prima facie charitable,[20] and, in particular, *Holmes v Attorney-General*, which had held a trust of the Brethren to be charitable in 1981.[21] In charity law, as in other areas of law,[22] the courts have refused to judge the truth and merits of individual religious doctrines, but have generally assumed that 'any religion is at least likely to be better than none'.[23] The Commission refused to register the Trust, partly on the basis that the applicant had not provided sufficient evidence

[16] *Special Commissioners of Income Tax v Pemsel* [1891] AC 531 (HL) 583 (apparently based, without acknowledgement, on the (almost identical) formulation put forward by Romilly, counsel in *Morice v Bishop of Durham* (1805) 10 Ves Jr 522, 532; 32 ER 947, 951). The fourth head comprised 'other purposes beneficial to the community'.

[17] See chs 3, 5 and (especially) 6.

[18] It will be seen that there is significant legal authority which stands in the way of the Commission's interpretation (see chs 4, 5 and 8).

[19] As prescribed by the Charities (Exception from Registration) Regulations 1996, SI 1996/180; but see Charities (Exception from Registration) Regulations 2014, SI 2014/242.

[20] Provided it was not subversive of morality, eg: *Thornton v Howe* (1862) 31 Beav 14, 54 ER 1042.

[21] *Holmes v Attorney-General*, *The Times*, 12 February 1981 (concerning a trust of the Brethren, sometimes described as the Exclusive Brethren and formerly, and more generally, known as the Plymouth Brethren).

[22] At least where there is no infringement of civil rights: *Kaira v Shergill* [2014] UKSC 33, [2014] 3 WLR 1 [45]–[59].

[23] *Neville Estates v Madden* [1962] Ch 832 (Ch) 853 (Cross J).

of the institution's beneficial impact on the wider public, but also because it had concerns that the precedent value of such cases 'may well be affected' by 'doubts about the extent to which the presumption was determinative' in them.[24] Regrettably, the Attorney-General refused to submit a Reference,[25] or to offer its wholehearted support to the Commission making a Reference,[26] on the basis that such a Reference might clarify the law in 'this and similar cases' but would be unable to give 'more comprehensive guidance in this area which would be of universal application'.[27] The Preston Down Trust, therefore, had little choice but to challenge the Commission's interpretation of the public benefit requirement at vast cost to both parties. Unfortunately its appeal was never judicially considered, because the Commission later affirmed the Trust's charitable status on the basis of an amended trust deed and so we lack any specific judicial pronouncement on the impact of the no-presumption provision in religious cases and, in particular, on the precedent value of existing case law.[28]

The idea that a presumption had existed previously appeared to be based primarily on a dictum of Lord Wright, that 'the test of benefit to the community goes through the whole of Lord Macnaghten's classification, though as regards the first three heads, it may be *prima facie assumed* unless the contrary appears' (emphasis added).[29] Apart from the fact that his Lordship used the word 'assumed' rather than 'presumed', and qualified any assumption by reference to evidence to the contrary, it goes too far to conclude from this that those purposes were presumed to be for the public benefit as a matter of law. A presumption is a legal device which operates to prove a secondary fact upon proof of a primary fact and the term is not always used correctly.[30] In *Holmes*, for example, the judge referred to a 'presumption' in three different ways, but went on to examine whether the purposes of the Trust were sufficiently public and actually applied no presumption at all.[31]

Judges are, of course, entitled (and expected) to assume, or take judicial notice of, some matters which they regard as incontrovertible without judicial evidence and the law had already recognised the purposes within the first three heads to

[24] Letter from Kenneth Dibble, Charity Commission, to Farrer & Co, 7 June 2012: www.parliament.uk/documents/commons-committees/public-administration/letterfromkennethdibble.pdf.

[25] 2011 Act, s 326.

[26] It is unclear whether the Commission formally requested consent under 2011 Act, s 325(2), but, after a lengthy consultation with the AG, it followed the suggestion of the Solicitor General that the matter should be dealt with by means of an appeal: Further supplementary evidence submitted by the Charity Commission to the Public Administration Committee (CH 63) December 2012, nos 2, 5.

[27] ibid, no 2; see also Decision (n 28 below) paras 4, 5 and text to n 26, ch 9.

[28] Decision of the Charity Commission in the Application for Registration by the Preston Down Trust (3 January 2014).

[29] *National Anti-Vivisection Society v IRC* [1948] AC 31 (HL) 42.

[30] eg, in referring to a presumption of innocence (which is no more than a statement of the burden of proof): W Swadling, 'Explaining Resulting Trusts' (2008) 124 *LQR* 72; Garton concludes that to describe the courts' practice 'as the operation of a presumption, a term with certain connotations, is overstating the case somewhat': J Garton, *Public Benefit in Charity Law* (Oxford, Oxford University Press, 2013).

[31] *Holmes* (n 21), citing *Gilmour v Coats* [1949] AC 426 (HL). Applying a presumption should not be confused with following precedent (see text to nn 88–91 below).

be beneficial to the community, so establishing legal precedent to that effect.[32] It seems entirely plausible that the courts would have felt justified in assuming, without proof, that the purposes of relieving poverty, advancing education and advancing religion were inherently and indisputably beneficial to a civilised society. Lord Simonds also emphasised that it was the courts which, 'one by one', had recognised purposes to be charitable by applying an 'overriding test' of public benefit, suggesting that the courts no more relied on a presumption than they relied on the donor's intention or motive.[33] That was not to say that all such purposes were necessarily charitable, however, and even purposes which were prima facie charitable could always be disqualified, or precedent distinguished, where the purposes were shown to be either political or illegal, contrary to public policy, or more detrimental than beneficial.[34] The need for multiple purposes to be exclusively charitable and for the required public character to be present still had to be satisfied.[35] Thus, a gift for the advancement of education where beneficiaries communicated with no one and left no record of the fruits of their learning, would not be charitable.[36] Such a cloistered community is more likely to exist in religious cases, of course, and here any inherent benefit to society may be denied where the intended (direct) beneficiaries deliberately shut themselves away from the public.[37] The bar has been set low, however, so that a closed synagogue whose members nonetheless mix with their fellow citizens does not render the institution more private than public.[38]

Turning to the statute itself, there appears to be no ambiguity on the face of it: there shall be no presumption that purposes are for the public benefit (presumably once it is established that they are prima facie charitable), rather the courts (or Commission) must ask themselves whether they are clearly within the listed purposes (and so beneficial in a way the law regards as charitable) and sufficiently public in character.[39] The statute does not purport to change the law of evidence, however, or require that judges should no longer make assumptions or take judicial notice where appropriate to do so.[40] Any ambiguity seems to revolve around whether a presumption existed or was applied previously, not how the

[32] Real evidence is not required in order to support all conclusions of fact: JB Thayer, *A Preliminary Treatise on Evidence* (Boston, Little, Brown, 1898) 279–80: 'In conducting a process of judicial reasoning, as of other reasoning, not a step can be taken without assuming something which has not been proved; and the capacity to do this with competent judgement and efficiency, is imputed to judges and juries as part of their necessary mental outfit'.

[33] *Anti-Vivisection* (n 29) 65, 67 (and see 63–67 generally).

[34] Saying masses for the donor's soul, for example, or the maintenance of tombstones outside a church are not charitable (*Anti-Vivisection* (n 29) 64); the disqualifying factors are explained in part III below.

[35] See part III below.

[36] *Gilmour* (n 31) 450.

[37] *Cocks v Manners* (1871) LR 12 Eq 574 (Ch); *Gilmour* (n 31).

[38] *Neville Estates* (n 23), where the synagogue was attended by members only, although it was acknowledged that non-members were not turned away.

[39] Reflecting the meaning of 'for the public benefit' in case law, as discussed in part III below.

[40] It seems appropriate that the provision should be interpreted according to its legal technical meaning, ie, a legal presumption, and not to signify a layman's assumption or presumption: *Fisher v Bell* [1961] 1 QB 394 (QB) (where 'offer for sale' was interpreted technically).

no-presumption provision itself is to be construed. If a presumption *had* existed previously, one might also have expected more explicit legislative wording to signal the abolition of a legal presumption, as in the Equality Act 2010 for example, which states categorically: 'The presumption of advancement … is abolished'.[41] And if the no-presumption provision was to set aside swathes of case law, it would seem somewhat curious to have defined 'public benefit' by reference to that same case law in the very next subsection.[42] If there were any ambiguity, legislation should be construed so as to involve the minimum interference with the common law.[43] Various submissions to Parliament had advised that this provision would not change the law,[44] although it seems that these failed to prevent a widely held view to the contrary. Although the Tribunal sought in places to restrict the scope of the decision in *Independent Schools Council v Charity Commission* to educational charities, many parts of the judgment had a wider impact, not least in the matter of the presumption, where it described Lord Wright's approach as nothing more than a 'predisposition' and concluded that no such presumption had existed.[45]

If one takes the view that no presumption existed previously, it follows that the no-presumption provision changed nothing. Its effect, therefore, is likely to be declaratory and procedural only, in that the courts may be more likely to articulate their conclusion in each case as to whether an organisation's purposes satisfy the tests of charitable status.[46]

III. Charitable Status and the Meaning of 'Public Benefit' in Case Law

An analysis of the pre-2006 case law[47] reveals that the test of charitable status was applied to the purposes of a trust or organisation, rather than its activities, and

[41] Equality Act 2010, s 199 (not yet in force).

[42] 2011 Act, ss 4(2), (3).

[43] *Shiloh Spinners Ltd v Harding* [1953] AC 691 (HL) 725. For a detailed discussion on statutory interpretation, see J Bell and G Engle (eds), *Cross on Statutory Interpretation*, 3rd edn (Oxford, Oxford University Press, 2005).

[44] H Picarda: Memorandum to Joint Committee (DCH 297, July 2004) para 9: 'Mere reversal of the "presumption" of public benefit cannot change the declared law on this point'; see also HL Deb 9 February 2005, vol 669, col 113 (Lord Phillips); P Luxton, Written Evidence to the Joint Committee (DCH 270, August 2004) paras 4–8.

[45] *ISC* (n 4) [67], [68], [71], [83], [88]; see too *AG v Charity Commission* [2012] UKUT 420 (TCC), [2012] WTLR 977 [39]. This is one of the many respects in which an Attorney-General's Reference in respect of religion would have been helpful in the Preston Down Trust case (see nn 24, 28 above).

[46] Or even each of the principles discussed in part III below (whereas a court might previously have addressed only those aspects of charitable status which were in issue before it). An organisation applying for registration might be advised to do likewise: P Ford, 'The Scottish Charity Test: Do We Really Need It?' [2004] *Edinburgh Law Review* 408, 411 (where he describes the statutory provision as merely shifting the onus of proof onto the applicant, the substantive law remaining 'a matter of applying the principles gleaned from the cases').

[47] In fact, the relevant provisions came into force on 1 April 2008, but this makes no material difference.

that it required those purposes to be both beneficial in a way the law regarded as charitable and to have a public character.[48] Not all good or beneficial public purposes were regarded as charitable but, as we have seen, those of relieving poverty, advancing education and advancing religion were readily accepted as prima facie charitable.[49] Whether these and other purposes were actually charitable was determined according to a strictly legal interpretation of what was charitable, rather than a layman's understanding or popular opinion, and this interpretation found its expression in a number of principles which were developed over a considerable period of time. At times, but not consistently, these principles were expressed in terms of 'public benefit'.

This chapter extrapolates various rules and principles from case law which, together, provide an adequate understanding of public benefit 'as that term is understood for the purposes of the law relating to charities in England and Wales'.[50] It is not the purpose of this book to examine the principles in detail, but to offer them as an alternative framework on which guidance on the public benefit requirement might have been based and to highlight points of particular difficulty or relevance.[51]

Rule 1 **A technical legal meaning of charity is to be employed**

Principle A Poverty is not an essential element

Rule 2 **The law requires that an institution's purposes satisfy two tests, namely that they are beneficial in a way the law regards as charitable and that they are public in character**

Test 1 **A charity's purposes must be beneficial in a way the law regards as charitable**

Principle B If a purpose is regarded as more detrimental than beneficial, it cannot be charitable

Principle C A political purpose cannot be charitable[52]

Principle D A purpose which is illegal, immoral or otherwise contrary to public policy cannot be charitable

Principle E The purpose of making a private gain cannot be charitable

Principle F If any of its main purposes is non-charitable, an institution cannot be charitable[53]

[48] eg, *Williams Trustees v IRC* [1947] AC 447 (HL) 455.
[49] *Re Strakosch* [1949] Ch 529 (CA) 536; *Anti-Vivisection* (n 29) 42.
[50] 2011 Act, s 4(3).
[51] The reader will find fuller explanations in specialist texts such as H Picarda, *The Law and Practice Relating to Charities*, 4th edn (Haywards Heath, Bloomsbury Professional, 2010); P Luxton, *The Law of Charities* (Oxford, Oxford University Press, 2001) and Garton, *Public Benefit* (n 30).
[52] This principle requires particular caution (see below).
[53] Commonly expressed by saying that the purposes must be 'exclusively charitable'.

Test 2 A charity's purposes must be for the benefit of the public or a section of the public

Principle G Except where the purposes are for the relief of poverty, a class of beneficiaries which is defined by a personal nexus cannot constitute a sufficient section of the public

Principle H A class which is numerically negligible may not constitute a sufficient section of the public[54]

Rule 3 Once a charity, always a charity[55]

Principles B–H are negative in nature and can be referred to as 'disqualifying factors'. Thus, if an institution's purposes appear to be charitable on the face of it, by satisfying the positive requirements of Tests 1 and 2, they might still be rendered non-charitable by the presence of one or more of these factors.

The Use of the Term 'Public Benefit' in Case Law

The test of public benefit has, I think, been developed in the last two centuries.

Lord Simonds[56]

Before looking at each of these rules and principles in turn, it may be appropriate to examine how consistently the term 'public benefit' was used in case law, as this may lead to a greater appreciation of its significance and also caution us against attempting to give the term a narrow or readily defined meaning.

It will be seen that the Commission refers to 'public benefit', first, as a concept derived from principles and, second, as something which is delivered to, and received by, the end user, both delivery and receipt needing to be demonstrated. The term 'public benefit' has had a long and varied application in case law,[57] but a study of case law reveals its predominant use to have been to denote a condition or description of charitable status and not the concept of social benefit which is inherent in the Commission's use of the term.[58]

[54] It should be noted that this principle refers to possible beneficiaries being negligible in number and not merely small in number (see below).

[55] This could be expressed as a principle, but its importance (particularly in the context of a comparison with the Commission's approach) merits its label as a rule. (No attempt is made here to enter the jurisprudential debate about, or to justify the labels of, 'rules' and 'principles' (see, eg, J Raz, 'Legal Principles and the Limits of Law' (1972) 81 *Yale Law Journal* 823): they are used here only to suggest a structural framework, essentially putting flesh (principles) on the bones (rules).)

[56] *Gilmour* (n 31).

[57] Early examples include *Blandford v Thackerell* (1793) 2 Ves Jr 238, 241; 30 ER 612, 614 and *AG v Hartley* (1820) 2 Jacob & Walker 353, 383; 37 ER 663, 674.

[58] See text to n 60, ch 1. Well in excess of 100 cases have been studied for this purpose.

Thus, the term 'public benefit' was used generally to define charitable status or charitable trusts,[59] or, at times, to denote more specifically either one or both of the two tests of charitable status, namely that an organisation's purposes must be beneficial in a way the law regards as charitable and also public in character.[60] The two tests might be distinct where purposes are either beneficial but not public in character or, alternatively, beneficial to the public but not in a way the law regards as charitable. The test of charitable status was met only where both tests were passed, however, and so a failure of either test could be expressed by saying that the purposes were 'not for the public benefit'.

Purposes of faith healing, for example, were described as 'a recognised activity of public benefit',[61] essentially meaning beneficial in a way the law regards as charitable, and the fruitless search for public benefit in the testator's collection of exhibits in *Re Pinion* indicated a failure, essentially, of the first test.[62] It was also the first test which was most relevant in consideration of the fourth head of charity, namely 'other purposes beneficial to the community',[63] and here the term 'public benefit' was sometimes used in lieu of, or synonymously with, that description.[64] Although the word 'public' was included, it was the requirement for purposes to be beneficial in a way the law regards as charitable which was in issue in these cases.[65]

On other occasions, 'public benefit' was used synonymously with the test of public character, the second test of charitable status. In *Oppenheim v Tobacco Securities Trust Co Ltd*,[66] for example, the issue before the Court was whether a class of persons defined by common employment could be regarded as a section of the community 'as to satisfy the test of public benefit'.[67] The charitable nature of the educational purposes was not in question and Lord Normand explained

[59] eg, *Bowman v Secular Society* [1917] AC 406 (HL) 441 (charitable trusts being 'gifts for the benefit of the public' (Lord Parker)); *Re Hummeltenberg* [1923] 1 Ch 237 (Ch) 240 (for the public benefit 'in order to establish that it is charitable in the legal sense' (Russell J)).

[60] See n 48. In this sense, the public benefit requirement can be equated with Rule 2 below.

[61] *Funnell v Stewart* [1996] 1 WLR 288 (Ch) 297.

[62] *Re Pinion* [1965] Ch 85 (CA); see also *Re Good* [1905] 2 Ch 60 (Ch); *Hummeltenberg* (n 59).

[63] The fourth head in the *Pemsel* classification (n 16), the first three having long been categorised as beneficial in a way the law regards as charitable.

[64] eg, *Inland Revenue v Peeblesshire Nursing Association* 1927 SC 215 (CSIH), 222; *Re Grove-Grady* [1929] 1 Ch 557 (CA) 587; *Anti-Vivisection* (n 29) 47 (although Lord Macnaghten's own wording was used in the vast majority of cases).

[65] The term was used liberally in *Anti-Vivisection* (n 29) for example, where it was the potential detriment which was in issue, not the public character. See also *IRC v Falkirk Temperance Café Trust* 1927 SC 261 (CSIH) (providing a temperance hotel) and *Good* (n 62) 66 (increasing the efficiency of the army).

[66] *Oppenheim v Tobacco Securities Trust Co Ltd* [1951] AC 297 (HL) 305, 306; see also *Re White's Will Trusts* [1951] 1 All ER 528 (Ch) 530; *Re Scarisbrick* [1951] Ch 622 (CA) 656; *Royal College of Surgeons v National Provincial Bank Ltd* [1952] AC 631 (HL) 654; *IRC v Educational Grants Association Ltd* [1967] Ch 993 (CA) 1009.

[67] *Oppenheim* (n 66) 306 (Lord Simonds).

'that the element of public benefit must be found in the definition of the class of persons selected by the truster as the objects of his bounty'.[68]

It was not always clear, or even necessary to identify, which test was failed when charitable status was denied. In *Coats v Gilmour*,[69] for example, money was to be held on trust for a Roman Catholic priory, but it was held that its purposes were non-charitable on the strength of precedent which established that a cloistered religious community is not charitable.[70] Lord Greene MR, 'for brevity', used the term 'public benefit' to refer to the public character test, in respect of which evidence of the greater benefit afforded by intercessory prayers and edification was placed before the Court.[71] His Lordship also noted, however, that the principle had been established on the basis that the purposes were neither within the letter nor the spirit of the Preamble to the Statute of Elizabeth, thus failing the first test.[72] Either way, to the extent that one can say that the Carmelite Priory in that case was not charitable, or lacked public benefit, there may be no need to be specific about which of the two tests of charitable status was failed.

The term was also used in the sense of public policy[73] and, commonly during the nineteenth century, to indicate purposes of general public utility, such as building or repairing bridges.[74] It is also worth noting that different judges have used the term in different ways within the same case[75] and that one judge might even use the term differently within one judgment.[76]

Put simply, the term 'public benefit' was not used consistently, nor at all in many cases, even where judges had used the term in previous cases and use of the term might have been expected.[77] It is a term which should, therefore, be used with caution, mindful of its many uses and potential ambiguity, and not as a term with a legal or technical meaning of its own. Essentially, 'public benefit' encapsulates the fundamental quality of charitable status and it is suggested that the term is best understood as offering a shorthand description of the two tests of charitable status, or whichever test is in issue before the court. The 'public benefit requirement', therefore, is a requirement to satisfy the tests of charitable status at

[68] ibid, 309 (Lord Simonds). His Lordship was also a member of the House of Lords in *Anti-Vivisection* (n 29) and *Gilmour* (n 31) (where the term was used to different effect).

[69] *Coats v Gilmour* [1948] Ch 340 (CA) (upheld by the House of Lords (n 31)).

[70] *Cocks* (n 37) 585.

[71] *Coats* (n 69) 344.

[72] ibid, 343, referring to the preamble to the Statute of Charitable Uses Act (1601) 43 Eliz 1 c 4 (the Preamble). For the significance of the Preamble, see text to nn 163–66 below.

[73] *AG v Andrews* (1749) 1 Ves Sen 225, 27 ER 996 (Ch); *Anti-Vivisection* (n 29) 42 (where Lord Wright indicated that it could not be for the public benefit to favour a trust contrary to the law).

[74] Which were later treated as part of the fourth head of charity: see, eg, *Townley v Bedwell* (1801) 6 Ves Jr 194, 31 ER 1008; *AG v The Haberdashers' Company* (1832) 5 Sim 478, 58 ER 417.

[75] eg, *IRC v Baddeley* [1955] AC 572 (HL) 597, 615.

[76] eg, Lord Wilberforce in *Re Resch* [1969] 1 AC 514 (PC), both to indicate the public character test (at 544) and the fourth head (at 540, 'provision of medical care accepted as a public benefit').

[77] eg, *Strakosch* (n 49); *Gibson v South American Stores* [1950] Ch 177 (CA); *IRC v City of Glasgow Police Athletic Association* [1953] AC 380 (HL); *Re Koeppler's Will Trusts* [1986] Ch 423 (CA).

common law, according to their legal meaning and as determined by the legal rules and principles outlined below.[78]

Rule 1: 'Charity' and 'Charitable' are to be Understood According to their Technical or Legal Meaning and not According to a Popular Meaning

This rule is fundamental to an understanding of what is charitable as a matter of law and has profound implications which are explored below. It will be seen in subsequent chapters that whilst the rule was acknowledged by the Commission, it was not always apparent in the regulator's interpretation or implementation of the public benefit requirement.

It is not uncommon for a word to have a distinct legal meaning,[79] but the disparity between the common and legal meanings of 'charity' is so great that the courts have felt it necessary to emphasise both the distinction between them and the fact that charitable status is strictly a matter of law. In *Morice v Bishop of Durham*, for example, Lord Eldon explained, in no fewer than a dozen references, that the courts had formed their own understanding of charity in a 'technical sense' and 'not falling within its ordinary signification'.[80] Accordingly, in this case, 'objects of benevolence and liberality' were not charitable in law, however beneficial they might appear. Later, Lord Macnaghten explained that the 'technical meaning' denoted something 'clear and distinct, peculiar to the law as understood and administered in this country and not depending upon or coterminous with the popular or vulgar use of the word'.[81]

In *Verge v Somerville*, where the legal meaning rendered the ostensibly beneficial purposes of helping soldiers *non*-charitable (due to there being a personal nexus), Lord Wrenbury chose emphatic language to demonstrate the fundamental and critical importance of Rule 1, describing the two meanings as 'so far apart that it is necessary almost to dismiss the popular meaning from the mind as misleading before setting out to determine whether a gift is charitable within the legal meaning'.[82] Similarly, Sachs LJ spoke of a 'natural allergy, stemming simply from the popular meaning of "charity"' that would need to be eliminated in order to accept that the business of producing and selling law reports could be charitable in law.[83]

The 2006 Act does not purport to alter this first rule, or to detract from its significance.

78 Subject to any change to the common law position brought about by the Act (see n 12).

79 'Agreement', 'consideration' and 'malice' are examples.

80 *Morice* (n 16) 542/955, 538/953.

81 *Pemsel* (n 16) 581; see too *Re Hood* [1931] 1 Ch 240 (CA) 243 ('The question is whether the trust is charitable in the eyes, not of a layman, but of a lawyer' (Bennett J)).

82 *Verge v Somerville* [1924] AC 496 (PC) 502.

83 *Incorporated Council of Law Reporting for England and Wales v AG* [1972] Ch 73 (CA) 90.

1. Legal Meaning: Clarity and Constancy

The interpretation and application of charity and charitable status by members of the judiciary, on multiple occasions and in a variety of contexts, may have 'baffled efforts to reduce the law to systematized definitions',[84] but it has also resulted in an authoritative and publicly available source of the meaning of charity, or public benefit. The use of a distinct legal meaning has also allowed the courts to avoid the vagaries of a popular meaning which is difficult to define,[85] since it changes from time to time and from one person to another,[86] even if it is, perhaps, most commonly associated with the need to help the poor. In his dissenting judgment in *Pemsel*, for example, Lord Halsbury conceived that 'the real ordinary use of the word "charitable" as distinguished from any technicalities whatsoever, always does involve the relief of poverty'.[87]

Most importantly, whereas a change in the prevalence of opinion could at once change the popular meaning of the word, a legal meaning, though capable of change, is constrained by the doctrine of precedent and more likely to be resistant to it.[88] At a basic level, this doctrine requires courts to follow principles laid down by courts previously, at least courts of the same or higher authority, and it is only in certain circumstances that a previous case may be departed from or overruled.[89] That is not to say that courts cannot have regard to surrounding circumstances, including the 'beliefs and knowledge' of the present time, and they do.[90] It is one thing to recognise that laws, morality and public policy might change, and also that time brings with it new human needs and new ways of meeting those needs. It is quite another, however, to portray charitable status as something which comes and goes according to changing social values or social and economic circumstances, especially when those values and circumstances (and any changes in them) are

[84] *Oppenheim* (n 66) 309 (Lord Normand); see also *Educational Grants* (n 66) 1009 ('shorn of logic, we can only go by the decided cases' (Lord Denning MR)); *Gilmour* (n 31) 443 ('degree of uncertainty in the law must be admitted' (Lord Simonds)).

[85] *Ashfield Municipal Council v Joyce* [1978] AC 122 (PC) 134 ('neither clarity or [sic] unanimity as to what this "popular" meaning is' (Lord Wilberforce)); see also *Pemsel* (n 16) 583 ('no one as yet has succeeded in defining the popular meaning of the word "charity"' (Lord Macnaghten)).

[86] *Pemsel* (n 16) 573 (where Lord Herschell pointed out that whilst some might consider almshouses and the giving of doles to be charitable, others might view them as more harmful than beneficial).

[87] *Pemsel* (n 16) 552; see also at 575 (Lord Herschell also dissenting); *cf* J Brunyate, 'The Legal Definition of Charity' (1945) 61 *LQR* 268, who suggests that some would define charity more widely, as 'any good cause for which people are willing to give away money'. Animal charities, of course, do not depend on poverty; see also ch 4.

[88] eg *Gilmour* (n 31) 444 (where Lord Simonds referred to a legal precedent 'accepted and approved in numerous cases' (and the added authority arising from legal texts)). A reformulation of the principles governing charitable status does not represent new law (*Re Macduff* [1896] 2 Ch 451 (CA) 474).

[89] Put simply, the previous case must be 'distinguished' on the basis of material facts being different or a decision of a lower court can be overruled on the basis of it having been wrongly decided. For a discussion of the doctrine of precedent, see M Partington, *Introduction to the English Legal System 2014–15*, 9th edn (Oxford, Oxford University Press, 2014) 51–53.

[90] eg, *Anti-vivisection* (n 29) 74 (Lord Simonds); see also at 42, which makes it clear that 'economic ideas and conditions and ideas of social service' will also be highly relevant (Lord Wright).

not explained.[91] Not only does this render an institution's status uncertain and unpredictable, but it also represents a radical departure from case law by rejecting the courts' inherent conservatism and resistance to allowing the legal definition or consequences of charity to be changed.

A legal meaning is derived from principles which are drawn in general terms and applied to particular facts and circumstances.[92] The principles themselves, however, and hence the definition, remain constant.[93] The legal principle that illegal purposes cannot be charitable, for example, means that changes in the law may result in charitable purposes becoming non-charitable (or vice versa), but the principle itself remains constant. Similarly, the emergence of a new principle may expand, or refine, a definition, but does not alter it. For example, the courts, after much debate, arrived at a principle that the purposes of relieving the needs of the aged or infirm were charitable without the need for the beneficiaries also to be poor.[94] The principle settled a debate, but did not reverse a previously held principle or change the definition of charity.[95] Nor does the continued expansion of potential and acknowledged charitable purposes represent any change in either the definition of charity or the test of charitable status.[96]

2. Legal Meaning: Surprising Results

If a popular meaning is to be disregarded, it follows that a significant proportion of people can be expected to show surprise at what is or is not charitable in law. Lord Macnaghten, for example, suggested that a 'person of education' might expect to see religious and educational charities included, but a layman 'would probably be amused if he were told that a gift to the Chancellor of the Exchequer for the benefit of the nation was a charity'.[97] More recently, a survey found that 73 per cent of respondents mistakenly believed that Eton School was non-charitable and 60 per cent that the Methodist Church was non-charitable.[98] The Commission's

[91] The Commission makes repeated references to the changing nature of charity and charity law (see ch 3).

[92] *Falkirk* (n 65) 267. There is nothing unusual in this: consider the application and development of the neighbourhood principle in the law of negligence, which determines to whom a duty of care is owed (stemming from *Donoghue v Stevenson* [1932] AC 562 (HL) 580).

[93] See *Re Diplock* [1941] Ch 253 (CA) 262, where Sir Wilfred Greene MR explained that changes in perception in charity law are 'not due … to any alteration in the legal meaning of the word "charitable"' but are more to do with 'a different appreciation of social questions and matters of that kind'.

[94] See text to nn 48–68, ch 4.

[95] ibid. The fact that the courts, in the earlier cases, had taken comfort from the intended beneficiaries happening also to be poor did not mean that they were required to be poor: the legal principle was simply that relieving the needs of the aged was, prima facie, a charitable purpose.

[96] Such expansion occurring by a process of analogy under common law or, now, under statute (n 13).

[97] *Pemsel* (n 16) 583; see also *Re Shaw* [1957] 1 WLR 729 (Ch) 736.

[98] *Report of findings of a survey of public trust and confidence in charities* 17 (Opinion Leader Research (for the Commission) November 2005) 17 (and see text to n 22, ch 1).

observations that the Register contained many institutions which people would not believe to be charitable were undoubtedly correct, but the implication that it should thus be amended to reflect that public perception, a view echoed by the former Prime Minister's foreword to the Strategy Unit Report,[99] does not respect Rule 1.

In fact, the adherence to established legal principles and a technical meaning of charity have sometimes resulted in decisions which are distasteful, and unfathomable, even to lawyers,[100] but neither discontent, nor surprise, nor public expectation (whether informed or uninformed) alone justifies or legitimises any deviation from established law. Any of these might prompt calls for legislative reform, but that is another matter.

3. Legal Meaning: Requires Legal Understanding

In its guidance on the public benefit requirement, the Commission suggested that there were only a 'limited number of cases' which offer an understanding of public benefit.[101] Members of the House of Lords, on the other hand, have referred to 'a great body of law'[102] and to cases being 'legion'.[103] At the same time, the abundant case law has been described as 'intricate',[104] 'difficult and very artificial'[105] and 'in a measure chaotic',[106] although Lord Porter attributed the difficulties of charity law to 'not the law but the diversity of subjects'.[107] It follows that the task of issuing guidance on the meaning of public benefit, a term which the 2006 Act defined by reference to that same case law, required a high level of legal skill. The Commission may have been misguided, then, to consider a public consultation sufficient and for its own staff engaged in policy development to write the guidance, when legal counsel or other charity law specialists would have been better placed to do so.[108]

[99] *Private Action, Public Benefit: A Review of Charities and the Wider Not-For-Profit Sector* (Cabinet Office, September 2002) (Strategy Unit Report); see too *The Review of the Register of Charities* (Commission, October 2001).

[100] eg, *Diplock* (n 93) 266 (and see n 206); *Re Tetley* [1923] 1 Ch 258 (CA) 266 (quoted in *Anti-Vivisection* (n 29) 44); but note too the effects of the subsequent Charitable Trusts (Validation) Act 1954 and Administration of Justice Act 1982, ss 20, 21.

[101] *Charities and Public Benefit* (Commission, January 2008) (the Guidance) H1.

[102] *Gilmour* (n 31) 443 (Lord Simonds).

[103] *Williams* (n 48) 455 (Lord Simonds).

[104] ibid, 460 (Lord Simonds).

[105] *Oppenheim* (n 66) 307 (Lord Simonds).

[106] *Baddeley* (n 75) (Lord Tucker quoting Andrews CJ in *Londonderry Presbyterian Church v IRC* [1946] NI 178 (CA) 188); see also *Strakosch* (n 49) 536 ('full … of anomalies' (Lord Greene MR)); *Grove-Grady* (n 64) 579 ('already sufficiently complex' (Lawrence LJ)).

[107] *Anti-Vivisection* (n 29) 52.

[108] See ch 1, n 80. Under the 2006 Act, s 4(4) the Commission was required to carry out 'such public *or other* consultation as it considers appropriate' (emphasis added) (2011 Act, s 7(3)).

4. The Relevance of Fiscal and Other Considerations

The tax exemption of charitable purposes has a long and interesting history[109] and lies at the heart of much of the opposition to independent schools having charitable status.[110] Essentially, the question as to which institutions should receive favourable tax treatment is a political one and, therefore, one for Parliament and legislation, not for the courts (or the Commission). Nonetheless, controversy over the extent to which fiscal privileges are, or should be, extended to charities has accompanied the development of charity law, and attracted varying degrees of attention, since 1853 if not before. In this year, William Gladstone sought, unsuccessfully, to remove the exemption which applied to charitable purposes generally and to replace it with government grants in certain circumstances, but Parliament declined to legislate.[111]

As a result, it fell to the House of Lords to clarify the scope of the charitable purposes exemption in 1891, when the tension between the legal and popular meanings of charity came to the fore in *Pemsel.*[112] Whilst Rule 1 might have had a narrowing effect on the scope of charity in some instances,[113] its application in this case ensured that the full range of fiscal reliefs was available to the ever-increasing range of purposes embraced by the legal technical meaning. Recently described as 'practically self-selecting as the leading case in charity law',[114] *Pemsel* involved a dispute between the Moravian Church and the tax authorities over income tax allowances on rents and profits received by a trust whose purposes included advancing missionary establishments among heathen nations. Tax rebates had been given for many years but the tax authorities then refused to grant a rebate of tax paid by the Trust, on the basis that the rents and profits were not being applied for charitable purposes.

The dispute was settled, but not without stark differences of opinion. Four of the six members of the House of Lords rejected the proposition that, for the purpose of the tax exemption, charitable purposes included only those aimed at relieving poverty. This had been the basis on which the majority had reached its decision in the Court below,[115] and it was also the basis for the decision of the

[109] Picarda points to the roots in Roman time of the 'use of tax exemption as an encouragement of charitable endeavour': H Picarda, 'Charity in Roman Law: Roots and Parallels' (1992/93) 1 *Charity Law & Practice Review* 9, 11; see also MJ Gousmett, *The Charitable Purposes Exemption from Income Tax: Pitt to Pemsel 1798–1891* (University of Canterbury, 2009), where the author, in the course of an interesting, but unrequited, search for the rationale behind the original exemption in 1799 (the 1798 exemption having been limited to hospitals), notes that charities were relieved from other fiscal duties for centuries prior to this. As Gousmett points out (ch 5), the precise wording of the exemptions varied between statutes and between the schedules of the income tax legislation but, for the reasons mentioned therein, it does not seem inappropriate to talk of a general charitable purposes exemption.

[110] See text to nn 24–37, ch 1.

[111] Gousmett, *The Charitable Purposes Exemption* (n 109) ch 6.

[112] *Pemsel* (n 16).

[113] eg, *Morice* (n 16); *Macduff* (n 88); *Diplock* (n 93).

[114] Sir John Mummery sets out 'at least five reasons' for this claim: 'The Commissioners' (n 12) 1–4.

[115] *Special Commissioners of Income Tax v Pemsel* (1889) LR 22 QBD 296 (CA) (Lord Esher MR and Lopes LJ). This was also the preferred view of Lord Coleridge (one of two judges in the Queen's Bench Division) and Lord Bramwell and Lord Halsbury in the House of Lords.

Scottish Court of Session in *Baird's Trustees v Lord Advocate*, which had considered the same statutory provision.[116] The House of Lords held, instead, that the way in which the term had been understood in the Courts of Chancery should also be employed in the fiscal context.

Pemsel makes an awkward backdrop for the Commission's description of a 'kind of covenant' between society and the charitable sector, pursuant to which organisations should demonstrate that they are deserving of the advantages conferred on charities.[117] The Commission's view may be a popular one, but the 'technical' definition of charity, which featured so prominently in *Morice*, *Pemsel* and other case law, imputes no such test:[118] charitable status is a matter of construction and fiscal consequences neither comprise nor compromise the factors which govern that construction and which define the scope of charity.[119]

The case set a powerful precedent which has never been reversed, even though it failed to silence the debate. Calls for matters of charitable status and fiscal policy to be separated continued to be heard, both in the courts and in Parliament,[120] and the matter also assumed a greater significance as both the number of charities and the incidences, and rates, of taxation increased.[121] It may have been 'no coincidence', for example, that the personal nexus test emerged at a time of rising rates of tax, to deny tax privileges which might otherwise have attached to schemes for the educational benefit of a donor's relations or a company's employees.[122]

In *Dingle v Turner*, a case concerned with the charitable status of an employees' benevolent fund, Lord Cross expressed his view that the courts had been 'pretty obviously influenced' by the fiscal privileges which automatically attach to charitable status, and suggested that charitable status had sometimes been denied in order to avoid 'an undeserved fiscal immunity'.[123] His Lordship also advocated that the courts 'must do what they can to discourage such attempts'.[124] It is worth noting, however, that three of the four remaining judges expressly distanced themselves

[116] *Baird's Trustees v Lord Advocate* (1888) 15 R 682, 25 SLR 533 (CSIH).

[117] Foreword to the Guidance (n 101); see also text to nn 7–9, ch 3 and nn 37–38, ch 9.

[118] *Morice* (n 16); *Pemsel* (n 16).

[119] It might be noted that in listing the privileges attaching to charity, Slade J omitted any mention of tax privileges: *McGovern v AG* [1982] Ch 321 (Ch) 331.

[120] eg, *Scottish Burial Reform and Cremation Society Ltd v Glasgow Corporation* [1968] AC 138 (HL) 153, where Lord Upjohn suggested that the use of charitable status to reduce tax liabilities may need to be reconsidered; see also *Report of the Radcliffe Commission on the Taxation of Property and Income* (Cmd 9474, 1955); G Cross, 'Some Recent Developments on the Law of Charity' (1956) 72 *LQR* 187, 202–08; N Gravells, 'Public Purpose Trusts' (1977) 40 *MLR* 397; *cf* J Warburton, 'One Definition for all Purposes in the New Millennium' [2000] *British Tax Review* 144.

[121] eg, income tax was levied at 6% in 1914, but 50% (plus a surtax of 48%) in 1945.

[122] P Luxton, '*Dingle v Turner* Forty Years On' (2013–14) 16 *Charity Law & Practice Review* 43, 48; see Principle G, below.

[123] *Dingle v Turner* [1972] AC 601 (HL) 624–25.

[124] ibid, 625 (following the article written earlier in his Lordship's career ('Some Recent Developments' (n 120)) and referring specifically to the decisions in *Oppenheim* (n 66) and *Re Compton* [1945] Ch 123 (CA) and the temptation for private employee schemes to seek the advantages of charitable status).

from his Lordship's comments in this regard[125] and the ratio decidendi of the case, as with the cases referred to, followed clearly established principles, unaffected by the fiscal position.[126] Whilst fiscal considerations may have influenced his Lordship's view that the law should not be *changed* by extending an apparent anomaly in respect of poverty trusts,[127] it was not suggested that judges should disapply established principles on the grounds of fiscal privileges, or that fiscal implications should be taken into account, as a general principle, in determining charitable status.[128]

Of course, the fact that a judge passes comment on the fiscal outcome should not be understood to indicate that it necessarily influenced the determination of charitable status, any more than where he or she refers to events since the testator's death,[129] or the testator's motive.[130] Thus, for example, where a court was clearly satisfied to refuse a trust admission 'to the favoured ranks of charity', the refusal of charitable status was because it had no educative value and was not beneficial to the public, not because it would otherwise have attracted tax privileges.[131] And to say that there must be public benefit in order that a gift may 'stand in the privileged position of a charitable gift' is to say no more than that a gift must satisfy the public benefit requirement in order to be charitable.[132] It is not to say that the court will measure the extent of public benefit in deciding whether it is sufficiently great to earn those privileges. Such errors of interpretation might easily be made, but that neither excuses nor legitimises them. The legal position is clear: if an institution qualifies as charitable, it also receives tax privileges.[133] Any decision to curtail such privileges in respect of certain charities is a political one for Parliament and legislative reform.

[125] Viscount Dilhorne, Lord MacDermott and Lord Hodson; the fifth, Lord Simon, expressed no view either way. See also *Pemsel* (n 16) 591 ('With the policy of taxing charities I have nothing to do' (Lord Macnaghten)); *Brighton College v Marriott* [1926] AC 192 (HL) 201.

[126] Indeed, his Lordship's decision to dismiss the appeal was, expressly, not based on these reasons.

[127] *Dingle* (n 123) 622–25; see text to nn 218–19 below. The anomaly was acknowledged to have arisen for non-tax reasons.

[128] And, if this had been his intention, it 'led nowhere': Luxton, '*Dingle v Turner*' (n 122) 57; *cf* G Jones, 'Charitable Trusts: What is Public Benefit?' (1974) 33 *CLJ* 63, 65; see also S Bright, 'Charity and Trusts for the Public Benefit—Time for a Re-think' (1989) *Conveyancer and Property Lawyer* 28.

[129] *Diplock* (n 93) 260: 'entirely immaterial' (Wilfred Greene MR).

[130] *Keren Kayemeth le Jisroel Ltd v IRC* [1932] AC 650 (HL) 661. To what extent the effects of the Mortmain Acts (which prohibited devises of land to charitable purposes) might have encouraged an expansion of religious purposes being charitable is sometimes debated, but the better view is that the findings of charitable status were based on legal principle and not sympathy for the heirs: H Picarda, '*Thornton v Howe*: A Sound Principle or a Seminal Case Past its Best Buy Date?' (2013–14) 16 *Charity Law & Practice Review* 85, 90.

[131] *Pinion* (n 62) 111 (Russell LJ). See also *Educational Grants* (n 66) 1013 (where Harman LJ expressly based his decision on the 'true rule' of law and not his sympathies regarding the tax consequences).

[132] *Davies v Perpetual Trustee Co Ltd* [1959] AC 439 (PC) 454 (Lord Morton).

[133] Subject to the provisions of the Finance Act 2010 (see ch 1, n 24).

Principle A: Poverty is not an Essential Ingredient of Poverty

Put simply, the relief of poverty is a distinct head of charity and other charitable purposes are not required to incorporate any element of relieving poverty. The principle is explored in detail in chapter four.

Rule 2: The Law Requires that an Institution's Purposes Satisfy Two Tests, Namely that they are Beneficial in a Way that the Law Regards as Charitable and also Public in Character

A Purposes Test

The principle that the charitable status of a trust or organisation depends on its *purposes* (rather than its activities or the motivation or belief of its founder) is so clearly established, and judicial authority so abundant, that it hardly needs to be cited.[134] It was also explicitly preserved by the 2006 Act.[135] Indeed, the Strategy Unit Report recognised that a 'stricter activities test would … imply a degree of state oversight and control of voluntary organisations that would be onerous and stifling of initiative and innovation' and that it would detract from the organisation's flexibility in choosing how to achieve its purposes.[136] The distinction between purposes and activities is critical. If purposes do not fall within the legal definition of charity, the institution is not charitable. If a charity undertakes activities which do not accord with its charitable purposes, this constitutes a breach of trust, but does not alter its status.[137] Like Rule 1, however, the fact that charitable status is a 'test of purposes' was acknowledged by the Commission but not, in fact, applied by it.[138]

In identifying an organisation's purposes, the courts have construed the express terms of the will,[139] constitution[140] or relevant legislation,[141] and asked whether they are for the public benefit, considering judicial evidence where appropriate. They have also proceeded on the basis that the trustees will act lawfully and in an appropriate manner as charity trustees and have not, therefore, been swayed by counter-arguments which are based on the hypothesis that trustees might not carry out the designated purposes.[142]

134 eg, *Hummeltenberg* (n 59) 242; *City of Glasgow Police* (n 77) 400.

135 2006 Act, s 1; 2011 Act, s 1.

136 Strategy Unit Report (n 99) 4.11.

137 Unless, perhaps, they provide evidence that the purposes were incorrectly identified when charitable status was determined (see Rule 3 below).

138 See chs 3, 5 and 6.

139 *Morice* (n 16); *Houston v Burns* [1918] AC 337 (HL).

140 *IRC v The Trustees of the Roberts Marine Mansions* (1926) 11 TC 425 (CA).

141 *Re Christchurch Inclosure Act* (1888) LR 38 Ch D 520 (CA).

142 *Koeppler* (n 77) 438; *AG v Ross* [1986] 1 WLR 252 (Ch).

The relevant time for determining the charitable nature of the purposes is the date on which those purposes were declared,[143] or the date of death in the case of a testamentary gift for purposes.[144] In asking whether a gift 'is or may be for the public benefit',[145] the courts are contemplating a prospective test, but not suggesting that a mere possibility is sufficient.[146] And since the question is one of law and of construction, the courts have been able to judge cases which have been brought to test the charitable nature of proposed purposes, even before any steps were taken for their fulfilment.[147] Insisting upon evidence of activities and resulting benefits, on the other hand, would lead to the 'deplorable' result that trustees would risk breach of trust by embarking on a scheme that they did not know to be charitable.[148]

Nonetheless, the courts have been willing, or compelled, to consider activities in limited circumstances, a fact acknowledged by the Commission, but not reflected in its generalised and extensive examination of a charity's activities.[149] Thus, the courts have had regard to surrounding facts and circumstances in order to identify the relevant purposes where written documentation has been missing,[150] for example, or where it has been ambiguous,[151] or imperfect.[152] Similarly, where the subject matter has been unknown to the court, further evidence has been admitted to enable a determination of the purposes' charitable nature to be made.[153] And where the relevant issue is the availability of tax privileges, which depend on the application of a charity's resources to charitable purposes, it is clearly necessary to consider the charity's activities, in order to see how its resources have been applied.[154]

Activities may also be relevant to distinguishing between a purpose and the means of achieving purposes,[155] or between purposes and their consequences.[156]

[143] *Smith v Kerr* [1902] 1 Ch 774 (CA).

[144] *Koeppler* (n 77) 435.

[145] *Hummeltenberg* (n 59) 242; *Anti-Vivisection* (n 29) 58.

[146] *Grove-Grady* (n 64) 582 (benefit to the community must be anticipated as the 'necessary result' of the execution of the trust (Russell LJ)); see also *Anti-Vivisection* (n 29) 47 ('the whole complex of resulting circumstances must be *foreseen or imagined in order to estimate* whether … beneficial to the community' (emphasis added) (Lord Wright)).

[147] *Grove-Grady* (n 64); *McGovern* (n 119); *Joseph Rowntree Memorial Trust v AG* [1983] Ch 159 (Ch).

[148] *Joseph Rowntree* (ibid) 165 (Peter Gibson J); see also *Re Shaw's Will Trusts* [1952] Ch 163 (Ch) 170; *Funnell* (n 61) 297.

[149] See chs 3 and 6.

[150] *Goodman v Saltash* (1881–82) LR 7 App Cas 633 (HL); *Resch* (n 76).

[151] *Keren Kayemeth* (n 130) 658; *McGovern* (n 119) 348.

[152] *City of Glasgow Police* (n 77) 395.

[153] *Scottish Burial* (n 120) 146: including a dictionary (*Hummeltenberg* (n 59)) or sworn evidence (*Funnell* (n 61)).

[154] eg, *Falkirk* (n 65); similarly where the test is whether land has been 'used' for charitable purposes in order to avoid development charges: *Abbey Malvern Wells Ltd v Minister of Local Government and Planning* [1951] Ch 728 (Ch).

[155] *Falkirk* (n 65); see also *Re Mann* [1903] 1 Ch 232 (Ch) 235; *Taylor v Taylor* (1910) 10 CLR 218 (HCt Australia).

[156] *McGovern* (n 119) 340.

And additional evidence may be considered for various other reasons, for example, to establish the nature of a legatee,[157] or how an unincorporated association's funds are held,[158] or whether there is evidence of poverty[159] or blasphemy.[160] It should be appreciated, however, that activities are taken into account in very limited circumstances and the courts' main task is to identify the main purposes and to apply to them the legal test of charitable status.[161] Generally speaking, other than in the types of situation outlined above, the courts have treated an organisation's activities as irrelevant, and even a 'heresy', for the purposes of determining charitable status.[162]

Test 1: A Charity's Purposes Must be Beneficial in a Way which the Law Regards as Charitable

The Statute of Elizabeth, 1601, was directed at remedying abuses and not defining charity, but the purposes listed in its Preamble, together with others within its 'spirit or intendment', became the benchmark for this test.[163] So it was that an organisation's purposes had to be either included in the Preamble or analogous to the same, or analogous to any purpose or purposes which had previously been considered to be charitable as analogous to any within the Preamble.[164] Whilst a view of the law as archaic might be understandable, it does not follow that it is necessarily 'outdated'.[165]

The process of analogy, and the application of principles according to the knowledge and understanding of the time and context of each case, provided significant flexibility and enabled the law to evolve and adapt to modern needs. As a result, the relief of poverty, once described as the 'principal manifestation' of the 'public benefit [which] was the key to the statute', took its place as simply one of a growing list of charitable purposes.[166] That same element of flexibility and evolution was

157 *Cocks* (n 37); *Mann* (n 155).

158 *Neville Estates* (n 23).

159 *Re Drummond* [1914] 2 Ch 90 (Ch).

160 *Thornton* (n 20).

161 Non-charitable purposes may be permitted provided they are subsidiary only (see Principle F below).

162 *Ulrich v Treasury Solicitor* [2005] EWHC 67, [2006] 1 WLR 33 [34] ('the heresy of construing the deed by reference to subsequent conduct under it' (Hart J)); see also *Ross* (n 142) 263.

163 See n 72; *Shaw* (n 97) 742 (Harman J); or 'spirit *and* intendment' (emphasis added), eg, *Anti-Vivisection* (n 29) 41 (Lord Wright).

164 This was the basis on which fourth head purposes (other purposes 'beneficial to the community') were construed, the first three heads possibly having been accepted as explicit in the Preamble (the relief of poverty and advancement of education) or analogous thereto (the advancement of religion (analogous to the 'repair of churches')): see G Jones, *History of the Law of Charity 1532–1827* (Cambridge, Cambridge University Press, 1969) for a historical account of the legal definition of charity; see also text to nn 32–33 above.

165 Strategy Unit Report (n 99) 5 (Tony Blair). And the principles described in this chapter have been regularly restated by the courts, so that it is seldom necessary to go back too far: O Wendell Holmes, 'The Path of the Law' (1997) 110 *Harvard Law Review* 991, 992.

166 Jones, *History of the Law* (n 164) 27.

preserved by the 2006 Act.[167] Notwithstanding the preservation of the common law meaning of 'public benefit', and the role that the term plays in alluding to this first test, however, it seems appropriate to regard the statutory list of purposes as replacing Lord Macnaghten's four heads of charity and the Preamble.

It is worth considering whether educational purposes were charitable because of the benefit afforded to the pupils receiving the education, or because of the advantage perceived to result to society as a whole, or both. The express inclusion of 'schools of learning, free schools and scholars in universities' in the Preamble perhaps rendered the point academic, but it seems likely that the broad benefit to society as a whole would account for the courts' 'predisposition' towards charitable status.[168] Of course, it is the indirect benefit to mankind generally which underlies the charitable status of animal welfare charities (by improving morality)[169] and which might also justify the apparently anomalous poor relations cases, where a personal nexus does not disqualify purposes from charity.[170] It is also worth noting that the courts have sometimes noted the benefit to the public of purposes which represent a saving to the public purse.[171] A founder of a school has in mind the benefits of education, no doubt to both society and scholars, but he need not know (or care) who those scholars will be. Thus, Brightman J regarded the personal benefit conferred on individual scholars as incidental only,[172] and Lord Macnaghten's fourth head of charity, which encompasses '*other* purposes beneficial to the community' (emphasis added), also supports this view.[173] The courts do not appear to have questioned whether the people attending an educational institution were sufficiently large or important.[174] Where individuals are named, or a class of individuals is described by reference to a personal nexus, however, the

[167] 2006 Act, s 2(4); 2011 Act, s 3(1)(m).

[168] See text to n 45; see also text to nn 32–35 above.

[169] *Anti-Vivisection* (n 29) 76; *Baddeley* (n 75) 590.

[170] See text to nn 218–23 below; the rationale may also apply to the advancement of religion (*cf Gilmour* (n 31) 357).

[171] See *Good* (n 62) 67, where Farwell J was also prepared to consider upholding a gift for an officers' regimental mess on the grounds of the relief to the public purse; and note the reference in the Preamble to 'the aid or ease of any poor inhabitants covering payments of fifteens, setting out of soldiers and other taxes'; see also M Albery, 'Trusts for the Benefit of the Inhabitants of a Locality' (1940) 56 *LQR* 49, 52; R Nobles, 'Selling Charity' (1983) 46 *MLR* 782, 784 (who suggests that it was the savings to the public purse which 'justified the provision of private services to the better off in *Resch* (n 76)); see too the savings to the public purse noted in the case of independent schools (text to n 33, ch 1).

[172] *London Hospital Medical College v IRC* [1976] 1 WLR 613 (Ch) 620; *Pemsel* (n 16) 583; see also PS Atiyah, 'Public Benefit in Charities' (1958) 21 *MLR* 138, 145 (where he describes a trust for the establishment or maintenance of an educational institution as for the benefit of the public as a whole, but a trust for the education of certain eligible persons as for the benefit of a section of the public); *cf* Jones, 'Charitable Trusts' (n 128) 63, who puts educational trusts with fourth head charities in requiring the class benefited to be a sufficient 'section of the community', although arguably this comment should be confined (by the context in which it is stated) to educational trusts for a specific class as in *Oppenheim* (n 66).

[173] *Pemsel* (n 16) 583.

[174] eg, *London Hospital* (n 172); *AG v Earl of Lonsdale* (1827) 1 Sim 105, 57 ER 518; *Abbey* (n 154).

law regards those purposes as essentially private and the wider benefits to society, even though still present, would not be enough to render them public.[175]

The proposition that schools must demonstrate indirect or wider benefits to those outside their student bodies, in addition to any general improvement to society, pays little heed, therefore, either to the express mention of schools within the Preamble or the fundamental benefit to the community which schools and universities provide. It also goes further than case law suggests.[176]

Principle B: If a Purpose is More Detrimental than Beneficial, It Cannot be Charitable

Cases where charitable status is contested on the basis of harmful purposes or consequences are likely to be rare, but they are not out of the question. In *National Anti-Vivisection Society v Inland Revenue Commissioners*, the House of Lords held that the purposes of promoting the abolition of vivisection, although potentially beneficial in terms of improving morality by tending to avert cruelty to animals, were more fundamentally detrimental, since abolition would deprive mankind of valuable medical research.[177] In an earlier case concerning the same society,[178] the High Court judge had taken the view that the court could not balance benefit and detriment and should 'stand neutral',[179] but the House of Lords disagreed.[180] The courts were required, it said, to weigh the injury to the community against the ostensible charitable purpose, even if that meant weighing the relative value of material and moral benefits.[181]

Despite the rarity of this principle in case law, it has surfaced in recent years but with limited impact and it seems that cases where charitable status is disqualified on the basis of detriment will continue to be rare. First in relation to education, it was argued (unsuccessfully) in *ISC*, that the independent schools sector was detrimental to society because it prejudiced social mobility.[182] Second, the potential detriment which was alleged to stem from the Plymouth Brethren's practice of its doctrine of separation was also clearly an issue in relation to the Preston Down Trust. In its initial refusal to register the Trust, the Commission noted that it was aware of allegations but lacked evidence and did not need to decide the issue since

[175] *Compton* (n 124) 137; *Oppenheim* (n 66); *Gilmour* (n 31); *City of Glasgow Police* (n 77).

[176] See chs 4, 5 and 8.

[177] *Anti-Vivisection* (n 29); the purposes were also disqualified on the grounds of seeking a repeal of legislation and, therefore, of being political.

[178] *Re Foveaux* [1895] 2 Ch 501(Ch); see also *Anti-Vivisection* (n 29) 42, where Lord Wright explained that the applicant was either the same society or a successor or 'substantially identical for all relevant purposes'.

[179] *Foveaux* (ibid) 503.

[180] Although it did not also say that Chitty J should have found the society non-charitable, it not being known 'how far he had appreciated the full force of the evidence' before him (in the form of a Royal Commission report on vivisection): *Anti-Vivisection* (n 29) 46.

[181] *Anti-Vivisection* (n 29) 47 (Lord Wright).

[182] *ISC* (n 4) [29], [108], [109]; see text to nn 121–26, ch 8.

it found inadequate public benefit in other respects.[183] Subsequently, however, the Commission did consider evidence and decided that there were 'elements of detriment and harm' emanating from the doctrines and practices of the Brethren which were 'in real danger of outweighing public benefit'.[184] Again, it did not need to decide the point, however, since the Trust amended its trust deed by setting out principles and practices which clearly offered sufficient reassurance to the Commission to enable it to register the Trust.[185]

The principle is also included in the Commission's guidance and requires no further comment at this stage.[186]

Principle C: A Political Purpose Cannot be Charitable

It is generally regarded as an established principle (also included in the Commission's legal interpretation) that political purposes cannot be charitable, however desirable or beneficial they might be. Indeed, Lord Simonds considered it so well established that the absence of legal authority was of little concern.[187] The term 'political purposes', however, is not straightforward and may be far too broadly stated or construed. In *McGovern v Attorney-General*, the purposes of the Amnesty International Trust (which included attempting to secure the release of prisoners of conscience and procuring the abolition of torture) were held to be non-charitable on this ground and Slade J sought to explain what was meant by 'political purposes' by listing five non-exhaustive categories:

> [E]ither (i) to further the interests of a particular political party; or (ii) to procure changes in the laws of this country; or (iii) to procure changes in the laws of a foreign country; or (iv) to procure a reversal of government policy or of particular decisions of governmental authorities in this country; or (v) to procure a reversal of government policy or of particular decisions of governmental authorities in a foreign country.[188]

This classification has been widely cited,[189] but it is arguable that it extended the scope of political purposes beyond either what was necessary in that case or justified on the basis of judicial authority, including dicta in *Anti-Vivisection*, where the purposes of abolishing vivisection necessarily involved seeking the repeal of existing legislation.[190]

Leaving aside the more limited and more widely accepted category of party political purposes, the reasons usually given for this principle are, first, that the

[183] Letter to K Dibble (n 24).

[184] Decision of the Charity Commission (n 28) [54], [91].

[185] ibid.

[186] Although application of the principle by both the Commission and the Tribunal may be open to question (see chs 6 and 8).

[187] *Anti-Vivisection* (n 29) [63]; see also *Bowman* (n 59) 442.

[188] *McGovern* (n 119) 340.

[189] Including by the Court of Appeal in *Southwood v AG* [2000] WTLR 1199 (CA).

[190] *Anti-Vivisection* (n 29); also going beyond *De Themmines v De Bonneval* (1828) 5 Russ 288, 38 ER 1035 and the authority offered by the obiter comments of Lord Parker in *Bowman* (n 59).

court has no means of judging whether a proposed change in the law will be for the public benefit or not and, second, that the courts should not usurp the functions of the legislature but accept the law in force as right (and, effectively, an expression of what Parliament regards as for the public benefit).[191] The extent to which either rationale is sound in principle or authority, however, is open to doubt and recent developments have highlighted the difficulties of an approach which relies too unquestionably on the *McGovern* classification. It seems that, whilst the principle should remain, the scope of 'political purposes' may need to be considerably refined. In a thorough study of this case, Alison Dunn subjects the five categories to close analysis and demonstrates how they lack both cogency and adequate judicial authority, and have also acted as an obstacle to further jurisprudential development of charity law in this area.[192] It is also worth noting that other jurisdictions have distanced themselves from the 'broadly expressed "political objects" doctrine' stemming from *McGovern*, both in the courts[193] and by legislation.[194]

In the context of education, purposes which appear to be educational may, on a true construction, constitute propaganda and so be non-charitable,[195] but education which encourages political awareness will not necessarily be rendered non-charitable as a result.[196] There is clearly a fine line between non-charitable political purposes and legitimate campaigning which is well beyond the scope of this book, and the principle is unlikely to be especially controversial in the case of independent schools, but it is suggested that Principle C illustrates very well two points of interest for our purposes: first, the dangers of drawing principles more widely than authority (or principle) requires and second, the scope for principles almost to take on a life of their own and, if not carefully tested, to risk becoming incoherent and adrift from a sound legal basis. The reader might ask, having reached the end of this book, whether these points possibly bear some resemblance to the way the public benefit requirement has been interpreted and applied in relation to poverty and fee-charging charities.

[191] eg, *Anti-Vivisection* (n 29) 50, 62.

[192] A Dunn, '*McGovern v Attorney-General*' (2013–14) 16 *Charity Law & Practice Review* 105; Garton also questions the principle on the basis that it deprives donors to political purposes of the protection which would otherwise be afforded by the imposition of trustees' duties on those carrying out the purposes (*Public Benefit* (n 30) 75–76).

[193] *Aid/Watch Incorporated v Commissioner for Taxation* (2010) 241 CLR 539 (HCt Australia) 557 (French CJ, Gummow, Hayne, Crennan and Bell JJ); see too *In Re Greenpeace* [2014] NZSC 105 (Sup Ct New Zealand) [114]. The First-tier Tribunal recently confirmed the charitable status of the Human Dignity Trust, treating its purposes as falling outside the *McGovern* classification: *Human Dignity Trust v Charity Commission* CA/2013/0013 (9 July 2014).

[194] Scotland expressly prohibits the promotion of party political purposes, but it is clear that the broader political purposes identified in *McGovern* are not also prohibited (see ch 7) (an approach which is also found, more explicitly, in Australia's Charities Act 2013, s 11).

[195] *Re Hopkinson* [1949] 1 All ER 346 (Ch) 350 ('political propaganda masquerading—I do not use the word in any sinister sense—as education is not education within the Statute of Elizabeth' (Vaisey J)).

[196] *Koeppler* (n 77); *Ross* (n 142).

Principle D: A Purpose which is Illegal, Immoral or Otherwise Contrary to Public Policy Cannot be Charitable

Lord Wright's comment that a society with an unlawful religious object might fail the test of public benefit may be unhelpful, even if it is not inaccurate, since the courts' refusal to regard illegal purposes as charitable is adequately, and more appropriately, explained as a matter of public policy rather than public benefit.[197] Likewise, even if one takes the view that a school for pickpockets is prima facie educational, it would offend public policy as being immoral, if not illegal, in any event.[198]

Public policy is a flexible doctrine which responds and adapts to changes in public opinion and social circumstances.[199] The principle, however, remains constant. Public policy dictates that a contract between an English company and an enemy company shall be void, for example, but which country constitutes an enemy of this country may change from time to time.[200] Laws and morality also change. When Lord Wright added that 'the test may vary from generation to generation as the law successively grows more tolerant', it seems evident that the test to which he was referring was the test of lawfulness of the religious object and not the test of public benefit in any wider sense.[201]

Public policy also dictates that a testator's property should not be used for 'fantastical, useless, or ludicrous' purposes,[202] so that a trust for purposes 'which the whim or caprice of a testator may prescribe' may be refused charitable status.[203] It is on this basis, rather than for reasons of 'public benefit', that one can say the law would not allow a trust in favour of a class which has no rational link with the purpose or which expressly excludes the poor, such as a trust for the education of sons of millionaires only.[204] It seems that greater clarity is achieved in all these instances by avoiding the use of the term 'public benefit' and stating instead that an institution's purposes, or the way they are expressed, offend public policy and are therefore non-charitable.

[197] *Anti-Vivisection* (n 29) 42.

[198] Luxton takes the view that it would 'patently not rank as education': P Luxton, 'Opening Pandora's Box: The Upper Tribunal's Decision on Public Benefit and Independent Schools' (2012–13) 15 *Charity Law & Practice Review* 27, 35.

[199] *Bowman* (n 59) 426.

[200] *Daimler Co Ltd v Continental Tyre & Rubber Co (GB) Ltd* [1916] 2 AC 307 (HL).

[201] *Anti-Vivisection* (n 29) 42. Lord Wright also referred to Lord Parker's judgment in *Bowman* (n 59) 448–50, in which his Lordship gave a historical discourse on religion and statutes which prescribed either penalties or tolerance.

[202] *Jeffries v Alexander* (1860) 8 HL Cas 594, 11 ER 562 (HL) 648 (Lord Campbell); see also *McCaig v University of Glasgow* 1907 SC 231 (CSIH) 242.

[203] *Grove-Grady* (n 64) 571 (Romer J); see too *Brown v Burdett* (1882) LR 21 Ch D 667 (Ch).

[204] See ch 4.

Principle E: The Purpose of Making a Private Gain Cannot be Charitable

This principle, and the related principle that a charity may charge for its services, is addressed in chapter four.

Principle F: If Any of the Main Purposes is Non-Charitable, the Institution Cannot be Charitable

It is a well-established legal principle, accepted by the Commission and explicit in the legislation that a charity's purposes must all be charitable in law, so that the 'charitable *or* philanthropic' purposes (emphasis added) in *Re Macduff*, for example, were not exclusively charitable because philanthropic purposes were not necessarily charitable in the legal sense.[205] The courts' willingness to uphold and apply the principle, even where the results have meant that it has been viewed 'with some distaste',[206] serves to illustrate the courts' strict adherence to a principle-based approach to defining charity.

The courts have sometimes adopted a more refined approach to interpreting an institution's purposes, however, and it is a matter of construction as to whether purposes are charitable in law or not. It might be, for example, that non-charitable purposes can be construed as incidental or subsidiary to the dominant purpose,[207] or as the method or means by which the general (charitable) purpose is to be effected.[208] It might also be appropriate to distinguish between purposes and the consequences of carrying out those purposes, so that, for example, the education received by a school's pupils can be classed as a consequence of the furtherance of charitable purposes (education) for the benefit of society as a whole.[209] In either case, the purposes can still be seen as exclusively charitable and entitled to charitable status. Such distinctions are not easily made, however,[210] and although the

205 *Macduff* (n 88); Garton suggests that the decision in this case was a lost opportunity, unnecessarily restricting the scope of the fourth head of charity and ignoring the philanthropic characterisation of the Preamble: J Garton, '*Re Macduff* and the Charity of the Wise' (2013–14) 16 *Charity Law & Practice Review* 21; see also *Morice* (n 16); *Diplock* (n 93); 2011 Act, s 1.

206 *Diplock* (n 93) 267 (Goddard LJ) aff sub nom *Chichester Diocesan Fund and Board of Finance Inc v Simpson* [1944] AC 341 (HL), where next of kin successfully challenged a testator's trust for charitable or benevolent purposes, with serious consequences for the trustees (and the charities (*Ministry of Health v Simpson* [1951] AC 251)).

207 *Yorkshire Agricultural Society* (n 9) 637 (the alleged 'purpose' of providing membership benefits not actually being construed as a purpose at all by Lawrence and Atkin LLJ); *Funnell* (n 61) (where private services were seen to be a part of the spiritual work (the predominant purpose) but subsidiary only).

208 *Falkirk* (n 65) 265; see also *Re Hetherington* [1990] Ch 1 (Ch), where a charitable purpose could be achieved by a charitable or non-charitable method and the court directed that the dominant purpose be implemented by means of the charitable method (public as opposed to private saying of masses).

209 See too *Law Reporting* (n 83) 93, 103; and see text to nn 168–74 above.

210 *McGovern* (n 119) 341; *Re Bushnell* [1975] 1 WLR 1596 (Ch) 1604; see also Dunn ('*McGovern*' (n 192)) 123–24 for an illustration of the difficulties of construction.

Commission acknowledges the need carefully to identify the 'purposes', it does not always make these distinctions clearly.[211]

The principle is critical. As a matter of English law, if a trust for purposes is not exclusively charitable then the trust will be void, subject to very limited exceptions (typically trusts for the maintenance of tombs and monuments, care of individual pets and the saying of masses).[212] This means that the property intended to be applied to the stated purpose will, instead, revert to the settlor or, if he or she is deceased, the settlor's estate. It could be that the trust has been operational for some time before the invalidity is discovered, in which case the redirection of assets is likely to be hugely problematic.[213]

Test 2: A Charity's Purposes Must be for the Benefit of the Public or a Section of the Public

Purposes which are aimed at the public generally will satisfy the test of public character, but it they are aimed at a section of the public only the law requires the section of the public to be 'sufficient'. Subject to the two principles stated below, there is little authority, or even debate, on what constitutes a sufficient (as opposed to insufficient) section of the public, however, and most cases have concentrated on a nexus of ancestry or employment between those intended to benefit.

In an attempt to explain the concept, distinctions have sometimes been made between a 'section of the public' and a 'fluctuating body of private individuals',[214] or, in respect of the quality that unites the potential beneficiaries, between one which is 'impersonal' and one which is 'purely personal'.[215] Such distinctions have not been received with a great deal of enthusiasm, however, and ultimately it may be that it is just a question of feel or instinct as to whether something is essentially public or private.[216] Charitable trusts are public trusts whose objects are purposes and not individuals and it may be that the common practice of adopting the term 'beneficiaries' or 'potential beneficiaries', to refer to the individuals who are intended to benefit directly, may have undermined or distorted the original basis on which purposes have been considered charitable.[217] The absence of consideration in the case law as to whether a body of school pupils constitutes a sufficient section of the public, for example, suggests that the pupils have been

[211] See chs 3, 5 and 6.

[212] A miscellaneous grouping, described as 'occasions when Homer has nodded' and which 'ought not to be extended': *Re Endacott* [1960] Ch 232, 250, 26 respectively; see, eg, G Virgo, *The Principles of Equity and Trusts* (Oxford, Oxford University Press, 2012) 220–22. (The position is different in Scotland (see ch 7).)

[213] It is different if a trust is once charitable but then becomes non-charitable, in which case the doctrine of cy-près applies (see Rule 3 below).

[214] *Goodman* (n 150) 650; *Verge* (n 82) 499.

[215] *Compton* (n 124) 129–30.

[216] Or a matter 'of degree': *Oppenheim* (n 66) 314 ff (Lord MacDermott); *Dingle* (n 123) 623 (also finding favour with the Commission: see ch 3).

[217] See also *AG v Charity Commission* (n 45) [60]; and see text to nn 32–33, 168–74 above.

clearly sufficient in numbers and importance (or both) in all cases or, perhaps more feasibly, that the courts have regarded the school's purposes as prima facie charitable because of the overriding benefit to society as a whole and that reference to the particular school or range of pupils has not deprived the trust of its public character.

Principle G: Except where the Purposes are for the Relief of Poverty, a Class of Beneficiaries which is Defined by a Personal Nexus Cannot Constitute a Sufficient Section of the Public

Case law established the principle that a trust for the relief of poverty may be for a class of beneficiaries defined by a personal nexus, whether by reference to a common ancestor or common employment,[218] although it was not entirely clear whether this was simply an anomaly or founded on the belief that there is sufficient public benefit inherent in a trust for the relief of poverty.[219]

Similarly, in the case of membership organisations, which are potentially non-charitable through not being sufficiently public in character, charitable status will be appropriate nonetheless if the purpose, or one of the dominant purposes, is to relieve poverty.[220] Thus, in *Re Hobourn Aero Components Limited's Air Raid Distress Fund*, where a fund was set up primarily for contributing employees who had suffered from air raids, the Court of Appeal refused to uphold it as a charitable trust, principally on the ground that it was of a private and not public nature.[221] It was clear, however, that had there been a requirement of poverty in those eligible for assistance, the Trust would have been charitable, whereas the purpose of relieving distress from air raids (which would be capable of being charitable in a public context) could not render a private arrangement charitable.[222]

On the other hand, all other purposes (including the advancement of education) will not be charitable if they are directed at persons who are joined by a personal nexus, such as contracts of employment or a common ancestry.[223] In *Compton*, for example, a trust for the education of the descendants of three named persons was non-charitable because it was not public, due to the intended beneficiaries being defined by reference to a personal relationship.[224] In *Oppenheim*,

218 *Scarisbrick* (n 66); *Dingle* (n 123) respectively.

219 *Scarisbrick* (n 66) 639; *Dingle* (n 123) 622; see also *AG v Charity Commission* (n 45) [65] where the Tribunal confirmed the continued charitable status of the poor relations cases post-2006 but declined to decide the point.

220 *Spiller v Maude* (note) (1881) 132 Ch D 158 (Ch); *Re Lacy* [1899] 2 Ch 149 (Ch); *cf Cunnack v Edwards* [1896] 2 Ch 679(CA).

221 *Re Hobourn Aero Components Limited's Air Raid Distress Fund* [1946] Ch 194 (CA) 203.

222 ibid, 210; nor will restricting a non-charitable purpose to a particular locality: *Williams* (n 48).

223 *cf Dingle* (n 123) 625 where Lord Cross suggested that a religious trust for a company's employees might be treated in the same way as a trust for the relief of poverty, provided the benefits were spiritual only.

224 *Compton* (n 124); note that a stipulation that the founder's kin are to be preferred does not constitute a disqualifying personal nexus in this way (eg, *Spencer v The Warden and Fellows of All Souls College, Oxford* (1762) Wilm 163, 97 ER 64).

similarly, a trust for the education of children of certain companies' employees was non-charitable because it was not public, due to the intended beneficiaries being defined by reference to employment by particular employers.[225] This is not to contradict the proposition that it is the benefit to society which explains why purposes for the advancement of education are charitable, but merely signals that, where the trust identifies intended beneficiaries who are bound by a personal nexus, that inherent public aspect may be curtailed or contradicted to such an extent that the institution is thereby deprived of its public character (and hence its charitable status). The courts have not suggested that the members of a school are defined by a personal or contractual nexus in this way, however, even where the school is for the sons of (non-specified) gentlemen or where it charges fees.[226]

Principle H: A Class which is Numerically Negligible May Not Constitute a Sufficient Section of the Public

Whilst a large number of beneficiaries will not render a private trust public, some dicta suggest that a class which is 'numerically negligible' cannot be charitable, although 'numerically negligible' is not further defined, nor the rationale explained.[227] It is, perhaps, best understood as an expression of the legal doctrine, *de minimis non curat lex*, and its only application, in a recent case where the number of direct beneficiaries was small, may be flawed.[228] The better view may be that a small class of intended beneficiaries will not necessarily deprive an institution of charitable status, provided potentially eligible beneficiaries are not prevented from seeking to benefit.[229] There might only be a small number who suffer from a particular disease for which research is to be undertaken, for example, or only a small number who suffer from a particular need in a remote locality. An approach which reflects this reasoning would also prevent charitable status from being affected by fluctuations in numbers which occur in response to inevitable variations in the institution's resources or other changing circumstances.[230]

[225] *Oppenheim* (n 66); *Re Koettgen's Will Trusts* [1954] Ch 252 (Ch).

[226] Luxton points out that the contractual relationship between parents and the school is entered into only after selection from a public class and does not define the class as such: Luxton, 'Opening Pandora's Box' (n 198) 48.

[227] eg, *Oppenheim* (n 66) 306; see also *Baddeley* (n 75) 606 (where Lord Reid suggested that some sects might not be 'sufficiently numerous to form an appreciably important class of a community'); *Peggs v Lamb* [1994] Ch 172 (Ch); *cf Cross v Lloyd-Graeme* (1909) 102 LT 163 (Ch).

[228] *Re Duffy* [2013] EWHC 2395 (Ch), apparently decided without careful consideration of principle or authority (and the doctrine referred to meaning 'the law does not concern itself with trifles'). M Synge, 'Charitable Status: Not a Negligible Matter', *Law Quarterly Review* (forthcoming, 2016).

[229] See, eg, *Webb v Oldfield* [1898] 1 IR 431 (CA) 446 ('[a] class worthy, in numbers *or* importance' (emphasis added) (FitzGibbon LJ), cited with approval in *Falkirk* (n 65) 271); see also *Baddeley* (n 75) 590 (where Viscount Simonds suggested that the fact that only a limited number of people are capable of availing themselves of the benefits of a trust should not affect its validity).

[230] See too *Oppenheim* (n 66) 308; *Perpetual Trustee Co v St Luke's Hospital* (1939) 39 SR (NSW) 408 (SC, NSW) 419, 421.

The principle is of limited application for our purposes, however: the Commission has not suggested that a low pupil intake might disqualify a school from charitable status, rather its concern over widening access appears to be greater the higher the fee (not the smaller the school).

Rule 3: Once a Charity, Always a Charity

> A charity once established does not die, though its nature may be changed (Lord Simonds).[231]

Can charitable status be lost, or removed, and, if so, what are the consequences for an organisation's validity and its assets? These questions are fundamental and were raised during the passage of the Charities Bill, but they were never satisfactorily resolved. The Joint Committee recommended that the legislation should make express provision, but the 2006 Act was silent on the issue.[232] It will be seen in the remaining chapters that the Commission's legal interpretation clearly envisages that existing charities might lose their charitable status in a wider range of circumstances than those described in this section, but also that its explanations of the consequences of such loss are confused and misleading in places.[233]

The law does appear to lack clarity, and the contents of this section are necessarily limited, but it is at least clear that distinctions should be made between situations where the charitable status of an organisation is being considered for the first time and those where the status of an existing charity is brought into question at a later date,[234] in which latter case, the legal position might also differ as between trusts and companies.[235] It is also necessary to distinguish between any alteration in the nature of a charity's purposes, on the one hand, and the carrying out of activities which are not in furtherance of its purposes, or which have the effect of transforming an ancillary (but permitted) non-charitable purpose into a main purpose of the organisation, on the other. In the latter case, trustees are likely to be in breach of the duties owed by them, but the charity's status should not be affected.[236] To remove charitable status in such circumstances would be to damage the interests of the intended beneficiaries, rather than to call to account those

[231] *Anti-Vivisection* (n 29) 74.

[232] Joint Committee on the Draft Charities Bill, *The Draft Charities Bill* (2003–04, HL 167-I, HC 660-I) para 105.

[233] See also R Meakin, *The Law of Charitable Status: Maintenance and Removal* (Cambridge, Cambridge University Press, 2008), where the author concludes that the Commission's limited powers of removal are in need of clarification.

[234] See below. This distinction is emphasised by Lord Simonds in the passage from which the above quote is taken (n 231), a passage which the Commission sets out in full but then appears to misinterpret and misapply (see ch 3).

[235] Considered below.

[236] *Ross* (n 142) 263–64 ('The carrying on by an organisation of ultra vires activities cannot possibly, in my judgment, be relevant to the question whether or not it was formed for a charitable purpose').

responsible for pursuing, or permitting, improper activities. Breach of duty may give rise to a personal liability, which is limited in the case of companies limited by guarantee and charitable incorporated organisations, but unlimited in the case of unincorporated charities, although trustees may be excused liability where they have acted 'honestly and reasonably, and ought fairly to be excused'.[237] Breach of duty might also prompt regulatory action by the Commission, which has extensive powers of investigation and protection, including the power to remove or suspend trustees and to appoint trustees and interim managers.[238]

1. New Applications

Generally speaking, if an organisation's purposes are charitable, it should be registered and, if not, registration should be refused.[239] If those purposes have been considered charitable or non-charitable on a previous occasion, the Commission or court is entitled to take the opposite view, although it is not easy to envisage many instances where this is likely to occur and the House of Lords has also made clear that there must be 'compelling reasons' for doing so.[240] In *Gilmour*, for example, the House of Lords considered whether the purposes of a cloistered religious community, previously regarded as non-charitable, could be charitable and decided against it on the basis of precedent and established principle.[241] On the other hand, a trust for the sole purpose of giving doles might have been regarded as charitable in 1640 but non-charitable in 1940.[242] It might be tempting to include *Anti-Vivisection*, where a society against vivisection was held charitable in 1895, but non-charitable in 1948, but it has already been seen that this was due to the earlier judge having erred in law (by refusing to weigh up considerations of benefit and detriment) and was not attributed to a changed view of vivisection prompted by changing values or social and economic circumstances.[243]

In fact, case law has demonstrated a generous expansion of charitable purposes and a marked resistance to regarding previously charitable purposes as non-charitable. This is evident, for example, in the courts' refusal to depart from earlier

[237] Trustee Act 1925, s 61. It is recognised that there are differences in the duties owed by trustees of incorporated and unincorporated charities, and that liability will be determined (at least in part) by reference to the governing document, but a broad outline of legal principle must suffice for present purposes.

[238] 2011 Act, Part 5 and ss 76–87.

[239] 2011 Act, s 30; but note the exceptions in s 30(2).

[240] *Gilmour* (n 31) 443.

[241] *Gilmour* (n 31) (the evidence of alleged benefits of intercessory prayer and edification being insufficient to justify a departure from established law).

[242] *Anti-Vivisection* (n 29) 70 (adopting the distinction made in *AG v Marchant* (1866–67) LR 3 Eq 424 (Ch), but noting that that case concerned a scheme (rather than a question of charitable status), where surplus revenues were diverted to other purposes because the giving of doles was no longer seen as beneficial). Note too that if doles are merely one method of relieving poverty, they can be discontinued without affecting the charitable nature of the dominant purpose (*Re Campden Charities* (1880–81) LR 18 Ch D 310 (CA) 328).

[243] *Anti-Vivisection* (n 29); see also text to nn 177–81 above.

decisions which held non-public trusts for the relief of poverty to be charitable, despite their apparently anomalous nature. The reasoning seems to be as pragmatic as it is theoretical. The fact that many such trusts had been 'carried on for generations' in the belief that they were charitable, meant that the courts were unwilling to take a different view of the poor relations and poor employees cases, even if they were seen as 'far from satisfactory'.[244] Similarly, in *Pemsel*, the House of Lords refused to affirm a change of practice by the tax authorities which, it was said, 'would leave the bulk of the charitable foundations of this country exposed to liabilities appalling in amount'.[245] Any suggestion that schools and religions which have been regarded as charitable for many years (even centuries) might now be non-charitable should be considered in this context.

2. Existing Charities

Nevertheless, the maxim 'once a charity, always a charity' requires some qualification, since charitable objects might be replaced by non-charitable objects expressly, or they might come to be regarded as non-charitable owing to a change in the law or morality or public policy, for example, or due to an increasing knowledge of their detrimental effects. These are the most likely circumstances in which charitable purposes might become non-charitable and were articulated by Lord Simonds in *Anti-Vivisection*, in which his Lordship stressed the distinction to be made between considering purposes on occasions many years apart and reviewing the nature of an existing charity:

> A bequest in the will of a testator dying in 1700 might be held valid on the evidence then before the court but on different evidence held invalid if he died in 1900. So, too, I conceive that an anti-vivisection society might at different times be differently regarded. But this is not to say that a charitable trust, when it has once been established can ever fail. If by a change in social habits and needs, or, it may be, by a change in the law the purpose of an established charity becomes superfluous or even illegal, or if with increasing knowledge it appears that a purpose once thought beneficial is truly detrimental to the community, it is the duty of trustees of an established charity to apply to the court … and ask that a cy-près scheme may be established … A charity once established does not die, though its nature may be changed.[246]

Although these circumstances were not expressed as an exhaustive list, the courts' approach has given every impression that charitable status is not apt to be withdrawn lightly and this might go some way towards explaining why the consequences of their occurring are not well understood. The position is considerably

[244] Although this would have removed the perceived anomaly: *Compton* (n 124) 139 (Lord Greene MR); see also *Dingle* (n 123) 610 (where the financial impact on existing trusts was calculated).

[245] *Pemsel* (n 16) 587 (Lord Macnaghten).

[246] *Anti-Vivisection* (n 29) 74; see also at 57 (Lord Porter).

more straightforward in the case of an institution which is included on the Register, so appearing to be a charity, but which, it later turns out, was registered in error (and, in fact, never was a charity): in such circumstances the Register needs to be rectified and the institution removed.[247]

It may be helpful briefly to consider the relevant statutory provisions before considering the consequences which should follow where the registration of a charitable trust or company is challenged as either erroneous or no longer justified.

3. Cy-près[248]

The equitable doctrine of cy-près was first put onto a statutory footing by the Charities Act 1960.[249] It empowers the court or the Commission to alter a trust's purposes to other, similar, charitable purposes and/or to direct the transfer of the trust's property to another charity with similar purposes, where the original purposes have been fulfilled or cannot be carried out.[250] Most importantly for present purposes, the circumstances set out in the statute include 'where the original purposes have ceased, as being useless or harmful to the community or for other reasons, to be in law charitable'.[251] The word 'useless', here, echoes the possibility included in Lord Simonds' passage of a 'change in social habits and needs' rendering purposes 'superfluous'.[252] The word 'harmful', likewise, reflects his Lordship's second example of where 'with increasing knowledge … a purpose once thought beneficial is truly detrimental to the community'.[253] The words 'or for other reasons' would appear to encompass the third example in his Lordship's explanation, where 'a change in the law' renders a purpose illegal.[254] Situations where purposes become immoral or otherwise contrary to public policy (through a change in morality or public policy) can also be treated as falling within this provision.

Trustees have a duty to apply to the court or the Commission for a scheme in appropriate cases,[255] and the similar purposes must be selected having regard to the spirit of the gift and to social and economic circumstances prevailing at the

[247] 2011 Act, s 34. The conclusive presumption that a registered institution is a charity does not apply for the purposes of rectification: 2011 Act, s 37.

[248] Broadly translated as 'as near as possible'.

[249] Charities Act 1960, s 13.

[250] Now 2011 Act, s 62(1)(a) (or cannot be carried out 'according to … the spirit of the gift' (s 62(1)(a)(ii)), a provision which might invite a challenge where a school was originally founded for the education of the poor (but see text to nn 21–28, ch 4 and the cases reviewed in ch 8, part III(1)).

[251] 2011 Act, s 62(e)(ii).

[252] *Anti-Vivisection* (n 29) 74.

[253] ibid (eg, having regard to that passage, the giving of doles).

[254] ibid.

[255] 2011 Act, s 61.

time.[256] A cy-près scheme does not, in itself, remove an institution's charitable status, although if its entire property is transferred to another charity, so that it is no longer able to operate, it should be removed from the Register on that basis.[257]

4. Removal from the Register

The Commission has a duty to delete from the Register:[258]

(i) any institution which it 'no longer considers is a charity';
(ii) any charity which has ceased to exist;
(iii) any charity which does not operate;
(iv) any charity which applied for voluntary registration and later applies for removal.

The second of these categories appears to be self-explanatory and the fourth can be disregarded for present purposes (although it is worth pointing out that charities cannot choose to be removed from the Register except in these limited circumstances).[259] The third ground is less straightforward and it seems possible that the Commission may have construed the provision so as to authorise the removal of merely inactive charities (despite such inaction suggesting a failure of governance rather than inappropriate status) without sufficient regard to its regulatory and protective duties.[260]

It is the first category which merits consideration here. It is worth noting that the draft Charities Bill was amended from 'considers is no longer a charity' to 'no longer considers is a charity', specifically to cover cases of rectification (following erroneous registration).[261] (The amended wording is closer to the original statutory provision and it is assumed that the original wording in the Bill was in error.)[262] Thus, where the Commission takes the view that the original registration was in error and that the institution was never charitable it has a duty to remove

[256] 2011 Act, s 62(2), reference to 'social and economic circumstances' having been added by the 2006 Act.

[257] 2011 Act, s 34(1)(b) (see below).

[258] 2011 Act, s 34.

[259] There is provision for certain excepted and small charities to seek voluntary registration (2011 Act, s 30(3)). The position is different in Scotland, where registration is essentially optional (see ch 7).

[260] Meakin describes the rather 'ominous' practice of the Commission removing inactive charities (n 233) 83–84; *Removal of charities from the register: inactive charities* (Commission, March 2012). See also Meakin's contextual interpretation of this provision ((n 233) 50–52); and note that a charity may legitimately have temporary, or even prolonged periods of inactivity, eg, where a trust continues to hold property which cannot be transferred to, but which is used by, a new merged or incorporated charity (eg, if a landlord's consent to assignment of a lease cannot be obtained).

[261] HL Deb 8 March 2005, vol 670, col GC269.

[262] Charities Act 1960, s 4(3) ('Any institution which no longer appears to the Commissioners to be a charity shall be removed from the register').

it from the Register.[263] Equally clear is that a charity should be removed under the first ground where there is an express change in the trusts, since the statute provides that, in those circumstances, the removal shall take effect from the date of the change.[264]

The question is whether the wording 'no longer considers is a charity' indicates that this ground for removal also applies where charitable purposes *become* non-charitable due to one or more of the circumstances mentioned above.[265] Such an interpretation would create a potential conflict, however, between the provisions regarding removal and those regarding cy-près. Put simply, if such a change leads to cy-près, this is within the jurisdiction of the Commission because the charity remains registered and the assets are applied to other charitable purposes. Whereas, if such a change leads to removal, the erstwhile charity is removed from the Commission's jurisdiction and it is then not clear what should happen to the institution's assets. For the reasons set out below, and somewhat unsatisfactorily, it seems that this potential difficulty may also be resolved differently, depending on whether the charity is incorporated or not.

Charitable Trusts

Where a decision is reached that a trust was never charitable, and so was wrongly registered, it must be removed from the Register.[266] Since the purposes were never charitable, there can be no question of a cy-près application of its assets.[267] There is a high risk, however, that the trust in these circumstances will be void, since, with very few exceptions, English law does not recognise trusts for non-charitable purposes.[268] In those circumstances, it would appear that the courts' inherent jurisdiction, which requires the existence of a (presumably valid) trust, cannot be invoked.[269] In that analysis, the practical implications of the property of the trust belonging to the settlor or his estate on a resulting trust could be immense, especially where the trust has been carried out over a long period of time and also

[263] Either because the Commission misunderstood the law, or due to inaccurate information being provided on application.

[264] 2011 Act, s 34(2). The following discussion will illustrate why it is suggested that the reference to 'a change in its trusts' in this provision should be understood to refer only to an express change.

[265] This was clearly assumed by Lord Hodgson who moved the amendment referred to above (n 261).

[266] 2011 Act, s 34(1)(a).

[267] *cf* Meakin (n 233) 68, 105–08, who suggests that cy-près might be available in limited circumstances where the court (but not the Commission) decides that its initial determination of charitable status was wrong.

[268] See text to n 212 above. Arguably *Re Denley's Trust Deed* [1969] 1 Ch 373 (Ch) could provide an alternative analysis in some situations, but by no means all; *cf* J Jaconelli, 'Independent Schools, Purpose Trusts and Human Rights' [1996] *Conveyancer and Property Lawyer* 24.

[269] *Re Bennett* [1960] Ch 18 (Ch) (although it was a gift, not a void trust, in that case which required to be applied under the Royal Prerogative).

where assets have already been applied to non-charitable purposes in the belief that they were charitable.[270]

As noted earlier, if a trust *becomes* non-charitable because one or more of its purposes become illegal or otherwise contrary to public policy or more detrimental than beneficial, the correct course is for the trustees to apply for a cy-près scheme. The trust property should then be applied towards the new objects, but the charity should not be removed from the Register unless, as a result of such a scheme, it no longer operates or ceases to exist.[271] If, on the other hand, the removal (rather than cy-près) provisions were to be applied in these circumstances, there would be uncertainty as to what should happen to the assets of the institution once removed and, since removal from the Register is not one of the occasions specified in the statute for the application of cy-près, a scheme would seem to be inappropriate.[272]

Incorporated Charities

As a general rule, a company owns property beneficially and not as trustee for the company's objects,[273] although there are circumstances in which a company's position as trustee has been assumed,[274] or conceded by counsel,[275] or in which a trust has been imposed by statute.[276] Even where a company's constitution places a legally binding obligation upon the company to apply its assets for exclusively charitable purposes, however, the better view would seem to be that whilst this might place the company in an analogous position to a trustee, it does not make it a trustee or non-beneficial owner except in a broad sense.[277]

The lack of clarity over a company's position raises difficult questions in considering the possible withdrawal of charitable status. Relatively straightforward is the position where a decision is reached that a company's objects were never charitable and so its inclusion on the Register was erroneous. In these circumstances, the company should be removed from the Register (of Charities), but its status as a registered company, and its beneficial ownership of the company assets, will not be affected.

[270] *Chichester* (n 206). It seems likely that there would be no liability to repay tax reliefs and allowances received whilst on the Register: 2011 Act, s 37; J Claricoat and H Phillips, 'Removal from the Register' (1997/98) 5 *Charity Law & Practice Review* 13, 14; *cf* Meakin (n 233) 69.

[271] 2011 Act, s 34.

[272] Nor, for obvious reasons, could removal from the Register be said to have had any place in the doctrine prior to the statutory provisions.

[273] *Bowman* (n 59) 441; *Liverpool and District Hospital for Diseases of the Heart v AG* [1981] Ch 193 (Ch) 209; see also J Hodgson and A McNeely, 'Trusteeship and the Charitable Corporation' (1984) 4(2) *The Philanthropist* 26; *cf* I Dawson and J Alder, 'The Nature of the Proprietary Interest of a Charitable Company or a Community Interest Company in its Property' (2007) 21 *Trust Law International* 3.

[274] *Re French Protestant Hospital* [1951] Ch 567 (Ch).

[275] *Soldiers', Sailors' and Airmen's Families Association v AG* [1968] 1 WLR 313 (Ch).

[276] *Re Manchester Royal Infirmary* (1889) LR 43 Ch D 420 (Ch); *Construction Industry* (n 8) 187.

[277] *Liverpool and District* (n 273) 209.

Where a company's objects *become* non-charitable for reasons of public policy or detriment, the position is less clear. The doctrine of cy-près applies to all charitable trusts, but its application in the context of companies is debateable. It has been suggested that a 'new cy-près doctrine divorced from strict trust principles may be developing',[278] and in *Liverpool and District Hospital for Diseases of the Heart v Attorney-General*, Slade J concluded that the court's jurisdiction to intervene and to declare a cy-près scheme did exist where the company was subject to a legally binding restriction to apply its assets for exclusively charitable purposes, whether such an obligation arose by a trust in the strict sense or under the terms of its constitution.[279] Where these limited circumstances do not apply, however, it seems that there may be no cy-près jurisdiction. In such cases, is the Commission required nonetheless to remove the company from the Register on the basis that it no longer appears to be a charity? This would appear to accord with common sense, but it would necessitate treating charities differently, on the grounds of their constitutional make-up, a situation which would be unlikely to find judicial favour.[280]

If removed from the Register, without any cy-près application, the company's status as a registered company would be unaffected, but the question arises whether the ownership and application of its assets is, or should be, affected. Legislation provides that where a company *expressly* alters its objects to include non-charitable objects, property previously given for the once charitable purposes must be ring-fenced and protected for charity.[281] There is no corresponding provision, however, where the nature of the objects changes in the circumstances described.

It has been suggested that a constructive trust should be imposed in these circumstances, on the basis that it would be unconscionable to allow the company to appropriate charitable property to non-charitable purposes, but this may be stretching notions of unconscionability too far and the issue has not been litigated.[282] It might also be argued, of course, that the company's investors intended to further the company's stated objects, whether or not the law called them charitable,[283] and/or that since legislation imposes a trust where objects are

[278] Hodgson and McNeely, 'Trusteeship' (n 273) 39.

[279] *Liverpool and District* (n 273) 214, where the constitution provided that the company should apply its assets for exclusively charitable purposes and also that, in the event of dissolution, the company's assets should be transferred to an institution with similar purposes; see also *Re Dominion Students' Hall Trust* [1947] Ch 183 (Ch), where a cy-près jurisdiction appears to have been exercised without consideration of whether the company was a trustee or not.

[280] *Re Finger's Will Trusts* [1972] Ch 286(Ch) 294; *Von Ernst & Cie SA v Inland Revenue Commissioners* [1980] 1 WLR 468 (CA) 475.

[281] 2011 Act, s 197.

[282] To the best of the author's knowledge. Meakin describes the imposition of a constructive trust as 'the better view' (n 233) 111; the Commission also adopts this approach: *Maintenance of an Accurate Register* (Commission, 2012) Annex E; *cf* Lord Goodhart, who doubted the accuracy of this analysis (HL Deb 3 February 2005, vol 669, cols GC8–10).

[283] J Dutton, 'Charitable Companies Ceasing to be Charitable' (2000) 7 *Charity Law & Practice Review* 31, 36.

altered expressly (but not otherwise),[284] the implication is that no trust is intended to arise in cases where they are altered by operation of law. It does not seem safe to assume either that the courts would exercise their cy-près jurisdiction, or that they would impose a constructive trust, in these circumstances.

These are questions which were acknowledged to exist during the passage of the Charities Bill, but they were not answered as they should have been. It is, perhaps, worth repeating that the absence of clarity and judicial authority regarding the consequences of charitable purposes becoming non-charitable may exist precisely because such a change in status has not generally been recognised by the law of charities, save in the exceptionally rare circumstances outlined.

[284] See n 281.

3

Charitable Status and Public Benefit: The Commission*

So, whilst public opinion cannot decide what is or is not charitable, it is an important factor to be taken into account in helping us to understand what modern social conditions are, and which in turn can enable us to shape the legal understanding of what is charitable in a way that is relevant for modern society.

The Commission[1]

I. Introduction

The Commission's view was that the pre-2006 law provided only '*a basis for* taking decisions on public benefit' (emphasis added), since it drew on only 'a limited number of cases'.[2] Nonetheless, its guidance on the public benefit requirement, published in 2008, put forward a number of principles which it described as 'contained in the existing case law'.[3] Those principles differed in material respects from the rules and principles described in the previous chapter. In particular, the Commission's legal interpretation treated the public benefit requirement as relevant to both charitable status and trustees' duties and also portrayed charitable status as a quality which should be reviewed from time to time and which was at greater risk of being lost or withdrawn. The other significant difference, regarding the importance of poverty and fee-charging charities, is examined separately in chapter five.

Although the 2008 guidance was replaced in 2013, it should not be discarded on the grounds that it is no longer relevant. It was this earlier version which guided the Commission's public benefit assessments of independent schools and other charities during 2008–11,[4] and which was challenged in judicial proceedings in 2011.[5]

* In this chapter, references to the 'Guidance' are to *Charities and Public Benefit* (Commission, January 2008) and numbered references to the 'Analysis' are to paragraphs of the *Analysis of the law underpinning Charities and Public Benefit* (Commission, December 2008).

[1] Analysis 1.10.

[2] Guidance H1.

[3] Guidance B3.

[4] See ch 6.

[5] *R (Independent Schools Council) v Charity Commission* [2011] UKUT 421 (TCC), [2012] Ch 214 (discussed in ch 8).

Its relevance is not merely historical, however. The publications which replaced it are considerably less detailed, but the basic legal principles have not been greatly altered and it seems entirely likely that the understanding and approach which is more amply revealed in the 2008 publications will prove material in filling in the gaps and resolving the ambiguities which exist in the later versions, should the Commission ever be called upon to do so. For these reasons, the focus of this chapter is on the 2008 publications, although reference will be made to the 2013 guidance as appropriate.[6]

II. Questions of Privilege, Changing Law and Public Benefit Duties

At the heart of the Commission's interpretation is the belief that charitable status is a 'privilege not a right',[7] but that proposition merits attention: charitable status is a quality possessed by a charity and an institution which is established for charitable purposes necessarily, and by definition, has charitable status because it *is* a charity.[8] Charitable status is an inevitable consequence of meeting the legal definition of charity and requires nothing more. In that sense, it might be appropriate to call it 'a right'. Contrasting notions of privilege with right, however, suggests that something more is required, essentially that the privilege must be *earned*, not bestowed as a matter of right, and that simply 'being' a charity is not enough to earn that privilege. Certainly charitable status ensures privileged treatment, not least tax advantages, but it is only a privilege in the sense that privileges have been attached to it by law. It might also be interesting to note that Disraeli, in successfully opposing Gladstone's attack on automatic fiscal privileges for charities, referred to charitable status as 'not a privilege—but a right'.[9]

Also significant in the Commission's interpretation is the notion of charity law being capable of change and development in response to a changing society, but this is not a characteristic which is unique to charity law, nor should it be taken too far. The Commission has no law-making powers of its own and, no less than the courts, is required to observe the doctrine of precedent and principles of statutory interpretation. Whilst charity law should not be described as static, it will be seen that the Commission may have relied on an exaggerated depiction of the

[6] Changes made by the 2013 publications are addressed in ch 9.

[7] Echoed by Lord Hodgson in his statutory review of the 2006 Act, *Trusted and Independent: Giving charity back to charities* (TSO, July 2012) (see ch 9).

[8] Provided it is subject to the control of the High Court (2011 Act, s 1).

[9] HC Deb 4 May 1863, vol 170, col 1128 (refuting the suggestion that tax exemption is a donation from the State); see also D Owen, *English Philanthropy 1660–1960* (Massachusetts, Harvard University Press, 1964) 332; text to nn 109–11, ch 2.

law's flexibility and evolution to justify a threat to the continued charitable status of existing charities. This threat, and the consequences of charitable status being removed, is clearly a matter of critical importance and is considered later in this chapter.[10]

The Commission's interpretation of the public benefit requirement went beyond questions of charitable status and identified three 'public benefit duties' owed by charity trustees.

(i) A Duty to Carry Out the Purposes for the Public Benefit

The Commission explained that trustees have a duty to carry out the purposes for the public benefit. It presented this as an entirely logical and straightforward representation of the public benefit requirement, that is to say that since purposes are required to be for the public benefit and since trustees have a duty to carry out those purposes, therefore they have a duty to carry out the purposes for the public benefit. On the face of it, this must be correct, but only if and to the extent that the meaning of 'for the public benefit' is not allowed to change. Judging purposes to be 'for the public benefit' is employing the term adjectivally, in ascribing to them a quality or description, and so requiring the purposes to be carried out for the public benefit is doing nothing more than requiring the purposes to be carried out, at the same time anticipating the manifestation of that descriptive quality as a consequence of that requirement being met. It will be seen, however, that the Commission attaches a new and different meaning to the term 'for the public benefit' in this context, most particularly in relation to fee-charging charities, by requiring trustees (in carrying out the purposes) to give opportunities to the poor and/or those unable to afford any fees charged.[11] This approach was also evident in the Tribunal's judgment and appears in the 2013 guidance and will be explained more fully in subsequent chapters. Essentially, the adjective is replaced by an adverb with a quite different meaning, which goes beyond the logical progression suggested and the public benefit requirement as defined in the 2006 Act. It is also worth noting that whilst certain duties were set out in the 2006 Act,[12] this duty was not one of them, either in respect of charity trustees generally or in the list of duties owed by trustees of charitable incorporated organisations.[13]

(ii) The Duty to Have Regard to the Guidance

This duty is expressly set out in the legislation, but its formulation is somewhat curious. The obligation is to have regard to the guidance whenever trustees 'exercise any powers or duties *to which the guidance is relevant*' (emphasis added),

[10] See part IV below.

[11] See ch 5.

[12] eg, a duty to file annual reports (now 2011 Act, s 162) or to apply for a cy-près scheme (2011 Act, s 61).

[13] 2011 Act, s 221. The 2006 Act did not seek to codify trustees' duties in the same way as the Companies Act 2006 codified directors' duties (ss 171–77).

rather than *where the public benefit requirement is relevant.*[14] The effect of this is that if the guidance goes beyond explaining the public benefit requirement, as that term is defined in the legislation, the legal obligation of trustees to have regard to the guidance is correspondingly enlarged, regardless of the relevance or irrelevance of that guidance to the public benefit requirement.[15] It is worth bearing this point in mind when considering the Commission's guidance.[16] The suggestion that trustees should confirm that regard has been had to the guidance 'in deciding what activities the charity should undertake', for example, was entirely unfounded.[17]

(iii) The Duty to Report

The Commission described a 'new requirement' for trustees 'to report on their charity's public benefit' and to explain *how* the charity's activities were carried out for the public benefit.[18] The Commission based these obligations on anticipated changes to reporting requirements which were made later in that year by the Charities (Accounts and Reports) Regulations 2008 (the Regulations).[19] These required trustees to include in their annual reports 'a review of the significant activities undertaken by the charity during the relevant financial year to further its charitable purposes for the public benefit'.[20] Although the term 'public benefit' is not defined, it seems likely that the Regulations were drafted on the basis of the Commission's interpretation. Nonetheless, Parliament's intention was made clear in the explanatory memorandum which accompanied the Regulations. This was that the reporting of activities (which was already required) should be set 'in the context of furthering the charity's purposes for the public benefit', but that trustees should not be required to explain *how* the activities and purposes are for the public benefit.[21] It was recognised that providing such an explanation would be unduly burdensome, particularly for small charities and where the benefit to the public is less obvious or tangible (as in cases of education and religion).[22] Whilst it was acknowledged that this might constitute best practice, it was specifically stated that it should not be a legal requirement, as the Commission presented it.[23] It follows that the Commission's description of the duty to

[14] 2011 Act, s 17(5).

[15] The Commission sought to justify this approach in the 2013 Analysis (see text to nn 103–06, ch 9).

[16] In this chapter and also chs 5 and 9.

[17] Guidance G3, G6.

[18] Guidance G2, G3; or even how education was advanced: *The Advancement of Education for the Public Benefit* (Commission, December 2008) F1 (which post-dated the Regulations (n 19 below)).

[19] Charities (Accounts and Reports) Regulations 2008, SI 2008/629.

[20] Or 'a brief summary' of the 'main activities' undertaken to further the charity's purposes for the public benefit and its 'main achievements' in the case of a non-auditable charity (Reg 40(2)(i)).

[21] Explanatory Memorandum to the Regulations (Cabinet Office, 2008) paras 7.2.5, 54 (p 19).

[22] *Summary of the consultation and changes made to the regulations following consultation*, annexed to the Explanatory Memorandum (n 21) paras 62, 78, 79.

[23] ibid, para 79.

comply with the Regulations may have given trustees a misleading impression of their statutory obligations.

'Public benefit reporting' was described as an important tool in enabling the public to appreciate 'just how much they benefit' in return for the privileges conferred on charities, but (as mentioned above) it would be wrong to suggest that the privileges in any way depend on that appreciation.[24] By stating that a breach of the reporting duty would not 'necessarily' result in the organisation being non-charitable, the Commission also presented loss of charitable status as a distinct possibility in the event of breach, further suggesting that persistent failure or unconvincing reporting would be likely to prompt it to undertake a detailed public benefit assessment.[25] Failure to comply with the Regulations, however, is a matter of governance and not status.

III. The Commission's Interpretation of Public Benefit

The 2008 Guidance and Analysis were extensive, running to 36 and 55 pages respectively, with several ancillary publications of sector-specific guidance, each over 20 pages in length (or 38 pages in the case of guidance for fee-charging charities).[26] In the author's view, these publications were excessively lengthy and repetitive, often illogical, and inaccurate in law. At times, they risked being patronising, for example, by suggesting that trustees should consider the charity's costs when setting fees, or that offering a loan provides less of an opportunity to benefit than a permanent waiver of charges.[27] More significantly, the Analysis, which one assumes was written by the Commission's legal staff and not by the Policy Division, was of a poor standard, repeatedly including quotations from cases without context, commentary or analysis.[28] This chapter addresses some of the more significant criticisms which can be made of the Commission's legal interpretation in 2008.

The Guidance was said to reflect 'changes in the law on public benefit arising from the Charities Act 2006', but did not specify what those changes were alleged to be.[29] The Analysis, on the other hand, suggested that the only change was the removal of a presumption of public benefit in certain cases.[30] Whilst it concluded from this that public benefit would now need to be shown in all cases, the

[24] Guidance G6.

[25] Guidance G7.

[26] *Advancement of Education* (n 18); *The Advancement of Religion for the Public Benefit*; *The Relief of Poverty for the Public Benefit*; *Public Benefit and Fee-charging* (all Commission, December 2008).

[27] *Fee-charging* (n 26) Annex A2 and B2 respectively.

[28] See ch 1, n 80.

[29] Guidance B1.

[30] Analysis Introduction, 3: otherwise 'the law on public benefit [was] unaltered' by the Act; elsewhere it was noted that the way charitable purposes had been articulated in the 2006 Act also represented change (4.17).

Commission's publications did not also conclude with any clarity that case law might no longer be relevant, as it later suggested in the Preston Down Trust case:[31] the Analysis merely included a somewhat ambiguous, and inadequate, statement that the intention of the 2006 Act had been that case law regarding public benefit should continue to apply 'apart from the removal of the presumption'.[32]

From the case law, the Commission extrapolated two principles which it said had to be met in order to demonstrate that an organisation's aims were for the public benefit.[33] These two principles were further divided into 'important factors that must be considered', or 'sub-principles', which were equally mandatory:[34]

Principle 1
1a: It must be clear what the benefits are.
1b: The benefits must be related to the aims.
1c: Benefits must be balanced against any detriment or harm.

Principle 2
2a: The beneficiaries must be appropriate to the aims.
2b: Where benefit is to a section of the public, the opportunity to benefit must not be unreasonably restricted by geographical or other restrictions.
2c: People in poverty must not be excluded from the opportunity to benefit.
2d: Any private benefits must be incidental.

On the face of it, the two principles appeared similar to the two tests of charitable status described in the previous chapter, but they differed in several respects.

Principle 1a: It Must be Clear what the Benefits are

The 2008 publications explained that it was 'the benefit', rather than an organisation's purposes, which had to be beneficial in a way the law regards as charitable,[35] and that 'way' meant capable of proof in a court of law.[36] The two formulations might amount to the same thing in many cases, but they are not the same. The use of the noun 'benefit', rather than the adjective 'beneficial', created a different emphasis and encouraged a focus, first, on the activities through which purposes

[31] See text to nn 19–28, ch 2.
[32] Analysis 4.17. This qualification is removed by the 2013 Analysis (see ch 9).
[33] 'Aims' were defined as an individual organisation's purposes, but those purposes were sometimes misrepresented (eg, Highfield Priory, where the constitutional object was 'the advancement of education … and in connection therewith to … carry on schools', but 'the aim' was expressed as 'to provide a school or schools for the advancement of education' (in the Commission's first round of public benefit assessments (see ch 6)). Holmes questions the lawfulness, and desirability, of the Commission's practice of refusing registration where a constitution includes only one or more of the statutory list of purposes: R Holmes, 'Purposes, Descriptions of Purposes and Drafting an Objects Clause' [2009] *Private Client Business* 295.
[34] Guidance C3. For convenience (and adopting the practice of the Commission), sub-principles are herein referred to as Principles.
[35] Analysis 2.15.
[36] Analysis Part 2.

are carried out and, second, the end result. This approach ran counter to the purposes test so unambiguously laid down by case law and is especially problematic where the purposes have not yet been carried out or where the 'benefits' are intangible.[37] Whilst resulting benefits are likely to constitute evidence that purposes are beneficial, the absence of proven benefits does not necessarily mean that purposes are not beneficial in a way the law regards as charitable.

In considering the Guidance and Analysis together, it was clear that institutions would be expected to satisfy the Commission of the benefits they offered by providing proof in most cases, although the publications differed in the detail. The Guidance stated that a benefit must be 'capable of being recognised, identified, defined, described', but may 'seem quite remote', and need not be 'capable of being quantified or measured', for example, the appreciation of a beautiful landscape or conservation of the environment.[38] No evidence would be needed if the benefit were obvious, but where the benefit was 'debatable or may depend on the circumstances', evidence *would* be required and the type of evidence would depend on the nature of the benefit:[39] it might comprise expert opinion, for example, or a 'general consensus of objective and informed opinion'[40] and third party evidence could be required to confirm or refute evidence put forward by the organisation.[41]

The Analysis, on the other hand, defined a benefit, not only as something identifiable and which the law recognises as beneficial, but also as 'something which produces demonstrable impact on the community or a section of the community'[42] and which, if necessary, must be 'demonstrated as fact'.[43] Despite acknowledging that charitable status was a 'pure question of law',[44] the Commission elsewhere described it as a 'question of fact'[45] and signalled that, like all questions of fact, it was to be answered by 'evidence cognisable by the courts'.[46] Crucially, benefits,

[37] Use of the noun was questioned by C McCall and M Smith: Joint Memorandum (submitted with the ISC's response to the consultation on the draft Guidance (5 June 2007) para 23). The 2013 guidance, more accurately, directs attention to the need for the purposes to be beneficial, but the questions over the need for, and the nature of, evidence remain.

[38] Guidance E2 (although the Commission's approach in assessing public benefit suggests otherwise (see ch 6)); see also the statement at Analysis 2.22, that 'a large amount of public benefit in relation to one aim cannot make up for a deficit in public benefit in relation to another', which has no counterpart in case law.

[39] Guidance E2.

[40] Although it was not clear how such opinion should be ascertained, nor how its objectivity and informed quality should be measured. It seemed to go further than the 'common understanding of enlightened opinion' referred to, specifically in the context of fourth head charities, in *National Anti-Vivisection Society v IRC* [1948] AC 31 (HL) 49 (Lord Wright).

[41] It was not obvious why third party evidence should be required to corroborate the organisation's evidence. (A similarly questionable need for third party verification is suggested in the public benefit assessments: see text to nn 18–19, ch 6.)

[42] Analysis 2.2.

[43] Analysis 2.1.

[44] Analysis 4.21 (citing Lord Nathan).

[45] Analysis 4.17.

[46] Analysis 2.2.

even intangible benefits,[47] were required to be 'capable of proof', where necessary by sufficient 'factual and positive evidence' which the courts must evaluate.[48] Whilst the Analysis acknowledged that there is no need to 'call for proof' if the benefit is obvious, the question of what was 'obvious' remained unclear.[49] Indeed, the Commission's extensive investigation and identification of benefits provided by a school gave every indication that the Commission's view of what amounts to 'obvious' differed materially from the courts' view.[50] And given that the benefit of providing a mainstream education appeared not to be 'obvious', all the signs were that the demand for judicial evidence of demonstrable impact was going to be the norm.

The proposition that a benefit which is 'not capable of proof … cannot be recognised',[51] so that the relevant institution cannot be charitable,[52] was drawn more widely than is justified by the cases which the Commission cited in support and would inevitably cause difficulties where benefits are intangible or remote. In *McGovern v Attorney-General*, for example, the fundamental reason for holding the purposes of the Amnesty International Trust non-charitable was that they were considered to be political in nature and, whilst Slade J accepted that one rationale for the relevant legal principle was that the public benefit in respect of intended changes in law and government policy could not be proven, the case did not warrant the Commission's much wider proposition.[53] Similarly, the suggestion that the Carmelite Priory in *Gilmour v Coats* was non-charitable because the alleged benefits of intercessory prayer were incapable of proof ignored the fundamental principle, which the case clearly illustrated, that no amount of benefit, whether capable of proof or not, can confer the necessary public character on a trust which is construed as essentially private.[54] To take the dictum from that case, which refers to a 'demonstrable impact on the community', and use it as the basis for defining 'benefit' was both unjustified and unhelpful. The need for 'demonstrable impact' in that case was in order to distinguish legal precedent which had established that a cloistered religious community, such as the Priory, could not be charitable. This was not to say that every benefit must be shown to have a demonstrable impact on a community. In *Funnell v Stewart*, for example, Hazel Williamson QC (sitting as a High Court judge) found faith healing to be charitable, without the need for evidence of its 'demonstrable efficaciousness'.[55] Similarly, in *Re Shaw's Will Trusts*,

[47] Analysis 2.16. Proof of something intangible is, of course, notoriously difficult.

[48] Analysis 2.4.

[49] Analysis 2.7.

[50] See the Commission's list of 'obvious' benefits in *Advancement of Education* (n 18) D2. (In assessing public benefit, the Commission listed numerous benefits, far beyond the principal benefit of providing an education (see ch 6).)

[51] Analysis 2.6.

[52] Analysis 2.6, 2.9.

[53] *McGovern v AG* [1982] Ch 321 (Ch) (see ch 2, part III, Principle C).

[54] *Gilmour v Coats* [1949] AC 426 (HL).

[55] *Funnell v Stewart* [1996] 1 WLR 288 (Ch) 297.

Vaisey J indicated that evidence of the beneficial aspects of improving citizenship 'could not be sought from any quarter' (and was not required in any event).[56]

Other propositions in the Analysis were similarly misleading and inaccurate. The statement that 'it is well established that the courts have recognised on numerous occasions[57] that whether there is a benefit "is a question to be answered by the court on forming an opinion upon the evidence before it"',[58] for example, misrepresented the judgment in question, where the 'question to be answered' was 'whether a gift is or may be operative for the public benefit' and not 'whether there [was] a benefit'.[59] The two are different. The Court did not seek to identify or prove an actual benefit in this case but to satisfy itself that the stated purpose (of training spiritualist mediums) would, *if* carried out, be beneficial for the community or would tend to advance education. The purpose of the statement was to emphasise the fact that the test was not one to be judged according to the personal beliefs of either the judge or the testator, but by the court, applying the normal rules of evidence. The Commission's failure to explain that the Court considered affidavits, and consulted dictionaries and other works, only because it was unfamiliar with the subject of the training of spiritualist mediums was likely to give the false impression that actual benefits should be demonstrated by evidence in virtually every case.

Likewise, the proposition that it was 'the role of the courts to determine in each case whether the benefit to the public necessarily results from the way in which the purpose is being carried out' was misleading.[60] To the extent that this suggested that the courts should examine the way in which an organisation carries out its purposes, or that the identified (and proven) benefit must result from that method and only that method, it was a serious misrepresentation. It also ignored the very relevant context of the case cited, which was that the purposes being considered had been proposed, but not yet embarked upon.[61] The actual description of the court's role, in the words of Russell LJ, was that it must determine 'whether the trusts are such that benefit to the community must necessarily result from their execution'.[62] The word 'necessarily' was used here several times in order to emphasise the point that purposes aimed at the welfare of animals were not necessarily (though commonly) charitable, or to indicate that purposes must be undoubtedly beneficial and not merely possibly beneficial.[63] The Commission further quotes a comment on the case made by Lord Wright, that 'there could not be a

[56] *Re Shaw's Will Trusts* [1952] Ch 163 (Ch) 170.

[57] The two ideas presumably being the same.

[58] Analysis 2.3.

[59] *Re Hummeltenberg* [1923] 1 Ch 237 (Ch) 240. Nor was the dictum in para 2.9 quoted entirely accurately: it was not the 'content of a benefit' which the court felt could not be precisely defined, but the test of public benefit (*Gilmour* (n 54) 446).

[60] Analysis 2.10.

[61] *Re Grove-Grady* [1929] 1 Ch 557 (CA).

[62] ibid, 588 (not 572 as stated).

[63] eg, *Re Wedgwood* [1915] 1 Ch 113 (CA).

legal charitable trust unless its execution involved a benefit to the community'.[64] This was also misleading in ignoring the context of the contemplated trusts in *Re Grove-Grady* and the distinction being made by Lord Wright, namely that there must be a benefit to the community and not just a benefit to the animals.[65]

The Commission also misquotes Lord Wright directly by saying that 'an assumed prospect or possibility of gain which is vague, intangible *or* remote' (emphasis added) could not be treated as establishing public benefit.[66] His Lordship actually said that 'the law may well say that … an assumed prospect or possibility of gain *so* vague intangible *and* remote' (emphasis added) could not be treated as a benefit to humanity.[67] The context is critical, as his Lordship was referring to the specific 'vague and problematical moral elevation', which had been pitched against the clear evidence of detriment which would result from suppressing vivisection, in a bid to establish charitable status under the fourth head (where there was a tendency towards tangible and objective benefits).[68] His Lordship was making it abundantly clear that the 'life and happiness of human beings must be preferred to that of animals'.[69]

Lastly, the statement that 'in the context of educational … purposes, unless it is obvious, the courts must receive evidence to support or negate the presence of educational value *and* public benefit' (emphasis added) suggested that a benefit, *apart from* educational value, had to be shown to have been delivered and it had to be shown by producing evidence to the courts.[70] In the case cited, however, Vaisey J specifically addressed the question of whether he was concerned to receive evidence of actual benefit and concluded that he was not. The question, he said, was whether the purposes were 'genuinely educational in their aim and scope' and he was not concerned with, indeed 'ought not to speculate', 'how far' the intended purposes would 'be considered to be, *or be in fact*, beneficial' (emphasis added).[71]

Principle 1b: The Benefits Must be Related to the Aims

This principle was fundamentally flawed and asked a question which did not need to be asked. The Commission maintained that both case law and the 2006 Act required the benefit to be 'related to the purposes', but cited no authority in support.[72] In fact, each provided simply that the purposes must be for the public benefit. The difference may be subtle, but it is not unimportant, the Commission's

[64] Analysis 2.26; *Anti-Vivisection* (n 40) 44.
[65] *Anti-Vivisection* (n 40) 44.
[66] Analysis 2.10.
[67] *Anti-vivisection* (n 40) 49.
[68] ibid.
[69] ibid, 48.
[70] Or, presumably, the Commission; Analysis 2.5.
[71] *Shaw* (n 56) 168, concluding (at 172) that the education proposed 'if corrected and augmented and amplified by other kinds of teaching and instruction, might have most beneficial results'.
[72] Analysis 2.20.

approach necessarily leading it to identify benefits which were both relevant and irrelevant to the aims and to question any benefits which arose incidentally, whereas the courts' approach was to consider only the beneficial (or detrimental) nature of the purposes or aims themselves, primarily as a matter of construction. The law required neither identification nor consideration of additional, unrelated benefits except, perhaps, where they were private and more than incidental so that charitable status should be denied, or where they signified a breach of the trustees' duty to carry out the proper purposes of the charity.[73] And the Commission's repeated assertion, that it was the courts' role to consider whether benefit 'results from the way the purpose is carried out', was not supported by the cases and dicta cited.[74] The need to consider 'the sphere in which [a charity] operates', for example, derived from a case where it was appropriate for the Court to construe a written memorandum in order to identify the institution's purposes (and to determine whether the purposes, once identified, were charitable)[75] and did not warrant a similar approach where the purposes of an independent school, or other institution, are clearly set out.[76]

Although the Commission correctly stated that it is the main purposes which are relevant, and not the means or consequences of carrying out those purposes, its explanations were sometimes confusing.[77] In considering an organisation with the aim of running a boys' school, for example, the Commission also considered the benefits which arose from the pupils running a luncheon club for old people and 'counted' the benefits to the boys but not those enjoyed by the old people.[78] And although the Commission's publications had suggested that activities would be relevant to charitable status only in exceptional circumstances,[79] the Commission's interpretation gave activities a much greater relevance, essentially linking them to the overriding question of public benefit in all respects,[80] including whether purposes will or may be carried out for the public benefit.[81]

[73] eg, where non-charitable benefits conferred by the means to the end are so substantial that it can no longer be said that the purposes are exclusively charitable: *IRC v City of Glasgow Police Athletic Association* [1953] AC 380 (HL) 402; Analysis 3.83.

[74] Analysis 2.24–2.28; see also text to nn 60–62 above.

[75] *Incorporated Council of Law Reporting for England and Wales v AG* [1972] Ch 73 (CA) 91, quoted at Analysis 2.25.

[76] Similarly, the expert evidence adduced in *Re Pinion* [1965] Ch 85 (Ch) (Analysis 2.28) addressed the quality of exhibits and concluded that they did not advance education (the possibility of a more selective exhibition being considered to be outside the terms of the will (at 110)); and the significance of the dictum at 2.27 was that the proposed trust (in *Grove-Grady* (n 61)) would need to be beneficial, not that a benefit had to be proved as a matter of fact.

[77] Analysis 2.23 (seemingly reversed in the 2013 Analysis (see ch 9, n 122)).

[78] *Advancement of Education* (n 18) 15. The distinction was also ignored in the Commission's assessment of independent schools (see ch 6).

[79] eg, Analysis 4.4, 4.6, 4.10, 4.11, the purposes test being emphasised at 4.1.

[80] Analysis 4.16.

[81] Analysis 4.6; for a similar emphasis on the analysis and evaluation of activities, see the First-tier Tribunal's decision in *Full Fact v Charity Commission* CA/2011/0001 (26 July 2011). (The Commission has since granted charitable status on the basis of the organisation having revised its objects: Decision (Commission, 17 September 2014).)

The notion of the courts using 'practical measures' to assess public benefit was also somewhat obscure.[82] By way of illustration, the Commission explained that the benefits arising from members of a sports club collecting money for disaster victims, or the health benefits of an ice rink in the grounds of a historic house, 'will not count' in a public benefit assessment.[83] But this is misleading. In truth, such benefits are simply *irrelevant* to the question of whether the identified purposes of furthering sport or preserving historic buildings are prima facie charitable and public in character. Collecting money for a good cause, or operating an ice rink are operational matters within the discretion of the trustees and do not need to be considered, or even identified, in determining charitable status.[84] There is also doubtful merit in the Commission's explanation that the measures differ between charities because, for example, the public benefit of conserving an endangered species is very different from that of relieving poverty.[85]

The Commission also maintained that both common law and statute provided that 'the remoter benefits of having a charitable purpose are not enough'.[86] The 'remoter benefits' were not explained and, more importantly, the Commission failed to cite any case law in support or to identify a relevant statutory provision. In fact, the Act did not make such provision, or even address the question.[87] If it was the Commission's intention to suggest that the purposes of advancing religion or education were not for the public benefit on the basis of their advantage to society as a whole, this should have been stated more clearly and supported by named cases. The proposition might also cast doubt upon the charitable status of animal charities which primarily assist animals but, more importantly (and more remotely) improve human morality. Furthermore, if an institution is established for exclusively charitable purposes, the test of public benefit, by definition, has been satisfied and so whether any remoter benefits (whatever they might be) are 'enough' would appear to be meaningless in any event.

More specifically, case law was said to show that broad benefits to the public which are unrelated to a charity's purposes are 'too remote' and 'will not count'.[88] But the authority cited did not support this proposition, the Commission stating (correctly) that, in *Oppenheim v Tobacco Securities Trust Co Ltd*, the advantage to society in having well-educated people 'did not save what was otherwise an insufficient section of the public'.[89] On a basic level, this failed to provide any logical

[82] Guidance E3.

[83] ibid.

[84] Unless, as explained above, there is evidence to suggest that they indicate non-charitable purposes.

[85] Guidance E3.

[86] Analysis 2.20.

[87] It is assumed that the remoter benefits are not limited to the general benefit which is 'sometimes argued' (by whom is not stated) to derive from being included in the statutory list of charitable purposes (Analysis 2.20). It is possible, but not beyond doubt, that the Commission had in mind the no-presumption provision (2011 Act, s 4(2)), but it is difficult to know.

[88] Analysis 2.21.

[89] ibid; *Oppenheim v Tobacco Securities Trust Co Ltd* [1951] AC 297 (HL).

illustration of the proposition itself, particularly since such an advantage to society could hardly be described as 'unrelated to' the purposes of advancing education. The Commission's legal reasoning was also misleading in suggesting that the House of Lords had been assessing the amount of benefit and had found it to be inadequate because it was obliged to disregard benefits stemming from accidental and unplanned activities. The trust in that case was not charitable because it was not public in character and it is well established that no amount of benefit can render a private trust charitable, whether it is direct or indirect, related or unrelated. Similarly, the conclusion that incidental activities, however beneficial, are not 'counted towards' meeting the public benefit requirement was said to be supported by *IRC v Yorkshire Agricultural Society*, whereas the correct principle to be drawn from that case is that a subsidiary purpose of providing incidental benefits to members of a society does not prevent the conclusion that it was established for charitable purposes only.[90] And to the extent that the law regards purposes as 'for the public benefit' because they are beneficial to the community as a whole, even if incidentally they also benefit individuals (such as scholars or religious followers), the Commission's proposition cannot be supported.[91]

In many cases, of course, purposes are prima facie charitable because the intended beneficiaries will clearly benefit *directly* and whether indirect or remote benefit alone is sufficient, or even relevant, will not arise. Furthermore, since incidental benefits of a *private* nature do not deprive purposes of their charitable nature, it seems both logical and sensible that non-private incidental benefits which only enhance the benefit to the intended beneficiaries or others should be immaterial to the question of charitable status.

Principle 1c: Benefits Must be Balanced Against Any Detriment or Harm

There was nothing contentious in Principle 1c, or the Commission's reference to the need for 'an overall or net benefit', and it is well illustrated by *National Anti-Vivisection Society*.[92] The Analysis in this respect was suitably brief.[93] The more lengthy expositions in the Guidance, however, appeared superfluous and potentially confusing, for example, the explanation that if benefits are 'overwhelming', then 'inconsequential detriment' is irrelevant: one might have assumed that *inconsequential* detriment could be disregarded even if benefits are less than overwhelming.[94] Similarly, the proposition that 'real evidence of detriment' is required,[95] and

[90] *IRC v Yorkshire Agricultural Society* [1928] 1 KB 611 (CA) (cited but not named: Analysis 2.30).
[91] See ch 2, part III.
[92] *Anti-Vivisection* (n 40); see text to nn 177–81, ch 2.
[93] Analysis 2.31.
[94] Guidance E4, assuming the benefits are not themselves inconsequential (and 'inconsequential' apparently meaning incidental, or relatively insignificant, in the example given).
[95] Guidance E4 (it 'cannot just be supposed').

weighed against 'benefits that are provided',[96] was also misleading: the weighing up may be done prospectively, and by 'foreseeing' and 'imagining' the beneficial and detrimental aspects of the purposes.[97]

In the context of education, the Commission noted examples of publishing a guide on money laundering or teaching computer hacking.[98] Clearly these are more detrimental than beneficial, but, like a 'school of pickpockets',[99] are also non-charitable on the grounds of morality or public policy, even if they are 'educational' at all.[100] The suggestion that, where an organisation promotes an extreme sport, there should be an investigation into steps taken to minimise risks of injury also appeared to confuse charitable status with concerns about health and safety regulation and compliance, and appears to have no basis in charity law.[101] More helpfully, the Commission might have offered guidance on the areas of detriment which had already been identified as potential areas of difficulty, for example, the prejudice to social mobility allegedly caused by independent schools or the doctrines or practices of certain religions which exclude individuals. But it did not.

Principle 2a: The Beneficiaries Must be Appropriate to the Aims

Principle 2b: Where Benefit is to a Section of the Public, the Opportunity to Benefit Must not be Unreasonably Restricted by Geographical or Other Restrictions[102]

The Analysis (but not the Guidance) merged Principles 2a and 2b in order to 'avoid unnecessary repetition and confusion',[103] but the Commission's failure to comment on the detailed types of restriction in Principle 2b, or to cite any authority for them, undermined its analysis and inevitably aroused the suspicion that there was no such authority.[104] It was also quite remarkable that fee-charging

[96] Analysis 2.31.

[97] The Analysis (2.31) set out the quote which referred to the resulting circumstances being 'foreseen or imagined' (*Anti-Vivisection* (n 40) 47); see also text to nn 55–56, 71 above.

[98] *Advancement of Education* (n 18) D2. The examples given in the general guidance were similarly unenlightening (Guidance E4).

[99] *Pinion* (n 76) 105 (Harman LJ) (also at 100).

[100] See n 198, ch 2.

[101] Guidance E4; the Commission also considered child protection issues in assessing an independent school's satisfaction of the public benefit requirement (see ch 6).

[102] Note the 'other restrictions' addressed by the Commission: restrictions based on charitable need, personal characteristics, access to facilities, eligibility for membership, trustees' discretion and the ability to pay any fees charged (Guidance F5–F10). The last of these is dealt with separately by the Commission and is considered in ch 5.

[103] Analysis 3.2 (also suggesting that the two principles are virtually the same).

[104] The restrictions were said to 'flow from' the case law supporting the principles generally (Analysis 3.2). In fact, where the restrictions in Principle 2b had merit, they were better dealt with on other grounds, eg, illegality (Guidance F6) or the requirement for purposes to be public in character (Guidance F5, F8). The reference to religious restrictions also raises the question of whether faith schools might have been challenged on the grounds of public benefit.

was not the subject of a separate principle, given that the treatment of charities which charge high fees had led to so much debate during the passage of the Charities Bill and had featured so prominently in the Commission's pronouncements, and also given that the specific guidance for fee-charging charities was so extensive.[105]

It is hard to conceive of how beneficiaries might be *inappropriate* to a charity's aims, other than on the grounds of the stated objects being capricious and contrary to public policy, for example a school for the deceased or a school for the sons of millionaires only. Indeed 'appropriate' here seemed to mean no more than that the aim should be intended to benefit the public, or a section of the public which is 'a public class' and 'sufficiently large or open in nature'.[106] Although the Commission stated that the number of potential beneficiaries should not be 'negligible', it went on to say that a class could be 'quite small', provided benefits were widely available to any eligible person, a sensible proposition which was not inconsistent with binding precedent.[107]

The Commission maintained that the principles applied differently, depending on the purposes concerned, but failed to indicate how the test might differ, save that it illustrated (at length) the fact that a personal nexus does not prevent a trust for the relief of poverty from being charitable.[108] There appeared to be no legitimate basis for its conclusion that the principles apply differently depending on (inter alia) the 'modern social and economic conditions in which the organisation operates', and its further comment that they depend on 'the law which applies to that purpose' seemed somewhat circular.[109] Both statements were difficult to understand and whether either offered 'guidance' to the reader is doubtful. Other propositions were set out with no legal authority, such as the suggestion that a balance should be struck between present and future generations,[110] or that an unreasonably restricted class should be widened,[111] or that a 'very narrowly defined class, although perhaps not as narrow as one having a personal family connection' might be sufficient for the relief of needs of the aged or disabled or to prevent social exclusion.[112]

In a rare piece of analysis, the Commission rejected as 'unhelpful' the concept of a 'class within a class', put forward (obiter) by Viscount Simonds in *Inland Revenue Commissioners v Baddeley*.[113] The Commission referred to the case as establishing, instead, that if the link between the purpose and the beneficial class is irrational, the restriction on the class will not be acceptable.[114] This may be unobjectionable

[105] As mentioned above, 38 pages long. One wonders whether the intention was to draw less attention to the subject.

[106] Guidance F2.

[107] The guidance predated *Re Duffy* [2013] EWHC 2395 (Ch); see ch 2, part III, Principle H.

[108] Analysis 3.5–3.8.

[109] Analysis 3.9.

[110] Guidance F2.

[111] ibid.

[112] Analysis 3.49. An example might have made this less obscure.

[113] *IRC v Baddeley* [1955] AC 572 (HL) 591; Analysis 3.12, 3.15.

[114] Analysis 3.10.

as a principle, and even preferable to the concept of a 'class within a class' (which failed to receive the support of the other judges),[115] but it should be noted that the trust in that case was non-charitable because the purposes were too vague and not exclusively charitable, not because there was no rational link. Nor was it suggested that the class was 'irrational', simply too restricted. The Commission also failed to cite any authority in which purposes were found to be non-charitable because of the absence of a rational link, and the statement that a class 'can' be sufficient where there *is* a rational link provided no support for the proposition either.[116]

The Commission commented that 'some purposes' *must* be available either to the public as a whole or inhabitants of an area.[117] Whilst this is likely to be the case with objects of 'general public utility',[118] there is no reason to suggest that the proposition extends to all fourth head charities.[119] It also stated that 'the issue becomes whether [the people intended to benefit] benefit',[120] but whether people actually benefit is more pertinent to the question of how effective the charity is in carrying out its purposes than it is a determining factor in establishing charitable status.[121]

The Commission may also have misconstrued Lord Simonds' comment that a gift for the advancement of education could not be charitable, where it is conditional upon the beneficiaries leading a cloistered life and not imparting the fruits of their study.[122] Certainly such purposes would not satisfy the test of public character,[123] but his Lordship's words did not justify the Commission's much wider conclusion, that, apparently in all cases, 'part of the consideration of public character is the extent to which the charity is beneficial to the wider community'.[124]

Citing no authority for its statement that the test of public character was 'for a long time' 'one of degree',[125] the Analysis concluded that the Commission 'should be both cautious and flexible in the application of the Compton test', a reference to *Re Compton*, in which the distinction was made between the intended

[115] Lord Reid, dissenting on the principal ground, nonetheless concluded that the intended class *was* a sufficient section of the public and Lord Porter and Lord Tucker expressed a preference not to decide the point. It might also be dubious as a possible disqualifying factor in light of *Goodman v Saltash* (1881–82) LR 7 App Cas 633 (HL) and *Verge v Somerville* [1924] AC 496 (PC).

[116] Analysis 3.16 (or 'more rational connection', 3.10).

[117] Analysis p 19, 3.17–3.21. A library, for example, should be open to all the inhabitants of a particular area as a minimum (p 19); *cf* para 3.24, which suggested that a library may be open to the partially sighted only.

[118] *Baddeley* (n 113) 592.

[119] Analysis 3.21 (which refers to a discussion but without stating the conclusion).

[120] Analysis 3.17; *cf Shaw* (n 56) 168.

[121] Although it may also provide evidence that purposes are beneficial (where there is uncertainty).

[122] Analysis 3.30, referring to *Gilmour* (n 54) 450 (being one of two limitations on a gift for advancing education being charitable, the other being that it is not a question of the testator's opinion (to which might be added that none of the disqualifying factors apply, such as an intention to make a profit)).

[123] As in religious cases: cp *Gilmour* (n 54) and *Neville Estates v Madden* [1962] Ch 832 (Ch).

[124] Analysis 3.31.

[125] Analysis 3.34 (but possibly referring to *Oppenheim* (n 89) 314 (Lord MacDermott)).

beneficiaries being defined by a personal or impersonal quality.[126] 'Cautious and flexible' were not explained,[127] but in light of judicial dicta post-*Compton*, it is not suggested that the Commission was unjustified in taking a critical view of the test, or in describing the question of whether a class constitutes a sufficient section of the public as one to be decided on the facts of each case.[128] Lord MacDermott, for example, had called the distinction 'arbitrary and artificial'[129] and his views had met with approval from Lord Cross, who had called the public character test a 'question of degree'.[130] In light of this conclusion, however, the Commission's 11-page analysis of Principles 2a and 2b appeared all the more superfluous.[131]

Principle 2d: Any Private Benefit Must be Incidental[132]

The Analysis set out a number of quotations from cases, which expressed in different ways the general principle that private benefit must be ancillary or incidental and must not represent a distinct and main purpose of the organisation.[133] The Guidance also explained that Principle 2d was not concerned with benefits received by beneficiaries, in keeping with case law where private benefit is normally associated with benefits accruing to trustees or founders or others (rather than potential beneficiaries).[134] The Analysis, however, suggested that if a beneficiary received a greater benefit than necessary to meet his need, or which did not directly relate to his need, charitable status 'will be affected'.[135] *Joseph Rowntree Memorial Trust v Attorney-General* was cited, but does not support the proposition.[136] This case tested the charitable status of several proposed housing schemes and the alleged 'profit' to a beneficiary, in realising the increased value of a purchased home, was held *not* to deprive the proposed scheme of its charitable nature. No authority was cited by the Commission to support the additional proposition that individual benefits should be 'appropriate and reasonably proportional to the need' or that 'the means used and the amount involved must be limited and determined by the charitable purpose'.[137] Such propositions may be unobjectionable, or even self-evident, but to the extent that they are accurate at all, they would have been better

[126] Analysis 3.45; *Re Compton* [1945] Ch 123 (CA) 129.

[127] But might suggest a freedom to ignore it.

[128] Analysis 3.50.

[129] *Oppenheim* (n 89) 317.

[130] *Dingle v Turner* [1972] AC 601 (HL) 623 (an approach which the Commission described as 'a proper basis' (Analysis, 3.14)).

[131] And twice as long as its analysis underpinning Principles 2b (fees) and 2c combined.

[132] Principle 2c is addressed in ch 5.

[133] Analysis 3.77–3.90. An excessive number were included and most had no further analysis or commentary.

[134] Guidance F12 (although the word 'reasonable' in the first paragraph leaves an ambiguity).

[135] Analysis 3.92 (presumably adversely and perhaps with luxury or 'gold-plated' education in mind, a point echoed by the Tribunal (see ch 8)).

[136] *Joseph Rowntree Memorial Trust v AG* [1983] Ch 159 (Ch).

[137] Analysis 3.93.

expressed in terms of the trustees' duty to exercise their powers properly in fulfilment of the charitable purposes and not as pertaining to charitable status.

IV. Once a Charity, Always a Charity?

The Commission's publications in 2008 presented significantly greater scope for charitable status to be denied or lost than was outlined in the previous chapter, but the legal basis for its interpretation appeared weak and its explanation of the consequences of failing to meet the public benefit requirement was unhelpful. The guidance, of course, was required to reflect the law and not the policy aims of the Government or the Commission, but it is worth bearing in mind that the Strategy Unit Report had indicated that inadequate access, or benefit, to the poor should result in removal from the Register,[138] and also that the Commission's own policy paper, in 2001, had made clear its view that what is charitable 'may change following trends in social and economic circumstances'.[139] Despite improvements made in 2013, the transience or permanence of a charity's status remains confused and open to doubt and the risk of removal from the Register has not disappeared altogether.[140]

In its 2008 Guidance and Analysis, and in its 'public benefit assessment programme',[141] the Commission was keen to give the impression that removal from the Register would be a last resort, suggesting that charitable status was unlikely to be affected by a review of a charity's public benefit,[142] for example, and that removal might result from a determination that the registered charity was never charitable 'in extreme circumstances'.[143] The Commission's approach was not entirely consistent, however,[144] and it also indicated that removal from the Register may be necessary following 'changes in modern social conditions' which alter perceptions of 'how ... purposes need to be carried out if they are to be for the public benefit'.[145] In its 2000 publication, *Maintenance of an Accurate Register*,[146] to which the reader of the Analysis was directed,[147] the Commission also indicated that a charity could be removed where 'changes in the values of society' lead to

[138] *Private Action, Public Benefit: A Review of Charities and the Wider Not-For-Profit Sector* (Cabinet Office, September 2002) (Strategy Unit Report), eg, paras 4.0, 7.75.

[139] *The Review of the Register of Charities* (Commission, October 2001) para 2.

[140] See ch 9.

[141] See ch 6 (which describes how two schools failed to meet the public benefit requirement but were not removed from the Register).

[142] Analysis 4.23; see also 4.21, 4.22.

[143] Analysis 4.25. *The Maintenance of an Accurate Register* (Commission, November 2000) (*Accurate Register*) also called removal a 'last resort' (para 8).

[144] cp Guidance H5 and Analysis 4.21–4.23.

[145] Analysis 4.18; see also 4.25.

[146] *Accurate Register* (n 143).

[147] Analysis 4.25.

the nature and effect of purposes being perceived differently,[148] or where a change in 'social circumstances or values' leads to purposes becoming non-charitable.[149] It was clear that the concept of social 'conditions', 'values' or 'circumstances' was critical to existing charities, as changes in any of them might cause their charitable status to be taken away. A proper explanation was called for as to what these terms meant, and what sort of change was contemplated, but none was given and the terms were left vague, perhaps deliberately.

Likewise, talk of trustees being in breach of trust or failing in their duties was bound to cause concern and any risk of new trustees being appointed, or the organisation's assets being taken out of the trustees' control, should have been unambiguously explained.[150] There was a distinct lack of detail, however, and the 2008 guidance sought to justify its absence on the basis that the Commission's approach was to be 'informed by the result of [its] future work',[151] a justification which was inadequate from the outset and which has proved to be manifestly inadequate in light of the Commission's work to date. The position was not much improved in 2013. Although the revised guidance attempts to distinguish more clearly between the issues of charitable status and trustees' duties, the level of detail is minimal and superficial and the reader is directed to a little-altered version of the 2000 *Accurate Register* publication.[152]

(1) The Legal Justification for the Commission's Review of Existing Charities and the Threat to their Charitable Status

The Commission maintained that a failure to meet 'any one or more' of its principles of public benefit meant that an institution 'cannot be a charity', whether the institution was already registered as a charity or applying for registration for the first time.[153] This interpretation necessarily threatened the charitable status of a registered charity and, therefore, its inclusion on the Register. It was also the basis on which the public benefit assessment programme was conducted and yet the results of those assessments revealed a reluctance to apply the Commission's legal interpretation in practice, as the two schools which failed to satisfy Principles 2b and 2c were not removed, but encouraged to offer more social benefit.[154]

The Commission's claim that it was required to 'ensure that registered charities are properly established for charitable aims, a necessary characteristic of which is

[148] *Accurate Register* (n 143) Annex A4.2.

[149] ibid, Annex D2.2.

[150] The removal of assets, by implication, also raises the possibility of removal from the Register; the ambiguity in the words 'appointing new trustees' (in addition to or in substitution for?) should have been avoided (assuming that the latter interpretation was not intended).

[151] Guidance H5.

[152] The updated version of *Maintenance of an Accurate Register* (Commission, December 2012) (*Accurate Register* 2012) contains some updated legislative references (although it fails to take account of changes made by the Companies Act 2006) and updated information on rights of redress.

[153] Guidance D3.

[154] See ch 6.

that the aims are for the public benefit' is not disputed.[155] Its further claim, however, that it was also required to ensure that those aims were administered 'solely in ways that further the purposes for the public benefit', is not accepted to the extent that it imported a new meaning of 'public benefit'.[156] Nor was it supported by the cases which the Commission cited in support, which tended, rather, to illustrate that where a gift is capable of a charitable or non-charitable interpretation, the court will favour the former, so that the means to be employed should be restricted to furthering those charitable purposes.[157]

The Strategy Unit Report had envisaged that the Commission should carry out a systematic review of registered charities, but the 2006 Act never made any provision for such a review.[158] The Commission went ahead with its public benefit assessment programme nonetheless, apparently continuing the 'rolling programme' which it had launched in 1998,[159] although it reviewed only 20 charities in total.[160] The fact that the charitable status of such a small proportion of registered charities was reassessed against legal criteria which the Commission regarded as new law (principally on the basis of a presumption of public benefit having been removed) raises serious questions about the reasonableness of the Commission's actions as a public authority and, in particular, its compliance with the statutory duty to have regard to best regulatory practice.[161]

In the absence of a statutory duty to review the charitable status of registered charities, the legal basis for the Commission's review of existing charities is open to doubt. Specifically, these assessments of public benefit were said to be justified on the basis of both the Commission's statutory functions and objectives and the purported removal of a presumption of public benefit, all stemming from the 2006 Act. The Commission also sought to justify its review of existing charities more generally, on the basis of its statutory duty to maintain an accurate register and in light of changing social conditions and perceptions of what is charitable. But it is suggested that none of these grounds provides an adequate legal basis.[162]

155 *Emerging findings for charity trustees from the Charity Commission's public benefit assessment work: 2008–09* (Commission, July 2009) 3. Nor is it suggested that such an obligation is restricted to the point of registration.

156 Analysis 4.23: a new criterion based on a meaning of public benefit which is not supported by case law (see text to n 11 above and see chs 4 and 5).

157 Analysis footnote 167 (eg, *Re Hetherington* [1990] ch 1).

158 Strategy Unit Report (n 138) para 4.18. The position was different in Scotland (see ch 7).

159 *Review* (n 139) paras 5, 19, a document to which reference continues to be made: *Accurate Register* 2012 (n 152) 2.

160 Representing approximately 0.0122% of all registered charities. The prospect of future assessments, though much diminished, should not be ruled out (see ch 9, part V).

161 2011 Act, s 16.

162 It is not intended to question the possibility of a registered institution's status being reviewed in other circumstances, such as in claims brought by next of kin or in proceedings regarding fiscal reliefs or breach of trust, for example.

(i) The Commission's Statutory Functions and Objectives

The 'public benefit assessment programme' was described as part of the Commission's statutory objective to promote awareness and understanding of the operation of the public benefit requirement.[163] This requirement, it will be remembered, is expressly defined by reference to the meaning of 'public benefit' in case law and, whilst the programme undoubtedly succeeded in raising awareness of it, the Commission's interpretation of the law relating to charitable status neither justified the assessment programme itself nor provided a true understanding of the legal requirement. The programme was also described as part of interpreting and applying the law on charitable status, and that, in turn, was described as part of promoting charities' compliance and accountability.[164] Charity trustees, however, must ensure that the charity operates for its stated purposes and complies with the various common law and statutory requirements which are applicable to it. Neither the common law nor the Act imposes any additional obligation to demonstrate the flowing of public benefit from its operations or the delivery of social benefit, as the Commission maintained, whether or not related to the question of charitable status.[165]

(ii) Removal of a Presumption of Public Benefit

The Commission put great reliance on the belief that there existed in case law a presumption that purposes for the relief of poverty, the advancement of religion and the advancement of education were for the public benefit, and that the effect of the 2006 Act had been to remove that presumption.[166] It was not alone in that interpretation.[167] It further maintained that this removal entitled (or required) it not simply to consider new applications without the aid of a presumption, but also to revisit all existing registered charities and to test their compliance with the public benefit requirement. If one accepts that there was no presumption of public benefit, however, and that the no-presumption provision said nothing new, this argument could not justify the review of existing charities.[168] The Tribunal's endorsement of the view that no presumption existed would also suggest that the Commission could no longer seek to justify any review of existing charities on this basis.[169]

[163] *Emerging findings* (n 155) 3; 2011 Act, s 14, no 2.

[164] *Emerging findings* (n 155) 4; 2011 Act, s 14, no 3.

[165] See chs 2 and 4.

[166] 2006 Act, s 3(2); 2011 Act, s 4(2); see ch 2, part II.

[167] See, eg, M Harding, 'Trusts for Religious Purposes and the Question of Public Benefit' (2008) 71 *MLR* 159; J Warburton, 'Charities and Public Benefit—from Confusion to Light?' (2008) 10 *Charity Law & Practice Review* 2; see also the Explanatory Notes which accompanied the 2006 Act, para 25 ('there is a presumption').

[168] See text to nn 29–46, ch 2.

[169] The Tribunal's comments in this regard were not confined to educational charities (*ISC* (n 5) [67], [68], [83]), as acknowledged by the Commission in the 2013 guidance (para 26); see also *AG v Charity Commission* [2012] UKUT 420 (TCC), [2012] WTLR 977 [39].

(iii) An Accurate Register

The Commission is required to maintain an 'accurate and up-to-date' register.[170] It must ensure, therefore, that names and particulars of charities, and any changes notified, are correctly entered and that any errors are rectified, which may involve removing incorrect entries. Whether an institution has ceased to be a charity is 'a pure question of law', however, and so any amendment to the Register on this ground must be justified on legal grounds.[171]

(iv) Changing Perceptions and Conditions

In 2001, the Commission justified its review of existing charities partly on the basis that since the 'understanding of what is legally charitable' had continued to evolve since the Register was established in 1960, it had grown to include charities which 'most people would not now regard as charitable and organisations not on it that perhaps they might'.[172] Although later publications acknowledged that charity has a legal technical meaning,[173] and that charitable status 'is not decided on the basis of popularity',[174] the Commission also described how popular opinion could be considered where public benefit was not obvious and, more generally, how public attitudes and opinions should aid an understanding of current social and economic conditions which 'in turn can enable [the Commission] to shape the legal understanding of what is charitable in a way that is relevant for modern society'.[175] It is difficult to reconcile the Commission's affirmation of Rule 1,[176] on the one hand, with this not inconsiderable influence of public opinion on the other.

The idea of charitable purposes and public benefit changing over time,[177] and changes in charity law being 'influenced by social values',[178] has been a common theme in the Commission's publications, where repeated words and phrases have depicted charity as a fluid concept and given charitable status something of an impermanent quality, subject to repeated re-examination and over which the Commission (and the courts) appear to have considerable discretion.

By way of example, the Commission frequently referred to its role in interpreting the law in light of 'modern conditions', 'modern social conditions' and 'changing social and economic circumstances'. It described using an 'evidence-based approach' to identify social and economic conditions,[179] and outlined its task of

[170] 2011 Act, s 15(4).
[171] Analysis 4.21 (indicating that the courts would not be influenced by the Commission's opinion).
[172] *Review* (n 139) para 1.
[173] Analysis 1.10.
[174] Guidance D8.
[175] Analysis 1.10.
[176] See ch 2, part III.
[177] Guidance D6.
[178] Analysis 1.10.
[179] Guidance D7 ('social and economic circumstances' here signifying, or including, 'indicators of social deprivation, local demographics and census results, government or sector reports or surveys etc').

judging what was 'relevant and appropriate' in those conditions in order to determine whether something was charitable.[180] Specifically what the relevant social conditions or values might be in respect of independent schools, or how (if such were the case) a change in such conditions or values might have led to a different view being taken of their purposes, was never explained however. Furthermore, and 'by analogy', the Commission suggested that what constitutes a section of the public or reasonable restrictions could also vary from generation to generation.[181] The risk, of course, is that as generalised and innocuous as such words may appear, they lend themselves to a more extensive interpretation which appears to license a greater discretion than that given by law.

The legal authority cited (at length) in this respect was the passage by Lord Simonds in *National Anti-Vivisection*, which was set out in the previous chapter.[182] It should be noted, however, that his Lordship referred to purposes '[becoming] *superfluous*' '*by* a change in social habits and needs' (emphases added), thereby giving vital context and meaning to the effect of those habits and needs changing.[183] It is not suggested that the circumstances outlined by Lord Simonds in that passage are exhaustive, but the Commission goes considerably further by suggesting that charitable status might be lost merely due to changes in social conditions, values or circumstances, particularly when the nature and extent of such changes is not explained.[184]

It is not inaccurate to refer to the changing nature of charity law, but the limited context in which such a description is appropriate should be understood.[185] First, a change in the law (or morality or public policy) may render charitable purposes non-charitable, and vice versa, but that is not to say that the law on charitable status has changed. Second change may be represented by growth, and more accurately described as such.[186] Thus, the 'ever widening scope' of charitable trusts and purposes[187] is a logical and natural consequence of several factors: new social needs and activities,[188] including an increasing number of lawful religions and a broadening view of 'education',[189] the process of construing purposes by analogy with existing charitable purposes and a judiciary which has given a benevolent construction to dispositions characterised by altruism.[190]

180 Guidance D6.

181 Analysis 1.5.

182 See text to n 246, ch 2.

183 *Anti-Vivisection* (n 40) 74; cited at Analysis 4.20.

184 See text to nn 144–49 above.

185 eg, *Re Diplock* [1941] Ch 253 (Ch) 261.

186 Adding plants to a garden may change its appearance, but not its definition as the cultivated area of land adjoining the house.

187 *Taylor v Taylor* (1910) 10 CLR 218 (HCt Australia) 238 (Isaacs J).

188 *IRC v Falkirk Temperance Café Trust* 1927 SC 261 (CSIH) 272.

189 *IRC v McMullen* [1981] AC 1 (HL) 15 (where Lord Hailsham attributed 'moving and changing' concepts of charity and education to 'changes in ideas about social values').

190 See, eg, *Williams Trustees v IRC* [1947] AC 447 (HL) 460, although less generous attitudes have also been noted to prevail at times: *Re the Estate of Forbes* (2003) NBQB 430 (QB, New Brunswick) [44] (citing AH Oosterhoff and EE Gillese, *Text, Commentary and Cases on Trusts*, 6th edn (Toronto, Carswell, 1998)).

Third, it may *appear* that the law on public benefit has changed, where a court considers a different question in similar circumstances,[191] or where a previous decision is overruled because it was wrongly decided.[192] The Commission also appeared not to distinguish between purposes and the means of achieving those purposes, for example, by suggesting that a supply of cigarettes to hospital patients would no longer be charitable, when it seems more likely that the (constantly charitable) purpose would have been to relieve suffering, although the means of fulfilling those purposes might have needed to change.[193]

The Commission acknowledged that a court would not take a different view of the charitable nature of an institution's purposes without 'a radical change of circumstances, established by sufficient evidence … compelling reasons',[194] and also that a change in the nature of an institution's purposes from charitable to non-charitable was, accordingly, a 'much less common occurrence'.[195] It has never made clear, however, whether the doubt which it cast upon the charitable status of fee-charging independent schools was due to a radical change of circumstances which meant that their purposes, whilst once charitable, had become non-charitable, or whether it considered that they had never been charitable.[196] As has been seen, the consequences of each conclusion are radically different and the Commission should have been clear in its reasoning.[197]

(2) The Commission's Explanation of the Consequences of a Failure to Meet the Public Benefit Requirement

(i) New Applications

The Commission explained that an application for registration would be rejected where an institution failed to demonstrate either that its aims were for the public

[191] cp the cases involving the Royal College of Surgeons (RCS) (*Re RCS* [1899] 1 QB 871 (CA) and *RCS v National Provincial Bank Ltd* [1952] AC 631 (HL)), the later case holding that a testamentary gift over to the RCS was charitable, notwithstanding the RCS's failure to secure an exemption from corporation duty in the earlier case (where exemption was sought (at least before the courts, although not before the Commissioners) only on the grounds of 'promotion of science' and not for education or other charitable purposes).

[192] As where *Anti-Vivisection* (n 40) overruled *Re Foveaux* [1895] 2 Ch 501 (Ch) (see text to nn 177–81, ch 2).

[193] Guidance D6 (like the example of giving alms: *Anti-Vivisection* (n 40) 69); *Clephane v The Lord Provost of Edinburgh* (1866–69) LR 1 Sc 417 (HL) 421.

[194] Analysis 1.3 (from *Gilmour* (n 54)).

[195] Guidance D6, where the necessary circumstances are described by the Commission as a 'radical change *of social and economic* circumstances' (emphasis added).

[196] Such clarity was not offered in respect of specific schools (see ch 6) or more generally. Similar confusion surrounds the removal of rifle clubs from the Register: P Clarke, 'The Charitable Status of Rifle Clubs: Out with a Bang?' (1992/93) 1 *Charity Law & Practice Review* 137; P Clarke, 'The Charitable Status of Rifle Clubs: the Explosion Occurs' (1993/94) 2 *Charity Law & Practice Review* 97; J Claricoat and H Phillips, 'Removal from the Register' (1997/98) 5 *Charity Law & Practice Review* 13.

[197] See ch 2, part III, Rule 3.

benefit, or that they would be carried out for the public benefit.[198] Whilst the first ground is uncontroversial, the second is arguably meaningless and superfluous, and unsupported by law, particularly to the extent that a different meaning is given to 'public benefit' in this context.[199]

(ii) Existing Charities

The 2008 guidance outlined a number of possible consequences for an existing registered charity whose activities did not comply with the stated purposes or which failed to meet the public benefit requirement by not carrying out its aims for the public benefit. The listed consequences are the same in each case and each is based on a concern with the operations of the charity, more than a construction of the institution's purposes:[200]

(i) alteration of objects;
(ii) alteration of the way in which the charity carries out its objects;
(iii) where trustees are in breach of trust, regulatory action including the appointment of new trustees and giving directions;
(iv) where it is not possible for the aims to be carried out in a way which is for the public benefit, the application of the institution's assets for other similar charitable purposes;
(v) where it is decided that the aims never were for the public benefit and registration was erroneous, a restructuring of the organisation or re-statement of its objects or removal from the Register.

Alteration of Objects

The indication that a charity's purposes 'would need to be changed' where they no longer satisfied the public benefit requirement failed to take into account the fact that a company may be formed to carry on specified purposes, whether or not the law regards those purposes as charitable.[201] The explanation that a charity's objects should be altered, or 'restated', where its activities fell outside those objects, also appeared to ignore, or even condone, the fact that such activities would necessarily have been carried on in breach of duty.[202]

Alteration in Operations

Altering a charity's activities where they are inconsistent with the charity's purposes would appear to be the appropriate course of action, certainly where the purposes remain appropriate and charitable, and might successfully avoid proceedings for

[198] Guidance H2.
[199] See text to n 11 above. It is not explicit in the 2013 guidance but could still provide a ground for refusal (see ch 9).
[200] Guidance D4, H5 respectively.
[201] Analysis 4.23; see ch 2, part III.
[202] Guidance D4.

breach of trust. To the extent that it was intended to mean that a charity should change its modus operandi in order to give sufficient opportunity to those who cannot afford any fees charged 'as a matter of law', however, the consequence was flawed.[203]

Regulatory Action

The Commission gave two *examples* of regulatory action, namely giving directions and appointing new trustees,[204] but it failed to explain adequately how and when the power to take such action arose or why either should be appropriate in the case of an institution's purposes not being for the public benefit.[205]

The Commission has power to direct any action which it considers to be expedient in the interests of a charity, but only after a section 46 inquiry[206] and provided it is satisfied either that there has been misconduct or mismanagement, or that such action is needed in order to protect property or to ensure its proper application.[207] A power to appoint trustees is restricted by the same criteria.[208] Section 46 inquiries, however, are undertaken only in 'the most serious cases of abuse and regulatory concern',[209] and it is worth noting that the public benefit assessments were not framed as section 46 inquiries, nor did they include expressions of 'misconduct' or 'mismanagement'.[210]

The Commission's conclusion, that a failure to satisfy Principles 2b or 2c amounted to both a breach of trust *and* the organisation being 'not in substance a charity', suggested that the trustees would be at risk of regulatory action *and* that the charity would be at risk of being removed from the Register.[211] The Commission's regulatory powers, however, are concerned with the protection of charitable property and there is no power to remove a charity from the Register on the grounds of breach of trust.[212] Although the appointment of new trustees, who represent a majority of trustees, may provide an effective means of securing the

[203] *Fee-charging* (n 26) E6. This argument will be made out in chs 4 and 5.

[204] Others include the appointment of an interim manager or removal of trustees (2011 Act, ss 76–83).

[205] The Commission's concurrent jurisdiction with the High Court (2011 Act, ss 69, 70(2)) is exercisable only upon the application of the charity or the Attorney-General, or the order of the Court, and its incidental power to do anything which is intended to assist the performance of any of its general functions or duties (2011 Act, s 20) would not appear to offer broader regulatory powers in this regard.

[206] 2011 Act, s 46 (previously a 'section 8 inquiry' (Charities Act 1993)).

[207] 2011 Act, s 84 (s 85 also contains a power to direct the application of property where someone is 'unwilling' to apply it and it is necessary or desirable to make the order).

[208] 2011 Act, s 76 (although a power of appointment also lies in certain other circumstances (s 80)).

[209] *Statutory inquiries into charities: guidance for charities* (Commission, December 2013).

[210] The process described by the Commission would not appear to enable it to describe a public benefit assessment as a section 46 inquiry after the event. Compare the position in Scotland, where the regulator conducted public benefit assessments as statutory inquiries (see ch 7).

[211] *Emerging findings* (n 155).

[212] The Commission states that it 'will not normally' remove an institution in such circumstances: *Accurate Register* 2012 (n 152) para 16 (save in the case of a sham charity, which would be removed as a matter of rectification (Annex B5)).

winding up of a charity and its subsequent removal from the Register,[213] that power of appointment can be legitimately exercised only in the circumstances described.[214]

Cy-près Application

The fourth consequence was that the Commission may need to ensure that a charity's assets were applied for similar charitable aims, where it was 'not possible for the organisation's aims to be carried out in a way that is for the public benefit'.[215] Since no such ground is included in the occasions for applying property cy-près,[216] it is assumed that the Commission was referring to occasions 'where the original purposes … have … ceased, as being useless or harmful to the community *or for other reasons*, to be in law charitable' (emphasis added).[217] It appears that the Commission interpreted 'other reasons' to include changes in 'social circumstances or values' notwithstanding that the authority on which this is based referred to changing social habits and needs *rendering purposes superfluous*.[218] In order to apply this outcome to an independent school, however, the Commission would need to conclude that changes in social circumstances or values had resulted in the school's purposes of advancing education no longer being charitable, or even, applying its own interpretation, that those changes had rendered it impossible, whereas it had once been possible, for the purposes to be carried out for the public benefit.[219] Despite the seriousness of such an outcome, the Commission offered no explanation of what those circumstances or values were or how they might have changed to have this effect. It should have done.

Rectification

In the event of the Commission concluding that the aims were 'never in fact for the public benefit',[220] so that registration was made erroneously, three alternative outcomes followed, the first two being that the institution's objects might be changed or that it might be 'restructured'.[221] Since the organisation would not be subject to the Commission's jurisdiction once the mistake had been recognised, it must be assumed that any amendment of its objects would not be of concern to the

[213] R Meakin, *The Law of Charitable Status: Maintenance and Removal* (Cambridge, Cambridge University Press, 2008) 116 (who describes the same result being achieved by the means of the appointment of an interim manager (at 117)). The appointment of additional trustees, rather than removing existing trustees, is also effective in avoiding appeals against removal.

[214] eg, where there is only one trustee or no trustees (2011 Act, s 80).

[215] Guidance D4.

[216] 2011 Act, s 62.

[217] 2011 Act, s 62(1)(e)(ii).

[218] *Accurate Register* 2012 (n 152) Annex D2, D3; see text to n 183 above.

[219] So that sufficient social benefit was provided. If it had never been possible, rectification of the Register (by removal of the school) would be the appropriate outcome.

[220] Guidance D4, H5.

[221] ibid; see also Analysis 4.25, which referred to an organisation being 'reconstructed' as a charity.

Commission.[222] The third alternative, namely removing the charity from the Register, accurately reflected the Commission's statutory duty in such circumstances and was the only appropriate consequence described in *Accurate Register*.[223] This explained that the institution's assets, never having been held for charitable purposes, would remain with the institution, subject to any adverse claims.[224] As explained in the previous chapter, however, whilst this may be correct if the charity was a company, the position of a trust is less straightforward.[225]

Although removal from the Register was mentioned specifically only in relation to such cases of erroneous registration (requiring rectification), it has been seen that the risk of removal was clearly envisaged in circumstances where the Commission takes the view that purposes have *become* non-charitable due to a change in society's values or social and economic conditions.[226] In these circumstances, it envisaged removal where a cy-près scheme involved the transfer of assets from a trust to another charitable institution. In the case of a company, the Commission stated its 'tentative conclusion' which 'lean[t] in favour of' the imposition of a 'constructive charitable trust' on the beneficially owned corporate property.[227] Recognising the absence of a 'definitive legal answer', it seems this conclusion was reached, at least in part, on the basis of responses to a public consultation.[228]

(3) Appealing Against an Assessment of the Commission

In its Guidance, the Commission maintained that anyone 'unhappy' with a decision 'regarding a charity's public benefit' could appeal, either by seeking an informal review, or to the Charity Tribunal and, ultimately, the courts.[229] This suggested a broad right of appeal against decisions concerning public benefit and one which extended beyond the two examples given in the Guidance, namely the refusal of an application for registration and the refusal of a request to amend objects. A public statement issued by the Commission also gave the impression that there was a broad right of appeal, but in fact restricted that right significantly to instances where the Commission had taken regulatory action:

> Where our decisions affect whether a charity remains as a charity, or indeed whether the way in which it operates is for the public benefit, the charity, or anyone affected by our

[222] Strictly, it should be removed and a new application made.

[223] *Accurate Register* 2012 (n 152) para 18.

[224] ibid para 19: eg, referring to claims of donors, or Revenue authorities in respect of tax benefits received during the period of registration (Annex C6).

[225] See text to nn 266–70, ch 2.

[226] See text to nn 144–49 above. There was also an ambiguity in the Analysis (4.18(a), 4.25), suggesting that removal was a possible consequence whether or not it was decided that the institution was never charitable.

[227] *Accurate Register* 2012 (n 152) paras 38, 39.

[228] *Accurate Register* 2012 (n 152) Annex E12–14.

[229] Guidance H6. Following The Transfer of Functions of the Charity Tribunal Order 2009, SI 2009/1834 the path would now be to the First-tier Tribunal (Charity) and then the Upper Tribunal (Tax and Chancery).

> decision, *who disagrees with the regulatory action that we take*, can challenge that action with the Charity Tribunal or the courts where appropriate (emphasis added).[230]

A determination that a charity had failed to meet the public benefit test, accompanied by an instruction to the institution to submit a plan showing how it intended to meet the requirement in the future, could not be appealed in the way described in the Guidance.[231] Such a determination may have appeared to be a decision which affected the charity in the ways mentioned, but in the absence of regulatory action, the determination itself was not an appealable decision within the legislation.[232] In order to challenge such a determination, therefore, a charity was forced either to consider seeking judicial review, or to refuse to submit a plan in an attempt to provoke regulatory action or possible removal from the Register. The potential for adverse publicity and damage to a charity's relations with the Commission ensured that such action was highly unlikely.[233]

[230] '*Public benefit: statement of the basis for the Commission's role and actions*' (Commission, December 2008).

[231] Two independent schools were among those charities which received such a determination (see ch 6). *Cf* the Preston Down Trust, which appealed against the Commission's refusal to register it (see text to nn 19–28, ch 2).

[232] 2011 Act, sch 6.

[233] D Morris, 'The First-tier Tribunal (Charity): Enhanced Access to Justice for Charities or a Case of David versus Goliath?' (2010) 29 *Civil Justice Quarterly* 491.

4

Poverty and the Charging of Fees: The Law

I entirely decline to limit the doctrine that a trust for the advancement of education is not charitable unless there be the element of poverty in it also. There is no foundation for it in authority, nor is there any foundation for it in reason.

Lord Cozens-Hardy, MR[1]

I. Introduction

To what extent poverty must be taken into account in determining charitable status or in carrying out a charity's purposes represents the most fundamental discrepancy between the law, as interpreted by this author, and the Commission's representation of the law. At the heart of the Commission's legal interpretation, broadly endorsed by the Tribunal, is the premise that people in poverty must not be excluded from the opportunity to benefit from a charity's services and that, where fees are charged, opportunities to benefit must be offered to people unable to afford them.[2]

The relevant principles which can be drawn from case law, on the other hand, are, first, that poverty is not an essential element of charity and, second, that a charity may charge for its services provided it is non-profit making.[3] These principles were unaltered by the 2006 Act. Furthermore, case law reveals no requirement in charity law for the poor to be given the opportunity to benefit from an organisation's charitable purposes.[4] As the Charities Bill took shape, many thought that such a requirement should exist, if it did not exist already, and several attempts were made during the legislative process to ensure that it would appear on the face

[1] *R v Special Commissioners of Income Tax ex p University College of North Wales* (1909) 78 LJKB 576 (CA) 578.

[2] There are some differences in language between the Commission's publications in 2008 and 2013, and the Tribunal's judgment in *R (Independent Schools Council) v Charity Commission* [2011] UKUT 421 (TCC), [2012] Ch 214, but this general proposition remains (see chs 5, 8 and 9).

[3] Principles A and E, ch 2, part III.

[4] At least none prior to the Upper Tribunal ruling discussed in ch 8 (in *ISC* (n 2) and, of course, except where purposes are to relieve poverty).

of the statute. A number of amendments were proposed which would incorporate specific reference to the effects of fee-charging on public benefit, including requiring the Commission to consider the extent to which fee-charging restricted access, and the 'public benefit consequences thereof',[5] or to exclude 'elite schools' from charitable status,[6] but none was successful.

II. The Relevance of Poverty in Charity Law

It is true that whether or not poverty, and the needs of the poor, must be addressed in all cases of charity has long been a source of contention in charity law. On the one hand, there have been clear authoritative statements to the effect that poverty does not always need to be considered. In 1924, for example, Lord Wrenbury made it clear that poverty is not 'a necessary element' in charities under the fourth head and, similarly, that education and religion 'do not require any qualification of poverty to be introduced to give them validity'.[7] On the other hand, it has sometimes been argued that poverty is, or should be, relevant and even that poverty is fundamental to the very essence of charity. These arguments have been heard principally, although not exclusively, in relation to charities dealing with the aged or infirm and where fees are charged for the charity's services.

To say that poverty is not an essential element of charity is to say, in its narrowest construction, that not every beneficiary need be poor and, in its widest construction that the purposes of the organisation do not need to be directed at the poor at all. To confer charitable status on an organisation even though few, or even none, of the people it benefits is in absolute or relative poverty may well not accord with popular notions of charity, but it has already been seen that 'charity' is defined according to a distinct and technical legal meaning and not according to popular sentiment. The question of whether an organisation *should* have charitable status in those circumstances is quite different and concerns policy not law. The two should not be confused.

It has already been noted that the objects of a charitable trust are its purposes, rather than individuals (as in a private trust), but it is appropriate here to refer to the intended beneficiaries of the institution's purposes.[8] Those beneficiaries might comprise all poor, all rich, or a combination of poor and rich. For our purposes, 'rich' means 'not poor' and 'poor' means 'not rich'. The two terms are thus mutually

[5] (Amendment 28) HL Deb 9 February 2005, vol 669, col GC110.

[6] (Amendment 9A) ibid, col GC63; Amendment 17 would have excluded secondary schools where at least two-thirds of pupils pay fees or have fees paid for them; see also n 52, ch 1.

[7] *Verge v Somerville* [1924] AC 496 (PC) 499–500, 503 respectively; see too *Re Compton* [1945] Ch 123 (CA) 139.

[8] See text to n 217, ch 2.

exclusive and require no further definition.[9] Whilst accepting the principle that a class need not be confined to the poor and that the rich may also benefit, it is in cases where all the beneficiaries *may* be rich, most notably because high fees are charged, that the Commission maintains that the poor must also be given opportunities to benefit which are more than tokenistic or minimal.

A class which comprises only the rich might arise in the following ways:

— by an indifference to whether those who actually benefit are rich or poor;
— by declaring that purposes are aimed at the rich or by including a proviso or qualification that the poor shall not benefit (an 'express exclusion on the terms');[10]
— by describing a class of beneficiaries in such a way that only the rich are likely to fall within it (an 'implied exclusion on the terms');[11]
— by declaring purposes which can (or do) only benefit the rich, typically, though not necessarily, because high fees are charged (an 'implied exclusion in practice').

Except where purposes are clearly aimed at relieving poverty, there is unlikely to be any intention on the donor's part that a potential beneficiary's wealth should be taken into account in considering his eligibility to receive the benefits of the charitable purposes: the services offered by a charitable lifeboat organisation, for example, are available to all distressed seamen, without regard to their means. This paramount concern with the purpose, rather than the financial means of those who might benefit from the purpose, has been reflected in the courts' attitudes. It seems particularly unlikely that an express exclusion on the terms would arise in practice and even less likely, if it did, that charitable status would be advocated or defended with any vigour.[12] An implied exclusion on the terms may be more likely to arise and, of course, an implied exclusion in practice is commonplace where fees are charged.

The relevance of poverty has been dealt with differently in relation to the various heads of charity and, for that reason, each will be considered in turn.

[9] Thus avoiding the inevitably tortuous problems of scope and definition which the Commission and Tribunal fail to resolve (see chs 5, 8): since the law does not rule out rich beneficiaries, there is no need to address varying degrees of wealth.

[10] An 'express exclusion on the terms' covers any exclusion of persons less rich than those included (so that there is no need to consider any other class on a sliding scale between the wealthy and the impoverished).

[11] Arguably less offensive than an express exclusion on the terms. The term is intended to describe circumstances where it seems likely that the intended beneficiaries will be wealthy rather than poor, even though a literal interpretation might not mean that the poor are excluded (eg, a 'school for the sons of gentlemen' or 'aged peers').

[12] Some judicial dicta (considered below and in ch 5), which suggest that charitable status would be denied if the poor were excluded, appear to be limited to such express exclusions, a view shared by Luxton: P Luxton, 'Making Law? Parliament v The Charity Commission' (Politeia, 2009) 22 and considered plausible at least by the Tribunal (*ISC* (n 2) [162]).

(1) The Relief of Poverty

It goes without saying that poverty is an essential element where the purposes are to relieve poverty.[13] It means that where those to be helped have been described by reference to their means, the courts have had to determine whether those means signify poverty. The law has not confined 'poverty' for these purposes to expressions of destitution, but has construed it as 'a relative matter, a matter of opinion',[14] and widely interpreted it to include beneficiaries 'in needy circumstances',[15] 'of moderate means',[16] or even comfortably off but needing 'a helping hand from time to time in order to overcome an unforeseen crisis'.[17] The effect of interpreting poverty in this way has been to admit greater numbers of institutions to the ranks of charity.

It is also worth noting that where incidental benefits are permitted to be conferred on an organisation's members, or others, without depriving the institution of charitable status, the wealth of those benefited is not a relevant consideration.[18]

(2) Advancement of Education

This head of charity derives from the inclusion in the Preamble of 'schools of learning, free schools, and scholars in universities'.[19] It may be tempting to suggest that this should be understood to refer only to schools which were founded for the poor, due either to the literal or historical context in which the Preamble was written, but this would be erroneous. The relief of poverty may have been the 'principal manifestation' of the public benefit which characterised the Preamble,[20] but the purposes included in it were not exclusively poverty-based, nor were they regarded as comprehensive. It may also be a misconception to assume that all schools were founded for the poor or that they were non-fee charging. The Tonbridge School, for example, was founded in 1553 for pupils who were already

[13] Or to prevent poverty (added by the 2006 Act): 2011 Act, s 3(1)(a).

[14] *Re Scarisbrick* [1951] Ch 622 (CA) 650.

[15] ibid; similarly 'in distressed circumstances' (*Re Buck* [1896] 2 Ch 727 (Ch)); 'in special need' (*Re Cohen* [1973] 1 All ER 889 (Ch)).

[16] *Re Clarke* [1923] 2 Ch 407 (Ch).

[17] *Re Segelman* [1996] Ch 171 (Ch); *cf Re Sanders' Will Trusts* [1954] Ch 265 (Ch). Whether or not a purpose constitutes the relief of poverty may also be decided on the basis of the amount of assistance offered (*Re Tree* [1945] Ch 325 (Ch)) or the income of the beneficiaries (*Re Lacy* [1899] 2 Ch 149 (Ch); *Re Lucas* [1922] 2 Ch 52 (Ch)).

[18] *Incorporated Council of Law Reporting for England and Wales v AG* [1972] Ch 73 (CA) 87 (where those benefiting were members of the legal profession); *IRC v Yorkshire Agricultural Society* [1928] 1 KB 611 (CA).

[19] The preamble to the Statute of Charitable Uses Act (1601), 43 Eliz 1 c (Preamble); see text to nn 163–66, ch 2. Arguably, it would be more accurate to say that the inclusion of the advancement of education in the Preamble simply reflected the fact that the law had already recognised the purpose as prima facie charitable.

[20] G Jones, *History of the Law of Charity 1532–1827* (Cambridge, Cambridge University Press, 1969) 27.

fluent in Latin and who were required to pay sixpence each on admission.[21] Both requirements would have ruled out the poor classes. It should also be noted that the term 'free school' did not denote a non-fee paying school, so much as a superior school or one independent of ecclesiastical power.[22]

A distinguishing feature of sixteenth-century grammar schools was their emphasis on the classical languages, in preparing pupils for public life and the literate professions,[23] and this, together with the widespread increase in fee-paying boarders, or 'foreigners', gave rise to a number of applications to court for schemes to be directed. The courts heard arguments that the education was being adapted to accommodate the boarders, to the prejudice of day pupils, and that boarders were favoured in the award of exhibitions and prizes. This presented the courts with an opportunity to mark out the boundaries of charitable status by reference to the imposition or level of fees and/or the opportunities offered to less wealthy children. The courts rejected that opportunity, however, preferring to comment positively on the benefits of mixing rich and poor.[24] Some of these cases will be considered in chapter eight.

In *Attorney-General v The Earl of Lonsdale*, the Vice-Chancellor, Sir John Leach, dismissed outright an argument by counsel that a free school 'for the sons of gentlemen' could not be charitable,[25] and it seems reasonable to suggest that this conclusion was based neither on the extensive endowment nor the 'free school' status by which the school was described. Conceding that such an object would not be charitable 'in popular language', his Lordship stated that 'in the view of the statute of Elizabeth, all schools for learning are so to be considered'.[26] Although a class of gentlemen's sons does not expressly exclude the poor, the likely correlation between class and wealth is not easily ignored: '"Good breeding", so-called, is not the same thing as old money, but they tend to go together'.[27] An account of the testator's life suggests that he may have made such generous provision for the sons of gentlemen in the belief, based on his own experience, that the considerable wealth and privilege attached to that status might usefully be constrained by a

21 S Rivington, *The History of Tonbridge School* (Rivingtons, 1869) 52–53; St Paul's School, London, reports that it was founded in 1509 for boys 'from all nacions and countres indifferently' without regard to means or race: www.stpaulsschool.org.uk/about-st-pauls.

22 Rivington (ibid) 48, fn 1 (quoting works of Knox and B Kennedy); *AG v Bishop of Worcester* (1851) 9 Hare 328, 68 ER 530; *cf AG v Earl of Devon* (1846) 15 Sim 193, 60 ER 591 (where the school was founded as 'a free school and not a school of exaction'). Of course, the effect of generous endowments was often to render the payment of fees inappropriate, but that generosity benefited the wealthy as well as the poor: see, eg, *Manchester School Case* (1866–67) LR 2 Ch App 497 (CA).

23 C Tyerman, *A History of Harrow School 1324–1991* (Oxford, Oxford University Press, 2000) 31.

24 *AG v Earl of Stamford* (1842) 1 Ph 737, 761, 41 ER 812, 822; *Worcester* (n 22) 540/347.

25 *AG v Earl of Lonsdale* (1827) 1 Sim 105, 57 ER 518.

26 ibid, 520. This reliance on the Preamble (n 19) was also critical in *Abbey Malvern Wells Ltd v Ministry of Local Government and Planning* [1951] Ch 728 (Ch) (discussed in part III below).

27 A Lejeune, in *Burke's Genealogical and Heraldic History of the Landed Gentry*, 18th edn (London, Burke's Peerage Ltd, 1964–72) Vol 3, xv; see also text to n 50 below (where the evident assumption seems to be that aged peers are rich). On this basis, it would seem that the case represents an implied exclusion on the terms.

more disciplined education.[28] And whilst we should not assume that sons of poor gentlemen would have been turned away, there is also nothing to suggest that there was any expectation that they should be included, or any obligation positively to include them.

The charitable status of all schools, regardless of pupils' wealth or status, was also affirmed by the courts where fees were charged and the proposition that the means of the students had to be taken into account was emphatically dismissed by the Master of the Rolls in 1909: 'There is no foundation for it in authority nor is there any foundation for it in reason'.[29] The House of Lords, too, accepted without question the charitable status of Brighton College, which charged substantial fees, without any mention of the school's provision of education or other opportunities to people unable to afford its fees.[30]

The courts have interpreted 'education' widely but not without limitation and, provided purposes are actually seen as tending to advance education,[31] they have been held to be charitable without any consideration of the presence or absence of poverty.[32] Where charitable status has been refused, however, refusal has not been attributed to considerations of poverty but other reasons, most notably lack of public character where education has been intended for relatives or employees,[33] or on the basis that purposes are more political than educational.[34] It seems entirely plausible that the law has attributed charitable status to schools on the basis of the general and unquestioned benefit to society and not the individual benefits to the schools' pupils, far less the individual benefits to non-pupils. This fundamental benefit to society can be lost if the school is 'cloistered', so that the fruits of its teaching and learning are not shared,[35] but it is not lost because the pupils are wealthy. And there appears to be no authority which has held a school's pupils to be an insufficient section of the public.[36]

[28] F Wrangham, *The Works of the Rev Thomas Zouch … With a memoir of his life* (York, 1820): archive.org/details/worksrevthomasz00wrangoog; Williams concludes from the case that 'making it difficult to gain access to the schools was unethical but legal': I Williams, *The Alms Trade* (London, Unwin Hyman, 1989) 61.

[29] *North Wales* (n 1).

[30] *Brighton College v Marriott* [1926] AC 192 (HL).

[31] *Re Shaw* [1957] 1 WLR 729 (Ch) (not so in the case of research into a 40-letter alphabet); *Re Pinion* [1965] Ch 85 (CA) (not so in the case of a testator's private art exhibits).

[32] eg, *Smith v Kerr* [1902] 1 Ch 774 (CA); *Re Gott* [1944] Ch 193 (Ch); *IRC v McMullen* [1981] AC 1 (HL); *Re Koeppler's Will Trusts* [1986] Ch 423 (CA). See also *Re Campden Charities* (1880–81) LR 18 Ch D 310 (CA), where the Court approved a scheme which added educational purposes (including exhibitions for higher education and lectures for scholars) to the original purposes of relieving poverty, without any qualification aimed at ensuring the poor benefited.

[33] *Compton* (n 7); *Oppenheim v Tobacco Securities Trust Co Ltd* [1951] AC 297 (HL); *IRC v Educational Grants Association Ltd* [1967] Ch 993 (CA).

[34] *Re Hopkinson* [1949] 1 All ER 346 (Ch).

[35] *Gilmour v Coats* [1949] AC 426 (HL) 450.

[36] See ch 2, part III, Test 2.

(3) Advancement of Religion

The idea that charity necessarily requires some element of relieving poverty was central to *Special Commissioners of Income Tax v Pemsel*, where the House of Lords, it will be remembered, held that no such requirement exists even where the issue is the availability of tax allowances rather than the validity of a charitable trust.[37] Lord Bramwell, in a forceful dissenting judgment, echoed the conclusion of Lord Esher MR in the Court of Appeal, that charity necessarily implies the relief of poverty and that the testator must be found to have had an intention to provide such relief. The majority, however, dismissed such a 'restricted' view[38] and found the purposes to be charitable, notwithstanding that there was no intention to discriminate between rich and poor in fulfilling the purposes of the trust.

As with education, any wider benefits to society are liable to be curtailed where a religious community is cloistered,[39] but the presence or absence of poverty has not been a relevant factor in determining charitable status.[40]

(4) Cases Falling Under the Fourth Head

After identifying the fourth head of charity in *Pemsel*, Lord Macnaghten added that trusts within that category 'are not the less charitable in the eye of the law, because incidentally they benefit the rich as well as the poor, as indeed, every charity that deserves the name must do either directly or indirectly'.[41] The statement is not entirely easy to understand. In itself, it tells us only that the beneficiaries of a charitable trust are not required to be exclusively poor and not that poverty is an irrelevant consideration. Whilst it is authority for the proposition that the rich may benefit incidentally, it is not authority for saying that the rich cannot benefit in ways which are not merely incidental,[42] nor that a beneficial class must include some poor who benefit directly. Indeed, the somewhat curious ambiguity in the last part of his Lordship's statement appears to suggest that it is the rich, and not the poor, who must benefit directly or indirectly and it is supposed that this envisages the rich either comprising some of the beneficiaries or being relieved of the financial burden which might otherwise fall on them.[43]

Later dicta address more explicitly the relevance of poverty in charities under the fourth head and find it to be inessential. In *Inland Revenue Commissioners v*

[37] *Special Commissioners of Income Tax v Pemsel* [1891] AC 531 (HL); see text to nn 112–17, ch 2.

[38] *Pemsel* (n 37) 571 (Lord Herschell).

[39] *Cocks v Manners* (1871) LR 12 Eq 574 (Ch); *Gilmour* (n 35). Some jurisdictions take a different view, including Australia and Ireland (see ch 9).

[40] eg, *Re Manser* [1905] 1 Ch 68 (Ch); *Re Hood* [1931] 1 Ch 240 (CA); *Farley v Westminster Bank* [1939] AC 430 (HL); *Cocks* (n 39).

[41] *Pemsel* (n 37) 583.

[42] Recognised by Lord Wrenbury in *Verge* (n 7) 503.

[43] The dictum does not condone a class of rich only, but it would be going too far to rely on it as expressly prohibiting such a prospect.

Baddeley, for example, trusts were declared to be non-charitable because the purposes were not recognised by law as exclusively charitable, but Lord Reid was clearly of the opinion that, even if the purposes had been exclusively within the fourth head, 'the element of poverty [was] not necessary to make them valid charitable purposes'.[44] And, in *Re Resch*, Lord Wilberforce referred to Lord Wrenbury's having 'held generally that poverty is not a necessary qualification in trusts beneficial to the community'.[45]

Again, numerous purposes have been found to be charitable under this head without any consideration of poverty[46] and charitable status has been denied on a number of grounds but not, it seems, on there being an absence of poverty.[47]

The Relief of the Aged or Infirm[48]

The significance of poverty has been especially prominent where purposes are directed at the aged or infirm, perhaps because the Preamble specified the relief of 'aged, impotent and poor people', but without indicating whether a conjunctive or disjunctive interpretation was intended. In these cases are to be found some of the most notable suggestions of a judicial reluctance, or 'great disinclination',[49] to accord charitable status to purposes which omit any element of poverty.

In the mid-twentieth century, academics debated whether a trust for the relief of 'aged peers' or 'impotent millionaires' would be charitable.[50] Robert Megarry noted the evolving cases of the time and identified the nub of the problem as it seeming 'to accord ill with the spirit of the Statute to open the doors of charity to those who are wealthy and well able to provide for themselves, merely because they are aged'.[51] John Brunyate, however, considered the example of a rich blind man and distinguished between making gifts of money on the one hand, which would not relieve a need in the charitable sense, and curing blindness or providing braille services on the other, which would.[52] Taking a bolder approach than some, he noted: 'to regard a rich man who is blind or maimed as in no sense a proper object of charity would surely be taking a very worldly view of human suffering'.[53]

[44] *IRC v Baddeley* [1955] AC 572 (HL) 604.

[45] *Re Resch* [1969] 1 AC 514 (PC) 543 (referring to *Verge* (n 7)).

[46] eg, *Re Good* [1905] 2 Ch 60 (Ch); *Re Gray* [1925] Ch 362 (Ch); *Scottish Burial Reform and Cremation Society Ltd v Glasgow Corporation* [1968] AC 138 (HL).

[47] eg, *National Anti-Vivisection Society v IRC* [1948] AC 31 (HL); *IRC v City of Glasgow Police Athletic Association* [1953] AC 380 (HL). Likewise, the 'animal cases' contain no consideration of poverty: eg, *Re Wedgwood* [1915] 1 Ch 113 (CA); *Re Grove-Grady* [1929] 1 Ch 557 (CA).

[48] There seems to be no reason to perpetuate the practice of treating these cases under the first head even though they 'should perhaps be considered to fall under the fourth head', noted in J Warburton, D Morris and NF Riddle (eds), *Tudor on Charities*, 9th edn (London, Sweet & Maxwell, 2003) 29.

[49] *Re Lewis* [1955] Ch 104 (Ch) 107.

[50] A class of 'aged peers', in the context of this debate, might be seen as an implied (not express) exclusion of the poor, but a class of impotent millionaires an express exclusion on the terms.

[51] RE Megarry (1951) 67 *LQR* 164 (note), referring to the Statute of Elizabeth (n 19).

[52] J Brunyate, 'The Legal Definition of Charity' (1945) 61 *LQR* 268.

[53] ibid, 272. See also PS Atiyah, 'Public Benefit in Charities' (1958) 21 *MLR* 138, 140.

The cases which addressed this issue over the following two decades reflected this view,[54] and to relieve the needs of 'aged' or 'impotent' persons came to be regarded as charitable without any need for poverty, just as other prima facie charitable purposes had not been disqualified through an absence of poverty.[55]

After a period of reticence, where judges appeared reassured by evidence which suggested that the testator had intended to benefit aged people who were also poor[56] or indigent,[57] a new confidence emerged in *Re Robinson*,[58] where Vaisey J did not hesitate to conclude that a gift to people aged over 65 was charitable without any need for poverty.[59] It was the relief of a *need* attributable to age which was important and this approach was emphasised in *Joseph Rowntree Memorial Trust v Attorney-General.*[60] Peter Gibson J, in that case, considered five schemes for the provision of special housing for the elderly, in which beneficiaries were required to purchase leasehold interests for a capital sum and which included one scheme where there was no express qualification that beneficiaries should be 'of moderate means'. The relief of the need for housing was held to be prima facie charitable without any qualification of poverty. Basing his decision on logic as well as judicial authority, his Lordship expressed his conclusion with utmost clarity: 'It would be as absurd to require that the aged must be impotent or poor as it would be to require the impotent to be aged or poor, or the poor to be aged or impotent'.[61]

The question of whether poverty is essential in gifts for the relief of the infirm had already been answered in a similar vein in *Re Lewis*, where the Court considered gifts of £100 to each of 10 blind girls and 10 blind boys.[62] Roxburgh J boldly decided to 'grasp the nettle' and decide whether or not the absence of 'any element of poverty whatsoever' was fatal to finding that the gifts were charitable.[63] He was also happy to endorse the disjunctive interpretation (and its necessary consequences) adopted by Danckwerts J and Vaisey J,[64] and pointed to the illogical

[54] Briefly, but helpfully, reviewed in *Joseph Rowntree Memorial Trust v AG* [1983] Ch 159 (Ch) 172–73.

[55] Interestingly, in all the cases studied in this area, the purposes were held to be charitable, the courts' willingness to give effect to a testator's charitable intentions perhaps overcoming any reluctance which might have stemmed from a lack of poverty.

[56] *Lucas* (n 17).

[57] *Re Glyn's Will Trusts* [1950] 2 All ER 1150n (Ch).

[58] *Re Robinson* [1951] Ch 198 (Ch); see also *Re Bradbury* [1950] WN 558 (Ch); *Re Neal* (1966) 110 SJ 549 (Ch).

[59] Although it failed to dispel all reluctance: *Re Cottam* [1955] 1 WLR 1299 (Ch) (even though the case was heard by Danckwerts J, whose disjunctive interpretation in *Glyn* (n 57) had been relied on in *Robinson* (n 58), to which latter case his Lordship also referred).

[60] *Joseph Rowntree* (n 54). This emphasis on need is also discernible in *Resch* (n 45) (discussed below).

[61] *Joseph Rowntree* (n 54) 171; see also *McGovern v AG* [1982] Ch 321 (Ch) 333, where the principle was reiterated without question.

[62] *Lewis* (n 49).

[63] ibid, 107 (noting that the dilemma was easier in respect of the infirm (as opposed to the aged) and citing a decision in which gifts for the blind in Inverness-shire had been held charitable (*Re Fraser* (1883) LR 22 Ch D 827 (Ch)), but unreported on that point).

[64] In *Glyn* (n 57) and *Robinson* (n 58).

nature of the counter-argument which would mean that a trust for poor people would not be charitable unless they were also aged or infirm.[65]

As a matter of charitable status, case law establishes that there is no need for relief to be confined to the poor sick and demonstrates that the law is not concerned to ensure that at least some of the beneficiaries are poor, or even to concern itself with whether they are rich or poor, but only that their needs as aged or impotent people are being relieved.[66] Furthermore, the law has not stipulated that trustees should nonetheless concern themselves with such matters in the proper performance of their duties. *Re Resch* is considered below in relation to fee-charging, but for present purposes it is worth noting the words of Lord Wilberforce in that case where, keen 'to dispose of a misapprehension', he said that 'it is not a condition of validity of a trust for the relief of the sick that it should be limited to the poor sick … there is no warrant for adding to the condition of sickness that of poverty'.[67] The first part of this statement is narrow and not contentious, but the second is much broader: whilst it clearly envisages a class of rich and poor, logically it must also embrace the possibility that all beneficiaries could be rich. In a case which concerned a private hospital charging high fees, if the court had meant to exclude such a possibility, it might be expected to have done so, but on the contrary (as will be seen below), a later dictum lent further support to this even broader interpretation.[68]

Locality Cases[69]

In *Mitford v Reynolds*, a bequest for the benefit of the native inhabitants of a named city was construed as being 'not for any particular class of the native inhabitants, but for all the native inhabitants in general, both rich and poor' and thus charitable.[70] Similarly, in *Jones v Williams*, a gift to supply water to the people of Chepstow was charitable as 'a gift to a general public use, which extends to the poor as well as to the rich'.[71] Neither decision *requires* that some poor must benefit,

[65] *Lewis* (n 49) 108.

[66] Of course the test of public character must still be satisfied and purposes must be exclusively charitable.

[67] *Resch* (n 45) 542.

[68] See text to n 163 below.

[69] Albery suggests that several cases in this category were wrongly decided: M Albery, 'Trusts for the Benefit of the Inhabitants of a Locality' (1940) 56 *LQR* 49; Luxton calls the category 'one of charity's rather more awkward anomalies': P Luxton, *The Law of Charities* (Oxford, Oxford University Press, 2001) 121.

[70] *Mitford v Reynolds* (1842) 1 Ph 185, 191; 41 ER 602, 604; see also *Howse v Chapman* (1799) 4 Ves Jr 542, 31 ER 278; *Re Mann* [1903] 1 Ch 232 (Ch). Nor is poverty considered to be required by Glennie J, in reviewing locality cases in both English and Canadian courts (*Re the Estate of Forbes* (2003) NBQB 430 (QB, New Brunswick)), nor H Picarda, *Law and Practice Relating to Charities*, 4th edn (Haywards Heath, Bloomsbury Professional, 2010) 197–98 (save to comment, in respect of a Hong Kong case, that poverty would have been necessary to save a trust which appeared to benefit a village but, in fact, was only aimed at the testator's clan in the village), nor *Tudor on Charities* (n 48) 113–16.

[71] *Jones v Williams* (1767) Amb 651, 652; 27 ER 422, 423. (This 'definition of charity' was attributed to Lord Camden by Mr Ambler, according to Lord Wilberforce in *Resch* (n 45) 543; similarly in *Nightingale v Goulburn* (1847) 5 Hare 484, 487; 67 ER 1003, 1005 and *Educational Grants* (n 33) 1011; but attributed to Lord Hardwicke LC by Lord Simonds in *Oppenheim* (n 33) 305.)

however, and it may be going too far to conclude (however reasonable it might appear) that the courts have granted charitable status to such trusts only because any given locality can be assumed to contain both rich *and* poor.

In fact, *Jones*[72] was cited by the House of Lords in *Goodman v Saltash* as authority for the proposition that a 'trust for the benefit of the inhabitants of a parish or town or a particular class of such inhabitants' is charitable, without making any reference to some being poor.[73] Similarly, in *Pemsel*, Lord Halsbury LC quoted the first part of the 'definition' from *Jones*[74] (as 'a general public use'), but omitted the words 'which extends to the poor as well as the rich'.[75] The use of the definition by the House of Lords in both cases suggests that the intention was to emphasise the *public* nature of the use, rather than any question of whether rich and poor or only the rich or only the poor were intended to benefit.[76] As was later pointed out, in *Nightingale v Goulburn*, many things of general utility were strictly matters of private right even though the public benefited indirectly from them, for example the construction of railroads or canals which were of general utility but not charitable.[77] Both the purpose and the effect of adding the reference to poor and rich, therefore, seems to have been to distinguish the truly *public* general use from the privately owned or privately sponsored provision of something for public use.[78]

In *Goodman*, the House of Lords concluded that the privilege of removing oysters from a fishery, practised over nearly 200 years, amounted to a charitable trust for the benefit of free inhabitants of ancient tenements in the borough of Saltash.[79] None of their Lordships was concerned to find any element of poverty. This case is significant because the charitable trust was tantamount to a trust for the rich alone and the potential or actual exclusion of the poor in practice did not prevent that conclusion.[80] The free inhabitants and beneficiaries of the charitable trust were hardly poor: Lord Fitzgerald understood the term to refer to persons 'on whom privileges were conferred in respect of their having erected houses within

[72] *Jones* (ibid).

[73] *Goodman v Saltash* (1881–82) LR 7 App Cas 633 (HL) 642 (Lord Selborne LC) where, in fact, it seems the beneficiaries were not at all poor (see text to nn 79–81 below).

[74] *Jones* (n 71).

[75] *Pemsel* (n 37) 543; see too *Taylor v Taylor* (1910) 10 CLR 218 (HCt Australia) 237, where Isaacs J described these additional words as 'merely explanatory'.

[76] This would appear to be the interpretation of Harman LJ in *Educational Grants* (n 33) 1011; see also *Oppenheim* (n 33) 305.

[77] *Nightingale* (n 71) 490/1006.

[78] Or to make clear the charitable nature of gifts of general public utility as an alternative to the usual relief of poverty: Luxton, 'Making Law?' (n 12) 21.

[79] *Goodman* (n 73).

[80] An implied exclusion in practice, attributable to long usage (there being no express terms) rather than fees; see also *Re Norwich Town Close Estate Charity* (1889) LR 40 Ch D 298 (Ch), where the Court held a trust for the freemen of Norwich (decreed by an earlier court) to be charitable (their wealth was not discussed in this case, but *if and to the extent that* the freemen might be assumed to have been wealthy at the time of the decree, the case could be said to represent an implied exclusion on the terms).

its limits, and being inhabitants or residents therein'.[81] The case has been subjected to criticism but not, it appears, on the grounds of the beneficiaries' wealth.[82]

In *Re Christchurch Inclosure Act*, the Court of Appeal considered the status of trusts of land which were made pursuant to an Act of Parliament and which benefited certain cottage owners by entitling them to cut turf from the land.[83] The Court was reluctant to find that the Act created a trust unless it could be framed as a charitable trust in line with existing judicial authority. It seems that some comfort was derived from conjecturing that the Act might originally have been aimed at poor people,[84] but this was said only to support (and not to prove) the view that the Court had already reached on the basis of features in common with those in *Goodman*,[85] namely that the Act gave rise to a charitable trust for the benefit of occupiers of the cottages.[86] The trust was neither limited to poor occupiers, nor qualified to ensure that some were poor.

(5) Charitable and Non-Charitable Purposes

Where the courts have ruled that 'public' or 'benevolent' purposes (for example) are not charitable as a matter of law, it has been on the basis of the potential breadth of those purposes and the absence of analogous links with the Preamble and not because the purposes have failed to address the needs of the poor.[87]

One case deserves particular mention, not least because of the significance attached to it by both the Commission and the Tribunal.[88] This is *Re Macduff*, where the relevance of poverty might appear to have been a prominent consideration.[89] Here, a bequest for 'charitable or philanthropic purposes' required the court to determine whether purposes could be 'philanthropic' without also being 'charitable'. Lindley LJ suggested that 'purposes indicating goodwill to rich men to the exclusion of poor men' would be philanthropic but not charitable.[90] He did not say that poverty, whilst clearly not an essential element of philanthropy, was an essential element in charity. Although the purposes of 'indicating goodwill' might be non-charitable in any event, his Lordship's comment by way of explanation, namely that he doubted 'very much whether a trust would be declared

[81] *Goodman* (n 73) 668.

[82] *Williams Trustees v IRC* [1947] AC 447 (HL) 460; see too Albery, who argues that the trust was not for the general benefit of the inhabitants but a special trust for a particular purpose ('Trusts for the Benefit' (n 69)); G Cross, 'Some Recent Developments in the Law of Charity' (1956) 72 *LQR* 187, 201.

[83] *Re Christchurch Inclosure Act* (1888) LR 38 Ch D 520 (CA).

[84] Based on the occupiers having been exempt from certain expenses and the fact that management and protection of the cottagers' rights was entrusted to the churchwardens and overseers of the poor.

[85] *Goodman* (n 73).

[86] *Christchurch* (n 83) 533.

[87] eg, *Morice v Bishop of Durham* (1805) 10 Ves Jr 522, 32 ER 947; *Houston v Burns* [1918] AC 337 (HL); *Chichester Diocesan Fund and Board of Finance Inc v Simpson* [1944] AC 341 (HL).

[88] See chs 5, 8.

[89] *Re Macduff* [1896] 2 Ch 451 (CA).

[90] ibid, 464.

to be charitable which excluded the poor',[91] does suggest that even a prima facie charitable purpose would not be charitable if it 'excluded the poor'. His Lordship did not articulate whether he had in mind an express exclusion or an implied exclusion, either on the terms or in practice, but it is only an express exclusion on the terms which falls squarely within the words he used. There is nothing to indicate that his Lordship was also contemplating an implied exclusion in practice, as there is no context of fees or other operating factor which would exclude the poor, and one must also assume that his Lordship would have been mindful of the implications of *Lonsdale*[92] and *Goodman*.[93] This may appear to be something of a pedantic exercise, but it is critical. The dictum can hardly be said to justify the proposition that a fee-charging charity should not exclude the poor by charging fees which are necessarily high because the cost of providing its services is high.

Of course, an express exclusion of the poor is a very different matter from an implied exclusion in practice, and not simply because it is highly unlikely to occur. At worst, it may be offensive or immoral and so contrary to public policy, rather in the same way as discrimination against race or gender. It may also mean that a class is defined, at least in part, by an attribute which bears no relation to the purpose, thereby appearing capricious and, as such, contrary to public policy.[94] Either reason would justify excluding charitable status where the poor are expressly excluded on the terms. In the context of a fee-paying school, an express exclusion of the poor would also prevent its trustees from accepting poor pupils, even where it had the means to give means-tested bursaries, for example, or if a pupil received a grant from elsewhere (without becoming 'rich' as a result).[95]

In the same case, Lopes LJ indicated that he would not consider to be charitable 'recreation grounds and grounds devoted to sport which are not for the poorer classes, but are generally for rich and poor alike'.[96] Unlike the example of Lindley LJ, this example distinguishes between a trust for the poor only, which might be charitable, and one for rich and poor, which would not, but it does not concern the exclusion of the poor. The comment was made in response to submissions from counsel and the significant point to bear in mind is that the purpose of providing such facilities was not (at that time) a prima facie charitable purpose, but *could* be rendered charitable only if provided specifically for the poor, because in those circumstances this would constitute the undoubtedly charitable purpose of relieving poverty.[97] His second example of purposes which are philanthropic but

[91] ibid.

[92] *Lonsdale* (n 25).

[93] *Goodman* (n 73).

[94] In the same way that allowing only Methodists to cross a bridge in a public place restricts eligibility according to a criterion with no rational link to the purpose and might be regarded as capricious: *Baddeley* (n 44) 592.

[95] And a trust for impotent millionaires may be less likely to be considered charitable than one for aged peers (see text to nn 50–53 above).

[96] *Macduff* (n 89) 469.

[97] To argue that the purpose is rendered non-charitable only because of the admission of some rich to the grounds would be to suggest that a class must be confined to the poor, a view not supported by authority (nor advanced by the Commission).

not charitable was that of a gift to landowners affected by agricultural depression whose incomes drop to £300 per annum.[98] Since the only possible charitable purpose would appear to be the relief of poverty, assuming the gift is of money, the wealth of the recipients is clearly relevant and there can be no charitable purpose of relieving the poverty of the rich,[99] including someone in receipt of an annual income of £300 in 1896. Hence, the gift is philanthropic but not charitable. Peter Gibson J made much the same point in 1983: 'a gift of money to the aged millionaires of Mayfair would not relieve a need of theirs as aged persons'.[100]

The third member of the Court of Appeal, Rigby LJ, illustrated his conclusion that some purposes may be philanthropic but not charitable by considering a gift of residue on trust 'towards advancing the happiness and the position in life generally' of the 'well-to-do or moderately well-to-do'.[101] Again, neither making people happier nor making them 'in some sense better than they now are' is likely to be construed as a charitable purpose in law, even if philanthropic.[102] If the aims were to advance the happiness or improve the position of poor people, these might be construed as ways of relieving poverty, but one cannot relieve the poverty of the 'well-to-do'.[103] Thus, the examples of Rigby and Lopes LLJ describe philanthropic but not charitable purposes. The mention of the class being rich may add emphasis but, unless coupled with charitable purposes, cannot be taken as authority that purposes, which are otherwise charitable, are rendered non-charitable if for the rich alone.[104]

Of course, logic alone would not demand that an express exclusion of the poor should render a purpose non-charitable that would otherwise be charitable.[105] Assuming, for the moment, that the gentry were people of wealth in the late-seventeenth century, there is no difference between a gift 'for the education of gentlemen's sons but not the poor' and one 'for the education of gentlemen's sons': if the latter is charitable, the exclusion of persons who could not fall within

[98] The nature of the gift is not specified but it does not appear unreasonable to assume that his Lordship had in mind a gift of money.

[99] *AG v Duke of Northumberland* (1877–78) LR 7 Ch D 745 (Ch) 752.

[100] *Joseph Rowntree* (n 54) 171; Brunyate, 'Legal Definition' (n 52).

[101] *Macduff* (n 89) 471.

[102] At least not unless by charitable means such as circulating religious and virtuous learning: *Browne v Yeall* (1791) 7 Ves 50n.

[103] Similarly, Harman J in *Re White's Will Trusts* [1951] 1 All ER 528 (Ch) 530 notes that a rest home for millionaires would not be charitable, but he appears to make this comment on the basis that a rest home is not charitable per se unless for the benefit of doers of charity (as in *Re Estlin* (1903) 72 LJ 687 (Ch) and *Re James* [1932] 2 Ch 25 (Ch)) or objects of charity (as in *Re Chaplin* [1933] Ch 115 (Ch)) and millionaires are neither. Picarda's statement that gifts for the exclusive benefit of the rich are not charitable (*Law and Practice* (n 70) 149), based in part on Rigby LJ's dicta and *Duke of Northumberland* (n 99) 752, appears not to make the distinction (which he goes on to describe) between gifts of money and other purposes, nor to distinguish between express and implied exclusions.

[104] Even if one suspects that their Lordships might have been sympathetic to the dissenting voices in *Pemsel* (n 37) and/or the views of the Commission and Tribunal, it should be remembered that *Macduff* (n 89) was a decision of the Court of Appeal which did not involve fee-charging and which came shortly after *Pemsel*.

[105] Provided the charitable purpose is other than the relief of poverty.

the stated class, logically, should not render it non-charitable.[106] And if a test of charitable status survives describing the class as, essentially, wealthy people, logic cannot demand that charitable status should be denied where the beneficiaries, though not described as such, would need to be wealthy in order to pay any contributions charged. Likewise, if the law tolerates an indifference to whether the rich or poor are likely to benefit, logic cannot demand a different approach where it seems more likely than not that some, or even all, of those will be rich.

III. A Charity May Charge for Its Services, Provided It is Non-Profit Making

It is recognised that charities face costs in fulfilling their purposes, which may exceed their income, and the ability of a charity to charge for the benefits and services it provides is a well-established principle of charity law, not confined to any particular head of charity and not disputed by the Commission.[107] Lord Upjohn put it simply: 'It is quite clear that the mere making of a charge for the services rendered does not prevent an organisation, otherwise charitable, from being charitable'.[108]

The inevitable consequence of fees being charged, however, is to highlight the distinction between rich and poor and it becomes entirely foreseeable that the beneficiaries of a charity which charges high fees may comprise a significant proportion of rich people. This makes the question of whether poverty is an essential element of charity more acute and the tension between the popular and legal meanings of charity more pronounced. It is not surprising, therefore, that the legitimacy of charities charging fees has been challenged. The courts' response, however, has been to affirm charitable status, notwithstanding fees (even high fees) being charged, provided that any surplus or profit is applied to the institution's charitable purposes.

Perhaps one of the most striking challenges was the argument put forward on behalf of the Minister of Town and Country Planning in *Abbey Malvern Wells Ltd v Ministry of Local Government and Planning*, that a school is not charitable unless tuition is free or at reduced fees.[109] Danckwerts J dismissed this as a 'startling proposition'.[110] 'Substantial fees' had been charged at all material times and

[106] To say 'for all children but not adults' means nothing more than 'for all children'.

[107] Clearly charges seem inappropriate where the purpose is to relieve poverty (but see *Re Monk* [1927] 2 Ch 197 (CA), where the purpose of providing loans without fees or interest to poor persons for the purposes of purchasing coal was considered charitable).

[108] *Scottish Burial* (n 46) 149; see also *Brighton College* (n 30) 204.

[109] *Abbey* (n 26) (discussed in ch 8, text to nn 59–69).

[110] ibid, 737. An argument that a school could not be a 'public school' within tax exemption legislation, unless education was free, was also rejected in *Blake v Mayor and Citizens of the City of London* (1887) LR 19 QBD 79 (QB).

there was no evidence to suggest that the poor were included, nor was an enquiry made.[111] The fee-charging institutions of Brighton College and the University College of North Wales were also charitable.[112]

Level of Fees

If an organisation's purposes are charitable, charitable status will not be denied because either the services are expensive to provide or the means of fulfilling those purposes involve the running of a business.[113] The test is essentially whether the venture is a commercial enterprise or a charitable one.[114] Fees are typically expressed to be in relation to cost,[115] or at a rate necessitated by the cost of providing the services,[116] and may vary in order to reflect different levels of services received[117] or different categories of beneficiary.[118] The courts have not considered it necessary to stress any objective requirement that fees should be fair or reasonable or necessary,[119] and, of course, the fees charged by a charity are likely to be lower than those charged by a non-charity (for the same services) since there is no element of profit, although the amount of any 'subsidy' will vary according to the organisation's charitable resources.

On the contrary, trustees are entrusted with a discretion in setting the level of fees and determining the basis on which they are charged. Even fees set on a commercial basis have not affected charitable status, whether they have been charged to some in order to subsidise others, or across the board. Thus, schools have been considered to be charitable despite 'substantial fees',[120] or fees fixed 'on commercial principles' and giving rise to fee receipts significantly exceeding working expenses.[121] Fees for the hospital in *Resch*, too, were substantial and produced surpluses but, in line with the common approach, the Court was more concerned with the application of the surplus than the level of fees and found the trust to be

[111] It is not clear to which case his Lordship was referring in saying that it had been held in the early eighteenth century that a school had to be a free school to be within the statute (*Abbey* (n 26) 737), but no reliance is placed on this by the Commission or Tribunal and, in the writer's view, rightly so (and see text to n 22 above).

[112] See text to nn 29–30 above.

[113] *Law Reporting* (n 18); see also *Brighton College* (n 30), where the House of Lords upheld the Commissioners' finding of fact that the whole purpose of the charitable school was the carrying on of a trade (although Lord Blanesburgh expressed some reluctance in doing so).

[114] *IRC v Falkirk Temperance Café Trust* 1927 SC 261 (CSIH).

[115] *Cottam* (n 59); *Clarke* (n 16).

[116] *IRC v The Trustees of the Roberts Marine Mansions* (1926) 11 TC 425 (CA); *Neal* (n 58).

[117] *Cawse v Nottinghamshire Lunatic Hospital Committee* [1891] 1 QB 585 (QB).

[118] *Roberts Marine Mansions* (n 116).

[119] Arguably the imposition of unfair, unreasonable or unnecessary charges could constitute breach of the trustees' charitable duties, in any event. (The Commission initially placed greater emphasis on the level of fees (see chs 5, 6).)

[120] *Abbey* (n 26).

[121] *Brighton College* (n 30).

charitable.[122] Nor does the level of fees appear to be relevant where they are to be paid by a grant-making organisation.[123]

The courts' approach is summarised in *Incorporated Council of Law Reporting v Attorney-General*, where the preparation and publication of law reports was considered to be beneficial to the community, notwithstanding that charges would be made for their use and that members of the legal profession would be assisted in their work.[124] Sachs LJ explained:[125]

> [I]t is clear that the mere fact that charges on a commercial scale are made for services rendered by an institution does not of itself bar that institution from being held to be charitable—so long, at any rate, as all the profits must be retained for its purposes and none can enure to the benefit of its individual members.

There was every opportunity for the Court here to consider the affordability of the charges or to insist that some provision should be made for people in poverty, but such considerations appear to have been irrelevant.

By contrast, a more restricted view of fee-charging is to be found in some academic texts. The view expressed in *Tudor on Charities*, for example, is that if charges are 'set at a level which deters or excludes a substantial proportion of the beneficial class the public benefit requirement will not be met',[126] but makes no particular mention of fees charged by schools in the context of education and public benefit, despite their being a type of charity very likely to deter or exclude a substantial proportion of the public.[127] No authority is cited for the proposition, however, and it appears to be out of line with case law. *Resch* is cited in support of the rather more accommodating proposition that 'charges may be set at a level which generates a surplus to assist the funding of a charity's other current or future activities', but no analysis of the case is provided.[128] Luxton suggests that a charity is not excluded from charging fees 'unless *perhaps* the charges are so high that the poor are effectively excluded' (emphasis added).[129] Picarda, on the other hand, describes the 'secure line of authority' which runs counter to the 'novel consideration of fees serving to exclude the poor'.[130]

[122] *Resch* (n 45); see also *Falkirk* (n 114).

[123] *Educational Grants* (n 33). It was not that some recipients of grants were rich, but that they were children of those joined by a contractual nexus of employment, that rendered the application of grants non-charitable in that case.

[124] *Law Reporting* (n 18).

[125] ibid, 90 (Sachs LJ).

[126] *Tudor on Charities* (n 48) 11. Reference is also made to *The Public Character of Charity* (Commission, February 2001) although it did not have force of law (and was superseded by the guidance).

[127] *Tudor on Charities* (n 48) 72; fee-paying schools are mentioned in relation to bounty, however: ibid, 33.

[128] Given the differing interpretations of the case, a commentary would have been welcome. It is assumed that *Resch* (n 45) is not cited as authority for the first part of the sentence, since 'a substantial proportion' of the public of New South Wales might be assumed to have been 'deterred' by the charges of St Vincent's Private Hospital.

[129] Luxton, *The Law of Charities* (n 69) 193.

[130] Picarda, *Law and Practice* (n 70) 85; Brunyate calls the advancement of education 'not a troublesome head of charity' and makes no reference to fees ('Legal Definition' (n 52) 272).

Intention to Make a Profit for Private Gain

An absence of any intention to make a profit for the private gain of its founders, managers, owners or members, does not lead to an inevitable conclusion that an institution *is* charitable, but the presence of such an intention will mean, conclusively, that an institution is *not* charitable. Even the potential for profit may be sufficient. Thus, the entitlement of preference shareholders to dividends and a return of capital was treated as a non-charitable purpose in the first instance decision in *Girls Public Day School Trust Ltd v Minister of Town and Country Planning*, even though the Trust had been conducted along charitable lines and by charitably-minded people who had asserted insignificant rights as preference shareholders (compared with the rights they were entitled to assert).[131] On the other hand, where dividends received were required to be applied towards a school's charitable purposes, charitable status was not denied.[132] Making accounting provision for reasonable surpluses or reserves is regarded as sensible practice and does not deprive an organisation of charitable status. It is the element of 'private gain' which 'must be eliminated',[133] not the making of any surplus.[134]

A slightly less rigid view may be apparent in the courts' interpretation of 'public school' within tax exemption legislation.[135] Whilst the allocation of shares in return for subscriptions, where those shares were saleable and sold, prevented one school from being a 'public school',[136] the payment of a 'rigidly limited dividend' to preference shareholders did not prevent Wimbledon High School for Girls from achieving that status.[137] The House of Lords identified a number of factors to be taken into account, none of which was said to be conclusive and none was concerned with providing opportunities to those unable to afford the fees. The existence of a perpetual foundation or portion of income derived from charity, for example, was undoubtedly a relevant factor but not essential.[138] Significance was also attached to the existence of a charitable endowment and eleemosynary character in the interpretation of 'hospital' within similar tax legislation so that, for example, an institution was a 'hospital' for these purposes where it was maintained in part by charity notwithstanding that it no longer catered only for 'the poorer

[131] *Girls Public Day School Trust Ltd v Minister of Town and Country Planning* [1951] Ch 400 (Ch).

[132] *Abbey* (n 26), where a trust deed required the shares to be held on trust.

[133] *Falkirk* (n 114) 268 (Lord Sands).

[134] *Scottish Burial* (n 46) 149.

[135] Although it is possible to argue that, on similar facts, an opportunity for profit (as in *Ereaut's* case (n 137) below, referred to in this paragraph)) might not disqualify the institution from charitable status either.

[136] *The Birkenhead School Ltd v Dring* 11 TC 273 (KB).

[137] *Girls Public Day School Trust Ltd v Ereaut* [1931] AC 12 (HL); see also *Dilworth v Commissioner of Stamps* [1899] AC 99 (PC) 108.

[138] Offering an interpretation of *Blake* (n 110). Other relevant factors noted in *Ereaut* (n 137) included the absence of private interests or profit-making motives and management by a public body. Lord Atkin also suggested that there should be no difference between a school which raises finance by debentures at interest and one which does so by preference shares at a limited rate of interest.

classes' but treated a 'very different … class of patients' whose payments produced surpluses in some years.[139]

Numerous cases and judicial dicta have noted the destination of profits to be the critical test in relation to charitable status, not the availability of opportunities for people unable to afford the fees. It is the application of profits to the charitable purposes which represents the 'element of unselfishness' at the heart of charity and 'the vital distinction' between it and non-charity.[140] Danckwerts J considered it a straightforward matter: 'as the whole purpose of this deed was to secure the education of girls at the Abbey School on a non-profit-making basis, the trusts are plainly of a charitable nature'.[141] Similarly, Buckley LJ concluded in the *Law Reporting* case that the fact that business profits were permitted but could only be applied in furtherance of its objects meant that the Council was '*consequently* not prevented from being a charity by reason of any commercial element in its activities' (emphasis added).[142]

Likewise, in *Re Smith*,[143] Upjohn LJ described two ways of treating the sick: the 'charitable' way, being a hospital where funds are applied exclusively to the relief of the sick, and the 'non-charitable' way, being an institution run for profit, where the funds are applied in part to the treatment of the sick and in part to earning profits. The position may be different, however, where the profit-making institution is not the purported charity itself, but another institution whose services might be engaged in order to carry out the charity's purposes. In *Taylor v Taylor*, for example, Isaacs J contemplated circumstances where founding or endowing a non-profit-making institution would not be practicable and expressed his view that the charitable intention to provide care and treatment of mentally afflicted persons could properly be carried out by providing financial assistance to an existing profit-making institution which would meet the needs of the beneficiaries.[144]

If an institution's purposes include the purpose of making a private gain, it cannot be granted charitable status because the purposes cannot be described as exclusively charitable. Once established as a charity, however, any application of the institution's surplus or profit for private gain will constitute a breach of trust. That is quite a different matter. It does not, at the same time, deprive the institution of charitable status.[145]

[139] *Cawse* (n 117) 589 (the Court not considering it necessary to question to what extent (if at all) fees were reduced or waived in individual circumstances); *cf Needham v Bowers* (1888) LR 21 QBD 436 (QB) ('self-supporting' on fee income and not a 'hospital', despite some patients being treated free of charge).

[140] *Law Reporting* (n 18) 86 (Russell LJ).

[141] *Abbey* (n 26) 738.

[142] *Law Reporting* (n 18) 104.

[143] *Re Smith* [1962] 1 WLR 763 (CA) 768.

[144] *Taylor* (n 75) 239 (in which circumstances, of course, the proper application of charitable funds would appear to justify a view that the charges should be fair, reasonable and necessary (*cf* text to n 119)).

[145] Although it could lead to a conclusion that the institution was never charitable and that the purposes had been misconstrued.

Reduction or Waiver of Charges

Any charitable source of finance, whether a founding gift or ongoing donations and legacies, enables trustees to extend services to beneficiaries at a subsidised cost, whereas a commercial operation will require payments which cover the costs of its services and provide profits in addition. Any subsidy may be directed towards all beneficiaries or only a few and the application of that bounty, or saving, is in the trustees' discretion (subject to any express provision in the constitution). Whilst an obligation or willingness on the part of an institution to reduce, or even waive, fees in some cases is likely to indicate a charitable intention where the charitable nature of the purposes is in question,[146] the courts have not required fee-charging charities to offer reduced or nil fees for their services as a condition to conferring charitable status.[147] In *Perpetual Trustee Co v St Luke's Hospital*, for example, a hospital was expressed to be for paying patients, but with a 'great objective' of admitting some who could not afford the ordinary fees, and was held to be charitable.[148] Nicholas J commented that 'a hospital is not excluded from the category of charitable institutions because it accepts no patients who do not pay fees' and also intimated that charitable status cannot depend on precise numbers of those receiving below-cost services or their proportion to the total number of beneficiaries or the precise level of fees.[149] Furthermore, case law demonstrates that neither evidence of reduced or waived charges,[150] nor an express power to reduce and waive charges,[151] is critical in establishing charitable status.[152]

Conversely, it is not suggested that generous gratuitous provision will be conclusive in favour of charity.[153] In both cases, this is a sensible and pragmatic approach: an institution's financial resources vary from year to year and the trustees must make operational decisions accordingly. If charitable status were to come and go depending on such fluctuating circumstances, it would cause great uncertainty

[146] *Roberts Marine Mansions* (n 116).

[147] *Ereaut* (n 137); *cf Blake* (n 110) 82 (Lopes LJ) (although his words regarding gratuitous provision can be taken to refer to a reduced cost for all, in light of the absence of evidence of free or reduced fees for some and the school's endowment; also his words are cited in *Cawse* (n 117) apparently to refer to 'reduced' fees for all due to a charitable endowment, rather than reduced or nil fees for some).

[148] *Perpetual Trustee Co v St Luke's Hospital* (1939) 39 SR (NSW) 408 (SC, NSW) 419; apparently representing an implied exclusion on the terms. Radan and Stewart cited the case as authority for charitable status being unaffected by the charging of fees, provided the income is applied towards the purposes of the hospital: P Radan and C Stewart, *Principles of Australian Equity and Trusts* (Chatswood NSW, LexisNexis Butterworth, 2009) 18.53.

[149] *St Luke's Hospital* (n 148) 421.

[150] *Falkirk* (n 114).

[151] *Roberts Marine Mansions* (n 116).

[152] See also *Cawse* (n 117), where the hospital's eleemosynary character was not dependent on fees being reduced or waived in individual cases.

[153] eg, private profits could still deprive a generous institution of charitable status; and see *Needham* (n 139), where 66 out of 158 patients paid reduced fees based on means (10 paying nothing at all), but it was not a 'hospital' within the tax exemption legislation.

and significant legal difficulties in respect of the institution's tax position and assets.[154]

The decision in *Resch* merits particular attention.[155] This was a Privy Council decision, on appeal from the Supreme Court of New South Wales, and involved a trust of income to be applied to the general purposes of St Vincent's Private Hospital. Described as a 'blancmange … a foundation for nothing but a sinking feeling',[156] the case has received markedly different interpretations and it was not until decades after the case was reported that it surfaced as the mainstay in the Commission's interpretation of the law relating to fee-charging charities.[157] After identifying the purposes of the hospital as prima facie charitable, the Privy Council went on to describe two 'disqualifying indicia' that might render it non-charitable: first, whether it was run for private profit and, second, whether it failed the necessary test of public character by not benefiting a sufficiently large section of the community.[158] It was not disqualified on either count.

There was evidence that some patients had been treated for nil or reduced fees 'from time to time',[159] but there was no constitution or written rules for the hospital (nor provision in the will) which required some services to be given *gratis*, or for reduced rates, and so the position could have varied from year to year and fees covering the full cost might legitimately have been charged to all. Counsel for the hospital did not seek to rely on such provision as there was for those unable to afford the fees, as one might have expected if the law had established this to be a necessary element of charitable status. And although Lord Wilberforce commented on this part of the evidence in summarising the facts of the case,[160] he can hardly be said to have attached weight to it and it is not a conclusive, or even critical, part of the Privy Council's decision.[161] It is striking that when his Lordship listed the constituent parts of the 'strongly present' public benefit in the case, the provision of reduced or free services was not included, nor was it suggested that such provision should be a qualifying factor of charitable status.[162]

Recognising the high cost of medical services, the Privy Council held that a trust for providing medical facilities would not be deprived of charitable status

[154] As demonstrated by the uncertainty caused by the Commission's approach (see chs 5, 6) and the uncertainty which the Tribunal acknowledges (see ch 8).

[155] *Resch* (n 45).

[156] HL Deb (n 5) col GC120 (Lord Phillips).

[157] Picarda notes that the case, 'after languishing without much academic or other comment for many years, has now become the touchstone for new generalised doctrine or dogma': *Law and Practice* (n 70) 155.

[158] *Resch* (n 45) 540. This was a case under the fourth head of charity.

[159] ibid, 539.

[160] ibid; and at 544 (patients who 'cannot get a reduction of or exemption from the charges' being some of those excluded from benefiting).

[161] Nor does it appear in the headnote to the case; Buckley calls the weight attached to this evidence 'negligible': C Buckley, 'The Charities Act 2006: Consolidation or Reform?' (2009) 11 *Charity Law & Practice Review* 1.

[162] See also *St Luke's Hospital* (n 148).

'merely because by reason of expense they could *only* be made use of by persons of some means' (emphasis added).[163] The fees were variously described in the case as 'substantial', 'not low' and 'expensive', and it is implicit that 'some means' must signify means which are sufficient to pay them.[164] The principle, then, appears to be significant in suggesting that a charitable purpose may be charitable even though the practice of charging high fees (as opposed to the existence of an express exclusion on the terms) means that only the rich can benefit.[165] Lord Wilberforce also suggested that to the extent that the poor could be said to be excluded, that would mean that the services were not open to all and not that they were non-charitable. Of course, the purpose could still be rendered non-charitable by an intention to make a profit for private gain or to apply monies to other non-charitable purposes, but the case does appear to offer persuasive authority for the proposition that charitable status is not denied on the basis that a class comprising only 'persons of some means' necessarily fails to benefit a large section of the public. On the contrary, such a class may constitute a sufficient section of the public.[166]

In deliberate contrast to this principle, however, Lord Wilberforce proposed that 'to limit admission to a nursing home to the rich' would not be charitable.[167] The reference to limiting admission needs to be construed as referring to an express exclusion on the terms if it is not to conflict with the principle outlined in the preceding paragraph. It is also possible that his Lordship was referring to institutions run for profit and which, therefore, are not charitable in any event.[168] On this basis, the dictum could be regarded as a 'belt and braces' approach, akin to the examples of philanthropic but non-charitable purposes in *Macduff*.[169] Five years earlier, Wilberforce J, as he then was, had been required to interpret the word 'hospital' in a will.[170] Since the word 'hospital' could be construed as including non-charitable institutions, he had held that the purposes were not exclusively charitable and that the gift failed. The Court of Appeal, whilst reversing his decision on the construction of the will, agreed that the word 'hospital' was capable

[163] *Resch* (n 45) 544.

[164] ibid, 542, 544 (Lord Wilberforce).

[165] Whether or not the case can be seen as illustrating an implied exclusion in practice must be open to debate, given Lord Wilberforce's comment that the poor were not excluded (because some poor might obtain gratuitous services or have contributed sufficiently to a medical benefit scheme (although counsel's argument that anyone who contributes to such a scheme cannot be poor has some merit)). It would appear, however, to be capable of being so construed.

[166] It is also worth noting that counsel was unsuccessful in arguing that a section of the community can only be selected on the basis of locality, occupation, trade or creed and not on wealth or membership of a benefit scheme: *Resch* (n 45) 523, based on *Baddeley* (n 44).

[167] *Resch* (n 45) 544. The two ideas are separated by a colon and joined by the conjunctive adverb 'on the other hand'.

[168] Although it should be noted that the example was given in the context of considering the poor being excluded and not in relation to considerations of commercial profit (the second and first 'disqualifying indicia' respectively).

[169] *Macduff* (n 89); see also text to nn 90–104 above.

[170] *Smith* (n 143).

of covering 'both voluntary hospitals, dependent on voluntary contributions, and also nursing homes run for private profit'.[171]

This review of the case law indicates that, with the exception of cases involving the relief of poverty and early cases concerning the needs of the aged and infirm, the courts have not looked for some element of poverty to be present, either in the limited means of actual or potential beneficiaries or in the expression or fulfilment of the organisation's purposes. Whilst the law might not tolerate a settlor *explicitly* excluding the poor as a matter of deliberate choice, it recognises that human needs are not always dependent on financial circumstances and also that trustees may need to exclude the poor, as an inevitable consequence of their having to charge fees in order to fulfil the charity's purposes. In so doing, the courts have not sought to formulate a legal principle, either as a matter of charitable status or in relation to trustees' duties, that the poor must also be considered or given opportunities to benefit, or that some services must be provided gratuitously or at reduced rates. The 2006 Act made no changes to this position.

[171] ibid, 766 (Lord Denning MR); see also *Robinson* (n 58) 201 (where Vaisey J intimated that aged persons in a 'nursing home' might be 'not at all in need of any sort of pecuniary assistance').

5

Poverty and the Charging of Fees: The Commission*

[T]he issue for charities that charge high fees is whether or not there is sufficient opportunity to benefit for those people who cannot afford to pay.

The Commission[1]

I. Introduction

The Commission's interpretation of the law relating to poverty and fee-charging, in both the 2008 and 2013 versions of its guidance, differs significantly from that set out in the previous chapter. Essentially, the Commission maintains that a charity cannot exclude the poor, either expressly or as a result of charging fees which the poor cannot afford. As a result, it says, charity trustees must also provide opportunities to benefit for people who cannot afford the fees charged, including the poor. The difficulties surrounding this interpretation include the definition of 'the poor', the nature and extent of the opportunities which should be offered and the consequences of a failure to provide sufficient opportunities.

This chapter considers the Commission's legal interpretation in its 2008 publications. The effect of changes made in 2013 (which did not resolve those difficulties entirely) is addressed in chapter nine.

II. The Commission's Legal Analysis

In every charity, the elements of public benefit must be present, but it is not the case that the measure or standard is uniform across the entire range of charitable purposes.

The Commission[2]

* In this chapter, references to the 'Guidance' are to *Charities and Public Benefit* (Commission, January 2008) and numbered references to the 'Analysis' are to paragraphs of the *Analysis of the law underpinning Charities and Public Benefit* (Commission, December 2008). References to *Fee-charging* are to *Public Benefit and Fee-charging* (Commission, December 2008).

[1] Foreword to the Guidance.

[2] Analysis 3.1.

The Commission's legal interpretation in 2008 was summarised in the following two principles which, for the most part, were merged for the purpose of explaining their legal justification and also their practical significance:

Principle 2b: Where benefit is to a section of the public, the opportunity to benefit must not be unreasonably restricted … by ability to pay any fees charged.[3]

Principle 2c: People in poverty must not be excluded from the opportunity to benefit.

The legal justification for these two principles was expounded in the Analysis. Admittedly described as 'a useful reference point for trustees' rather than a 'comprehensive legal digest',[4] the level of legal justification and analysis which appeared in the Analysis in support of Principles 2b and 2c was nonetheless poor and inadequate. In the absence of direct authority for its interpretation, the document proffered 'the Commission's interpretation of'[5] *Re Resch*,[6] the Privy Council case concerning an Australian private hospital, and included quotations from obiter comments in other judgments without also providing any comment or context in respect of those comments.[7]

Several cases were cited in support of the basic and uncontested proposition that charitable status is not denied simply because fees are charged, but the legal foundation for Principles 2b and 2c was said to rest on the following cases:[8]

— *Re Resch*[9]
— *Jones v Williams*[10]
— *Special Commissioners of Income Tax v Pemsel*[11]
— *Oppenheim v Tobacco Securities Trust Co Ltd*[12]
— *Re Macduff*[13]
— *Taylor v Taylor*[14]

Resch was put forward by the Commission as the principal authority for its statement of legal principles, the other cases being cited in support.[15] The case is the only one of the six cases which directly involves a fee-charging charity, although

[3] The other restrictions were considered in ch 3 (see n 102).
[4] Analysis Introduction 2.
[5] Analysis 3.65.
[6] *Re Resch* [1969] 1 AC 514 (PC); see text to nn 155–71, ch 4.
[7] Save to their 'wider context' (Analysis 3.64) and general effect alongside *Resch* (ibid) (Analysis 3.68). Specific page references were given in respect of only two of the five cases.
[8] *Re Coulthurst* [1951] Ch 661 (CA) 666 was referred to with regard to the definition of poverty in relation to Principle 2c.
[9] *Resch* (n 6).
[10] *Jones v Williams* (1767) Amb 651, 27 ER 422.
[11] *Special Commissioners of Income Tax v Pemsel* [1891] AC 531 (HL).
[12] *Oppenheim v Tobacco Securities Trust Co Ltd* [1951] AC 297 (HL).
[13] *Re Macduff* [1896] 2 Ch 451 (CA).
[14] *Taylor v Taylor* (1910) 10 CLR 218 (HCt Australia).
[15] *Resch* (n 6). Although dicta from the cases were set out in the section of the Analysis dealing with Principle 2c, they were also referred to as authority for Principle 2b (Analysis 3.60, 3.64, 3.68).

Taylor does make reference to fee-charging.[16] Both of these cases were Australian, the first reaching the Privy Council and the second the High Court of Australia (on appeal from the Supreme Court of Tasmania) and are thus of persuasive authority only.[17] Only one of the cases concerned advancement of education.[18]

(1) *Re Resch*[19]

The Commission extrapolated three principles from the case:[20]

(i) that providing charitable services mainly to people who can afford the fees charged, does not necessarily mean that it is not set up, and does not operate, for the benefit of the public;

(ii) that an organisation 'which wholly excluded poor people from any benefits, direct or indirect' would not be set up, and operate, for the benefit of the public;

(iii) that both direct and indirect benefits may be taken into account in consideration of public benefit.

The first of these principles is not contested, although the interpretation of the word 'mainly' is as critical as it is ambiguous and should be replaced by the word 'only' in order more closely to reflect the words of Lord Wilberforce, who spoke of expensive services not losing their charitable nature because they 'could *only* be made use of by persons of some means' (emphasis added).[21]

It is convenient to address the third principle, which is not disputed, before the second, since the words are very close to Lord Wilberforce's own.[22] The Commission took the view that indirect benefits should be 'looked for first', based on his Lordship's comment that 'indirect *as well as* direct benefit enters into account',[23] a process of deduction which may be flawed but also insignificant. It also considered that the juxtaposition of the two hospitals made indirect benefit 'particularly prominent' in this case.[24] This is not disputed either, save to the extent that it risks overstating the factor's significance and suggests that some such juxtaposition, or

[16] *Taylor* (n 14).

[17] Which may explain why *Resch* (n 6) was introduced in the Analysis by way of its mention in a first instance case before the English courts (Analysis 3.53).

[18] *Oppenheim* (n 12); but see text to nn 50–51 below.

[19] *Resch* (n 6).

[20] Analysis 3.59. It might be worth noting at this stage that the Commission's reliance on *Resch* is replaced by a reliance on *R (Independent Schools Council) v Charity Commission* [2011] UKUT 421 (TCC), [2012] Ch 214 in the 2013 legal analysis (see ch 9).

[21] *Resch* (n 6) 544, assuming 'some means' refers to the fees charged (see text to nn 163–66, ch 4). The Scottish regulator cited a similar principle (see text to nn 65–66, ch 7).

[22] 'The test is essentially one of public benefit, and indirect as well as direct benefit enters into the account': *Resch* (n 6) 544.

[23] Analysis 3.66.

[24] ibid.

collaboration, between state and private institutions is necessary in order to satisfy the public benefit requirement.

To argue, as the Commission did, that indirect benefit alone would render the public benefit test ineffectual, on the basis that a nursing home limited to the rich would then be charitable, is an unsophisticated argument.[25] It assumes that a test of indirect benefit, unlike a test of direct benefit, would not be overridden by an express exclusion of the poor or other disqualifying factors, such as a personal nexus or profit-making motive.[26] It also suggests that the Commission may have misunderstood the point being made by counsel, to which it referred and on which its argument was based. Counsel's argument was not that indirect benefit was enough, without consideration of direct benefit, but that the indirect benefit of relieving the demand on public hospitals was enough to demonstrate a benefit to the public beyond the class of beneficiaries *if* such a wider benefit needed to be shown.[27]

The second principle is the most significant and, unlike the Commission's first and third principles drawn from this case, does not closely resemble wording in the judgment itself. It is also ambiguous: must an organisation exclude all poor from all benefits (both direct and indirect) in order to fall foul of the principle, or is the exclusion of all poor from any part of the overall benefits (direct or indirect) sufficient? It would seem difficult, if not impossible, to exclude the poor (or rich) from indirect benefit. And, perhaps more importantly, does it matter *how* the poor are 'wholly excluded' from those benefits, that is to say whether expressly on the terms of the constitution, or by high fees being charged in practice? It is implicit that the Commission regards any such exclusion as within this second principle. The better view, however, is that the principle can only be reconciled with the case itself, and the Court's interpretation of other cases, if the meaning is restricted to express exclusions on the terms.

The Analysis reported, not quite accurately, that Lord Wilberforce had confirmed that 'limiting services to the rich, excluding those who could not afford the fees, could not be charitable'.[28] This was to misrepresent his Lordship's words, 'to limit admission to a nursing home to the rich would not be [charitable]',[29] both by replacing the term 'nursing home' (with its possible connotation of commercial profit) with the infinitely more general word 'services' and by broadening what might reasonably be construed as a reference to an exclusion on the terms to a situation where the poor are excluded in practice because of fees which cover the cost of expensive services.[30] The idea of 'limiting admission' might also be seen as

[25] Analysis 3.67.
[26] *cf* Analysis fn 124.
[27] *Resch* (n 6) 529.
[28] Analysis 3.57.
[29] *Resch* (n 6) 544. (Although this dictum was included (Analysis 3.63), it was not commented upon directly.)
[30] See text to nn 167–71, ch 4.

narrower than 'limiting services', the possible implication of the former being that admission is limited by the settlor's choosing, rather than (as in the latter) by the necessary cost of providing services. The reported principle was supported neither by the passage of the judgment, which was set out in full in the Analysis, nor by the decision itself.[31]

Furthermore, the wording of the Commission's conclusion (drawn from the case) that an organisation 'limited to benefit only those who could afford the fees … would not be a sufficient section of the public',[32] replaced 'the rich' (the term used by Lord Wilberforce) with 'those who could afford the fees', thereby extending the proposition to instances where lower fees are charged, in fact to all fee-charging charities except those whose fees are affordable to all.[33] More importantly, it failed to distinguish between exclusions on the terms and exclusions in practice. It is assumed that the Commission intended to encompass both and certainly the statement that an organisation's purposes, and the way it carried out those purposes, 'must not be so as to help only those who by reason of their wealth are able to afford the fees', is a much broader proposition which cannot be restricted to instances of express exclusions.[34] It also appears directly to contradict the Privy Council's interpretation of the authorities and to contradict what is no more than the logical conclusion of accepting that fees do not deprive otherwise charitable purposes of their charitable nature. Both statements seemed to ignore the Court's conclusion that the test of public character was met, because 'so far as its nature permits' the service was open to all, and to place too great an emphasis on the conclusion that the poor were not excluded.[35]

The Commission made no comment on the fact that the Court included people with inadequate insurance in its understanding of 'the poor',[36] even though this could include wealthy people who, through choice or accident, have not taken out sufficient insurance and the concept of 'the poor' having medical insurance at all seems questionable.[37] It is doubtful whether this can be reconciled with the Commission's suggestion that the term 'people in poverty' signified people who are destitute, together with those 'who cannot satisfy a basic need without assistance'.[38]

[31] Analysis 3.57, quoting from '[t]he test is essentially one of public benefit' to 'which arises from the juxtaposition of the two institutions' (*Resch* (n 6) 544).

[32] Analysis 3.65.

[33] The Scottish regulator suggested that £1,500 pa might be regarded as affordable to all, but the Commission offered no such guidance (see ch 7).

[34] Analysis 3.65 (described as 'the test in *Re Resch*' (presumably the public benefit requirement)).

[35] See the discussion of *Resch* in ch 4 (text to nn 155–71).

[36] Which would appear to cover 'those who have (a) not contributed sufficiently to a medical benefit scheme or (b) need to stay longer in the hospital than their benefit will cover' (*Resch* (n 6) 544).

[37] Counsel calls the proposition that the benefit is open to all because they can insure 'an invasion of the approach to the law of charity which has always been fundamentally related to some need to help the poor' (ibid, 526). (The explanation may be open to question, but the implication, that those who can insure are not poor, is not.)

[38] Guidance B4.

With regard to the question of the provision of services for reduced or nil fees, the Commission acknowledged that this factor was 'not explicitly analysed', but then concluded that the provision afforded by St Vincent's Private Hospital was 'clearly more than minimal or nominal access or access that occurred merely by chance'.[39] Such a conclusion was unwarranted by the judgment. In fact, counsel for the next-of-kin had argued that the level of such provision was 'relatively small', limited to cases of 'extreme urgency', with only 'a few patients' being treated free of charge,[40] and it will also be remembered that counsel for the hospital did not suggest that more was given, nor was it an area of inquiry or deliberation by the Court. The Commission's further conclusion, therefore, that 'it was therefore clear that there were sufficient benefits to poorer people who could not afford the fees in this case', seems equally problematic.[41]

(2) Other Judicial Authority for the Second Principle Extrapolated from *Re Resch*[42]

Dicta from the five other cases referred to above were put forward in support of the second principle, on the basis of the courts having made statements that 'although the rich can be included as beneficiaries, poorer people cannot be excluded'.[43] The same five cases were also said to support the broader proposition that 'charities must in all cases ensure that poorer people are not excluded from the opportunity to benefit from each of their purposes'.[44] The Commission clearly considered these cases to show that neither exclusions on the terms nor exclusions in practice are permitted, but it will be seen that the cases offer no such authority. The dicta were set out in the Analysis, but the Commission made no attempt to give any comment or analysis in respect of them. Each dictum is considered below, before examining how these were interpreted by the Privy Council in *Resch*.[45]

(i) Jones v Williams

> Definition of charity: a gift to a general public use, which extends to the poor as well as to the rich.[46]

The Commission's reliance on this dictum suggests that it interpreted the relative clause as a conditional one, which applied to purposes directed at a section of the

39 Analysis 3.58.
40 *Resch* (n 6) 521.
41 Analysis 3.58.
42 *Resch* (n 6); Analysis 3.60, 3.71–3.76.
43 Analysis 3.60.
44 Analysis 3.76 (suggesting an ongoing obligation owed by the charity, whereas the first might be construed as limited to the settlor's class description (although it is not suggested that that was the Commission's intention)).
45 *Resch* (n 6).
46 *Jones* (n 10) 652/423.

public in addition to those directed at the public generally (which more obviously embraces both rich and poor). This interpretation is not supported by case law, however, and, as a definition of charity, the significance of the dictum has been diminished by a number of factors: the instances where it has not been cited in full, the numerous cases where judges have shied away from offering a definition at all, the particular context of the case, and the fact that the current legislative definition of charity makes no reference to issues of poverty and riches.[47]

(ii) *Pemsel*

> The trusts last referred to [the fourth head] are not the less charitable in the eyes of the law, because incidentally they benefit the rich as well as the poor, as indeed every charity that deserves the name must do either directly or indirectly.[48]

The ambiguity inherent in this dictum has already been addressed.[49] Even interpreting it to mean that trusts must benefit the poor, however, as it seems the Commission did, the further interpretation that such benefit may be indirect, or even incidental, seems unavoidable but also contradicts any contention that the poor should be included among the class of beneficiaries directly.

(iii) *Oppenheim*[50]

The Analysis stated that support was also provided by the judgment of Lord Simonds in this case, but gave no indication of where or how such support was to be found. Lord Simonds did refer to both of the above cases, but not in connection with whether the poor were excluded, by fees or otherwise. Poverty in *Oppenheim* was only relevant in the sense that, had the purposes been the relief of poverty rather than the advancement of education, the personal nexus (arising from common employment) would not have prevented the purposes from being charitable.[51] This was a regrettable flaw in the Commission's legal analysis.

(iv) *Macduff*

> I am quite aware that a trust may be charitable though not confined to the poor; but I doubt very much whether a trust would be declared to be charitable which excluded the poor.[52]

For reasons given in the previous chapter, the significance of this obiter dictum (and the obiter dicta of Rigby and Lopes LLJ which the Commission does not

[47] See also text to nn 71–78, ch 4.

[48] *Pemsel* (n 11) 583 (Lord Macnaghten).

[49] See text to nn 41–43, ch 4.

[50] *Oppenheim* (n 12).

[51] It might also be noted that, in contrasting the private circumstances of the case with the public (and therefore charitable) nature of colleges and universities, his Lordship made no reference to poverty or fees (ibid 306).

[52] *Macduff* (n 13) 464 (Lindley LJ).

include) appears to be limited to express exclusions of the poor and has no relevance to the effect of fees excluding those unable to afford them.[53] In light of the Commission's insistence that principles in respect of one head of charity should not automatically be applied in another, it might also be worth noting that the three members of the Court of Appeal made no reference to either the advancement of education or fee-charging charities.

(v) *Taylor v Taylor*

> The prima facie impression that the words convey to my mind is that the testator intended the establishment of what may be called private lunatic asylums for the benefit of well-to-do persons who could pay for their treatment, or at any rate to include institutions for the exclusive benefit of such persons. If this were the true construction I doubt very much whether the gift could be supported.[54]

Having already made clear that the word 'private' signified homes offering greater privacy and not profit-making ventures, Griffith CJ considered the dicta of Rigby and Lindley LLJ in *Macduff* and appeared to confine their relevance to express exclusions of the poor, since he identified only an express exclusion by the settlor as a reason for depriving the gift of charitable status: the 'prima facie impression' of the testator having contemplated institutions for the exclusive benefit of 'well-to-do' persons was said to be dispelled on the grounds that the testator had 'certainly not expressly excluded the poor from the benefit of this trust' and, therefore, the gift could not be said to be non-charitable for reasons of excluding the poor.[55] He did not suggest, as he could easily have done, that another reason might have been the effect of fees in excluding the poor. His Honour also had no doubt that a gift to a private fee-charging, but non-profit making, 'lunatic asylum' would be good 'unless, perhaps, if the poor were excluded from its benefits'.[56] His reliance on *Cawse v Committee of Nottingham Lunatic Hospital*, where there was no inquiry into the affordability of fees or insistence upon gratuitous services, reinforces the view that he had in mind only an express exclusion on the terms and not an implied exclusion in practice.[57]

[53] See text to nn 89–104, ch 4.

[54] *Taylor* (n 14) 226 (Griffith CJ).

[55] ibid, 227; his Honour regarding any possible ambiguity as not sufficient to deny charitable status, an approach which stands in stark contrast to that of the Commission (in particular in relation to the Preston Down Trust (see text to nn 20–28, ch 2)).

[56] *Taylor* (n 14) 227 (whilst acknowledging that *Cawse* (n 57 below) was decided on a particular statute, his view was clearly that a private hospital for the insane was a recognised form of charitable institution); see also text to n 144, ch 4.

[57] *Cawse v Nottingham Lunatic Hospital Committee* [1891] 1 QB 585 (QB).

(3) The Privy Council's Interpretation of the Judicial Authorities Considered

Returning to the discussion of *Resch* in the Analysis,[58] the Commission stated that Lord Wilberforce had considered 'some of these cases' and had 'expressly confirmed that they were correct'.[59] In fact, his Lordship referred to each of them except *Oppenheim*[60] and confirmed that the Court accepted the correctness of what was said in those cases (which is not the same as to confirm the correctness of the cases), but stressed that they should be 'rightly understood'.[61] What the cases did *not* say, he explained, was that providing medical services would not be non-charitable 'merely because by reason of expense they could only be made use of by persons of some means'.[62] The dictum was included in the Analysis, but without comment.[63] The further proposition that providing medical treatment, which is expensive but otherwise inaccessible, might well be charitable, was also referred to without comment (and omitting the important caveat 'without any profit motive').[64] Instead, the Commission chose to place greater emphasis on his Lordship's comment that 'to limit admission to a nursing home to the rich would not be [charitable]'.[65] The ways in which these two ideas differ and how they are juxtaposed in deliberate contrast by Lord Wilberforce, however, were not addressed as they should have been.[66]

The Analysis concluded that *Resch* and 'the wider context of the previous cases' supported the proposition that a restriction based on ability to pay fees 'affects public benefit', the implication being that charitable status may be denied.[67] None of the cases support this conclusion, however, nor any proposition that an implied exclusion in practice, where only the wealthy may benefit, cannot be charitable. The fees in *Resch* were unaffordable to those who could not afford to pay them outright or could not afford adequate insurance and fee waivers were occasional and discretionary, but the gift was charitable nonetheless.[68] If there had been no evidence of some people being treated free of charge, for example, or if there had not been the general hospital nearby, would the decision have been different? It cannot be presumed that if any one or more of the benefits described by the Court were absent, its decision would have gone the other way, and the case

[58] *Resch* (n 6); Analysis 3.61.
[59] Analysis 3.61.
[60] *Oppenheim* (n 12).
[61] *Resch* (n 6) 544.
[62] ibid.
[63] Analysis 3.61.
[64] Analysis 3.62; *Resch* (n 6) 544.
[65] Analysis 3.63 (which began: 'However, crucially').
[66] See text to nn 167–69, ch 4.
[67] Analysis 3.64; *Resch* (n 6).
[68] *Resch* (n 6).

cannot support the proposition that any fee-charging charity must offer benefits to people who cannot afford the fees.[69]

According to the Commission, the extent to which the law requires charitable services to be made available to those unable to afford the fees charged, including the poor, was said to depend on a variety of factors, including the exclusory nature of the fees, the extent to which they are moderated to give access and the modern context in which the charity operates.[70] In support of this, the Commission cited the six cases already considered, together with *Re Clarke*[71] and also, by way of example, *Attorney-General v Earl of Lonsdale*,[72] *Brighton College v Marriott*,[73] *Abbey Malvern Wells Ltd v Ministry of Local Government and Planning*[74] and *Smith v Kerr*.[75] It has been seen in the previous chapter, however, that the first three of these latter cases actually undermine, rather than support, the Commission's position, and the Analysis did no more than list them in a footnote.[76] Particularly in light of the focus which the Commission placed on independent schools as a high risk category in its public benefit assessments,[77] the three schools cases were significant and should have been addressed.

III. The Commission's Guidance

Principle 2c, that people in poverty must not be excluded from the opportunity to benefit, was described as 'most likely to be an issue for high fee-charging charities',[78] but it was not in fact confined in that way. In relation to all charities generally, it was expressed as a limited obligation to ensure that people in poverty are *not excluded* from the opportunity to benefit from a charity's aims, but its expression was transformed into a positive duty in the case of fee-charging charities. It is here that Principles 2b and 2c were merged and the obligation became one *to provide* sufficient opportunities to benefit in a material way for those unable to afford the fees, *including people in poverty*.[79] Care should be taken, however: an obligation not to expressly exclude something is not an obligation expressly to include it,

[69] The decision would have gone the other way, of course, if the institution had been profit-making or private in character.

[70] Analysis 3.68. Other factors included the purpose, the need for and nature of the services, the nature of the benefit, including its duration, and the general circumstances.

[71] *Re Clarke* [1923] 2 Ch 407 (Ch).

[72] *AG v Earl of Lonsdale* (1827) 1 Sim 105, 57 ER 518.

[73] *Brighton College v Marriott* [1926] AC 192 (HL).

[74] *Abbey Malvern Wells Ltd v Ministry of Local Government and Planning* [1951] Ch 728 (Ch).

[75] *Smith v Kerr* [1902] 1 Ch 774 (CA).

[76] Nor does *Smith* (ibid) provide authority in support (an Inn of Chancery held to be charitable, notwithstanding incidental benefits to its members).

[77] See ch 6.

[78] Guidance F11.

[79] *Fee-charging* B4.

but an obligation to allow it to be included. Similarly, a duty not to discriminate against certain types of people is not to say that persons of that type must be selected, but that they must be considered for selection or, at least, that consideration of them should not be refused. And if an obligation not to deny opportunities in practice *could* be converted into a positive obligation to provide those opportunities, the legal basis for the primary obligation would first need to be established. Whilst the Supreme Court might see fit to make such a leap, the Commission is not in a position to do so, especially when faced with conflicting legal authority.

Principle 2b: Regarding Restrictions Based on Ability to Pay Fees Charged

The entire guidance in this area was based on a truism. This was the premise that certain consequences must follow where a charity charges fees which, in practice, restrict the benefits to only those people who can afford to pay them. Thus, for example, the Commission explained that it would assess 'whether the levels at which fees are set have the effect of preventing people who are unable to pay the fees from benefiting from the services or facilities'.[80] *All* monetary charges must have this effect. Only if the charges are waived, is the restriction removed. Even a reduction in the charges only increases the number of people who can pay them and lessens the number who cannot, but does not remove the restriction altogether.[81] The truism would have been avoided if the Commission's intention had been that 'the levels' should include some at zero per cent, but this would have contradicted other parts of the Guidance, where it was said that charities do not have to offer services for free.[82]

The Relevance of Fees to Public Benefit and Charitable Status

The purported legal rationale was that if only those able to afford the fees could benefit, they might not constitute a sufficient section of the public and, therefore, fail the second principle (or second test) of charitable status.[83] The Commission offered no clarity, however, as to when (if at all) those who could afford the fees *might* have sufficed. Clearly, the higher the fees, the smaller the class, but it was not clear at what point the test of public character would fail to be satisfied, nor did the test appear to depend on the size or importance of the class or the presence or absence of any personal nexus.[84]

[80] Guidance F10; *Fee-charging* E3.

[81] These latter two points were acknowledged by the Commission but the essential truth on which they were based was not.

[82] Guidance F10.

[83] ibid.

[84] And the concept of numerical negligibility in case law would not appear to be on a par with the sorts of numbers that might be applicable in the scenarios outlined in the Guidance.

The Foreword to *Fee-charging* suggested that it was only when high fees were charged that the obligation to provide sufficient opportunities for people unable to afford them could arise. Hence, low fees were said to be 'unlikely to give rise to public benefit difficulties'.[85] It was only in 'most' (not all) cases, however, that charities which charged low fees would not need to demonstrate further opportunities to benefit and 'a public benefit issue' may also have arisen where the service or facility charged for formed a significant part of the charity's aims (no reference being made to the level of fees in such cases).[86] It was not the case, therefore, that the obligation to provide opportunities to those unable to afford any fees charged depended entirely on whether fees were high or low. It *was* clear, however, that the higher the fees, the more the charity would be expected to do to provide those unable to afford them with sufficient opportunities to benefit and also that more would be required where 'relatively high fees' were charged for ongoing services than 'relatively low fees' for more infrequent services.[87]

High and Low Fees

'High fees' and 'low fees' were described as 'technical terms', which were defined as 'fees that many people could not afford' and 'fees that most people could afford' respectively, although the latter was also said to depend on a charity's circumstances and the social and economic circumstances of the people in the country in which it operated.[88] Whilst the term 'most people' offered some degree of certainty (over 50 per cent), 'many people' was almost meaningless in this context and risked an overlap where fees were affordable by, say, 55 per cent or even 80 per cent. This was wholly unsatisfactory and could easily have been avoided by specifying a monetary amount (which could be subject to review)[89] or improved by defining 'high fees' as 'fees which most people could not afford'.

Examples of low fees included a 'small entry fee', 'low hourly costs', a 'small subscription fee', 'low entry fees' and 'small charges' to fund activities.[90] Only one example suggested a monetary amount of 'a few pounds'.[91] Although it was sometimes possible to guess the approximate cost from the context, such as small entry fees to events at community centres, others were less obvious, such as subscription fees for a youth club or mobile units providing services and equipment to local

[85] *Fee-charging* C1. Or even more categorically, 'low fees do not prevent people from having the opportunity to benefit' (ibid); but note that a tennis club, charging fees up to £339 pa, failed the Commission's public benefit assessment (*The Radlett Lawn Tennis and Squash Club: A Public Benefit Assessment Report by the Charity Commission* (Commission, February 2011)).

[86] *Fee-charging* C1.

[87] *Fee-charging* Annex A5.

[88] *Fee-charging* B9 (or which 'the vast majority' could afford (Annex A3)).

[89] As Scotland did (see n 33 above).

[90] *Fee-charging* C1.

[91] ibid.

people in deprived areas in developing countries. It seemed evident, however, that even the lowest fees charged by an independent school would be classed as high fees.

Generally speaking, fees were described as 'high' or 'low' or 'affordable', without reference to the costs which they were designed to cover.[92] Fees charged in excess of the cost of providing the services, however, were required to be 'reasonable and necessary'.[93] The proposition is not contested, in so far as unreasonable or unnecessary charges (whether in excess of cost or not) might represent a breach of the duty to exercise powers for proper purposes or to act in the best interests of the charity, but their relevance to charitable status is questionable. One wonders whether the Commission might have placed any reliance on the words of Isaacs J in *Taylor*, who referred to a home 'limited to a favoured class or to the rich, either by the caprice of the proprietor, or by reason of prohibitive charges' and to the need for 'fair and reasonable' fees, which enabled the rich and the 'comparatively poor, not the very poorest' to avail themselves of its services.[94] Both comments, however, referred to a profit-making home to which financial assistance might be given as an acceptable way of fulfilling the testator's charitable intention. His Honour concluded that such an institution which charged prohibitive fees, or fees that were not fair and reasonable, would not come 'within the generality of the terms of the will', by which it appears he meant that the testator had intended mentally afflicted persons generally, both rich and poor, to benefit. The dicta provide no authority, therefore, for the proposition that fees charged by a charity must be fair and reasonable.

Whereas the courts have regarded it as reasonable and necessary to charge fees where services are expensive to provide, the Commission's approach was to insist that, 'however reasonable the fees charged might be' in relation to the cost of providing them,[95] the obligation to provide social benefit remained paramount. Thus, the Commission explained that it would consider whether the amount of a charity's reserves was reasonable, or whether they should be used to provide financial assistance.[96] The courts, on the other hand, have consistently directed that any surplus should be applied to the charity's purposes. If the two approaches are to be reconciled, the provision of social benefit becomes a purpose of the charity, and yet the Commission preferred to regard it as a question of the adequacy of

[92] Although the example of a library card, which permitted free use of books and reading rooms 'whilst ensuring that the charity can administer and monitor their use', suggested that other services might be provided which were not free and pointed to the correlation between fees and cost found in case law.

[93] Guidance F10.

[94] *Taylor* (n 14) 239. And counsel for the hospital trustees in *Resch* suggested (perhaps unnecessarily) that charitable status was not threatened by the imposition of charges unless those charges were 'prohibitive' ((n 6) 527), but this suggestion was not adopted by the Court.

[95] *Fee-charging* Annex A5.

[96] ibid.

the section of the public and not as an aspect of the charity's aims.[97] To say, as the Commission did, that those unable to afford the fees must still be given either facilitated access or other opportunities to benefit, however reasonable the fees might be, would also appear to go against authorities such as *Clarke*, where potential benefits were limited to persons of moderate means who could pay 'some moderate contribution' for their medical treatment.[98]

Whether to charge fees, at what levels to charge them and the kinds of opportunities to be made available, were all described as matters for the trustees' discretion,[99] subject to the proviso that they were sufficient to satisfy Principles 2b and 2c (principles which, it should be remembered, determined charitable status).[100] Subject to this, however, the exercise of the trustees' discretion was said to be subject to a duty to act reasonably and to a test of 'whether trustees have exercised their discretion properly', so that their decisions could be regarded as 'within the range of decisions which a reasonable body of trustees could have made'.[101] The implication was that whether trustees were acting properly and exercising an appropriate standard of care was to be judged by the level of social benefit they provided. Unless case law or the 2006 Act could be shown to support such an obligation, however, this went beyond the common law duty to exercise powers (discretionary or otherwise) within the terms of the trust and in compliance with any statutory or common law requirements.

Affordability

Even though the application of the test was not dependent solely on whether fees were high or low, the question of their affordability was crucial. And yet the Commission failed to set out the criteria on which affordability was to be measured, neither distinguishing between or explaining the significance of a person's capital and income, nor addressing the possible reasons for his reduced means (which could stem from either low earning capacity or extravagance). Instead, whether fees were affordable was to be assessed 'on an individual basis'.[102] Examples were given which tended to state the obvious but offered little elucidation. Thus, 'a substantial number of people' would be unable to pay £20,000 for a vocational training course but 'few in number' would be unable to afford a 50 pence entry fee to a community centre; likewise, 'most people' would be able to afford a theatre

[97] Guidance F11. It might also be noted that *Charities and Reserves* (Commission, June 2010) indicates that reserves should be applied to a charity's purposes, but does not mention using them for making provision for the poor (although it is suggested that a charity with excess reserves should contact the Commission for advice).

[98] *Clarke* (n 71); see too the dictum of Lord Wilberforce (see text to n 21).

[99] *Fee-charging* Annex A1.

[100] *Fee-charging* C3.

[101] *Fee-charging* Annex A2 (noted here in respect of fee-setting, but described as a 'usual test').

[102] *Fee-charging* Annex A3.

ticket of around £10, but 'many people' would find a ticket price of £100 'less affordable'.[103] A test which determines matters of charitable status or trustees' personal liability should not depend on such vague criteria.

'To afford' means simply 'to meet the expense of'. What a person can afford depends, not only on his capital and income, but also on what expenditure he is committed to make and what expenditure he chooses to make, both of which will be variable and dependent on a whole range of considerations. The level of committed expenditure will be partly determined by others, for example, income tax and national insurance contributions, and partly by his own choice and actions, such as mortgage payments or rent, council tax and utility payments, which depend on his choice of accommodation. The level of optional expenditure will depend on choices and priorities he makes in relation to cars, holidays and interests, for example. Someone who considers the benefits of private education to be a high priority may be able to afford fees because he borrows and/or minimises other expenditure. Another person, with the same income, may appear to be unable to afford the same fees, because he chooses to give greater priority to other matters. Yet another may opt for state education and health services even though he can afford both privately, but it will be seen that such a person could benefit from the Commission's approach to the same extent as those receiving state services through necessity rather than choice.[104] Affordability is straightforward where the cost is greater than the income of a person with no capital, but is otherwise both subjective and complex. It is not something with which the courts have been concerned.[105] The Commission's attempts to explain affordability as a criterion which is central to the charitable status of fee-charging institutions are less than clear. An indication that fees of, say, £1,500 per annum, would be considered affordable, would have provided a better starting point.[106]

Opportunities to Benefit

As mentioned above, in respect of fee-charging charities the negative language of Principles 2b and 2c was turned into a positive obligation to provide opportunities to benefit for people unable to afford the fees, including people in poverty.

These opportunities were described as being by way of 'free or subsidised access' and/or by 'other significant opportunities' and were required to be 'sufficient'.[107] A 'sufficient amount' of facilitated access could satisfy Principles 2b and 2c, but there was no 'one-size-fits-all amount or percentage',[108] and more could be needed if other benefits were not also offered.[109] Where both types of provision were

[103] Guidance F10.
[104] See ch 6.
[105] Nor, in all probability, something with which they would wish to be concerned.
[106] As indicated by the Scottish regulator (see n 33 above).
[107] *Fee-charging* C3.
[108] *Fee-charging* C4.
[109] *Fee-charging* C5.

offered, the Commission would take into account 'the totality of benefits' arising from the charity's activities.[110] Although the possibility of a charity providing only other opportunities and no facilitated access was contemplated, it was clear that the onus of showing that the other opportunities were sufficient would be significantly greater, and might not be possible, where fees were high.

Both unpredictable and uncertain as a subjective term, it appeared that only assessment by the Commission, of whether a charity's level of social benefit was 'sufficient', would afford the objective measurement which might reassure trustees that they were not in breach of trust and assure them of the institution's charitable status. That imposed an unrealistic burden on the Commission, which did not have the resources to provide such individual reassurance, and created a lamentable degree of uncertainty for trustees. The opportunities were also described as needing to be 'genuine and meaningful' and to allow people to benefit in a 'material' way, that is in a 'significant, important, relevant and tangible' way, rather than in a 'minimal or tokenistic' way or in a way 'which happens by chance'.[111] The expression 'by chance' might suggest 'without design or intention', or 'beyond the charity's control', or in some way which lacks reliability. The proposition that opportunities arising by chance are inadequate, however, may be difficult to reconcile with the lack of obligation to provide services for reduced cost in *Resch* and also the likely fluctuations in the origin and scope of any charity's resources.[112]

It was acknowledged that 'small charities with smaller resources' were unlikely to offer as much as 'large charities with larger resources',[113] and a charity's resources would be taken into account in determining what was 'reasonable and appropriate' in each case.[114] It seemed, however, not that the level of provision was to be judged in light of the charity's existing resources, but that the charity's resources would need to be increased, as necessary, in order to facilitate the level of provision which, based on other considerations, the Commission regarded as sufficient.[115] Such increase could be by fundraising activities, seeking funding from other sources and/or by raising fees for some in order to subsidise the fees of others.[116] But the extra burden on trustees in initiating and pursuing fundraising activities,[117] and the fact that increasing fees would make them unaffordable to an even greater

[110] *Fee-charging* C3. The difficulty of reconciling this approach, which focused on a charity's activities and identified and weighed up resulting benefits, with case law has already been noted (see ch 3).

[111] *Fee-charging* C2.

[112] *Resch* (n 6) (the benefit derived from the proximity of the two hospitals, however, appears to have been deliberate (*Resch* (n 6) 539)); see too *Perpetual Trustee Co v St Luke's Hospital* (1939) 39 SR (NSW) 408 (SC, NSW), where such provision was merely an 'objective'; see also ch 6.

[113] *Fee-charging* E2.

[114] *Fee-charging* C4.

[115] This lack of focus on what might actually have been reasonable and appropriate in each case was also reflected in the public benefit assessments carried out by the Commission (see ch 6).

[116] *Fee-charging* E2.

[117] The need to devote additional time and financial resources was acknowledged (*Fee-charging* Annex B3).

number,[118] could have significant consequences and even affect the viability of the charity, particularly where organisations have insignificant, or no, endowment income. The Commission acknowledged that there was no 'general legal requirement' either to fundraise or to increase fees,[119] and that it 'may not be desirable or feasible' in every case,[120] but added that where it was the only way in which a charity could ensure it met the public benefit requirement, an unreasonable failure to do so would constitute breach of trust.[121] Charity trustees were unable to take much comfort from any assurance that having limited resources would be taken into account.

Facilitated Access

Whilst it was acknowledged that free or subsidised access 'costs money', this form of social benefit was noted to be an 'obvious and, in many cases, the simplest way' to satisfy the Commission's test.[122] It was also said that this would avoid a 'two-tier' service, where those unable to afford the fees are offered a less comprehensive service.[123] Several ways in which organisations might provide facilitated access were identified, including concessionary tickets or means-tested bursaries or securing sponsorship or funding by state or other voluntary sector bodies.[124] The extent to which third party funding would be taken into account would depend (inter alia) on the extent to which it was targeted at people in poverty and on its 'reliability',[125] even though the availability of such funding is typically beyond a charity's control and, to that extent, would appear to be 'by chance'. Making available free use of its facilities to other charities or public service providers, who in turn would provide free or subsidised access to those facilities, was also noted to be a way in which the charity might provide facilitated access.[126] Medical benefits and other insurance schemes might also be relevant, depending on their cost and terms of cover.[127] The potential for the premiums to be unaffordable to many and/or for the cover to be inferior where premiums are reduced, however, led the Commission to suggest that it might be 'unwise' to rely on insurance for the purposes of satisfying the public benefit requirement.[128] Whilst this note of caution might be consistent with an aim to extend benefits to 'people in poverty', it is not easily reconciled with the Court's interpretation in *Resch*.[129]

[118] At the same time compounding the problem which the Commission appeared to be trying to address.
[119] *Fee-charging* Annex B3.
[120] *Fee-charging* Annex A10.
[121] *Fee-charging* Annex B3.
[122] *Fee-charging* C4.
[123] ibid.
[124] *Fee-charging* C4, C5.
[125] *Fee-charging* Annex B4.
[126] *Fee-charging* C4.
[127] *Fee-charging* Annex B3, B6.
[128] *Fee-charging* Annex B6.
[129] *Resch* (n 6).

It was also clear that the Commission might consider the act of reducing fees to be inadequate, where the discounted rate meant that many would still be unable to afford them. In respect of a museum or gallery in a socially and economically disadvantaged area, for example, the Commission suggested that free passes to local families might be required, even though it seems unlikely that the normal charges would have been very high.[130] Similarly, it was said that reducing high fees marginally (or, presumably, substantially) would not be sufficient if people in poverty were still excluded from the opportunity to benefit.[131] The indication was that reduced or waived fees would have to be such as to reach people in poverty (and not merely people unable to afford the fees), at least unless other benefits were sufficient. In the context of independent schools, where fees are high, the inference was that reduced fees for all (due to charitable income) would be insufficient and that significantly discounted fees, including some at 100 per cent, would be required.[132]

Of course, in the absence of waiving charges altogether, providing means-tested access was the only way of ensuring that access would be given to those unable to afford the fees, including people in poverty. It cannot be assumed that all students and pensioners are unable to pay the full price for tickets, for example, or that non-fee paying NHS patients are unable to afford private hospital fees or private medical insurance. And 'lottery-based' systems for allocating cheaper tickets seemed significantly at odds with an intention to assist people in poverty.[133] The Commission gave little guidance, however, as to how, or to what extent, charity trustees should means-test prospective recipients, except to suggest that trustees should 'think about' how they would assess a person's ability to pay the fees and whether they would use a means test or 'generic indicators of poverty' (which were not defined).[134] The suggestion of providing free entry passes to a museum to families within the local area, for example, could require invasive inquiry to establish that a family was unable to afford the museum's charges or difficult decisions in drawing boundaries within local areas which reflected generic indicators of poverty.[135] Trustees were subjected to a difficult and unwelcome burden, with little in the way of guidance.

130 *Fee-charging* C5.

131 *Fee-charging* Annex A1.

132 The Commission was keen to dispel this interpretation and it is at least theoretically possible that 'the other benefits' might be so generous as to deny the inference, but it was the emphasis on means-tested bursaries in the Commission's public benefit assessment programme (see ch 6) which prompted the judicial review application by the Independent Schools Council (see ch 8).

133 *Fee-charging* Annex C (p 36).

134 *Fee-charging* Annex B2.

135 *Fee-charging* C5.

Other Benefits

Providing additional services, working with an outside body and offering the use of facilities to others were all suggested as means of providing other significant opportunities to benefit.[136] In the context of an independent school, for example, the Commission suggested allowing state school pupils to use its educational facilities, or to attend lessons and events at, and otherwise benefit from collaboration and partnership with, the school.[137] Trustees of the school were encouraged to liaise with local state schools, in order to 'target the charity's assistance to state schools … in ways that are likely to make most difference to their students' and to 'achieve the maximum impact from sharing resources'.[138] It could not be assumed, however, that all parents of state school pupils would be unable to afford independent school fees. There will always be some who are unable to pay them, some who are able to pay them but choose not to and some who would be able to pay them if they were to re-prioritise their spending in other areas.

Offering services indiscriminately to both rich and poor would appear to fall short of what the Commission was trying to achieve and yet the Commission's approach was sometimes based on little more than probability, in the sense that the greater the number of potential beneficiaries, the greater the chance that some might be poor.[139] It would, of course, be difficult for an independent school, or other fee-charging charity, to ascertain the means of those to whom opportunities were to be extended, in order to be satisfied that they were unable to afford the fees, but the Commission regarded the relative wealth of the beneficiaries as paramount. Hence, for example, whilst 'additional weight' would be given to the value of providing for the additional educational needs of dyslexic pupils, none would be given if 'only more affluent dyslexic pupils' benefited.[140]

The indirect benefit to society of having educated students, or the encouragement of voluntary work and charitable giving, was said not to contribute to public benefit within Principles 2b and 2c,[141] and yet it is arguable that the charitable nature of the advancement of education rests on its benefits to society as a whole.[142] Furthermore, the indirect benefit of relieving the public purse was

[136] Presumably here offering facilities for a charge, since free use of facilities was included as a means of offering free or subsidised access, although there was sometimes confusion (cp, eg, *Fee-charging* Annex B1, paras 4 and 5). It is noted that extending opportunities to people in poverty did not mean that there had to be 'no financial barriers to accessing benefit', despite the fact that charges would continue to have the effect of excluding some (unless the barrier was so minimal as to be illusory) (Guidance F10).

[137] *Fee-charging* C6.

[138] ibid, so that only 'relevant, desired and valued' services were offered. The suggestion of using 'peer review or other forms of quality assessment' was not explained.

[139] See ch 6.

[140] Guidance F10.

[141] *Fee-charging* C2.

[142] Provided that the inherent benefit is not denied by describing a private class or by the scholars being separated from society (see text to nn 35–36, ch 2).

described as potentially relevant to establishing benefit under Principle 1a but was said to be irrelevant to Principles 2b and 2c, even though this appeared to restrict the third principle (discussed above) which the Commission itself had extrapolated from *Resch*, without any explanation or authority and may also ignore the effect of judicial authority to this effect.[143] The Commission's tendency to place reliance on its own publications has sometimes been criticised,[144] and here was another example as it sought to justify its proposition by pointing out that it was consistent with the (main) Guidance.[145] The Commission described itself as acting in the same way as the courts, but there is no parallel between relying on its own publications, which do not have force of law, and the doctrine of precedent.

Principle 2c: People in Poverty Must not be Excluded from the Opportunity to Benefit

The Commission made no attempt to distinguish between express and implied exclusions of people in poverty. With regard to non-fee charging charities, the effect of this principle in prohibiting express exclusions on the terms was not objectionable, but its possible application to implied exclusions on the terms or implied exclusions in practice lacked authority and could not, therefore, be supported.

In relation to fee-charging charities, it is noteworthy that much of *Fee-charging* referred to 'people who cannot afford the fees' rather than 'the poor' or 'people in poverty'. The effect of merging Principle 2c with Principle 2b, however, was that trustees of fee-charging charities were required to ensure that their provision of opportunities extended to people in poverty and not simply those unable to afford the fees. The two are not the same.

The Commission explained that the meaning of 'poor' in charity law included people 'lacking the means to procure the comforts or necessities of life', the 'financially disadvantaged', the 'destitute' and 'also people who cannot satisfy a basic need without assistance',[146] perhaps suggesting a greater degree of poverty than appears in some cases.[147] More specifically, it was suggested that the poor in developing countries would be those who lack adequate clean water, food and shelter but that, in England and Wales, the poor 'might typically' mean households living on less than 60 per cent of average income or people living on or below the level of

[143] *Resch* (n 6); see text to n 23 above and text to n 171, ch 2 (although it is not suggested, of course, that such authority supports Principles 2b and 2c).

[144] See, eg, P Luxton and N Evans, 'Cogent and Cohesive? Two Recent Charity Commission Decisions on the Advancement of Religion' (2011) 75 *Conveyancer and Property Lawyer* 144 (in respect of the Commission's consideration of applications for registration by the Gnostic Centre and the Druid Network).

[145] *Fee-charging* C2.

[146] Guidance F11; *Fee-charging* B4. The distinction between poverty in s 3(1)(a) and 'financial hardship' in s 3(1)(j) of the 2011 Act remains to be drawn: H Palmer, 'Trustees' Responsibilities and the Public Benefit Requirement' [2008] *Private Client Business* 413, 418.

[147] See text to nn 14–17, ch 4.

income support.[148] The precise boundaries were left vague, however, and gave little guidance as to when a charity might fail to satisfy Principle 2c: 'people in poverty' in any individual case would thus be considered in the context of the organisation's aims, the intended beneficiaries and where the aims were carried out, regard also being had to modern social conditions and the nature of the benefits.[149]

The Commission maintained that the obligation to ensure that people in poverty are not excluded from the opportunity to benefit from each of a charity's purposes was not to say that all beneficiaries must be poor.[150] This is not in doubt. Nor is its statement that the court in *Resch* was concerned with the 'narrower proposition' concerning the exclusion of the poor, although the proposition was described, and dealt with, very much as the basis of the appellants' argument, rather than the Court's own concern.[151] Its further conclusion, however, that the effect of Principles 2b and 2c 'is not to introduce a qualification of poverty into each of the thirteen descriptions of charitable purposes' is difficult to reconcile with the content of its publications.[152] The requirement for charities to provide opportunities to the poor and others who cannot afford the fees requires the trustees to consider questions of poverty regardless of the institution's principal purpose or purposes and especially, but not solely, where fees are charged. That *does* introduce a qualification of poverty. It may also impinge upon the trustees' duties to exercise their powers in fulfilment of the charity's purposes.

Given the explanation of Principles 2b and 2c, and the extensive range of factors which were said to be relevant in determining whether they had been satisfied,[153] it was not surprising that the role which the Commission described, and later carried out, was one which was heavily investigative, highly discretionary and, inevitably, very resource intensive. This role represented a radical departure from the courts' approach and risked an unwarranted intrusion into the discretion of charity trustees.

148 Guidance F11.

149 Analysis 3.69.

150 Fn 1, which appeared in the analysis dealing with the law underpinning *Fee-charging*, but not in the (general) Analysis from which that analysis was said to be extracted (see n 76, ch 1).

151 *Resch* (n 6) 543.

152 Fn 1 (n 150).

153 *Fee-charging* E3. These included the extent to which there was a public need for the benefit offered; how the services compared in scope, cost and quality from those provided by other sources; the level of fees in relation to cost; any level of subsidy; the charity's position in the market; the extent to which a charity might reduce its costs; and for what it used any surpluses.

6

The Commission's Implementation of the Public Benefit Requirement*

I asked what did we have to do and they talked in riddles. I expect the process will be one of consultation with the Commission. It will be like a game of ping pong. We will propose something and they will say yes or no and go back and forth. It will be a guessing game for us which will take up a lot of our time.

Headmaster of S Anselm's School[1]

I. Introduction

The practical application of the Commission's 2008 guidance began in October 2008, when the Commission commenced 'public benefit assessments' of 12 registered charities, including five independent schools.[2] This was part of its rolling programme, which it had launched in 1998 and which received support from the Strategy Unit, but which was not enacted in the 2006 Act.[3] The Commission published its findings nine months later, in July 2009, in 12 individual reports and a composite report, herein referred to as *Emerging findings*.[4] The Commission was sometimes keen to avoid the language of success and failure,[5] but two of the five schools were reported not to have met Principles 2b and 2c and it seems appropriate, therefore, to refer to them as having 'failed' to satisfy the public benefit requirement. Although this would suggest that the Commission no longer regarded them as charitable, or perhaps that they had never been charitable, they were not removed from the Register.

* In this chapter, footnote references to the names of schools are to the public benefit assessment reports in respect of each institution (Commission, July 2009). References to the 'Guidance' are to *Charities and Public Benefit* (Commission, January 2008).

[1] Civil Society, 'Charities start talks on public benefit with the Commission', 14 October 2009: www.civilsociety.co.uk/governance/news/content/5234.

[2] The other seven comprised four charities for the advancement of religion and three fee-charging care homes.

[3] See text to nn 158–60, ch 3.

[4] *Emerging findings for charity trustees from the Charity Commission's public benefit assessment work: 2008–09* (Commission, July 2009).

[5] See, eg, Suzi Leather's speech to the Headmasters' and Headmistresses' Conference (7 October 2009): apps.charitycommission.gov.uk/Charity_requirements_guidance/Charity_essentials/Public_benefit/schoolspeech.aspx.

It had been the Commission's intention that its assessments of these five schools would be the first of many, but it was not much more than a year later when the Commission announced that it would not be conducting further assessments.[6] By this time, it had assessed only 20 charities and no more independent schools.[7] A total of five of the 20 had 'failed' to meet the public benefit requirement, four on the basis of their practices in charging fees.[8] The reason given for cancelling the assessment programme was said to be a lack of resources, rather than any lack of authority or capability, which suggests that the possibility of further assessments should not be ruled out, however remote that might now appear (and despite the 2013 guidance making no reference to individual assessments being carried out). It is also worth noting that, notwithstanding the Tribunal's criticism of the 2008 guidance and its subsequent withdrawal, the Commission has not sought to review any of its findings in the public benefit assessment programme, either in respect of individual charities or more broadly.[9] Although their value must be increasingly open to question in view of *R (Independent Schools Council) v Charity Commission* and the revised guidance,[10] the individual assessment reports remain on the Commission's website, as assessments against 'the principle in our then current public benefit guidance', and the public is still invited to read them.

The legitimacy of assessing the public benefit of existing registered charities was addressed in chapter three and found lacking.[11] This chapter takes a break from the legal issues and examines the detailed working out of the Commission's legal interpretation in practice. It will consider the assessment process, with particular reference to the five independent schools, and consider what conclusions might be drawn regarding the Commission's interpretation and implementation of the public benefit requirement.

II. The Assessment of Public Benefit

This is about ensuring that as many of our children as possible benefit from the opportunities to learn which charitable independent schools have offered for so long.

Suzi Leather[12]

[6] Third Sector, 'Charity Commission shelves public benefit assessments for hospitals and health charities', 31 August 2010: www.thirdsector.co.uk/charity-commission-shelves-public-benefit-assessments-hospitals-health-charities/article/1024971.

[7] Publishing on its website further reports in respect of four arts charities (July 2010) and four recreation and leisure charities (February 2011).

[8] Two independent schools, a tennis club and a care home; the fifth, another care home, failed because its activities were not consistent with its aims. All have since passed the Commission's test.

[9] Including those in *Emerging findings* (n 4).

[10] *R (Independent Schools Council) v Charity Commission* [2011] UKUT 421 (TCC), [2012] Ch 214.

[11] See ch 3, part IV.

[12] Suzi Leather (then Chair of the Commission), Brighton College conference speech (8 May 2008): apps.charitycommission.gov.uk/Charity_requirements_guidance/Charity_essentials/Public_benefit/bccspeech.aspx.

Recognising that it was 'not practical' to examine the 'continued claim to charitable status' of each organisation on the Register, the Commission set out to assess groups of charities where questions of public benefit were likely to be most pronounced.[13] Fee-charging charities were obvious candidates and religious charities were also included because of the Commission's view that the 2006 Act had changed the law by removing a presumption of public benefit.[14]

Scope of the Assessments

The Commission described the purposes of the assessments as fourfold:[15]

(i) to assess whether the organisation's aims fell within the list of potentially charitable purposes in s 2(2) of the 2006 Act;
(ii) to establish that the charity was capable of being operated in accordance with those potentially charitable aims;
(iii) to determine whether the charity's aims were capable of being carried out for the public benefit;
(iv) to assess whether the charity's trustees were in practice carrying out those aims for the public benefit.

The first of these was a legitimate consideration and was said to be satisfied in the case of each school, the aim being the advancement of education and capable of being charitable, subject to meeting the public benefit requirement. In so far as it required an assessment of the charity's operations and financial viability, however, the second stated purpose was difficult to reconcile with the courts' approach to determining charitable status, although the Commission reported that the requirement was satisfied in each case because the charity's operations were 'fully within this aim'. If it is to mean anything more than that the institution was a functioning school, this comment appears simply to confirm that the trustees were exercising their duties and powers within the charity's aims, which is more a regulatory matter (but possibly conflicts with the Commission's conclusions as to breach of trust by the two 'failed' schools). The third purpose was not separately considered in the reports, perhaps because it is hard to imagine that any potentially charitable purposes would be *incapable* of being carried out for the public benefit, except that an express exclusion of the poor, presumably, might have failed the Commission's assessment at this stage.

[13] *The Review of the Register of Charities* (Commission, October 2001) para 20. With over 163,000 charities on the Register, such a Herculean task was barely feasible.

[14] All four charities for the advancement of religion passed the test and questions of precedent were not in issue (see ch 2, part II).

[15] *Emerging findings* (n 4) 4.

The fourth purpose of the assessment, therefore, was the most significant and required an investigation into the operation and activities of each organisation. In considering the individual reports of independent schools below, it will be seen that the Commission was essentially testing compliance with a requirement to deliver social benefit, framed as a duty to carry out the charity's aims for the public benefit.

The Assessment Process

The Commission carried out the assessments using materials in the public domain and information provided by the charities involved.[16] It also visited each charity in order to 'understand the context within which the charity operate[d]', although it is not clear quite what this meant in the case of individual schools or how the understanding that it gained influenced its findings.[17] Its desire for reports by other regulators and independent assessors, in order to enhance and provide 'third party validation' of information submitted by the charity,[18] suggested a questioning, or even distrust, of charity trustees' information, which differed markedly from the approach taken by the courts.[19] It was acknowledged, however, that such reports might not be necessary or applicable in some cases, in religious charities for example, where benefits are difficult to quantify or measure and there are no independent assessors.

The Commission's claimed adherence to better regulatory principles, in making its activities 'proportionate, accountable, consistent, transparent and targeted only at cases in which action is needed', may be questionable.[20] The Commission reported extensively, and inconsistently, on matters which were not material and its failure to give clear guidance to the two failed schools, together with the fact that the schools were unable to appeal against the Commission's decisions,[21] cast doubt upon the transparency and accountability of its assessment process, both issues which are crucial to maintaining trust and confidence in the sector.[22] It is also questionable whether nine months spent on 12 charities was

[16] The methodology is described in *Emerging findings* (n 4) 28–30.

[17] ibid, 29.

[18] ibid, 8.

[19] Possibly a hangover of the 'slightly high-handed approach' acknowledged by Andrew Hind, outgoing chief executive of the Commission in June 2010: Third Sector '"Huge change in organisational culture" of the Charity Commission, says outgoing chief executive', 28 June 2010: www.thirdsector.co.uk/huge-change-organisational-culture-charity-commission-says-outgoing-chief-executive/governance/article/1012644.

[20] 2011 Act, s 16.

[21] 2011 Act, sch 6 (and see text to nn 229–33, ch 3).

[22] Lord Hodgson made the same point regarding transparency (of both charities and the Commission) in his review of the operation of the 2006 Act: *Trusted and Independent: Giving charity back to charities*' (TSO, July 2012) para 6.19.

proportionate or compliant with the statutory duty to 'have regard to the need to use its resources in the most efficient, effective and economic way'.[23] And whether assessing Manchester Grammar School, with its manifestly generous and extensive financial provision, was targeting the Commission's activity where action was needed is also open to question.[24]

III. The Reports

> *[W]here it does not meet the requirements, we would expect that being clear about the solution would also be helpful to the charity so that it could operate confidently in the future.*
>
> The Commission[25]

Although each report followed a standard format, repeated material led to unnecessary length and there was inconsistency, both within individual reports and between reports, which made it all the more difficult to draw any conclusions from them as to what it was that charity trustees were required to do in order to satisfy the public benefit requirement.[26] Each report addressed the principles of public benefit outlined in the Guidance, before setting out any required or recommended actions based on the conclusion reached.

Principles 1a (It Must be Clear what the Benefits are) and 1b (They Must be Related to the Aims)

The provision of education to the pupils of each school was described as the charity's primary benefit. In considering sub-principles 1a and 1b together, however, the reports identified various additional activities which were carried on by the schools and which also gave rise to 'identifiable benefits', both to the pupils themselves, as secondary to the main benefit of providing them with an education, and other benefits for the pupils and other children. Benefits were further categorised as relevant or not relevant to the aims. It is hard to understand, however, why it was felt necessary to list all benefits, including incidental benefits, to pupils in addition to the identified benefit of providing an education.[27] If these

[23] 2011 Act, s 16 (although it did acknowledge that it might not be necessary to visit every charity being assessed in the future (*Emerging findings* (n 4) 29)).

[24] The Commission would undoubtedly justify it as an illustration of good practice.

[25] Public Benefit Assessment Information (Commission, October 2008).

[26] eg, the S Anselm's report listed placements for gap year students as a relevant benefit (and related to the aims) in Section D1 but as an irrelevant opportunity (and unrelated to the aims) in Section 4 of the Annex. Several inconsistencies are highlighted in tables below.

[27] If a rule states that provisions must include liquid, it is enough to say that there is a bottle of water and no merit in adding that there is also milk or whisky.

added benefits had not been identified, would Principle 1 not have been satisfied in any event?

The relevant benefits of the first type were, typically, the sorts of activities carried on by most, if not all, schools, such as extra-curricular clubs, school trips, musical performances and charitable fundraising.[28] These were activities in furtherance of the schools' purposes and which, in the normal running of a school, would be subject to change from time to time, inevitably raising the question of how frequently assessments would need to be carried out.

Further benefits to the pupils and other children comprised activities which were extracted from the annex to each report, the annex also forming the basis for consideration of whether opportunities to benefit were provided to people unable to pay the fees, including those in poverty.[29] The lists of benefits were often extensive, but included benefits which would necessarily be subject to change and sometimes short-term, further casting doubt upon their relevance to a determination of charitable status.[30] Interestingly, the following benefits, which were pivotal in the assessment of the Church Mission Society, were not referred to in respect of independent schools, notwithstanding their potential relevance: namely those benefits 'arising from contributing towards the development of civil society through imparting positive values, attitudes and skills … encouraging altruism and volunteering … encouraging people to live with … a commitment to serve other people … opportunities for intercultural enrichment and international understanding'.[31]

Presumably in light of Principle 1b, which required the identifiable benefits to be related to the aims, the Commission also listed benefits which it considered to be *irrelevant*.[32] Typically these involved use of the school's facilities for purposes other than education, such as film projects or weddings (even though the income derived from such activities might prove critical in enabling the school to satisfy Principles 2b and 2c). Some benefits for the wider community were also disregarded, for example, opening the school for local council meetings or a local or national organisation,[33] or allowing public use of grounds maintained by the school.[34] Similarly, benefits to the wider public, such as enhancing or improving the local environment, were disregarded as irrelevant to the aim of

[28] Rugby coaching provided by a local club was also included (Manor House), apparently without questioning the sponsorship provided to the club by the school.

[29] 'Annex A' (although no report contained an Annex B). The use of extracts in sections B and D5 to each report resulted in undue repetition and often inconsistency.

[30] eg, see text to n 116 below.

[31] Church Mission Society, which was successful in meeting the public benefit requirement in the first round of assessments: *Church Mission Society: A Public Benefit Assessment Report by the Charity Commission* (Commission, July 2009).

[32] Annex A to each report, perhaps also to correct the charity trustees' view of them as *relevant*.

[33] Manchester Grammar, 14.

[34] Pangbourne College, 14.

education.[35] Only activities and opportunities which benefited other children outside the school (and only children of the same gender in the case of a single-sex school) were treated as relevant.[36] The Guidance, however, had failed to make clear that benefits for the community as a whole would not be positively assessed.

The indirect benefit of relieving the taxpayer of the cost of educating the schools' pupils was also listed as irrelevant, notwithstanding legal authority which might suggest otherwise,[37] and, perhaps more significantly, notwithstanding the Commission's own statement that whilst such matters might not be relevant to Principles 2b and 2c, they could be relevant to Principle 1a (unless in this regard they were seen as not related to the aims).[38] Supporting the armed forces by providing secure family-like boarding services and, more generally, enabling local employment were also disregarded. And, given the Commission's attention to learning support provision in each of the schools' reports, its disregard of a school providing places for pupils in need of learning support was surprising.[39]

Principle 1c (Benefits Must be Balanced Against Any Detriment or Harm)

Each report concluded that there was no evidence of detriment or harm, but the Commission's concern with the management of risk and harm to vulnerable children stood in stark contrast to the courts' approach in weighing the relative advantages and disadvantages of an institution's purposes.[40] The child protection issues considered in respect of S Anselm's making available its facilities to other users, for example, suggested a level of inquiry which is arguably outside the Commission's statutory duties and overlaps unnecessarily with the responsibilities of child protection authorities.[41]

Principle 2a (Beneficiaries Must be Appropriate to the Aims)

The Commission concluded that appropriate beneficiaries comprised children, primarily the school's pupils but also other children within the class specified.[42]

[35] eg, planting more than 1,000 trees (S Anselm's) or preserving historic buildings.

[36] Manchester Grammar; see also *Emerging findings* (n 4) 13, which suggests that benefits to girls are a legitimate but incidental aspect of the school's operations.

[37] See n 171, ch 2.

[38] *Public Benefit and Fee-charging* (Commission, December 2008) 10.

[39] Manor House, 14 (whereas the number or percentage of pupils receiving learning support was included (at least once) in three of the five reports and the existence of a learning support department was noted in a fourth).

[40] See ch 2, part III, Principle B.

[41] *Emerging findings* (n 4) 12.

[42] Boys only in the case of Manchester Grammar, 7.

Inconsistently, however, the reports included the benefits of providing placements for adults who were training as teachers.[43] Also included were the benefits of providing Year 10 pupils from the state sector with work placements in a school for 2–11 year olds,[44] and opportunities for Brownies and primary school children which were provided by a school for 11–18 year olds.[45]

Principle 2b (The Opportunity to Benefit Must not be Unreasonably Restricted by Geographical or Other Restrictions)[46]

Each report considered whether there were any geographical, age, gender, academic or religious restrictions. The significance, or worth, of considering these limitations was doubtful, however, given that there appeared to be no question of public benefit being affected adversely by either a restriction to a named city,[47] an upper age limit,[48] a gender restriction,[49] a religious direction,[50] or selective admission policies.[51] The Commission's conclusion in each case, namely that any restrictions noted were 'rational and justifiable', might have been more briefly and adequately dealt with by reporting only that there were 'no unusual (or unjustifiable) restrictions on the opportunity to benefit'.

Principles 2b and 2c (Sufficient Opportunity to Benefit in a Material Way, Related to the Charity's Aims, Must be given to those Who Cannot Afford the Fees, Including those in Poverty)

Each report combined Principles 2b (regarding fees) and 2c, and compliance with them was assessed by considering two factors, namely the level of fees and the moderation of those fees.[52]

43 Manchester Grammar, 13, 14; S Anselm's, 14.
44 Highfield Priory, 15 (Year 10 children are typically aged 14–15).
45 Pangbourne College, 13.
46 Restrictions due to fees are dealt with separately below.
47 Manchester Grammar (and the consideration given to the extent to which opportunities to benefit were known to people outside a local area seemed inconsistent with its acknowledgement that day pupils would, in practice, be drawn from the local area (*Emerging findings* (n 4) 13)); see also *Review* ((n 13) 6) which states that a charity for people in Bradford should not spend money for the benefit of people in Bristol.
48 Manor House.
49 Manchester Grammar.
50 Manchester Grammar was required to provide religious instruction in accordance with Christian principles and assemblies and prayers at S Anselm's were rooted in Christian values. There was nothing to suggest that this played any part in S Anselm's failure of the public benefit test.
51 Either expressly in the governing document (Pangbourne College) or in a school's policy (Manchester Grammar).
52 At Section D5 of each report, apparently disregarding the other two factors mentioned in *Emerging findings* (n 4) 17 (namely the need for, and nature of, the services and facilities and, inter alia, the current social and economic circumstances in which the school operates). The factors were said to be derived from case law, which is contested (see ch 4).

Asking whether the 'level at which fees are set have the effect of preventing people who are unable to pay the fees from benefiting from the services or facilities' highlighted the truism mentioned in the preceding chapter: that people who cannot pay the fees are, by definition, prevented from benefiting from the services where fees are charged, unless those fees are waived. Since all schools were said to have charged 'high fees', the level of detail about each school's fees was also unnecessary and cumbersome. The Commission noted in each case that the fees were set at a level designed to cover costs, including, where appropriate, the cost of providing bursaries. It appears that it was acceptable to report that fees were kept as low as possible but 'consistent with the need to maintain an appropriate level of education',[53] or to ensure that a current level of debt for upgrading facilities was serviced,[54] or to generate a surplus to meet the costs of both bursaries and capital investment.[55]

The second factor was said to relate to those who could not afford to access the services because of the charges made, although it will be seen that the Commission also took into account non-means tested reductions and other opportunities which, without discrimination, were provided to those who could not afford the fees *and* to those who could. It considered the extent to which those charges were 'moderated (in whole or in part)', first, in order to permit access to the services charged for and/or, second, in order to give other access to the benefits of the charity.

Whilst moderation might have been achieved by way of an individual reduction or waiver of the fees in order to achieve the first of these, it seems that any moderation would have had to have been by way of an *increase* in the aggregate fees in order to achieve the second. This was not spelt out and although the factor was divided in this way, the Commission went on to address it as a whole by considering the aggregate 'mix of opportunities' and 'totality of benefits' that were listed in the annex to each report, namely details of means-tested *and* non-means tested fee reductions, together with other measures to provide access to the benefits provided by the school. These will be looked at in turn, before examining the Commission's explanation of how they were considered and any conclusions that might be drawn.

Principles 2b and 2c: Means-Tested Assistance

The following table illustrates the inconsistency between the information collected and provided in respect of each school (blank boxes indicating that no information was given).

[53] Manchester Grammar, 8.
[54] Pangbourne College, 8.
[55] S Anselm's, 8. Although this school did not satisfy the public benefit test, there is no suggestion that this surplus was a factor in that assessment.

Table 1: Principles 2b and 2c: Means-Tested Assistance

Information	Manchester Grammar	Highfield Priory	Pangbourne College	Manor House	S Anselm's
Number of means-tested bursaries (MTBs)	203 (20–35 new MTBs pa in recent years)	None			2
As % pupils	14				0.8
Total value	£1,665,756				Not published[56]
% Gross Fee Income (GFI)	14.3				Less than 1% 'fee income'
% Gross Income (GI)	12.4				
Number @100%	120		2		0
As % pupils	8				
Number of Hardship Awards (HAs)[57]	45				
As % pupils	3				
Total value					£20,000 £20–35k pa over 5 years[58]
Range MTB/HAs %	10–100		0–50:76 50–75:12 75–90:8 100:2	0–50:20 50–75:7 75–90:2 Over 80:3[59] 100:2	Up to 90% (bursaries)
Number of MTBs + HAs			98	31	
As % pupils			24	19[60]	
% GFI			9.7	5	

(*Continued*)

56 In order to protect confidentiality.

57 Reductions in fees for existing pupils who face an unforeseen change in financial circumstances.

58 The previous year (£20k) was apparently the lowest for 5 years, but no explanation was given and the value of MTBs is not known.

59 This extra breakdown figure was provided at p 8 of the report.

60 Appearing as 19% in three places and 21% in one.

Table 1: ***(Continued)***

Information	Manchester Grammar	Highfield Priory	Pangbourne College	Manor House	S Anselm's
% GI			8.7	5[61]	
% total income					1
Total value			£722,861	£99,139	
No @100%				2 (HA probably)[62]	
As % pupils			Less than 1	1.3	
Other assistance			HMC place[63] £1.3m total assistance	66% pupils receive fee reduction	JET: 2 in 10 years[64]
Extras	Free meals if income support or jobseekers' allowance Travel depending on income and postcode		Uniform and trips if necessary	Bursaries include learning support (LS) costs	50% compulsory extras; 90% LS included

It was unhelpful not to provide the same type of information in respect of each school, especially given the undoubted importance of means-tested provision in the Commission's assessment of public benefit. The information was incomplete in several sections and the terms used were inconsistent. Amounts were expressed as a percentage of one or more of 'gross fee income', 'gross income' and 'total income', for example, but none of these terms was included in the Commission's glossary, despite their significance. Furthermore, the income margins and sliding scale which were used in means-testing calculations, and described as good

[61] Noted as 5% GFI and 5% GI.

[62] See n 70 below.

[63] Headmasters' and Headmistresses' Conference (HMC) scholarship for pupils from Eastern Europe. Under the scheme, fees charged depend on a means test conducted by the HMC. The statement that 'the charity fully funds this place' suggested that no fees were charged, but it was not clear whether, if so, this was one of the two 100% bursaries noted. It was also stated that one place per year was available, but it was not reported how many places had been taken up, or for how long.

[64] Two places were said to have been 'either partly or fully funded' over the past 10 years by JET, a charitable trust. Although the school appeared simply to have accepted pupils referred to it, the Commission stated that 'this type of help' had counted towards meeting Principles 2b and 2c.

practice in *Emerging findings*, were given only in respect of Manchester Grammar School,[65] and the effect on a recipient of means-tested assistance of having to pay a fixed percentage of compulsory extra costs was not considered.[66]

Hardship Awards and Means-Tested Bursaries

Hardship awards were said to provide an opportunity for those unable to pay the fees, including people in poverty, but 'to a lesser extent than bursaries' because they were available only to existing families and, therefore, to a very limited class.[67] Whilst schools' accounts may not always differentiate between bursaries and hardship awards, the Commission might have been expected to separate the two, rather than simply taking into account the 'combined effect' of hardship awards and other financial assistance, and stating the percentage or sums available.[68] It also failed to explain the significance of hardship awards being available only if funds remained after awarding means-tested bursaries, although this was sometimes recorded.[69] Here, as elsewhere in these reports, the Commission missed an opportunity to explain its thinking so that trustees, whose questions remained unanswered by the Guidance, would have a better understanding of the Commission's approach and their prospects of satisfying the public benefit requirement.

In the case of Manor House, for example, two 100 per cent awards appeared to have been made as hardship awards,[70] but the two further awards over 75 per cent might have been either.[71] The information supplied in respect of Pangbourne College combined means-tested bursaries and hardship awards, making it unclear how many of the 98 awards were of each type, although the two 100 per cent awards were described as bursaries.[72] The Commission also explained that not all fee assistance needed to be 100 per cent remission on fees but that such provision should be 'available where needed'.[73] It was precisely *when* it was 'needed', however, that charity trustees wished to know.

Principles 2b and 2c: Non-Means Tested Assistance

The account which the Commission took of non-means tested assistance, including scholarships, sibling discounts and publicly funded contributions towards fees

[65] But possibly in existence at the other schools?

[66] S Anselm's, 12.

[67] Manor House, 8

[68] *Emerging findings* (n 4) 25.

[69] Pangbourne College offered hardship awards from its bursary fund only once other awards had been made, whereas Manor House was noted for use of 'its available funds as necessary'.

[70] 'In awarding 100% hardship awards': Manor House, 8; it thus appears that each of the two 100% 'bursaries' awarded was a hardship award.

[71] Although the notes to the school's 2008 accounts introduced reference to means-tested bursaries, as part of an objective to widen access where possible, they were mentioned alongside armed forces families' discounts and scholarships.

[72] The ambiguity relating to the HMC award has already been noted (n 63).

[73] *Emerging findings* (n 4) 20.

appeared to contradict the rationale behind Principles 2b and 2c. A successful assessment depended on 'material opportunities to benefit' and yet the Commission acknowledged that the extent to which those unable to afford the fees might be helped by non-means tested assistance was less certain and more likely to occur by chance than by design, at the same time explaining that 'an opportunity to benefit that occurs by chance was not a 'material' opportunity to benefit'.[74] Furthermore, the very fact that such assistance was offered without regard to a recipient's financial circumstances meant that those who benefited *could* have comprised only those who were able to afford the fees in any event, and none in poverty.

The Continuity of Education Allowance (CEA), for example, is paid out of public funds to pupils in armed forces families. It is non-means tested and pupils are required to pay a minimum 10 per cent of the fees charged by the school attended. The Commission's reports indicated that a school which accommodated such pupils was regarded favourably, even though it also acknowledged that the allowance was not certain to assist those unable to afford the fees. Indeed, the Commission seemed content that a very high percentage of pupils receiving CEA meant that there was greater potential for families in the armed forces who could not afford the fees to be benefited in this way.[75] The Commission also made no comment on the affordability (or otherwise) of the 10 per cent which still had to be paid, and yet a sum of £2,495 per annum (payable in the case of Pangbourne College) would appear to be unaffordable by many. The information provided was as follows (Table 2).[76]

Table 2: Principles 2b and 2c: Non-Means Tested Assistance

	Pangbourne College	Manor House	S Anselm's
Number	19	40	9
As % pupils	4.6 or 4.7[77]	27 or 29[78]	3.7 or 4[79]
Further reduction	25%	0	20%
Value	£101,896		£30,800
%	1.4 GFI		Less than 1% 'charity's income'; 0.8 total income
Year	2007–08	2008–09	2007–08

Pangbourne College and S Anselm's were both reported to have reduced the fees further, on a non-means tested basis, by 25 per cent and 20 per cent respectively.

[74] ibid, 23 (the Commission sometimes referred to 'material opportunities to benefit' and sometimes 'opportunities to benefit in a material way').

[75] Manor House, 8.

[76] The Manchester Grammar report made no mention of CEA and Highfield Priory is a day school.

[77] Both numbers appeared (pp 3, 12).

[78] Both numbers appeared. Given the figures provided, 27% would appear to be more accurate.

[79] Both numbers appeared, the latter may have been simply a rounding-up.

Manor House, on the other hand, was said to have set its fees so that no further reduction was necessary. It was not clear whether this was a deliberate policy to assist the armed forces families, even though it would have impacted on the fees charged to all pupils, or whether the school was able to operate efficiently with fees at that level in any event. The Commission described the two methods of assisting, but failed to comment on the significance of either or their relative merits.

The 'levels of assistance' provided at Pangbourne College and the 'specialism' at Manor House were both highlighted in the Commission's conclusions regarding Principles 2b and 2c. In the former case, it was noted that 'a number' of families were assisted who could not otherwise have afforded the fees, but the number of pupils and the extent to which they could not afford the full fees were not specified. This lack of information, and the absence of any such assessment in the case of the other two schools, was unsatisfactory. The further reduction in fees and the percentage of pupils who benefited were not significantly less in the case of S Anselm's, a smaller school without the reserved funds of Pangbourne College, but it 'failed' where the College 'succeeded'. In light of these similarities, a clearer explanation of the divergent outcomes was called for.

Similarly, government-funded and non-means tested Early Years Entitlement (EYE) grants were included in the reports for two of the three schools which took nursery-age children, despite being described as only potentially capable of providing opportunities to those unable to afford the fees.[80] Again, their significance in determining public benefit was not explained.

Non-means tested scholarships were also taken into account, the *possibility* (or chance) of assisting those unable to afford the fees apparently being sufficient. (See Table 3 below.) Although the amount of scholarship funding was part of the total value and total percentage figures appearing in the conclusions regarding Principles 2b and 2c, once again the information provided in respect of the schools was inconsistent and the weight attached to scholarships in the Commission's assessment of public benefit was not made clear.[81]

Table 3: Non-Means Tested Scholarships

	Pangbourne College	**Manor House**	**S Anselm's**
Range	5–40% or 5–50%[82]	Junior: £900–40% Senior: up to 20%	Pre-prep to Junior: 10%
Number	83	12	7
As % pupils	20	8	3
Value	£351,033		£11,600
%	4.7 GFI		0.3 total income

80 But not mentioned in respect of S Anselm's.
81 It is assumed that Manchester Grammar and Highfield Priory did not award scholarships.
82 Both ranges appeared in the report (pp 3, 13).

The Commission recognised that sibling discounts were 'unlikely' to afford opportunities to people in poverty, but also commented that family discounts went 'some small way' to enabling those who could not otherwise afford the fees to ensure 'that all their family members who are eligible to benefit have the opportunity to do so'.[83] On this basis, they were included in the reports, either by specifying the number of sibling discounts in place[84] or the percentage allowed,[85] but their significance was not explained. Likewise, savings schemes, which allow the cost of fees to be spread, were described as relevant to Principles 2b and 2c, despite having 'little bearing' where the weekly or monthly costs remained high,[86] but none was mentioned in the reports.

The Source of Means-Tested and Non-Means Tested Assistance

The Commission maintained that a charity's financial circumstances were 'an important part of the extent to which it can satisfy principles 2b and 2c',[87] and that it 'did not expect smaller charities to be able to do as much as larger charities'.[88] In determining what was 'reasonable and appropriate' for each school to provide, the Commission purportedly took into account the level of fee income, the extent of reserves and endowments, including whether these were in the form of savings and investments or property (ie, the extent to which they could be used to subsidise fee assistance) and the ability of the school to make any necessary changes within a reasonable time frame to provide sufficient opportunities to benefit.[89] Explaining that assistance could be funded from third parties, such as a separate endowed charity, it also acknowledged that the amount of external funding available to independent schools would be limited, and less than that available to residential care homes, for example.[90] As a result, the Commission recognised that most schools would be required to fund bursaries and other fee assistance from their own resources, and that this would mean either having trust funds or endowment funds or setting fees at a level which would, 'over time', provide a fund for assisting those unable to pay the fees.[91]

These were all considerations which one might have expected the Commission to consider important and, in view of their purported significance, it was reasonable

[83] *Emerging findings* (n 4) 25.
[84] Manor House, 12.
[85] Highfield Priory, 14.
[86] *Emerging findings* (n 4) 25.
[87] ibid, 16.
[88] ibid, 22.
[89] ibid, 20.
[90] Where local authority funding is usually significant: *Emerging findings* (n 4) 18.
[91] Noting that 'having dedicated funds for fee assistance' is good practice is not entirely helpful: *Emerging findings* (n 4) 16.

to expect that the Commission would have tried to explain the relative value of each source of finance and how much less a smaller school (or one without dedicated funds) might have been expected to provide. It gave no such explanation, however, and the information presented in respect of each school was cursory. (Table 4 below.)

Table 4: Source of Means-Tested and Non-Means Tested Assistance

	Manchester Grammar	Highfield Priory	Pangbourne College	Manor House	S Anselm's
Details as to funding sources	Restricted funds (RF) and endowed funds (EF)	No RF, no EF	RF 'bursary fund'	No RF, no EF	RF for bursaries and capital projects
Named source of financial assistance	Restricted bursary fund, separate charitable trust and other educational trust		MTBs from fee income; HAs from bursary fund; bursaries supplemented from 'charity's income'	Fee income	50:50 bursary fund and fee income

Of course, schools' financial profiles vary considerably[92] and accounts are not always capable of easy interpretation.[93] It goes without saying that a richly endowed school with dedicated funds can fund means-tested bursaries a great deal more easily than one which is forced to increase its fees in order to do so. By way of a simple example, a school with a gross fee income of £2,000,000 per annum would need either to invest £5,000,000 at two per cent per annum or increase its fees by 5.26 per cent in order to fund bursaries worth five per cent of its gross fee income. In the absence of any legal requirement for a school to fundraise or to increase fees in order to subsidise additional places, however, the Commission could only *encourage* schools to do so.[94] And the lack of any evidence as to how

[92] From the £154m endowment fund of Eton College to the zero endowments of many independent schools: Caritas Data, *Independent Schools Financial Yearbook* (2009/10) (Caritas Data, 2009).

[93] The 76% fee income given in bursaries by Christ's Hospital School, for example, stemmed from a change in governance structure which resulted in endowed funds being paid to the school by a separate foundation and also a rise in its ranking from 409 to 2 in the Independent Schools' Table of Bursaries: ibid, 2.157.

[94] *Fee-charging* (n 38) 30.

(if at all) the Commission had assessed either the ability of a school without dedicated funds to raise sufficient money by these means, or the impact of charging higher fees on the intake of pupils who paid full fees, was unsatisfactory. These were two of several relevant considerations which the Commission had said it would take into account, but it was not clear that it had done so.[95]

None of the extensive means-tested awards given by Manchester Grammar, for example, appeared to have been provided from fee income, even though the value of bursaries was stated as a percentage of 'gross fee-income' (which was not defined).[96] The statement that the school had a fundraising department which was 'instrumental' in the programme of fundraising for bursaries told us little and the fundraising might have been limited to the encouragement of donations and legacies to dedicated funds. It might have been better to express the value of bursaries as an amount *equivalent to* x per cent of fee income.[97]

On the other hand, the five per cent gross fee income expended by Manor House in its provision of means-tested assistance was clearly sourced from its fee income and the charity had no restricted or endowed funds. Bursary places at S Anselm's were said to be funded 50:50 by an appeal fund and 'existing income', but there was also reference to a bursary scheme set up in 2007 and a foundation that was established in 2004, in part for bursary funding.[98] This gave a confusing picture of precisely how the means-tested bursaries were financed and it was not clear to what extent their source was important, nor how the Commission had taken account of the school's financial resources in this respect. Arguably, these two schools were doing more than Manchester Grammar to respond to the Commission's thinking on public benefit, and yet S Anselm's failed the test.

If a school offers financial assistance from funds which are made available for that purpose, it will do so because it is legally bound to do so by the terms of the governing document and the Commission's position on public benefit is not material. In expending the school's fee income, however, charitable trustees are bound to exercise their powers only in furtherance of the charitable purposes and could justifiably question, therefore, the extent to which they could legitimately provide financial assistance out of income, when such provision would necessarily be detrimental to existing beneficiaries (by increasing fees) and not actually required in order

[95] ibid.

[96] The report stated that bursaries were funded from a restricted bursary fund, a separate charitable trust and other educational trusts, but the funding of hardship awards was not specified. The school's accounts suggested that unrestricted funds had been partially applied toward bursaries in the year ending 2009 but not in the preceding year.

[97] Or perhaps as 100% of funds restricted to that purpose. Further confusion was caused by giving the value of bursaries in 2008/09 as a percentage of the gross fee income in 2007/08.

[98] The school's website indicated that the bursary fund was part of the foundation and appealed for donations, the reinvestment of a modest annual surplus being insufficient to fund the two existing bursaries.

to provide an education.[99] Furthermore, the more fees are increased, the further they move from being as close to cost as possible, a factor often commented upon in case law.[100]

Principles 2b and 2c: Other Measures which Provide Opportunities to Benefit for Other Children whose Families May not be able to Afford the Fees, Including those in Poverty[101]

In this section of the reports, reference was made to additional, non-financial, opportunities, which were listed in the annex to each report, such as hosting sporting fixtures and putting on local concerts. The way activities were listed was not consistent, however, and there was a risk that a longer list of individual activities might have appeared more 'worthy' than a single bullet point which, in fact, mentioned several activities at once.[102]

Despite the Commission's indication that charging for use of facilities may 'affect' the resulting public benefit,[103] presumably by reducing it, the reports rarely specified whether a fee was charged in respect of the listed activities, or whether non-fee paying state schools were accommodated, or whether people unable to afford the fees actually benefited. An assumption that parents of state school pupils are unable to afford independent school fees was evident in many of the entries and was sometimes made more explicit, for example by stating that an orienteering programme for local state schools was 'a benefit open to those who could not afford the fees',[104] or that providing work experience placements to students from state schools was a benefit 'open to those who could not afford the fees'.[105] Such an assumption is not justified, however. Some events were noted to benefit local state *and* independent schools, or state schools only, or simply local schools without reference to their status. The report for Pangbourne College even listed use of the College's facilities by local independent schools (only) as an opportunity relevant

[99] Put simply, relief of poverty is one head of charity, the advancement of education is another (a point more fully considered in ch 4); see also *The Hallmarks of an Effective Charity* (Commission, July 2008) D5, where the Commission notes that trustees are required to use funds 'in the most effective way to the benefit of the charity'.

[100] See also text to nn 53–55 above.

[101] The words 'may not be able to' represent a change of language from the more usual 'cannot' or 'are unable' and arguably places an even greater burden on trustees, or at least greater uncertainty, although it was probably not intended to be significant. It does accurately reflect, however, the Commission's approach to accepting only a possibility of opportunities reaching those unable to afford the fees, including people in poverty, and also the uncertainty over who can and who cannot afford the fees.

[102] cp, eg, S Anselm's fourth bullet point (offering use of facilities to local schools, clubs and youth and Church groups who regularly use the school's swimming pool, sports hall, theatre, hall, music block and dining room (p 14)) with Manor House's single item of hiring out badminton facilities for a badminton club (p 13).

[103] Guidance F10.

[104] Pangbourne College, 9.

[105] Manor House, 9.

to Principles 2b and 2c.[106] Notwithstanding its acknowledgement that such a contribution towards satisfying Principles 2b and 2c was 'in general terms … likely to be very limited',[107] this does appear somewhat difficult to reconcile with the Commission's own guidance on public benefit.

It seems that the activities did not need to have been undertaken *in order to* extend opportunities to those unable to afford the fees, including those in poverty; rather it sufficed that such benefits could have arisen incidentally. Hosting public music examinations, for example, is most convenient for a school's own pupils, their parents and teachers, and certain events, such as academic lectures and local or national competitions, provide good marketing opportunities by inviting prospective pupils and their parents to the school. A school might also undertake some activities primarily for the benefit of its own pupils, for example, including local state schools in its sporting fixtures so as to increase opportunities for competitive sport (particularly if the school is rurally located), or putting on local concerts in order to give its musical students greater experience in performing. It might also offer facilities because they are not commonly available, such as those needed for a national sculling competition.[108]

Perhaps most significantly, an independent school is likely to allow use of its facilities in order to supplement its income. The Commission mentioned schools 'making facilities available' or even 'hiring out' facilities, apparently without differentiating between (or even recognising) opportunities which were profitable for the school and those which were not. Even where a discount for local or children's groups,[109] or renting at below market rents,[110] was mentioned, it did not appear to be particularly significant. Taking into account only the free, or subsidised, use of premises might have been more consistent with the Commission's interpretation of public benefit, at least in so far as there was no apparent correlation between deriving income from letting out a school's facilities and its increasing the amount of financial assistance for the poor.

Also surprising was the fact that some activities were listed as contributing to public benefit, even though they would appear to have been primarily of advantage to the individuals involved: the fact that teachers acted 'as markers of Key Stage 2 exams', for example,[111] or the fact that members of staff wrote syllabus material or acted as assessors for exam boards.[112] Such work is normally paid and it is hard to imagine the courts ever being influenced by such matters in determining charitable status.[113] Some opportunities were also necessarily limited, for example

106 Pangbourne College, 13.

107 Pangbourne College, 9.

108 Pangbourne College, 13.

109 S Anselm's, 14.

110 Highfield Priory, 14, renting its premises to a profit-making children's club.

111 Highfield Priory, 15; even though this school failed to satisfy the public benefit test, this item was nonetheless a positive contributing factor to the assessment.

112 Manchester Grammar, 14.

113 By contrast, being a trustee of another charity or a member of a professional body was 'irrelevant' (or more difficult to show that the opportunities were targeted): Manchester Grammar, 9.

providing work placements,[114] and some were particularly infrequent or impermanent, such as a member of staff acting as an EYE coordinator in the area,[115] or a school offering its swimming pool as an alternative to a municipal pool which was closed for two months.[116] The decision to attach significance to such occasional or short-term benefits, however, is highly questionable, all the more so where private benefits are involved.

Measuring the Totality of Benefits for Principles 2b and 2c

Noting that high fees required some 'mitigation' in order to show that the opportunity to benefit was not unreasonably restricted, the Commission purported to explain how each category of assistance had been 'looked at'.[117] In fact, any 'explanation' amounted to little more, in most cases, than commenting that non-means tested assistance had less impact than means-tested assistance and that sharing facilities and resources with state schools could provide opportunities to benefit to those unable to afford the fees. This was not particularly enlightening.

The Commission reported that it had taken into account circumstances specific to each charity, including the steps taken to provide opportunities to benefit.[118] The large size and resources of Manchester Grammar, for example, were described as underlying the sufficient opportunities offered. On the other hand, the impact of a school having a 'relatively small size' was not elaborated upon, although it was said to have been taken into account.[119] In the case of each of the two 'failing' schools, the Commission also acknowledged that the school's ability to mitigate the fees was, or may have been, influenced by its location and financial situation.[120] It failed to explain, however, how any of the school's locations were relevant and the act of noting the influence of a school's financial situation was not to explain its significance in terms of public benefit.

The matters which were reported to have been taken into account in reaching a conclusion regarding Principles 2b and 2c are summarised in the following table (Table 5).

[114] The opportunities provided by Manchester Grammar were extensive, but the inclusion of helping teaching assistants with their PGCE applications and training and mentoring PGCE students (none of whom was actually of school age) was questionable.

[115] Highfield Priory, 15.

[116] S Anselm's, 14.

[117] The change from 'moderation' to 'mitigation' suggested a greater emphasis on reducing or waiving fees than increasing them in order to provide extended opportunities.

[118] It was not clear if this meant anything more than a consideration of the matters listed in the annex, but may have suggested that credit was given for a school's willingness to alter its practices in an effort to comply with the Commission's approach to public benefit.

[119] Manor House passed but Highfield Priory failed the assessment, both 'relatively small'; the size (without more) was also said to have been taken into account in the other reports.

[120] Highfield Priory, 9: '*may* be influenced by'; S Anselm's, 10: '*is* heavily influenced by' (emphases added).

Table 5: Measuring the Totality of Benefits

Manchester Grammar	Highfield Priory (fail)	Pangbourne College	Manor House	S Anselm's (fail)
		Very high fees		
Relatively large size	Relatively small size	Size (not specified)	Relatively small size	Size (not specified)
	Policy of keeping fees down			
		Circumstances[121]	Circumstances[121]	
	Location			Location
	Financial situation			Financial situation
	Steps taken to provide opportunities	Steps taken to provide opportunities	Steps taken to provide opportunities	Steps being taken to provide opportunities
	Totality of benefits			
		£1.3m assistance	66% pupils receive assistance	
Bursary scheme		Means-tested bursaries (MTBs) from fee income for 24% pupils, 9.7% GFI	MTBs for 19% pupils, 5% GI	
		100% bursaries	100% bursaries	
			100% hardship assistance	
			Number of means-tested awards	
		Assistance for armed forces families	Specialism in assisting armed forces families, so that 40 pay 10% fees	
Extensive additional opportunities		Links with state schools	Links with state schools	

[121] Exactly what circumstances was not indicated.

By reporting that it had taken into account what was 'reasonable and appropriate in the circumstances' of each charity in determining whether Principles 2b and 2c had been met, the Commission implied that it had actually formed a judgement as to what would have been reasonable and appropriate. Indeed, it was entirely reasonable to expect that such a judgement would have been arrived at in an assessment process as detailed as this was, but the Commission failed to give any indication of what *was* 'reasonable and appropriate' in its view in any case. Whilst it can be assumed that the successful schools achieved or exceeded whatever level the Commission judged to be reasonable and appropriate, some idea of what it considered reasonable and appropriate in the case of the two failing schools would have been particularly valuable and might have given all charity trustees a much greater understanding and confidence in knowing what was expected of them.

Principle 2d (Private Benefits Must be Incidental only)

Each report recorded that staff discounts were available, as part of the employment terms offered to staff, and concluded that these were legitimate private benefits and incidental only.[122]

No other private benefits were mentioned, save in respect of Highfield Priory. In this report, the Commission described how the school's governing document required a majority of parent-governors (and how, in practice, all governors were also parents) and so resulted in them facing a potential conflict of interest that could not be managed in the normal way (by excluding the votes of conflicted trustees). The risk of non-incidental private benefit was identified as both a breach of trust (but capable of remedy) and as failing to satisfy Principle 2d, thereby constituting a failure to meet the public benefit requirement and impacting on charitable status.[123] It might have been more appropriate, however, to view the document as giving rise to a risk of breach of trust which might prompt regulatory action, but not as a failure to meet the public benefit requirement.

IV. Results of the Assessments

Three reports concluded that the subject school was a charity and that it was operating for the public benefit.[124] Two, however, concluded that the subject school was not operating for the public benefit, a situation which the Commission had

[122] *Emerging findings* (n 4) 25.

[123] Explaining that it was unable to judge to what extent 'unmanaged private interests, and the possibility of unauthorised private benefit, can be regarded as incidental': *Emerging findings* (n 4) 28.

[124] Manchester Grammar, Pangbourne College and Manor House.

previously explained would mean that the trustees were 'operating in breach of their charity's trusts' *and* that an organisation was 'not, in substance, a charity',[125] or (more emphatically) 'cannot be a charity'.[126] Neither school was entitled to appeal against these findings, since they were not 'decisions' within the statutory framework for appeal.[127]

S Anselm's was said to be 'a charity but … not currently operating for the public benefit'.[128] To say that an institution is a charity means, by definition, that the public benefit requirement has been met, but the Commission maintained that the public benefit requirement had not been met as a result of the school's failure to satisfy Principles 2b and 2c. This illustrates the confusion, which permeates the whole of the 2008 guidance, between charitable status (to which the public benefit requirement is necessarily linked) and trustees' duties.[129] Critically, the conclusion that the school was 'not currently operating for the public benefit' also failed to indicate whether the school had ceased to operate for the public benefit or whether it had never done so, but there was no suggestion that there had been any change in either the purpose or (if relevant) the section of the public, nor were any changing social values or circumstances noted. To declare that the trustees were in breach of their charity's trusts, by not operating for the public benefit, also meant that each trustee was personally liable and, at least theoretically, might even have faced removal from office.

In the case of Highfield Priory, on the other hand, its aim was said to be '*capable* of being charitable, subject to the public benefit requirement being met' (emphasis added), suggesting that it was not in fact charitable at that time (although the school was referred to as 'the charity' throughout the body of the report).[130] Again, it was not evident whether the Commission considered that the school's registration as a charity had been in error, or that the school's purposes had since changed to ones that were not for the public benefit, or that the intended beneficiaries no longer comprised a section of the public. In fact, it was clear that the Commission was not concerned with the purposes for which it was established so much as its operations at the time of the assessment, the charitable status being ostensibly questioned because it was not 'operating for' the public benefit. It is hardly surprising that, faced with the risk of liability or removal from the Register, and no right of appeal, the trustees of both schools cooperated fully with the Commission.

[125] *Emerging findings* (n 4) 12. The meaning of 'in substance' was unclear: no distinction was made between 'in substance' and 'in law' or 'in fact'.

[126] Guidance D3.

[127] See n 21 above.

[128] S Anselm's, 11.

[129] The position is improved in the 2013 guidance, where the duty to operate for the public benefit is clearly separated, but the confusion persists to some degree (see ch 9).

[130] Highfield Priory, 12.

Actions where the Public Benefit Requirement was not Met

Notwithstanding that both schools were said not to satisfy the public benefit requirement, the Commission sought neither to remove them from the Register, nor to suggest that a cy-près scheme was appropriate.[131] Instead, the governors of Highfield Priory were required to produce a plan to demonstrate how they would ensure that sufficient opportunities to benefit were provided to those unable to afford the fees, including the poor, and the governors of S Anselm's were required to produce a 'revised' plan, showing a totality of benefits which could be regarded as sufficient. The governors of S Anselm's needed to 'do more' and 'take further action', making access to the school's benefits 'more extensive and targeted'. Exactly what they should do, or the minimum requirements they should consider, however, were not set out, despite the indications that the Commission would have made an assessment of just what would have been 'reasonable and appropriate' in its case.[132]

The need for the said plans to be produced within 12 months meant a significant period of uncertainty, with adverse implications for all, both in terms of potential liability for breach of trust and also the risk of charitable status being denied or removed. In fact, the charitable status of each school was confirmed in June 2010, on the basis of the schools' projected positions after five years. Highfield Priory's plans, for example, revealed an intention to increase 100 per cent bursaries from nought to 3.3 per cent of pupils and to award 4.9 per cent of its gross fee income in means-tested bursaries.[133] The Commission noted the school's desire to avoid drawing on the school's resources and identified 'several possible sources of funding' for the bursary scheme, including developing a fundraising strategy seeking donations and sponsorship.[134] The plan was also said to be 'based on changing economic circumstances' and was subject to annual review by the governors.[135] Other opportunities offered by the school were 'materially the same' and not developed further.[136]

S Anselm's had taken some measures already (including advertising bursaries of 'up to 100%' rather than 'up to 90%' fees) and planned to increase the number of pupils receiving means-tested financial assistance from 1.2 per cent to 4.6 per cent and from 0.8 per cent to 2.5 per cent of gross fee income.[137] Most of the bursaries would be funded from a bursary fund with some funds coming from reserves,

[131] See ch 2, part III.
[132] See p 151 above; see also text to n 1.
[133] See Highfield Priory 2010 report, para 3a.
[134] ibid.
[135] ibid.
[136] ibid, para 3b. The school's failure to meet Principle 2d was resolved by a plan to have 4 out of 10 non-parent governors with a majority vote on fee-setting decisions.
[137] See S Anselm's 2010 report, para 3a; again 'changing economic circumstances' were noted (in addition to a decline in pupil numbers and income).

but no detail was given.[138] The school also introduced a 'strategic approach' to its provision of other benefits for local children and committed to run at least one coaching event for children free of charge and to 'explore' further opportunities.[139] Plans to develop an astroturf pitch and to let the swimming pool (presumably for a charge) were also noted but, in other respects, the plan made no material change to the opportunities offered by the school.[140]

Although confirmation of the schools' charitable status is to be welcomed, the fact that it was given simply on the basis of the schools' intentions, and not conditional upon any further assessment in order to monitor whether the plans were, in fact, implemented, suggests that the transition from failure to success was rather easily made.

Actions where the Public Benefit Requirement was Met

It was reported that Pangbourne College and Manor House, although satisfying the test of public benefit, 'should' take some steps in order to demonstrate that they were meeting key good practice 'requirements' in the Commission's guidance. The subsequent setting out of three good practice 'recommendations', however, confused words of requirement and recommendation and this was unhelpful.[141]

The first recommendation was that the trustees should 'publicise more clearly' their means-tested awards,[142] although no specific direction was given as to what further steps trustees should take and it was acknowledged that more extensive advertising would attract more applications and so incur added costs and administrative burden.[143] Pangbourne College, for example, already advertised on its website (explicitly referring to the availability of 100 per cent bursaries), in the local press, annually in the national press and directly to local state and independent schools. Its trustees might have considered, therefore, that they had satisfied the requirement in the guidance to take 'reasonable steps to advertise [free or subsidised access] widely and publicly',[144] and the suggestion in *Emerging findings*, that publishing the availability of fees assistance on a school's website was sufficient (at least if it was made clear that funded places (presumably fully funded) were available), appears to be at odds with its direction to the school in this case.[145] Were the trustees of Pangbourne College to assume that they should take the additional steps, as Manchester Grammar had done, of advertising on buses and in shopping malls? Or could they not assume that something less would suffice, since

[138] ibid.

[139] ibid, para 3c.

[140] ibid.

[141] The Commission has been frequently criticised for its failure to distinguish between what was legally required and what was 'good practice'.

[142] Pangbourne College, 10; Manor House, 10.

[143] *Emerging findings* (n 4) 21 (plus the cost of advertising, of course).

[144] *Fee-charging* (n 38) 33; *Emerging findings* (n 4) 17.

[145] *Emerging findings* (n 4) 17 (but note the alternative, of advertising 'ideally through a range of media which reaches a socially diverse audience' (p 21)).

that school (unlike Pangbourne College) was not reported as advertising in the national press or explicitly mentioning the availability of 100 per cent bursaries? Manor House, likewise, publicised financial assistance on its website, through the local press and through other promotional literature.[146] Should its trustees also have advertised through the national press and on buses? The Commission's refusal to indicate what further measures it regarded as appropriate left trustees guessing.

The second recommendation was that the governors should consider increasing the relative number of higher percentage awards.[147] It was not clear whether this meant relative to the total number of pupils or relative to the total number of awards or whether the Commission required the school to increase the total value of awards. Again, this level of ambiguity and lack of direction was unhelpful and fell a long way short of the guidance that might have been given. Of course, the obligation to review the scope for offering more high percentage awards was not as onerous as a straightforward obligation to offer more, but it was unclear what level of review was required or what level of scrutiny of that review would be pursued by the Commission. Since the reports concluded that the level was sufficient at that time, the trustees might reasonably have questioned the merits of such a review and, indeed, might have considered that any further expenditure for these purposes, rather than directly on the school's main charitable purposes, would have been unnecessary and not in the best interests of the charity.

The third recommendation was to keep under review the extent to which the opportunities to benefit were actually taken up by people who were unable to afford the fees, including people in poverty.[148] It was not clear, however, how trustees were to conduct that review in the case of non-means tested assistance and other benefits. How were the trustees to measure whether people in poverty were actually members of the local cricket club or Brownie pack, for example, or that they were attending the sculling and orienteering events at Pangbourne College?

Nor did the Commission give any explanation for its decision to review the trustees' progress with these recommendations within 18 months in the case of Manor House, but not at all in the case of Pangbourne College, even though the recommendations were identical.

Guidance to be Drawn from the Reports

The value to be gained from having assessment reports in respect of only 20 of the 163,000 or so registered charities is necessarily limited, but it is also the case

[146] '[F]rom September each year … in advance of the school's Open Day', but without stating when the Open Day was held, thus making it difficult to assess the level of publicity by this means (Manor House, 11).

[147] Pangbourne College, 10; Manor House, 10.

[148] ibid.

that drawing conclusions from the reports themselves is not easy.[149] The Commission was keen to insist that it could not lay down a formula or any minimum requirements or criteria which would enable trustees to be sure of satisfying the test, but preferred to regard the assessment programme as 'a learning process for everyone'.[150] In view of its role as adviser, and as regulator in the event that trustees failed to provide sufficient opportunities, however, a far greater degree of clarity should have been provided, even though this might have been designed to allow for some margin of flexibility. A minimum requirement of a stipulated percentage of gross fee income to be expended on means-tested bursaries, for example, would have provided some degree of certainty. And even without clearly measurable criteria, the Commission could have explained the weight attached to each of the benefits listed, whether financial or otherwise, and the significance of each type of a school's financial resources. At the very least, it could have revealed what it had considered 'reasonable and appropriate' in each case. Such explanations and illustrations would have gone some way towards equipping the trustees of all fee-charging charities to gauge their own prospects of satisfying the Commission's public benefit assessment process.

Perhaps only the following principles can be extrapolated from the reports:

- that means-tested assistance below one per cent of a school's income was 'minimal' and insufficient on its own;
- that non-means tested assistance was not sufficient on its own;
- that means-tested bursaries for prospective pupils and hardship awards for existing pupils would be treated equally;
- that the motivation behind the provision of opportunities to benefit to pupils and other children was immaterial;
- that it was immaterial if the school charged for the use of its facilities;
- that commonly encountered restrictions on age, gender, location and academic selection would not detract from public benefit;
- that it was not necessary to show whether, or how many, pupils receiving CEA were actually unable to afford the usual fees.

And, more tentatively:

- that it might not be sufficient to identify benefits based on a charitable purpose listed in the statute;
- that opportunities to benefit would only be considered to the extent that they were provided to other children (but not necessarily children of the same age as pupils at the school) or adults concerned in education;
- that the level of operating surplus was not material;
- that advertising fee assistance on a school's website and in the local press was not sufficient;

149 And compares unfavourably with the position in Scotland (see ch 7).

150 *Emerging findings* (n 4) 2.

— in respect of non-means tested assistance, the provision of further assistance to armed forces families (beyond CEA) would be more favourably regarded than scholarships or sibling discounts.

In conclusion, it seems that the compilation of the reports was a time-consuming and expensive exercise, for both the Commission and the charities concerned. Containing unwarranted assumptions and unexplained conclusions, the reports demonstrate an approach which is intricately concerned with detail and yet fails to recognise or to include some matters of significant import. Above all, the assessments focused almost entirely on the charities' operations or activities and were not transparent or convincing in taking into account a school's size or resources. The conclusions in respect of the two failed schools are difficult to reconcile with the Commission's own conclusions and its legal interpretation in respect of an institution which fails to meets its own principles of public benefit. The plans on which charitable status was subsequently affirmed also revealed a lack of transparency and substance and suggest that the Commission viewed removing a charity from the Register not so much as a last resort as something to be avoided at all costs.

7

Charitable Status in Scotland*

At the moment the two sets of legislation (that of England & Wales and that of Scotland) only differ slightly, but it is possible that the definition of what is charitable or what public benefit means might differ more widely in the future.

The Commission[1]

I. Introduction

The Charities and Trustees Investment (Scotland) Act 2005 (the Scottish Act) received Royal Assent 16 months before the (English) Charities Act 2006.[2] It established the Office of the Scottish Charity Regulator (OSCR)[3] and made significant changes to Scottish charity law. It charged OSCR with determining whether bodies are charitable and with keeping a public register of charities (the Scottish Register).[4] Coming within the first decade of devolution,[5] the statute also signalled a readiness to depart from English law and to introduce a new test of charitable status that was 'good for Scotland',[6] even if that gave rise to an inconsistency between the two jurisdictions.[7] It is fair to say that Scotland's new definition of charity was 'clearly derivative of its English equivalent', but gave scope for 'widely divergent interpretation'.[8]

* In this chapter, footnote references to the names of schools are to the relevant parts of the Phase 1a Report (n 41 below) unless otherwise stated. References to the 'Scottish Guidance' refer to *Meeting the Charity Test: Guidance for Applicants and for Existing Charities* (OSCR, August 2011) (see n 10 below).

[1] *English and Welsh charities working in Scotland* (Commission, undated) para 7.

[2] In July 2005 and November 2006 respectively.

[3] Like the Commission, OSCR is a non-ministerial government department.

[4] Scottish Act, s 1(5).

[5] By virtue of the Scotland Act 1998.

[6] The benefits of a 'common or compatible definition' were acknowledged, but only if it was 'also right for Scotland': *Charities and Trustee Investment (Scotland) Bill: Policy Memorandum* (Scottish Executive, 2004) para 65. The intention expressed in Westminster, however, had been that the definitions of charity in the two jurisdictions should be 'fully compatible' (HL Deb 20 January 2005, vol 668, col 885 (Baroness Scotland)).

[7] Under the Law Reform (Miscellaneous Provisions) (Scotland) Act 1990, the test of charitable status had previously been compatible with the test in England and Wales.

[8] P Ford, 'The Scottish Charity Test: Do We Really Need It?' (2004) 8 *Edinburgh Law Review* 408, 414.

In accordance with the Scottish Act, OSCR consulted[9] and then published guidance (the Scottish Guidance)[10] on 'how [OSCR] determines whether a body meets the charity test'.[11] So far as independent schools and other fee-charging charities are concerned, charitable status depends, in part, on the level of social benefit provided to people unable to afford the fees.[12] The regulator has also carried out over 100 public benefit assessments as part of its statutory obligation to verify the inclusion of entries appearing on the Scottish Register, a process known as the 'Rolling Review'.[13] More than 30 of these have been independent schools.

II. The Charity Test

The Scottish Act defines a charity as 'a body entered on the [Scottish] Register'.[14] OSCR is obliged to register any body which applies for registration and which meets the 'charity test', and also to remove any registered charity which does not meet that test.[15] It describes the test as 'a complex one',[16] and one which requires OSCR to arrive at a 'holistic view of the charity'.[17] Although 'charitable purpose' and 'public benefit' are the defining characteristics of charity in Scotland,[18] as they are in England and Wales, the tests used to determine charitable status in the two jurisdictions differ significantly. The charity test in Scotland is prescribed by section 7(1) of the Scottish Act:

(1) A body meets the charity test if—
  (a) its purposes consist only of one or more of the charitable purposes, and
  (b) it provides (or, in the case of an applicant, provides or intends to provide) public benefit in Scotland or elsewhere.

[9] OSCR conducted focus groups and received written representations from charities, professional organisations and others: *Meeting the Charity Test: Proposals for Consultation, Findings from Winter 2007/08 Consultation* (OSCR, undated) (Consultation Evaluation Report) section 1.

[10] *Meeting the Charity Test: Guidance for Applicants and for Existing Charities* (OSCR, first published in 2008 and amended in August 2011, though not substantially (see 2008-09-05/BOARD/138, 25 August 2008)).

[11] Scottish Act, s 9.

[12] The Scottish Act uses the terms 'public benefit' but, in the context of fee-charging charities, the term 'social benefit' is appropriate (see text to n 60, ch 1).

[13] See part III below.

[14] Scottish Act, s 106. (Companies are similarly defined by reference to registration in England and Wales (Companies Act 2006, s 1).)

[15] Scottish Act, ss 5, 30.

[16] Particularly, it seems, in relation to independent schools: the High School of Dundee was 'the most complex and challenging' of all the pilot assessments: *Rolling Review Pilot Study Report* (PSR) (OSCR, August 2007) para 5.6.

[17] *Policy Statement Restrictive Conditions* (PSRC), App 4 PSR (ibid) conclusion (p 86).

[18] OSCR describes them as 'the key concepts': Scottish Guidance, p 4.

The first limb of the test is assessed on the basis of a body's constitution, the second on the basis of its activities.[19] The two features which most clearly distinguish the Scottish charity test from the English test concern public benefit: first, the requirement is not that charitable *purposes* must *be* for the public benefit, but that a charitable *body* must *provide* public benefit, taking into account fees and charges,[20] and second, public benefit is not defined by reference to existing case law.[21]

(1) The First Limb: Charitable Purposes

As in England and Wales, a body's constitution defines its purposes and these must be exclusively charitable.[22] 'Charitable purposes' are defined as those purposes listed in section 7(2) of the Scottish Act and they are similar (but not identical) to the purposes listed in the English Act.[23]

Any of three 'disqualifying factors' may prevent a body from being a charity, regardless of its provision of public benefit. First, a body's constitution must not allow any of its property to be distributed or otherwise applied (on being wound up or at any other time) to purposes which are non-charitable under the Scottish Act, even if they might be charitable under English law or for tax purposes.[24] Second, charitable status will be denied where a constitution allows Scottish Ministers to 'direct or otherwise control' the body's assets or activities.[25] The third factor disqualifies any body with a purpose of advancing a political party.[26]

(2) The Second Limb: Public Benefit

The term 'public benefit' is not defined, but, unlike the English Act, the Scottish Act specifies three factors to which regard must be had in determining whether a body provides or intends to provide public benefit.[27] These concern private benefit, detriment and restrictive conditions (including fees and charges) and are discussed below.[28] Like its English counterpart, the Scottish Act provides that no

[19] Scottish Guidance, pp 8, 15.

[20] Or 'intend to provide' in the case of an applicant for registration (Scottish Act, s 7).

[21] The term is not defined but certain factors (considered below) must be taken into account.

[22] 'Constitution' is defined by reference to a written document (Scottish Act, s 106).

[23] The 'English Act' refers to both the 2006 Act and the 2011 Act, where no distinction is needed between the two statutes; it includes 'the advancement of amateur sport', whereas the Scottish Act names the advancement of public participation in sport, for example; and the English Act (but not the Scottish Act) includes the promotion of efficiency of the armed forces.

[24] Scottish Act, s 7(4)(a).

[25] ibid, s 7(4)(b); eg, John Wheatley College, where governing legislation (the recognised constitution) permitted Scottish Ministers to remove trustees and to close colleges (PSR (n 16) para 5.5). (Remedial delegated legislation has since been enacted.)

[26] Scottish Act, s 7(4)(c); on the other hand, purposes of campaigning for a change in legislation, which are non-charitable in English law, may be charitable (Scottish Guidance 5.3).

[27] Scottish Act, s 8 (the term does not appear in the general interpretation section, s 106).

[28] In fact these three factors are set out as two, the first being to balance public benefit against each of private benefit *and* public detriment.

particular purpose is to be presumed to be for the public benefit.[29] It might have been more appropriate to provide that no particular purpose[30] shall be presumed *to provide* public benefit,[31] but there seems little merit in attaching any significance to such a mismatch in the wording.[32]

In sharp contrast to the English Act, there is nothing which obliges OSCR to interpret and apply the term 'public benefit' by reference to case law, even though at least some of the statutory factors clearly stem from judicial authority.[33] OSCR is thus at liberty, it appears, to interpret the term 'public benefit' and each of the three factors as it sees fit. The absence of any clear direction to take existing case law into account has been criticised for causing uncertainty and for giving OSCR 'the next best thing to a clean sheet'.[34] However, it seems that any dependence on case law, Scottish or otherwise, is necessarily curtailed by a reformulation of a test which sets out new definitional criteria and, in some respects, renders case law redundant.[35] Notwithstanding the statutory provision, however, the Scottish Guidance states that OSCR will follow normal rules of legal interpretation, which will include 'looking at' the Scottish Act, Scottish case law and 'case law in other jurisdictions (for instance in England and Wales)', but adds, as if for good measure, that such non-Scottish case law will be 'persuasive rather than binding'.[36]

Like the Commission, OSCR lays down no minimum threshold of benefit, declaring that it 'does not operate an absolute volume or impact threshold' and that, in the Scottish context of many small charities in small communities, setting a minimum would not be reasonable or appropriate.[37] It is not clear why the size of the charity or, even less, the size of the community, should preclude guidance as to how much benefit is expected,[38] but OSCR's desire to retain a wide discretion on the issue is quite apparent.[39]

[29] Scottish Act, s 8(1).

[30] Or no body, regardless of its purposes.

[31] OSCR does in fact state that 'none of Scotland's 15 charitable purposes brings with it the presumption that public benefit is automatically provided' (PSR (n 16) para 4).

[32] A presumption that public benefit is delivered may appear inappropriate in any event.

[33] Those relating to private benefit and detriment.

[34] Ford, 'The Scottish Charity Test' (n 8) 412.

[35] Case law might still be applicable with regard to detriment, private benefit and public policy, but less so regarding political purposes or fee-charging charities, for example.

[36] Scottish Guidance, p 4; if not simply asserting its autonomy, OSCR might also have been attempting to allay concerns over the blatant rejection of case law or to offer reassurance to those concerned about inconsistency in charity law throughout the UK.

[37] ibid, 7.2; the notion of public benefit being 'sufficient' is used rarely in OSCR publications (although the assessment of public benefit as sufficient or insufficient is clearly discernible in OSCR's assessments of independent schools (see below)); OSCR does, however, indicate a minimum fee level, below which the charity test is unlikely to be failed on the basis of fees (see text to n 80 below).

[38] On the contrary, one might argue that small charities are most in need of the clearest guidance.

[39] A literal interpretation of the provision should make any amount of benefit sufficient (at least where it is not outweighed by private benefit or detriment or affected by restrictive conditions), but the failure of a number of schools (below) demonstrates that this is not OSCR's interpretation of the provision.

OSCR notes that benefit must be related to the purposes,[40] but that it may be tangible, intangible, direct or indirect, for example, noting 'increased social solidarity' to be an indirect benefit of religious bodies.[41] Whether or not the indirect benefit of relieving the public purse is relevant was initially described as a complex issue 'which requires relevant statistical and sociological evidence' and 'an area that will merit further research and consideration in the context of the charity test'.[42] OSCR later concluded, however, that 'a link between the purposes set out in section 7(2) of the 2005 Act and relief to the public purse is not immediately clear', suggesting that indirect benefit in this sense is unlikely to be taken into account.[43]

Factors for Considering Public Benefit

The three factors to be taken into account in assessing public benefit are not intended to be conclusive and OSCR rejects a 'box-ticking approach' in favour of one which is prepared to consider and weigh up sometimes complex and variable considerations.[44] Private benefit, public disbenefit[45] and conditions which are 'unduly restrictive' are clearly three such factors which oppose or detract from public benefit and the regulator suggests that the factors' relative importance might depend in part on the type of body and purpose, adding that 'such issues will become clearer and more predictable as case law under the 2005 Act builds up'.[46] Experience thus far, however, suggests that case law will be elusive[47] and, since each factor is equally capable of precluding charitable status, their relative weighting may be insignificant in any event.[48]

1. Private Benefit

The first factor to be taken into account is how any benefit, gained or likely to be gained by members of the body or any other persons (other than as members of the public) in consequence of the body exercising its functions, compares with the benefit gained or likely to be gained by the public in that consequence.[49] In itself, this provision gives no indication of the extent to which private benefit might be

[40] Scottish Guidance 7.1.

[41] ibid (indirect benefit is defined as benefit extended to those 'beyond the immediate beneficiary group'); similarly the 'maintenance and improvement of the heritage value of property held in trust' constitutes public benefit (National Trust of Scotland, Rolling Review—Phase 1a Report (OSCR, October 2008) 16).

[42] PSR (n 16) para 3.3.

[43] In response to a Freedom of Information request made by the author (22 August 2011).

[44] Scottish Guidance 7.7.

[45] Meaning detriment or harm (ibid 7.5).

[46] Scottish Guidance 7.7.

[47] In light of OSCR's broad discretion and dearth of cases to date (see text to nn 129–32 below).

[48] OSCR also states that no one element takes precedence or has greater weight than another (Scottish Guidance 7.7).

[49] Scottish Act, s 8(2)(a)(i).

tolerated, if at all, but OSCR explains that any benefit, other than to individuals as direct beneficiaries, must be 'necessary and/or incidental' to the body's purposes.[50] Whilst necessity can be more objectively judged,[51] the quality of being 'incidental' might be assessed either quantitatively, where benefit might be tolerated up to a given threshold of 49 per cent or less, or qualitatively, for example, as being a 'secondary consequence'[52] (but which could, in fact, exceed the public benefit in quantitative terms).

In assessing the public benefit provided by the University of Dundee, OSCR examined the effect of academics carrying out privately funded research and considered that there could be a risk of dissemination of that research to the public being curtailed and of the funder obtaining a competitive advantage in the marketplace.[53] Not addressing whether such sponsorship was 'necessary', OSCR nonetheless concluded that the eight per cent research income from private sponsors (not all of which would necessarily result in private benefit) amounted to less than one per cent of the University's total budget and did 'not outweigh' the benefit that was provided to the public.[54] Noting the income received as a proportion of the University's budget, however, appears to equate the University's expenditure with the quantum of public benefit and to weigh benefit to the University against this rather than the benefit to the sponsors (which had been identified as potentially benefiting privately). Nor was it clear what the regulator's assessment would have been if, instead, the level of private funding had been, say, 40 per cent of either the research income or the University's budget or expenditure. The case study offers little clarity on its own but illustrates well the considerable scope for flexibility which is given in the statute.

2. Public Disbenefit or Detriment

The second factor requires OSCR to have regard to how any disbenefit, incurred or likely to be incurred by the public in consequence of the body exercising its functions, compares with the benefit gained or likely to be gained by the public in that consequence.[55] Not surprisingly, if the disbenefit 'outweighs the benefits' or is 'of such a serious nature as to negate the benefit provided', the charity test will not be satisfied.[56] At the same time, however, it is said that 'some disbenefit' may be acceptable,[57] apparently allowing a significant level of disbenefit, provided the

[50] Scottish Guidance 7.4 (which offers comprehensible and sensible definitions of 'necessary' and 'incidental').

[51] And judged sympathetically, perhaps, in recognising that a charity might only be able to operate by means of running a business (as in *IRC v Falkirk Temperance Café Trust* 1927 SC 261 (CSIH)).

[52] Scottish Guidance 7.4.

[53] PSR (n 16) para 5.7.3.

[54] ibid.

[55] Scottish Act, s 8(2)(a)(ii).

[56] Scottish Guidance 7.5 (a balancing calculation in this way is perhaps more suited to questions of disbenefit than questions of private benefit (and reflects case law)).

[57] Scottish Guidance 7.5.

benefit remains greater.[58] Essentially, maximum discretion is reserved to OSCR in respect of the undoubtedly rare cases where detriment might be in issue.

The argument that independent education has a negative and detrimental impact on state schools in the same area, and/or that independent schools are a 'divisive influence in society', was considered in the public benefit assessment of the High School of Dundee, but OSCR declined to adjudicate on the argument in the absence of 'strong evidence' in support of it.[59] Later, it made clear its decision that the relative merits of fee-paying schools would not be taken into account, on the basis that the argument was relevant to the sector as a whole.[60] Whilst a desire to avoid the issue might be understandable, this rationale does not seem entirely to justify ignoring its narrower, but consistent, application to individual schools within the sector. Like the Commission, however, OSCR seems keen to sidestep what is an inherently political argument, regardless of whether such a weighing up exercise might be merited by the Scottish Act.[61]

3. Unduly Restrictive Conditions

This statutory provision represents a significant departure from English law in respect of fee-charging charities in particular. It requires OSCR, where benefit is (or is likely to be) provided to a section of the public only, to consider any restrictions which narrow the beneficial class and to determine whether any condition on obtaining that benefit is 'unduly restrictive'.[62] Charges and fees are highlighted by specific mention, but other conditions may also be relevant, such as an academic selection process.[63] Generally, restrictions may be constitutional, in describing the eligible class, or practical, in regulating how a charity operates (for example, restrictions on opening hours or access).[64] Although restrictions imposed by an institution's trustees may change from time to time, the ongoing obligation in the charity test to provide public benefit justifies their consideration. All conditions are restrictive by definition, of course: the test is whether they are *unduly* restrictive and OSCR is the arbiter.

In a sentence which is striking in its contrast with the statement of Lord Wilberforce in *Re Resch*,[65] OSCR states that

58 Suggesting a 49%/51% balance, although this is undoubtedly over simplistic.

59 PSR (n 16) para 5.6.3.

60 Scottish Guidance 7.5 (likewise the 'general arguments for or against religious bodies').

61 And by *National Anti-Vivisection Society v IRC* [1948] AC 31 (HL), which has persuasive authority for these purposes (see text to n 36 above).

62 Scottish Act, s 8(2)(b).

63 Although this was not unduly restrictive in the case of the High School of Dundee (PSR (n 16) para 5.6).

64 Scottish Guidance 7.6(b) (which restrictions must be reasonable and appropriate and not prevent access for the majority without alternative arrangements or adjustments being made).

65 *Re Resch* [1969] 1 AC 514 (PC). Equally striking is its similarity to the Commission's first principle from the case (see text to n 21, ch 5).

> the fact that a (prospective) charity provides benefits that will be charged for and will be provided *mainly* to people who can afford and choose to pay the charges does not necessarily mean that the body does not provide public benefit (emphasis added).[66]

There is an implication that charitable status will be denied where *only* those who can afford the fees benefit and this would appear to be OSCR's interpretation, at least where fees are relatively high.[67] However, as a regulatory body with considerable discretion, unhindered by much legal authority and responsible for informing the public of its intended approach, it is unfortunate that OSCR failed to put the matter beyond doubt.[68]

OSCR defines an 'unduly restrictive' condition as one which is 'excessively restrictive, or restrictive in contradiction of general moral or legal standards, or is unreasonable or is not justifiable'.[69] Of these judgements, only one is truly objective and certain, namely a restriction which contradicts legal standards, such as anti-discrimination laws.[70] OSCR is otherwise at liberty, it seems, to decide what is excessive, immoral, unreasonable or unjustifiable.[71]

Morality is an uncertain and shifting territory, however. Is it immoral, for example, when only children of wealthy parents are able to attend a fee-charging independent school and is it immoral that those parents also pay general taxes in respect of state education? And what are the moral considerations where fees are increased, thus making them unaffordable to more, in order to fund means-tested bursaries for a few? The concept of conditions being 'unjustifiable' presents similar difficulties. Is not every measure capable of being justified by its proponent? Justification by itself, without a requirement for the justification to be on moral, reasonable or legal grounds, for example, appears meaningless in this context. The third criterion is reasonableness, which represents a more objective standard and a common term in the legal arena, although the familiar 'man on the Clapham omnibus'[72] might feel less accustomed to opining on questions of moral justification or social policy.

OSCR indicates that a restriction may be 'undue' if it is irrelevant to the purpose and not otherwise justifiable.[73] On this basis, defining a class by reference to a

[66] Scottish Guidance 7.6(d).

[67] See below.

[68] Possibly missing an opportunity to set out the clear parliamentary intention 'to prevent access … being restricted to the well-off', according to the Scottish Council for Voluntary Organisations (Consultation Evaluation Report (n 9) 16).

[69] Scottish Guidance 7.6; the PSRC defines the term similarly but omitting the word 'unreasonable' ((n 17) para 5).

[70] OSCR says that such conditions are unduly restrictive (Scottish Guidance 7.6(c)); of course they are also unlawful and subject to enforcement.

[71] Subject to normal rules of statutory interpretation and binding Scottish precedent (and see text to n 36 above).

[72] A term used to denote the 'reasonable man', popularly attributed to Lord Bowen (see, eg, *Healthcare at Home Ltd v Common Services Agency for the Scottish Health Service* [2014] UKSC 49, [2014] PTSR 1081 [2]).

[73] Scottish Guidance 7.6(b); eg, where membership of a sports club depends on being proposed and seconded and no reason is given for the trustees' decision.

personal connection, or describing a class of named beneficiaries, might be unacceptable,[74] but a restriction on numbers need not be unduly restrictive, provided the benefits are potentially available to anyone who satisfies the criteria for eligibility.[75] Although OSCR adds that, in such cases, direct benefit to a small number might also indirectly benefit the public as a whole, this appears to be expressed as a consequence and not as an essential requirement.[76]

Principles Regarding Fee-Charging and Unduly Restrictive Conditions

The Scottish Guidance aims to provide 'a clear indication of what OSCR expects',[77] by setting out six general principles which are intended to be 'capable of being applied across this whole range of bodies and contexts'.[78] The first addresses the need for fees and the arrangements for facilitated access to be well publicised and the second makes clear that it is for the trustees to decide how best to avoid conditions being unduly restrictive, but for OSCR to decide on whether public benefit is delivered. The remaining four principles deserve particular mention.

1. Proportionality

The greater the fee, the more evidence that might be required to show that the conditions are not unduly restrictive and the more important it will be to mitigate the impact of the fees. It is not clear, however, whether the *proportion* of facilitated access is also to increase as the fees increase. For example, if providing means-tested bursaries equivalent to seven per cent of fee income is sufficient where fees are £x per annum, will seven per cent also be sufficient where fees are £x+y per annum?

Having commissioned research on affordability,[79] the regulator published its conclusion that fees under £1,500 per annum would be unlikely to cause failure of the charity test, since this amount would be unlikely to impact significantly on the ability to pay for the vast majority of Scottish families.[80] Providing a benchmark in

[74] At least paving the way for preserving the personal nexus test in English law (see text to nn 223–26, ch 2).

[75] Scottish Guidance 7.6(a).

[76] ibid; eg, research into a rare disease. OSCR's concern appears to be with open access to all potential beneficiaries, rather than their actual number or the extent of any indirect public benefit.

[77] PSRC (n 17) conclusion.

[78] Scottish Guidance 7.6(d).

[79] *Assessing the ability to pay for the fees charged by charities, Phase 1 Report* (Virtual Worlds, October 2008); OSCR emphasised, however, that quantitative information should not replace taking a holistic view of the charity and the benefits it offers to the public.

[80] Third Sector Online, 'OSCR reveals 'affordability' level for fee-charging charities' (21 October 2009): www.thirdsector.co.uk/Governance/article/947394/OSCR-reveals-affordability-level-fee-charging-charities/?HAYILC=RELATED.

this way compares most favourably with the Commission's ambiguous measures of 'high' and 'low' fees and fees which 'most' or 'many' can or cannot afford.[81]

2. Level of Fees

OSCR notes that it will balance the fees against the benefits (both those charged for and any not charged for) and indicates that it will take into account other benefits which are provided free of charge.[82] Benefits for only a nominal charge may also be taken into account, but not all benefits for which a charge is made (as appears to have been the case in the pilot study).[83] This policy is consistent with a policy of extending benefits to the less well off and, arguably, should have been followed by the Commission.

3. Facilitated Access

Where fees may affect access to the benefits,[84] OSCR will 'expect some kind of facilitated access or other mitigation' and will assess the cumulative impact of support to help potential beneficiaries, such as discounts, bursaries and fee waivers, taking into account people 'with a wide range of incomes, including low incomes', in order to see how much 'should be expected'.[85] (It is noteworthy that OSCR does not use the terms 'poor' and 'people in poverty'.)

OSCR goes some way towards indicating the relative significance of the various means of facilitating access, although it resolved that the source of funding should not be 'a factor on its own in determining accessibility'.[86] Thus, means-tested assistance is said to have the 'greatest impact', but assistance based on non-financial need, such as local authority housing or specialised education, will also have 'significant impact'.[87] Financial assistance from a body not connected with the charity may also be taken into account, depending on its effectiveness, reliability and impact,[88] and the extent of a charity's active engagement in facilitating access and assistance provided by the charity itself will be regarded as a 'positive

[81] The ambiguity has not been removed by the Tribunal's judgment or the 2013 guidance (see chs 8, 9).

[82] This is ambiguous, but it appears to suggest that benefits to non-direct beneficiaries are taken into account only if they are not charged for (subject to n 83 below).

[83] PSRC (n 17) para 6.

[84] Presumably (generally speaking) fees over £1,500 pa (thus avoiding the truism inherent in the Commission's publications (see ch 5, part III)).

[85] Scottish Guidance 7.6(d).

[86] Minutes 30 May 2007, quoted in OSCR Board Minutes RR310508/Board/128, para 4(c) (but emphasising that whatever the source of funding, all arrangements should be publicised).

[87] As in England and Wales, primary and secondary legislation provides for financial assistance for residential care and university fees, for example, but not for school fees.

[88] Government funding of the CEA, for example, has 'considerable impact' but other employer-based assistance is unlikely to have impact unless it is based on the beneficiary's need: Minutes/128 (n 86) para 4(c).

contribution'.[89] The inference is that OSCR will favour a manifest and proactive commitment which might be satisfied by fundraising efforts, including increasing fees in order to subsidise reductions or waivers for some, but perhaps not by channelling funding which has been given by third parties for the specific purpose of providing financial assistance. It is impossible to judge whether, or at what point, a lesser amount of assistance from a charity's own resources may be equated to a greater amount of dedicated funding from other sources.

OSCR does not insist on 100 per cent assistance, perhaps reflecting its references to people on a range of incomes, including low incomes, rather than the Commission's consideration of 'the poor'. Thus, OSCR held that public benefit was provided by a residential care home, where the maximum assistance available was 80 per cent and funded entirely by external sources, leaving all residents to pay a minimum of £4,732 per annum, even though this represents a figure well in excess of the 'affordable' rate and necessarily excludes those on the lowest incomes.[90] The charity itself provided no financial assistance and no other benefits. It appears that the high proportion of residents assisted was significant, but OSCR gave no indication of whether the expected proportion and scope of facilitated access might differ between, say, the residential care and education sectors.[91] Would a school, where every pupil paid at least £4,732 per annum, for example, pass the test?[92]

4. Cost

OSCR recognises that a charity must be able to cover its costs and states that it will assess to what extent access may be restricted 'in the context of the cost of providing the benefit(s) (direct and indirect)'.[93] Keeping costs low by covering costs from other sources (for example donations) might be 'an appropriate means of ensuring that fees are not unduly restrictive' and regard will be had to conditions attached to external funding.[94] The difficulty lies in the failure to make clear the relationship between the principle regarding facilitated access and this principle concerning the cost of provision. The first suggests that the imposition of *any* charges (unless regarded as affordable) necessitates arrangements for facilitated access, but the second suggests that reduced fees for all may be sufficient. If the former is correct, then this principle, which acknowledges the need to cover costs, may have little impact, except to signal an understanding that some charities provide high-cost services, or possibly to warn that excessive operating and capital reserves will not be tolerated.

[89] The Board minutes indicate that such provision 'would be regarded positively' (ibid); the implication seems to be that it is regarded *more* positively than applying funds from other sources (since the alternative interpretation, that other sources should be regarded negatively is not feasible).

[90] Isobel Fraser Residential Home, Phase 1a Report (n 41) 17; see text to n 80 above.

[91] Out of 27, 24 were assisted (although OSCR acknowledged that the proportions of assisted and self-funded residents would fluctuate).

[92] ie, around 40% higher than the fees at Regius School, which passed the test with no facilitated access (see below).

[93] PSRC (n 17) para 5.

[94] Scottish Guidance 7.6(d).

This dilemma was brought to the Board's attention in 2008, but was not resolved.[95] The Board's view was that the weighting given to the criterion of cost exceeding fee income should be 'used with caution', suggesting that it has little significance.[96] A consistent reduction for all will mean a smaller reduction than that extended to the few where fees are waived or partially waived. It may be that where fees are relatively low, reduced fees for all are sufficient, but where they are not, facilitated access must be provided.[97] Or is the extent to which fees are subsidised for all by a charitable source of income (other than fees) significant? Whether or not there is any correlation between the extent of the subsidy for all and the need for facilitated access for a few appears uncertain.

III. The Scottish Register and the Rolling Review

When OSCR was created in 2006, all organisations previously recognised as charitable by HMRC[98] were automatically transferred to the new Scottish Register.[99] There are now over 23,000 charities[100] on the Scottish Register, of which around three to four per cent are cross-border charities.[101] A proposal that charities registered with the (English) Commission should automatically be entered on the Scottish Register was rejected and charities which have 'significant operations in Scotland' must register separately with OSCR.[102]

Rolling Review

Unlike the Commission, OSCR has a statutory obligation to review each entry from time to time and to make any necessary amendments.[103] Since charitable status is not a test which centres on the purposes for which a charity was established, but depends on registration, which itself depends on meeting a test that demands the provision of public benefit on a continuing basis, it follows that periodic

[95] Minutes/128 (n 86) para 3(a).
[96] ibid, para 1.
[97] See Regius and Steiner Schools, below.
[98] Or the Inland Revenue.
[99] Around 31,000 were registered under the transitional arrangements (Scottish Act, s 99). OSCR has since granted new applications, but also removed large numbers of dormant charities.
[100] According to the OSCR website (approximately one-seventh of the number on the Register (for England and Wales)).
[101] There do not appear to be any independent schools or groups of schools which constitute cross-border charities.
[102] *Seeking Charitable Status in Scotland* (OSCR, May 2009) 4.1.
[103] Scottish Act, s 3(6).

reviews of the public benefit (or 'social benefit') delivered by registered charities are both justified and necessary.

In light of the discretion vested in OSCR in respect of a new test of charitable status, such reviews were also 'an essential element in the ongoing development of how OSCR interprets and applies the charity test' and an opportunity to 'increase public confidence in charities, while allowing a greater understanding of the variety, complexity, and impact of charities in Scotland'.[104] The review process was also noted to allow charities to demonstrate their delivery of public benefit, and so meet 'an expectation that has always been at the heart of public understanding of charities'.[105] Such objectives, based on public education, expectation and satisfaction, were also evident in the Commission's publications, but they appear somewhat more justified where the test of charitable status is original, largely undefined and demands an assessment of the public benefit delivered through a charity's activities.

Adopting a risk-based strategy, OSCR targeted charities which it considered to be most at risk of failing the charity test, including independent schools and care services, due to their fees potentially constituting unduly restrictive conditions.[106] In contrast to the Commission's modus operandi, assessment was by means of a paper-based exercise, with visits being the exception rather than the rule,[107] and they were conducted as statutory inquiries.[108] OSCR also seemed to work more quickly, completing eight pilot assessments in nine months and a further 30 in 13 months,[109] although the timetable for assessing compliance with the charity test was not without delays.[110] After reviewing 15 independent schools, any further reviews were postponed as OSCR expressed its confidence that the messages which Phase 1a had delivered would produce the desired result without the regulator's 'very resource intensive' intervention.[111] Indications were that future reviews would be more broadly based and that individual assessments would be conducted only rarely,[112] but in fact the Rolling Review continues and many more schools have been assessed (individually). Lists of ongoing and completed assessments are published regularly on OSCR's website.

[104] PSR (n 16) para 1.11.

[105] ibid, para 8.3; it might seem curious, therefore, that a successful assessment is not noted on the Scottish Register (but only directions and removals).

[106] It had been intended that Phase 1b of the Rolling Review should include universities and private hospitals (Phase 1a Report (n 41) para 8a).

[107] Unlike the Commission which visited every charity in the first round.

[108] Scottish Act, s 28 (unlike the position in England and Wales); *Inquiry and Intervention Policy* (OSCR, September 2010); the follow-up reports on the failing schools are described as 'section 33 reports' accordingly (and directions (see below) as 'section 30 directions').

[109] Although if its list of current reviews is accurate, it suggests that some have not proceeded with such efficiency.

[110] eg, Phase 1b was one year late starting and the large number of charities originally identified for Phase 1b was later reduced to 40: Board Minutes RR080508/Board/123, para 8.

[111] ibid, para 8(a).

[112] *Protecting charitable status: a report on individual charity reviews 2006–11* (OSCR, January 2012).

Removal from the Scottish Register

The consequences for a Scottish school of failing to provide public benefit are a great deal clearer and more straightforward than under either English law or the Commission's guidance. Where it appears to OSCR that a charity no longer meets the charity test, it must either direct the charity to take such steps as OSCR considers necessary in order to satisfy the test or remove it from the Scottish Register.[113] Such directions are likely to require changes to the charity's activities, but might also direct the charity to apply to OSCR for approval of a reorganisation scheme, designed to ensure that its resources are applied to better effect, having regard to the spirit of its constitution and social and economic circumstances.[114] If such a direction is given but not complied with, OSCR must remove the entry.[115]

The Scottish Act also makes clear how property is to be dealt with when a charity is removed, by providing that an organisation must continue to apply its previously acquired property, and income arising therefrom, in accordance with its purposes as they were entered on the Scottish Register.[116] OSCR may, however, apply to the court for approval of a scheme to transfer that property to a charity, but the court must be satisfied that those purposes would be better achieved by such a transfer and that it is necessary or desirable in order to protect the property or income or to ensure that it is properly applied to those purposes.[117]

A 'failure to meet the charity test' might describe a failure to provide *sufficient* public benefit,[118] or failure to provide *any* public benefit, as where a charity has become obsolete or never become active in the first place.[119] It might also apply where a charity was registered by virtue of transitional provisions and was thus never required to meet the charity test.[120] It is assumed that an organisation which OSCR concludes was registered in error would also be subject to removal under this provision, although it would be inappropriate in such circumstances to require that the assets continue to be applied to the purposes appearing on the Scottish Register. In addition, and in contrast with England and Wales, any charity may apply for removal at any time and, since Scottish law does not prohibit non-charitable purpose trusts, removal from the Scottish Register is unlikely to threaten a trust's continued existence.[121]

Charities are given a 'realistic timescale for compliance',[122] similar to that allowed in England and Wales, except that OSCR specifies that a charity has an

[113] Scottish Act, s 30(1).
[114] ibid, ss 30(2), 39 and 42.
[115] ibid, s 30(3).
[116] ibid, s 19 (and certain provisions (regarding enquiries and accounts for example) continue to be applicable).
[117] ibid, s 19(5).
[118] As in the case of the four schools considered below.
[119] Including in circumstances where there is a breach of statutory obligations and allegations of mismanagement (The Largo Trust, section 33 report (OSCR, September 2009)).
[120] eg, the Isle of Gigha Heritage Trust (where the purposes of promoting trade and industry had been accepted by HMRC, but were rejected by OSCR (although the issue was resolved without removal): Phase 1a Report (n 41) 11.
[121] Scottish Act, s 18; see text to n 193 below.
[122] Scottish Guidance 8.2.

additional two years, after submitting a plan, in order to implement that plan. This appears to be a more robust and appropriate course of action than the way in which the Commission affirmed the charitable status of the two failed schools (on the basis of mere intentions and projections) in England.[123]

Removal from the Scottish Register means that the organisation loses the benefits associated with the charity 'brand' and also entitlement to business rates relief, since that entitlement depends on inclusion on the Scottish Register.[124] Whether or not it loses entitlement to other tax reliefs, however, is a matter for HMRC which, it will be remembered, applies an English definition of charitable purposes. This means that it must be theoretically possible for an organisation to continue as a non-charitable organisation but with the benefit of reliefs from central taxation: a fee-charging school, for example, whose purposes are undoubtedly for the public benefit but which fails to satisfy OSCR in respect of the public benefit provided.[125] Conversely, it must also be possible for an organisation to be denied those reliefs, but at the same time to qualify as a Scottish charity, perhaps because its purposes are political in a way which is tolerated in Scotland, but not in England and Wales.[126]

Where the charity test is passed but other shortcomings are noted, a 'recommendation' or 'suggestion' of good practice may be issued and failure to comply with a recommendation will result in OSCR's Compliance Support Team being informed and possible further action being taken. For example, where a charity has pursued purposes other than those set out in its constitution, OSCR has issued a recommendation, but not withdrawn charitable status.[127] This, correctly, and in contrast to the Commission's approach, treats mission drift as a breach of trust and not a matter of charitable status.[128]

Decisions and Appeals

The Scottish Act established the Scottish Charities Appeals Panel (SCAP). Although its abolition was announced in November 2008, on the basis that it had heard only one case in its first two years,[129] it was reinstated in November 2010[130] (since when only a handful of appeals have been considered).[131] Only specified decisions and directions could be appealed, first by a process of review by OSCR, then by appeal

[123] See ch 6, part IV.

[124] Mandatory relief of 80% with the remaining 20% being within the discretion of the local authority: Local Government (Financial Provisions etc) (Scotland) Act 1962, s 4.

[125] And, even applying the Commission's interpretation of the public benefit requirement, the same discrepancy will exist where OSCR's threshold of public benefit is higher than the Commission's.

[126] See text to n 26 above.

[127] Coalburn Miners Welfare Charitable Society (PSR (n 16) para 5.3).

[128] The distinction has been recognised more clearly in the 2013 guidance, following the Tribunal's judgment in *R (Independent Schools Council) v Charity Commission* [2011] UKUT 421 (TCC), [2012] Ch 214, but the Commission's approach may still be muddled (see ch 9).

[129] Against a projection of 50–100 cases per year (and regarding a change of name, not public benefit).

[130] Following a consultation which led to a decision to retain the Panel while a review of the Scottish tribunal system was undertaken.

[131] The SCAP website suggests that of seven appeals registered, only four were heard.

to SCAP and, thereafter, to the Court of Session.[132] Under the Scottish Act, as in the English Act, these omitted directions to take steps to comply with the charity test, but Scotland was quick to remedy this shortcoming, passing amending legislation in 2010.[133] This gave OSCR the power to vary or revoke such directions and also allowed the recipient to appeal against a direction in the same way as against a refusal of an application for registration.[134]

Pilot Study

As a trial for the Rolling Review, and as part of the consultation process, OSCR assessed eight charities, including a university, an independent school and a further education college.[135] Two failed the charity test, though not on account of charging fees.[136]

The independent school was the High School of Dundee. It passed the charity test, but not easily, even though means-tested bursaries were allocated to 13 per cent of the pupil roll and accounted for over six per cent of its annual income, 55 per cent of which was funded by the school from fee income.[137] The majority of OSCR's Board felt initially that the school should not pass the test and draft directions were prepared which set out specific targets (for example, increasing the overall monetary value of bursary and grant support to at least 10 per cent of annual turnover).[138] The Board, however, was persuaded to make a favourable assessment after all, due (at least in part) to the considered likelihood of the school applying for judicial review of any directions issued, or refusing to comply with such directions and lodging an appeal with SCAP.[139] It suggests that OSCR may have intended to set a higher threshold than the Commission in England and Wales, but it also raises some questions about the transparency and integrity of OSCR's assessment process, and whether a school with identical, or near-identical, provision would pass or fail the charity test today.

Phase 1a

The 30 charities in Phase 1a comprised 23 of those in 'at-risk' categories, including 11 independent schools, and seven randomly-selected charities.[140] The result was

[132] Scottish Act, ss 71–78, as amended.

[133] Public Services Reform (Scotland) Act 2010.

[134] ibid, s 121 (in force from 1 August 2010). These changes post-dated the directions given to the four failing schools, referred to below, each of which complied with the directions given.

[135] PSR (n 16). OSCR had already applied the charity test in applications for registration since 2006.

[136] One failed due to ministerial control and the other due to its constitution allowing distribution of property to non-charitable purposes.

[137] Although only 1.3% pupils received 80% or more and only half of these received 100%, a figure which OSCR describes as 'low'.

[138] Attached to Board Minutes RR160607/Board/80 (App 2), although it was made clear that this was not the only way for the school to satisfy the test.

[139] ibid, paras 3.2 and 4.

[140] The 'at-risk' categories included four care homes, three museums and five membership organisations (Phase 1a Report (n 41) section 4).

that four bodies, all of them independent schools, failed the charity test due to fees being unduly restrictive, an outcome which OSCR found 'not surprising'.[141]

Conditions based on catchment areas were accepted as not unduly restrictive and conditions which required agreement with a school's ethos were also regarded as reasonable and justifiable 'in view of the type of education being provided'.[142] Restrictions on eligibility based on academic ability had already been accepted and were not mentioned in the Phase 1a reports.[143]

In most cases, however, the relevant condition was the levying of school fees. Although the diverse range of financial support mechanisms was noted as making it difficult to establish the impact of each type, the consistency of information provided for each school stands in stark contrast to the Commission's reports. Each school's fees were categorised as either 'relatively high' or 'relatively low' or 'average', compared with both state and independent education. Relativity was expressed only in terms of the level of fees, however, and so focused on cost and affordability, without paying attention to the type, quality or scope of education offered, nor the associated costs.[144] Moreover, the comparison between state and independent sectors is based on cost in the former and revenue (fees) in the latter, and costs are not usually reported on the same basis in each: the cost of a state education is typically reported on the basis of revenue expenditure only and does not include the capital costs which independent school fees also cover. The purpose of the comparison appears to have been to warrant a demand for greater facilitated access where fees were described as relatively high. To explain principles in terms of 'greater' or 'lesser', or 'higher' or 'lower', however, only offers guidance where comparisons can be made between consistent measures: a principle that a plant needs relatively more care if it is relatively rare can be understood in general terms, but not in specific terms.

Relatively Low Fees

Although more than double the 'affordable' rate of £1,500 per annum,[145] the fees charged by Regius School were described as 'substantial', but also as low, relative to state and independent education, and there were no reduced fees in individual cases or other benefits provided. 'Most' beneficiaries were said to pay the fees of £3,360 per annum and the lack of information regarding those who did not (if any) indicates that facilitated access for individuals was not considered important. It seems to have been enough that the school sought to keep the fees as low as possible, by low staff costs, donations and grant income, but it is not clear whether it was the level of fees or their relationship to cost, ie, the amount of subsidy to all, which dispelled the need for the school to provide facilitated access to individuals who were unable to afford

[141] ibid, section 1.

[142] One was a Christian school, the other a Steiner school.

[143] *cf* High School of Dundee, PSR (n 16) para 5.6.

[144] A school's fees might be relatively high in the sector but its educational provision relatively low (or inferior) or vice versa; it is not suggested that OSCR should extend its analysis in this way, but the value of such an unsophisticated comparison of fees is doubted.

[145] See text to n 80.

the fees. Regrettably, the proportion of total income comprising fees on the one hand and donations and grants on the other was not specified.[146]

Glasgow Steiner School also charged substantial fees which were relatively low (compared with both state and independent education) and provided no other benefits. However, in this case, not only were fees for all kept lower than cost by parental involvement, fundraising and donations, but all pupils were means-tested and more than 70 per cent of pupils received assistance. Not surprisingly, the school was judged to provide public benefit.

Specialist Schools

The study included two specialist schools with relatively high fees and additional benefits which were not inexpensive.[147] In both cases, it appears that since the principle of facilitated access was overwhelmingly satisfied, the principle regarding the cost of services became redundant and the fees' relativity to cost was not noted. It also seems that the fees were not regarded as unduly restrictive because the Government provided means-tested funding and because further remissions were provided from an external source and some by the school itself (although no details of the school's provision were included).

Relatively High Fees

The fees of six schools were described as 'substantial', high relative to state education and average or high relative to independent education.[148] The Phase 1a reports for each school presented consistent and relevant information and were significantly shorter than the reports prepared by the Commission.[149] Sibling discounts were disregarded unless means-tested,[150] and OSCR noted that the publicity offered by each school was appropriate.[151] Fees were noted to be less than cost,[152] but the suggestion was that facilitated access was expected because they were nonetheless relatively high.

The information relating to these schools can be summarised as follows (Table 6):[153]

[146] The report merely gives one example of an amount received from an external source, but an annual fee income of less than £60,000 might suggest that external funding was not insignificant.

[147] eg, instrumental lessons costing £50–£150.

[148] Merchiston and Gordonstoun are described as high relative to independent education but low relative to independent boarding.

[149] Both consistent within and between reports; there is occasional lack of clarity in the details but only one discernible error (in respect of St Mary's Music School, although the correct figure can be calculated).

[150] Gordonstoun only.

[151] The availability of information on websites was noted in each case to be sufficient, and contrasts with the detail provided by the Commission, and in the pilot study on High School, Dundee (PSR (n 16) para 5.6). (And availability on request can surely be assumed even where not explicitly stated.)

[152] Except in the Lomond School report (which was silent on the point).

[153] The consistency of information can be seen at a glance.

Table 6: Relatively High Fees

	George Heriot	Hutcheson	Lomond	St Leonard's	Merchiston	Gordonstoun[154]
Public benefit provided?	Yes	No	No[155]	No	No	Yes
No. MTB	130	45	2	3	16	At least 80
% pupil roll	8	2.6	Less than 1	Less than 1	3.7	13.4
No. @100%	70	15	Available (but no number specified)	Available (but no number specified)	4	16
% @100%	4	*	*	*	*	2.7 (nearly 4% at over 80%)
Value MTB	£707,848	£291,552	£17,100	£17,690	£100,838	£1.1m (including £215,181 external sources)
Total income MTB	Just under 7%	Less than 2%	Less than 1%	0.5%	Less than 1.5%	8.8%

* The figure can be assumed to be 0% or can be calculated but it is not given (perhaps reflecting the lesser emphasis on 100% provision)

154 OSCR noted that the wide range of facilitated access and the depth of information made presentation of information regarding Gordonstoun School particularly difficult.

155 A paper presented to the Board, in May 2008, indicated that OSCR should pass Lomond School (presumably influenced by the high level of non-means tested assistance) and issue a recommendation that the school consider increasing its means-tested provision. The Board took a sterner line, however (Minutes/123 (n 110)).

No. non-MTB (% pupil roll not given)	80	4[156]	38 school scheme+ up to 64 external	11	116 'concessions'+ 36 non-MTB+ 12 armed forces concessions	1 scholarship up to 100% (sport) and others (unspecified) up to 10%
Value non-MTB (% total income not given)	£203,632 (source unspecified)		£24,510 + up to £823,845 external	£54,471 (+ estimated £165,000 external)	£383,197 (sport/ academic concessions) + £141,665 (non-MTBs) + £23,518 (armed forces concessions)—apparently school-funded	£287,838 (+ other £56,726 external)
Total no. MTB + NMT	210	49	At most 104	14	180	At least 190
% pupil roll	12	2.8	17.5	3	More than 41	32
Total value MTB + NMT	£911,480	£312,115	£865,000	At most £237,161	£649,218	£1.446m
% total income	9	2.1	18.5	5.5	Just under 9	Over 11.5

[156] It appears to be assumed (having regard to percentage of roll figures) that the four in receipt of external trust funding were non-means tested (the terms are not known).

As in the Commission's assessments, and despite its apparent significance, information regarding the source of funding was sometimes ambiguous. For example, the George Heriot School offered means-tested bursaries, only some of which were '"Foundation" and James Hardie awards' and presumably met by dedicated funding. It is not clear what proportion was met in this way, or how the other means-tested and non-means tested awards were funded.[157] On the other hand, means-tested bursaries at Hutcheson School were provided out of 'income from its endowed funds', although it was not said whether this was included in the amount of 'charitable donations and fundraising income' used to offset the cost of services.[158] OSCR sometimes noted that details of external funding were unknown, signifying its lesser importance.[159]

It appears, however, that in the three cases where the percentage of means-tested assistance against fee income was lowest, the school itself funded the assistance, although to what extent this was by increased fees, fundraising, legacies or donations is not clear.[160] The schools were reported to be developing their assistance schemes, in line with OSCR's general observation of a 'clear and very encouraging trend' that 'the schools on the whole are working hard to respond to the requirements that the charity test puts on them', whilst also noting that they 'may take some time to be realised'.[161] In relation to Gordonstoun School, it was 'the school itself' which provided the significant proportion of financial assistance,[162] but the exact nature of the funding source was never explained. It is notable that three of the four 'failing' schools showed significantly high proportions of non-means tested financial assistance compared with means-tested assistance.[163]

Other Benefits

In its guidance, OSCR indicates that it will take into account, in particular, activities which further the purposes of education of a certain age group and only benefits which are provided for no fee or charge.[164] OSCR's reports, however, contained very little detail regarding other benefits provided to non-pupils, in stark contrast to the detail provided by the Commission,[165] even though it seems likely that the

[157] Nor how the After School Club was subsidised (which was specifically mentioned).

[158] Noted to endure for as long as the pupil is at the school, apparently regardless of any increase in the pupil's means.

[159] 'External funding sources' supported nine pupils at Lomond School and 'six external trusts' supported four pupils at Hutchesons.

[160] It is not impossible that endowed funds might also have been included, although the express mention in other cases suggests otherwise; the proportion of endowed income in the 2% offered at Hutcheson was not specified

[161] Phase 1a Report (n 41) section 5b.

[162] The phrase is used four times.

[163] Approximately (in percentages of total income): Lomond 17.5:1; St Leonard's 5:0.5; Merchiston 7.5:1.5; whereas the two successful schools show 2:7 (George Heriot) and 2.7:8.8 (Gordonstoun).

[164] Scottish Guidance 7.6(d) (in contrast to the pilot study where charged-for benefits were also taken into account); but see text to nn 82–83 above and 172 below.

[165] And, to a lesser extent, to the assessment of the High School of Dundee.

schools would have provided similar benefits. Exceptionally, there was said to be 'good evidence' of other benefits at Merchiston Castle School, but more significant measures were needed in view of the scale of fees.[166] An 'altogether different approach to engaging with the wider educational community' was described in Gordonstoun's links with an academy school in Leicester, but few details were provided, probably because the extensive financial assistance offered was enough on its own to ensure that the test was passed.[167] It is impossible to deduce to what extent, if any, such other benefits might have been sufficient if the fees had been lower or the facilitated access less generous.

Rather than focusing on other benefits, OSCR concluded that the extent and nature of benefit was similar among the schools reviewed and also 'neither significant enough nor closely enough related to the charity's purposes to have critical impact in our assessment of public benefit'.[168] It also acknowledged that other benefits were not expected where the school was small.[169] Typically the examples given were teaching placements and participation in examination setting, moderating and marking,[170] such evidence being noted to 'partly extend to the wider educational curriculum'.[171] Use of an all-weather pitch for a 'nil *or reduced* charge' (emphasis added),[172] and the undertaking of community projects with pupils from a state school,[173] were also included.

The Failing Schools

Four schools failed the charity test and were directed to submit plans which showed an improved level of provision. Like the Commission's directions, and unlike the draft directions which had been prepared in respect of the High School of Dundee,[174] these were non-specific. Each school increased significantly the amount offered in means-tested bursaries and also increased the range of activities for no fee and, following a period for implementation, charitable status was confirmed.[175]

[166] Staff and senior pupils provided mentoring to pupils at a local state primary, the same were invited to attend the independent school for up to 2.5 hours per week and reciprocal visits took place between the school and a school in China.

[167] More material had been provided in an appendix to Minutes 123 (n 110) (but was presumably omitted from the report as immaterial to its conclusion).

[168] Phase 1a Report (n 41) section 5(b).

[169] Regius and Steiner Schools.

[170] As in England and Wales, the fact that teachers may receive remuneration for such services appears to be of no relevance.

[171] The meaning is not entirely clear, but it suggests a closer adherence to benefits reflecting the main purpose of providing education (ie, contributions to curriculum and professional development of teachers) rather than purposes of promoting sport, for example (*cf* High School of Dundee and use of facilities by the Dundee Asian Society which seeks to promote sport (and which may not be limited to school-age children): PSR (n 16) para 5.6.2).

[172] George Heriot (a reduced charge might be neither nil nor notional).

[173] Hutchesons.

[174] See n 138.

[175] *Protecting charitable status* (n 112) 20–27. The figures suggest that much of the increase in means-tested bursaries might have been achieved by redirecting non-means tested assistance.

Of the additional schools assessed since Phase 1a, a further five initially failed the charity test due to inadequate public benefit. Each of these schools subsequently passed the test, having increased the level of available income dedicated to means-tested bursaries, but more notably because the schools increased the availability of means-tested bursaries representing greater proportions of the fees.[176] The provision of more regular and scheduled activities available to non-pupils was also significant in one case.[177] With so many reports now available, and with the greater clarity they offer, it is fair to say that trustees in Scottish schools are significantly better equipped than their English and Welsh counterparts to assess their compliance or non-compliance with their regulator's demands regarding public benefit.

IV. Charitable Status in the Two Jurisdictions

The Charity Commission guidance on public benefit, issued since the [Scottish] 2007 Rolling Review Pilot, demonstrates a marked convergence with how OSCR has developed its approach to public benefit.

OSCR[178]

It is only in Scotland that registration itself determines charitable status, but in both jurisdictions, registration confers all the benefits of the charity 'brand' and attracts the facilitative, advisory and supervisory functions of the charity regulator. However, if a Scottish body neither wishes to be called a charity, nor wishes to obtain the benefits which accompany charitable status, it may elect not to register or to apply for removal from the (Scottish) Register.[179] In England and Wales, on the other hand, if a body qualifies as a charity, it *is* a charity and it *must* register and be subject to the Commission's regulation and supervision: it cannot opt out of charitable status.[180]

Although, simplistically, both jurisdictions use 'charitable purpose' and 'public benefit' to characterise charity, the obligation to provide public benefit, together with the broader scope for defining that term, means that the tests of charitable status are significantly different north and south of the border.[181] Unlike the English test, charitable status in Scotland necessarily demands an inquiry into whether

[176] See, eg, OSCR's Inquiry Reports under s 33 Scottish Act regarding St George's School for Girls (19 November 2013) and Loretto School Ltd (17 June 2014).

[177] St Columba School (ibid).

[178] OSCR, noting the influence of its approach on the Commission: Minutes/123 (n 110).

[179] Many Scottish charities were reported to have chosen, or to have been forced to accept, removal due to costs involved in charities' accounting and reporting obligations: *Herald Scotland*, '£400 fee is forcing charities to give up status' (28 September 2010): www.heraldscotland.com/news/home-news/400-fee-is-forcing-charities-to-give-up-status-1.1057923.

[180] Save for exempt or excepted charities or charities with gross incomes not exceeding a specified threshold, currently £5,000 pa.

[181] The Scottish Guidance notes that the differences 'have a number of possible consequences', although the suggestion is that these are limited to the first disqualifying factor described above (Scottish Guidance, p 4). The problems for cross-border charities are obvious.

public benefit is, in fact, delivered, and that necessitates an examination of the organisation's activities. For fee-charging charities, there can be no question that the fees may, in some circumstances, mean that an institution cannot be charitable.

The English courts have repeatedly stressed that charitable status is a question of law. In Scotland, although the first limb of the charity test is a question of law, the second has become a question of fact, properly determined by OSCR. OSCR is authorised to assess the level of social benefit offered by an organisation and to judge whether access is sufficiently open and the services sufficiently advantageous. It is not bound by a vast body of case law which has both made the wealth of the beneficiaries irrelevant and rejected demands that benefits be extended to the poor. As a result, the Scottish regulator is at liberty to require not just that public benefit is delivered, as required by the Scottish Act, but also to be satisfied as to what extent and to whom it is delivered. The process of public consultation prior to publishing guidance was entirely appropriate.

The two tests differ in more specific respects. The Scottish test, for example, permits purposes which are political but not party political, but also disqualifies on grounds of ministerial control, and there appears to be potential for OSCR to adopt a different approach regarding detriment and private benefit, although a radical departure from case law is not anticipated in either case. And the considerable scope for denying charitable status on the grounds of fees or other conditions which OSCR considers unjustified, whether imposed by the constitution or by the trustees, represents, perhaps, the greatest distinction between the two jurisdictions.

The requirement for a Scottish charity to provide public benefit, and OSCR's statutory duty to review each registered charity's compliance with the charity test from time to time, stem from legislative provisions which represent bold and deliberate departures from English law. Those provisions also mean that it is unnecessary to impose a statutory duty on trustees to have regard to the Scottish Guidance in conducting the charity's activities, although clearly they would be ill-advised if they failed to do so.

The regulators produced very different publications.[182] OSCR's guidance is predominantly coherent and clear,[183] and lacks the repetition and ambiguity which was prevalent in the Commission's significantly lengthier publications in 2008. It also offers substantially more guidance than that offered by the Commission's publications in 2013.[184] The same is true of OSCR's published reports in respect of individual charities and general findings, which are notable for their consistent presentation of information and relevant content.[185] And, although neither

[182] The Scottish Guidance was written 'for an audience of professional advisers' (Consultation Evaluation Report (n 9) 4).

[183] It explains the use of figures from different years, for example; *cf* n 97, ch 6.

[184] See ch 9, part V.

[185] Phase 1a reports in respect of individual charities are typically one to two pages whereas the English school reports ran to at least 16 pages each; the PSR also concentrates on only 'the most pertinent and relevant areas of interest' in order to avoid repetition and to focus attention on OSCR's policy response and areas of uncertainty (PSR (n 16) para 15).

jurisdiction initially allowed appeals against directions, Scotland's amending legislation was passed promptly and improved significantly the position of those charities which are told that they do not satisfy the charity test. Like the Commission, however, OSCR is less than clear with regard to the relevance and significance of sources of funding and declines to indicate acceptable ratios of fees to free or discounted places, or to stipulate acceptable ratios of fees in relation to indirect benefit.[186] Whilst this protects OSCR's discretion, it may be that setting parameters could come closer to fulfilling its objective of giving clear guidance as to what is expected.[187]

With the exception of relief from local government taxation, which depends on charitable status under the Scottish Act,[188] the fiscal burdens and privileges of Scottish charities are a matter of UK tax law, and this depends not on the Scottish test of charitable status but the English definition of charity. This adds further complexity to the difficulties already faced by cross-border charities in connection with registration and compliance with accounting regulations.[189] Arguably, OSCR's wider discretion will enable it to take into account the fiscal consequences of its decisions, although it remains to be seen whether that will be the case.[190] The undoubted difference between the definitions of charity north and south of the border may have been misunderstood or ignored by the Commission, but they were noted to be 'highly undesirable' by the Calman Commission which reviewed the operation and effectiveness of Scottish devolution following the Scotland Act 1998 and saw a single definition, which would require UK primary legislation, as the 'only acceptable solution'.[191]

In England and Wales, generally speaking, trusts for purposes (as opposed to individuals or a class of individuals) are void, save where those purposes are charitable within the English definition of charity.[192] Scottish law, by contrast, recognises trusts for 'public purposes', known as 'public trusts', which do not need to meet the charity test in order to be valid. Public purposes are far broader than charitable purposes, generally encompassing any purposes which are lawful and useful, but excluding any that are illegal or immoral or contrary to public policy.[193]

[186] The omission of such information was conscious even if not deliberate: Minutes/123 (n 110).

[187] See text to n 77 above.

[188] See n 124.

[189] O Breen, P Ford and G Morgan, 'Cross-border Issues in the Regulation of Charities: Experiences from the UK and Ireland' (2009) 11(3) *International Journal of Not-for-Profit Law* 5; see also ch 9.

[190] HMRC's working practice is to take into account whether an organisation is on the Scottish Register (*Memorandum of Understanding* (OSCR/HMRC, March 2008) para 12).

[191] *Serving Scotland Better: Scotland and the United Kingdom in the Twenty-first Century: Final Report* (Calman Commission, June 2009) 5.61. It further recommended that charities should be subject to the reporting and accounting requirements of one regulator only and that cooperation between the regulators should be directed to the detection and sanctioning of fraud and misfeasance.

[192] See text to nn 268–70 (and n 212), ch 2.

[193] See, eg, *McCaig Trustees v Oban Magistrates* 1915 SC 426; P Ford, 'Supervising Charities: A Scottish-civilian Alternative' [2006] *Edinburgh Law Review* 352 (who is critical of the 'half-way house' nature of the charity test and argues that development of Scottish charity law should have been allowed to reflect the inclusive nature of public trusts, with no requirement for purposes to fall within, or be analogous to, lists of purposes (provided tax reliefs are dealt with separately)).

Failure to meet the charity test in Scotland or electing not to be a registered charity does not, therefore, threaten the very validity of a trust for purposes. This is a fundamental distinction between the two jurisdictions which has a significant impact on the question of charitable status being lost and charities being deregistered. It should have featured more prominently in the regulators' collaborations.

Summing up, it is easy to see similarities between the approaches and legal interpretations of OSCR and the Commission, but many of these are entirely inappropriate in view of the differences which exist between the two jurisdictions. The Scottish Parliament, as it was entitled to do, deliberately freed Scottish charity law from English case law and invested its regulator with considerably more authority and discretion. It prescribed a charity test which is more restrictive than both the test for public trusts in Scotland and, at least regarding fee-charging charities, the test of charitable status stipulated by the English Act. The Commission, it seems, paid lip service to those differences and its claim that 'the two sets of legislation … only differ slightly'[194] was quite wrong.

[194] *English and Welsh charities working in Scotland* (Commission, undated) para 7.

8

The Guidance is Challenged: The Upper Tribunal*

The non citation of learned articles or apposite authorities in the Independent Schools Council case was a major hindrance to the secure emergence of an intellectually respectable decision in a case expected to be an authoritative important and defining case.

Hubert Picarda[1]

I. Introduction

Objecting to the emphasis which it perceived had been placed on means-tested bursaries during the Commission's first round of public benefit assessments, the Independent Schools Council (ISC) took steps to challenge the accuracy of the Commission's guidance in judicial review proceedings. At the same time, the Attorney-General lodged a Reference with the Tribunal, which sought clarification of the law specifically in relation to independent schools and public benefit.[2]

Both applications were heard in the Upper Tribunal (Tax and Chancery) (the Tribunal) by Mr Justice Warren, sitting with Judge Alison McKenna, originally President of the Charity Tribunal,[3] and Judge Elizabeth Ovey.[4] The case lasted for a week[5] and seven members of counsel represented the parties and two interveners.[6]

* In this chapter, footnote references to numbers in square brackets are to paragraphs of the judgment in *R (Independent Schools Council) v Charity Commission* (n 7).

[1] H Picarda, '*Thornton v Howe*: A Sound Principle or a Seminal Case Past its Best Buy Date?' (2013–14) 16 *Charity Law & Practice Review* 85, 95.

[2] Pursuant to the Charities Act 1993, s 2A(4)(b), as amended (now 2011 Act, s 326). The Reference sought clarification, but did not overtly *challenge* the guidance.

[3] Judge McKenna was previously employed as an in-house legal adviser to the Commission (1997–2002). As a partner at Wilsons (solicitors), she also represented Salisbury NHS Foundation Trust in an unsuccessful application for registration by Odstock Private Care Ltd (September 2007).

[4] A barrister in Radcliffe Chambers, who describes her practice as incorporating 'a hint of charity': www.radcliffechambers.com/barrister-profile/elizabeth-ovey/overview.

[5] 17–24 May 2011.

[6] Apart from the ISC, the Commission and the Attorney-General, the Education Review Group and the National Council of Voluntary Organisations were admitted as interveners in the judicial review proceedings and permitted to make representations in respect of the Reference: [9] [10].

The Court's decision, published in October 2011,[7] gave no outright triumph to either the ISC or the Commission but was welcomed by both. Whilst the Commission was able to celebrate the Tribunal's confirmation of its interpretation of the law on the 'key issues',[8] the fact that the Tribunal also criticised aspects of the Commission's legal interpretation, together with its assurance of some relief to the ISC, meant that the challenger was able to claim victory.[9]

The questions posed by the Attorney-General's Reference covered multiple scenarios involving a number of hypothetical independent schools, each varying in the type or amount of financial and non-financial assistance offered and in the descriptions of their purposes.[10] In each case, the Attorney-General asked the Tribunal whether the school was 'operating for the public benefit' within charity law, a question which itself has been seen to be possibly misguided.[11] It is unfortunate that the questions were not rejected on this basis and one wonders whether their being drawn in those terms may have influenced the Tribunal's thinking.[12] The Tribunal declined to answer each question categorically, saying that each 'real case' would depend on its factual circumstances and that many factors would need to be taken into account, including the school's business plan and class sizes, so that a school in Hackney would be likely to be treated differently from a school in Guildford, for example.[13] Nonetheless, in answering them so far as it was able, the Tribunal attempted to show what principles might be relevant in considering how the duty on trustees (which it described) to operate for the public benefit should be performed. It is in this respect that the answers to the Attorney-General's questions (which appear separately in the penultimate section of the decision) will be drawn from here in considering the decision as a whole.[14]

The case was hugely significant and expectations were high that it would bring much needed clarity to the law. It was disappointing, therefore, that the decision ran to 116 pages, lacked any clear summary and demanded careful study in order to establish quite what was decided. After reviewing the Tribunal's consideration of case law, this chapter will suggest an analysis of the decision which identifies, and critically examines, the four key elements on which it appears to be based. It will also consider the Tribunal's application of those elements and question the decision's legal justification.

[7] *R (Independent Schools Council) v Charity Commission* [2011] UKUT 421 (TCC), [2012] Ch 214.

[8] In a press release which is no longer available on the Commission's website, but reproduced at: www.hillingdonconnected.org.uk/news/charity-commission-statement.

[9] [236]; see, eg, the ISC's press release (14 October 2011): www.isc.co.uk/press/press-releases/2011/2011-10-14.

[10] The various permutations within the questions posed offered over 50 scenarios.

[11] See chs 3 and 5. Asking whether the public benefit requirement was met in each scenario would have been more pertinent to the issues raised by the 2006 Act perhaps (although it cannot be assumed that the answers would have been materially different).

[12] P Luxton, 'Opening Pandora's Box: The Upper Tribunal's Decision on Public Benefit and Independent Schools' (2012–13) 15 *Charity Law & Practice Review* 27, 49–50.

[13] [243].

[14] [237]–[258]; see part IV, (3) and (4), below.

II. The Decision in Summary

Despite noting two 'senses' of public benefit, the decision betrays a third sense, which imports a test of social benefit akin to the Commission's interpretation and which is significantly closer to the popular meaning of charity than the legal or technical meaning repeatedly emphasised in case law and acknowledged by the Tribunal.[15] And although the Tribunal purported to confine its considerations to independent schools and Principles 2b and 2c,[16] its comments were far broader and the impact of the judgment more far-reaching, as will be seen below.

In summary,[17] the Tribunal ruled that an independent school, which provides a mainstream education, may be a charitable institution, unless either its constitution expressly excludes those who cannot afford the fees which it charges or, in the absence of such an express exclusion, where it appears to be capable of operating only by charging full fees. Furthermore, trustees owe a duty to operate in a way which is for the public benefit and, in this context, the term 'public benefit' is used to denote social benefit. The fulfilment of this duty is an implicit, if not explicit, part of the school's objects, but the nature and extent of provision for those who are unable to afford the fees and the wider community, whilst being more than tokenistic, is a matter for the trustees' discretion and the proper exercise of their powers, and is neither subject to a test of reasonableness nor a matter for the courts or the Commission. Thus, whilst the existence of a duty to provide social benefit received the endorsement of the Tribunal, there appears to have been a desire both to curtail the role of the Commission in policing the performance of that duty and to separate questions of charitable status on the one hand and trustees' duties on the other.

Confining its deliberations to educational charities only,[18] the Tribunal declared Principles 2b (in relation to fees only) and, 'at least as explained in the Guidance', 2c to be 'wrong'[19] and ordered the parties to agree what relief should be afforded to the ISC.[20] It was clear, however, that the guidance needed to be corrected. And although the Tribunal did express some sympathy with the difficult task the Commission had faced,[21] it was not prepared to accept the Commission's suggestion that it should simply declare the Commission to have taken a reasonable view of the law, in framing the guidance as it did, and leave it to the Commission to amend or withdraw parts as it (the Commission) saw fit. The parties failed to reach any agreement as to relief, however, and a further decision was published

[15] [14].

[16] [15], [225], [235].

[17] Various qualifications to this summary are noted below.

[18] [15]; also noting that the extent of fiscal advantages had no bearing on the decision [34], this being for 'Parliament to grapple with' [260].

[19] [235].

[20] [236].

[21] ibid.

on 2 December 2011, declaring that the relevant parts of the guidance would be quashed, unless withdrawn by the Commission.[22] The Commission subsequently withdrew the affected parts (including the whole of the specific guidance for fee-charging charities) on 21 December 2011, thereby further extending the impact of the court proceedings beyond educational charities.[23]

III. The Tribunal's Analysis of Authorities

> *The Tribunal must decide as a matter of fact whether the class with which we are concerned—those able to afford to pay school fees—is a sufficient section of the community. There is no authority which binds us in this regard.*
>
> The Tribunal[24]

The Tribunal concluded that there was no binding authority either on the question of whether a class of those able to afford the fees charged by an independent school constituted a sufficient section of the public,[25] or on the question of whether the poor should be included, or not excluded.[26] And although it explained that there was no precedent value in an earlier decision which was reached either by applying a presumption or after failing to address, or assuming, a point of law,[27] it did not actually reject any cases on this basis.[28] It did not, for example, suggest that the legal precedent value of cases such as *Attorney-General v Earl of Lonsdale*,[29] *R v Special Commissioners of Income Tax ex p University College of North Wales*,[30] *Brighton College v Marriott*,[31] or *Abbey Malvern Wells Ltd v Ministry of Local Government and Planning*[32] should be doubted or denied.[33]

(1) Educational Cases

The Tribunal referred to a number of the nineteenth century cases concerned with the admission of fee-paying boarders in addition to non-paying pupils. Not

[22] *ISC v Charity Commission* TCC-JR/03/2010, available at: www.bailii.org/uk/cases/UKUT/TCC/2011/B27.html.

[23] Until the revised publications in 2013, the 2008 general guidance (*Charities and Public Benefit* (Commission, January 2008)) remained accessible online but with appropriate markers inserted to show that the relevant parts had been withdrawn. The sector-specific guidance (in respect of poverty, religion and education) remains accessible in this way pending replacement.

[24] [89].

[25] ibid.

[26] [178].

[27] [92].

[28] Although it sometimes raised questions (eg, see text to nn 100–01 below).

[29] *AG v Earl of Lonsdale* (1827) 1 Sim 105, 57 ER 518.

[30] *R v Special Commissioners of Income Tax ex p University College of North Wales* (1909) 78 LJKB 576 (CA).

[31] *Brighton College v Marriott* [1926] AC 192 (HL).

[32] *Abbey Malvern Wells Ltd v Ministry of Local Government and Planning* [1951] Ch 728 (Ch).

[33] These cases were considered in ch 4.

surprisingly, none of the cases involved an express exclusion of the poor,[34] nor was charitable status challenged (as the Tribunal acknowledged).[35] In *Attorney-General v Earl of Clarendon*, for example, it had been alleged that the admission of fee-paying boarders had rendered it 'impossible for such poor children to remain' and many were reported to have left as a result.[36] The Tribunal appeared content to note that 'it was not suggested that the poor were excluded', apparently confining its attention to the absence of any express exclusion of the poor and disregarding those arguments which had suggested that the poor were being excluded in practice.[37]

Likewise, commenting that *Attorney-General v Earl of Stamford*[38] shed 'little light on the question whether an educational institution the purposes of which exclude the poor can be charitable',[39] the Tribunal appeared to ignore the arguments in that case that the education provided had been 'adapted almost exclusively for the wealthier classes', with the implication that the poor were being excluded or that their educational needs were not being met in practice.[40] The observation that the case had suggested that 'there ought to be some limit on the number of fee-paying boarders' also risked giving a misleading impression.[41] The reference to the Master in that case, as to whether restrictions or limitations on boarders ought to be imposed, was not concerned with their number, but with their eligibility to participate in exhibitions and to benefit from the charitable funds.[42] Nor was it made 'in the light of inconclusive evidence' of possible partiality being shown to boarders in the award of exhibitions.[43] In fact, Lord Lyndhurst was satisfied that there was no such evidence, the greater proportion of awards to boarders having been entirely expected.[44]

[34] But fee-paying boarders were considered to have been excluded by the founder in *AG v Earl of Devon* (1846) 15 Sim 193, 60 ER 591.

[35] [122], [117].

[36] *AG v Earl of Clarendon* (1810) 17 Ves Jr 491, 493; 34 ER 190, 191.

[37] [117].

[38] *AG v Earl of Stamford* (1842) 1 Ph 737, 41 ER 812.

[39] [120].

[40] *Stamford* (n 38) 743/815 (it being argued before the Master that instruction in Latin, for example, was 'wholly unnecessary and useless' for those not destined for the learned professions (reported at (1849) 16 Sim 453, 460; 60 ER 950, 953 but not referred to by the Tribunal)). The school's charitable status was not questioned.

[41] [120].

[42] *Stamford* (n 38) 760/822. This was the matter on which Lord Cottenham and Lord Lyndhurst had disagreed ([119]). It is worth noting that the Attorney-General opposed any restriction on the number of boarders (as a matter of regulation as opposed to what was practicable), but a restriction was imposed in order to avoid interference with the performance of the school masters' duties ((1849) 16 Sim 453, 465; 60 ER 950, 954). In fact, boarders were later excluded altogether on the basis that Lord Lyndhurst had mistakenly understood their admission to have been made lawfully (ibid, 472/957), but then admitted again in the *Manchester School Case* (1866–67) LR 2 Ch App 497 (CA). (Interestingly, in *Earl of Clarendon* a reduction in the number of 'foreigners' was refused on the basis that any reduction would not remove the alleged evil in any event ((n 36) 502/195).)

[43] [119].

[44] *Stamford* (n 38) 759/821. The matter was not argued before the Master ((1849) 16 Sim 453, 466; 60 ER 950, 955).

The Tribunal commented that the cases of *Attorney-General v Earl of Devon*[45] and *Attorney-General v Bishop of Worcester*[46] 'illustrate the need for caution in approaching decisions based on an understanding of social and class structure and what promotes the welfare of society as a whole and of classes within it'.[47] It failed, however, to make the more significant point that the decisions in these cases (as with other cases of this type) were in fact based on the construction of the specific statutes of the schools involved, something which the courts had been keen to emphasise.[48]

The Tribunal concluded that *Lonsdale*[49] did no more than illustrate the proposition that not all beneficiaries must be poor.[50] On the basis that 'a gentleman may be poor',[51] it rejected the suggestion that a school 'for the sons of gentlemen' excluded the poor by implication. Whilst it might, literally, be correct that a poor gentleman might exist, the Tribunal should, perhaps, have considered the significance of the judge's failure to suggest that any qualification might be appropriate (if that were the case), in order to ensure that the sons of some poor gentlemen were included.[52] The Tribunal also dismissed the case on the basis that not all, or perhaps none, of the prospective pupils were to be charged fees covering the *full* cost of the education.[53] In fact, it seems likely that no fees were charged at all, the wording of the indentures suggesting that all costs were to be met by the testator's provision.[54] If the Tribunal considered that some fees were payable, however, it might have given greater consideration to how the case demonstrated, or satisfied, any legal principle that the poor should be included. Likewise, although the case report does not make clear the specific grounds on which a school for the sons of gentlemen might not be 'in popular language, a charity', the unambiguous assertion that, nonetheless, 'all schools of learning are so to be considered' tends to suggest that the Court regarded the reason for such an objection as immaterial in any event.[55]

With regard to *University College of North Wales*, the Tribunal suggested that the Court of Appeal rejected only the proposition that all beneficiaries should

[45] *Devon* (n 34).

[46] *AG v Bishop of Worcester* (1851) 9 Hare 328, 68 ER 530.

[47] [121].

[48] *Devon* (n 34) 608/236; *Worcester* (n 46) 363/548.

[49] *Lonsdale* (n 29).

[50] [118].

[51] ibid.

[52] The judge was the Vice-Chancellor, Sir John Leach; see too *Clarendon*, where the fee-paying boarders complained of were described as 'chiefly the sons of the nobility and gentry of this kingdom' ((n 36) 493/191).

[53] [118].

[54] An account of the testator's life described its liberal endowment (see ch 4, n 28); it was also described as a free school (although that term does not necessarily suggest that no charges at all were made: *Worcester* (n 46) 358/545 and see text to n 22, ch 4).

[55] *Lonsdale* (n 29) 109/250; the potential wealth of the sons of gentlemen must surely be a likely ground.

be poor,[56] whereas the Court in that case went further than this and rejected the much broader proposition which had been argued, that the means of the beneficiary should be taken into account in education cases.[57] If the pupils' means are irrelevant, it follows that all might be rich and/or able to afford the fees, but the Court made no qualification in rejecting the argument. The Tribunal's assertion that it was 'tolerably clear' that the Court contemplated the poor being included is not reflected in the case reports,[58] but, even if that were the case, and if the Tribunal's interpretation is to be supported, one might have expected the Court to have expressed some concern, or qualification, to ensure that it should remain the case.

The school in *Abbey Malvern Wells* contained no express or implied exclusion on the terms,[59] and so the Tribunal's conclusion that it is 'not a decision on the issue of the express exclusion of the poor' is unquestionably correct.[60] To say that the case was 'not concerned *in any way* with exclusion of the poor' (emphasis added),[61] however, ignores the implications of the substantial fees which could be charged (and were noted to have been charged at all material times), with the necessary consequence that the poor were excluded in practice.[62] Significantly, and despite the lack of any evidence that fees were reduced or waived in any circumstances, the Tribunal did accept that the 'charging of substantial fees in practice and at least as a general rule' did *not* mean that the school could not be charitable.[63]

The Tribunal supposed that the Ministry had argued, or that the Court had understood it to have argued, that all fees had to be reduced or waived. Undoubtedly this is correct, his Lordship summarising counsel's submission as being that an education could not be charitable 'unless … for persons who pay less than the full value of the services which they receive'.[64] The Tribunal appeared to suggest that the Court would not so emphatically have rejected an alternative argument that only some of the fees should be reduced or waived. The emphatic rejection of counsel's submissions, however, can be construed to mean that payment of 'full value',[65] by all pupils, *would* be acceptable, subject of course to no profits being applied other than to the educational purposes, but, once again, the Tribunal omitted to comment on the absence of any direction or enquiry as to social benefit being provided.

Although not suggesting that Danckwerts J was wrong to rely on *Lonsdale* in indicating that a school need not be a free school in order to be charitable,[66]

[56] [131].
[57] *North Wales* (n 30) 578/413.
[58] [129] (although the report in Tax Cases contains a closing comment by counsel, that any compunction felt over the tax exemption allowed by the judgment might be negatived by the fact that 'really poor scholars attend this college' (n 30) 417)).
[59] *Abbey* (n 32).
[60] [144].
[61] ibid.
[62] *Abbey* (n 32) 732. The Tribunal did not consider *Brighton College* (n 31).
[63] [144].
[64] *Abbey* (n 32) 737.
[65] Or 'full fees' (Upjohn KC, counsel for the school (*Abbey* (n 32) 735)).
[66] *Lonsdale* (n 29).

the Tribunal appeared to suggest that his Lordship had wrongly relied on that case to support his further proposition that 'all schools of learning are charities unless they are profit-making ventures'.[67] That proposition, however, had sufficient standing, and was intended to stand, on the strength of the Preamble, which referred both to free schools *and* schools of learning.[68] The Tribunal did not declare the proposition itself to be wrong, even though that would appear to be implicit in its decision. The issue of profit-making was central to *Abbey Malvern Wells*, because the company had power to make profits and to distribute dividends, but the Court held that the trust deed, which required the shares to be held on trust for the benefit of the school (and for dividends to be applied to the school's purposes) meant that charitable status was not denied.[69] Nor is there any suggestion that the decision in *Lonsdale* was wrong on the facts, or that Danckwerts J held the Abbey School to be charitable because he understood *Lonsdale* to have held an exclusion on the terms to have been charitable.

The Tribunal described *Inland Revenue Commissioners v Educational Grants Association*[70] as not 'entirely easy', but its premise, that the association's objects were 'wholly charitable' may go too far.[71] The company in this case had objects of providing grants for education, but without making it clear to what extent it was intended that children of the company's employees should benefit. The charitable status of the company, and whether its purposes were wholly charitable, had been conceded by the Crown and so was not in issue before the Court, but it was also clearly doubted by each of their Lordships nonetheless, albeit on diverse grounds.[72] The weakness of the premise makes questionable the conclusion drawn from it, namely that the company had to 'operate … for the public benefit'.[73] The Court was unable to say that the monies had been applied for exclusively charitable purposes (so as to qualify for a tax exemption under the relevant legislation) because too great a proportion had been applied to children of the company's employees, and they represented beneficiaries joined by a contractual nexus of employment. The case may not be easy, but the decision was based on the relationship between the recipients of the grants and not a failure to offer sufficient grants to the poor or less wealthy. If the stated purposes had been charitable, as was conceded, this would have pointed to a matter of breach, but their Lordships declined to say that the grant-making decisions had been ultra vires and the point was not in issue.

[67] [144].

[68] 'Schools of learning, free schools, and scholars in universities' having been interpreted disjunctively (referring to the Preamble to the Statute of Charitable Uses Act (1601) 43 Eliz 1 c 4).

[69] *Abbey* (n 32).

[70] *IRC v Educational Grants Association Ltd* [1967] Ch 993 (CA).

[71] [154].

[72] *Educational Grants* (n 70) 1008, 1013 and 1015.

[73] [154a] (and quite apart from any argument that such a proposition, with the intended meaning of social benefit, is flawed in any event); the conclusion at [154b] is flawed for the same reason. The Tribunal actually identified the nub of the problem [para 154c], suggesting that the tax exemption conceded in the case was probably wrong.

(2) Non-Educational Cases

Despite confining its deliberations to educational cases,[74] and despite warning against applying legal principles from one head of charity to another,[75] the Tribunal did not hesitate to consider cases involving non-educational charities, placing particular reliance on *Re Resch*, the Privy Council decision (having persuasive authority only) which found a fee-charging hospital in Australia to be charitable, notwithstanding the high fees that were charged.[76]

The Tribunal described *Jones v Williams*[77] as the 'foundation stone of the Commission's argument that poor people must not be excluded',[78] but seemed to attach no significance to it itself, apparently content to conclude that the House of Lords' reference to the case in *Goodman v Saltash*[79] did no more than indicate that a class need not be confined to the poor.[80] A closer analysis might have been expected, however, especially in light of the Tribunal's acknowledgement that the freemen of Saltash, who enjoyed the privilege of removing oysters from a fishery, were the sole beneficiaries, and probably 'not among the poorest members of the community'.[81] The Tribunal's refusal to 'draw any further inferences' about their relative wealth or poverty also suggests a reluctance to address the decision's significance in terms of the poor having been excluded in practice during the 200 year period of use which gave rise to the trust.

Likewise, the case of *Verge v Somerville*,[82] where a residuary estate was bequeathed for the repatriation of New South Wales soldiers, was said to be limited to illustrating the principle that a trust need not be administered solely for the poor.[83] Commenting that the case 'expressly put to one side the question of the charitable nature of a purpose which excludes the poor', however, the Tribunal ignored the extensive consideration which Lord Wrenbury gave to the relevance of poverty in that case, and the implications of his Lordship's conclusion that education and religion require no qualification of poverty.[84]

The Tribunal examined the words of Lord Macnaghten in *Special Commissioners of Income Tax v Pemsel*, concerning charity incidentally benefiting the rich as well

[74] See n 16 above.

[75] [15], [45] and [212].

[76] *Re Resch* [1969] 1 AC 514 (PC); see text to nn 105–12 below. It will be remembered that Lord Wilberforce said that the provision of medical facilities was not deprived of charitable status 'merely because by reason of expense they could *only* be made use of by persons of some means' (emphasis added) (at 544).

[77] *Jones v Williams* (1767) Amb 651, 27 ER 422.

[78] [124].

[79] *Goodman v Saltash* (1881–82) LR 7 App Cas 633 (HL).

[80] The '*Jones v Williams* line' appearing to mean only that both rich and poor might be included: [124].

[81] [124]; see text to nn 79–82, ch 4.

[82] *Verge v Somerville* [1924] AC 496 (PC).

[83] [134].

[84] *Verge* (n 82) 500–04 (see ch 4, text to n 7 ff).

as the poor.[85] It suggested that the effect of this dictum was that any charity must be 'capable, at least, of benefiting the poor as well as the rich', but acknowledged that the poor might benefit only 'indirectly' and that the meaning of 'indirectly' was unclear.[86] As a result, the case offers little authority for a principle that the poor should be included, or even not excluded, and the Tribunal did not attempt to suggest otherwise.

The Tribunal also identified a consensus in the three judgments in *Re Macduff*, that a trust for a purpose 'confined to those above a certain income level', so that the poor are excluded, could not be charitable.[87] Although interpreting the case more widely than was indicated in chapter four, and without questioning whether the restriction might be reasonable on objective grounds or the purpose non-charitable for some other reason, it is worth noting that the Tribunal did not suggest that the principle should be applied other than in the case of an express exclusion on the terms.[88]

Its suggestion that *Davies v Perpetual Trustee Co Ltd*[89] supports the view that there must be 'some link between any qualifying characteristic and the educational need' is misleading if and to the extent that it suggests that a positive link must be established.[90] It will be recalled that the Privy Council declared non-charitable a trust for the establishment of a college for the youth of Presbyterians in New South Wales who could establish a certain line of descent from the North of Ireland. The fact that certain class-defining characteristics may render a trust for the specified class *non*-charitable, however, does not justify a stipulation that other defining characteristics, whether evidencing some other link or otherwise, need positively to be shown. It is also worth noting that the particular eligibility criteria in this case, which were described as 'somewhat capricious' and 'in some respects wholly irrelevant', relied principally on a personal nexus, which is a well-established disqualifying factor.[91]

The Tribunal suggested that the statements which the House of Lords had made about charging fees, in *Scottish Cremation and Burial Society Ltd v Glasgow Corporation*,[92] should be 'treated with some circumspection', on the basis that it

[85] *Special Commissioners of Income Tax v Pemsel* [1891] AC 531 (HL) 542, where his Lordship talked of trusts within the fourth head of charity being 'not the less charitable in the eye of the law, because incidentally they benefit the rich as well as the poor, as indeed, every charity that deserves the name must do either directly or indirectly' (ibid, 583); see text to nn 41–43, ch 4.

[86] [126].

[87] *Re Macduff* [1896] 2 Ch 451 (CA) (although it is doubtful whether that makes the dicta any less obiter: [128]).

[88] [128]; see also text to nn 89–104, ch 4. Regrettably there is no explanation of the suggestion that the level at which those above it would exclude the poor might depend on 'the purposes of charity law as applied to the relevant purpose'.

[89] *Davies v Perpetual Trustee Co Ltd* [1959] AC 439 (PC).

[90] [147].

[91] *Davies* (n 89) 456; see too ch 2, part III, Principle G.

[92] *Scottish Cremation and Burial Reform Society Ltd v Glasgow Corporation* [1968] AC 138 (HL) (essentially statements to the effect that charitable character is unaffected by fee-charging where the charity provides services and not financial relief).

was not argued in that case either that charging should affect charitable status, or that the poor were excluded.[93] That neither argument was heard is not in doubt, but it is regrettable that the Tribunal failed to assess the significance and implications of their Lordships having so emphatically affirmed the parties' consensus that charitable status was not lost because of fees being charged.[94] Circumspection was also urged on the basis that the fees were not 'high fees', as that term was used in the Commission's guidance, but this would seem to attach a significance to the very thing the accuracy of which the Tribunal was being asked to judge.[95]

Although it described *Perpetual Trustee Co v St Luke's Hospital*[96] as establishing that a hospital is not denied charitable status because it admits no patients who pay no fees,[97] the Tribunal emphasised that that was not to say that a hospital 'which charges full fees for all of its patients (*and is required to do so by its constitution*) is charitable' (emphasis added).[98] There was no such requirement in the hospital's constitution, but by adding the words in parenthesis, the Tribunal limited the significance of the case to express exclusions only and ignored the significant impact of the case without those words. Its 'reasonable' conclusion that a token provision for those unable to afford the fees would not be sufficient to satisfy the public benefit requirement, 'if otherwise it was not satisfied', tells us little.[99] It might indicate, for example, that such provision is not sufficient if the class is personally selected or if the institution is intended to make a profit, but that is not contested in any event. It does not tell us whether it would be sufficient in the absence of such disqualifying factors, or indeed whether, and if so how much, provision is a necessary part of meeting the requirement.

The Tribunal comments that the judge in *Joseph Rowntree Memorial Trust v Attorney-General*[100] did not address the fact that the financial commitment necessary to purchase a lease necessarily restricted the class of potential beneficiaries, and yet such a result was inevitable.[101] The reasoning is not entirely clear, but the Tribunal appeared to suggest that charging fees to cover the whole cost was acceptable, provided the poor were not excluded, although that would appear to beg the question (unless limited entirely to express exclusions). It also acknowledged that neither the need to pay full price for a leasehold interest, nor (in relation to Scheme 3) the absence of any restriction to people 'of modest means', was inconsistent with charitable status.[102] It seems that the Tribunal reconciled Scheme 3

[93] [157].

[94] There is no suggestion that the concession was wrong in this case (*cf Educational Grants* (n 70); text to n 72 above).

[95] [157] (not being fees unaffordable to the 'vast majority').

[96] *Perpetual Trustee Co v St Luke's Hospital* (1939) 39 SR (NSW) 408 (SC, NSW).

[97] 'in [Lord Wilberforce's] view', although there appears to be no suggestion that the Tribunal did not share that view; [161].

[98] ibid.

[99] [165].

[100] *Joseph Rowntree Memorial Trust v AG* [1983] Ch 159 (Ch).

[101] [170].

[102] [172].

with its proposition that the poor cannot be excluded, by saying that although beneficiaries were not restricted to persons of modest means, the scheme was nonetheless open to them, but it failed to address how it was 'open to persons of modest means' to afford the accommodation at the prices charged.[103] And although reliance appears to have been placed on the lack of similar services on the open market, and the particular needs being relieved, the failure to address the potential for the charges in practice to exclude the poor is disappointing.[104]

The Tribunal admitted that clear principles are not easily derived from *Resch*.[105] Accepting that the case makes it permissible to levy charges so that only persons 'of some means' can enjoy the services provided, the Tribunal rejected the interpretation of the expression 'some means' as 'in the sense of "substantial means"' and interpreted it, rather, as 'of means sufficient to pay moderate charges',[106] despite the fact that the fees were not described as 'moderate' in the case, but rather as 'not low', 'high', 'substantial' and 'expensive'.[107] The expression 'persons of some means', in this context, surely signified persons with means substantially greater than 'moderate'. Although its observation that 'the service was open to all'[108] may have disregarded Lord Wilberforce's important proviso 'so far as its nature permits',[109] the Tribunal did accept that references to the poor being excluded in this and other cases appeared to be limited to express exclusions.[110] In addition, the Tribunal's deduction that 'some element of subsidy' was 'by no means rare' appears to be based on a sense that there is no smoke without fire: in this case, a conclusion reached by the judge at first instance and said to be 'without basis', that more than half of the patients were accommodated at less than full cost.[111] Nor is it clear what 'element of subsidy' the Tribunal understood had been made, except that it must have been more than negligible, nor how reliable from year to year it was considered to be.[112]

It is hard to avoid the conclusion that the Tribunal's 'lengthy review' of what it saw as 'diverse, and often irreconcilable, case law' lacked the sort of detailed analysis that might have been expected and which was surely merited.[113] Nor did it consider any academic commentaries. Seeming to prefer to ignore the significance of case law which touches on implied exclusions on the terms and implied exclusions in practice, the Tribunal confined its deliberations and conclusions to questions of the potential beneficiaries not being confined to the poor and to the poor being expressly excluded on the terms. Much more was needed.

[103] ibid.
[104] [171].
[105] *Resch* (n 76); [162].
[106] [162].
[107] *Resch* (n 76) 544.
[108] [163].
[109] *Resch* (n 76) 544.
[110] [162].
[111] [165].
[112] [164], [165].
[113] [13].

IV. The Four Elements of the Ruling

We have explained the principles as best we can and must leave to others the difficult task of applying them.

The Tribunal[114]

The Tribunal identified the central issues as both constitutional and operational, that is to say concerned with each of charitable status and trustees' duties, a vital distinction which had not been made adequately by the Commission.[115] Four key elements appear to form the basis of the decision:

(i) public benefit in the first sense;
(ii) public benefit in the second sense;
(iii) the proposition that a charity may not exclude the poor;
(iv) a duty to carry out the charity's purposes in a way which is for the public benefit.

The first two elements relate to charitable status only. It will be seen that the fourth element (and therefore the third on which it was based), although ostensibly relating to trustees' duties, may nonetheless also impact on charitable status, the performance of the duty being described as an implicit (if not explicit) part of a school's objects (on which charitable status depends).

(1) Public Benefit in the First Sense

The Tribunal explained that the common law meaning of 'public benefit', expressly preserved by the 2006 Act, had two aspects, or 'senses',[116] which had come to be identified as separate elements.[117] The first of these was that the nature of the purpose should be beneficial.

Whilst recognising that not *all* educational purposes are necessarily charitable,[118] the Tribunal nonetheless confirmed that the educational purposes of mainstream independent schools should be regarded as being for the public benefit in the first sense,[119] a conclusion which it reached as a 'finding of fact', not based on a presumption and without the need for judicial evidence.[120] It rejected arguments raised by the Education Review Group (ERG), an intervener in the proceedings, that the independent schools sector causes social divisiveness and obstructs social mobility.[121] Distinguishing *National Anti-Vivisection Society v Inland Revenue*

114 [224].
115 [13].
116 [44].
117 [51].
118 [49], [52]; although the example of a 'cloistered' school would appear to fail public benefit in the second sense rather than the first ([49b] *cf* [50]).
119 [94]; see too [69], [113].
120 [95].
121 [108].

Commissioners,[122] somewhat unconvincingly on the grounds that the alleged disbenefits in this case depended on 'value judgements influenced by social and political agendas',[123] the Tribunal declared that no balancing of the relative benefits and disbenefits of independent education was required.[124] As if embarking on such an exercise, however, it also concluded that ERG's arguments represented 'a manifesto as much as anything',[125] which only began to 'scratch the surface' and came 'nowhere near' establishing the alleged detriment.[126]

(2) Public Benefit in the Second Sense

The second sense of public benefit was said to be 'the real issue' in the proceedings and required the purposes to be directed at the public or a sufficient section of the public.[127] It has been seen that 'sufficiency' in this context is normally expressed by reference to the intended beneficiaries being sufficiently numerous or important and, more clearly, not being defined by a common attribute which is based on a personal relationship or common employment.[128] The Tribunal, however, used the term 'a sufficiently *wide*' section of the public (emphasis added),[129] appearing to suggest a width in terms of the beneficiaries' wealth or class, although if this was the meaning intended, no attempt was made to cite legal authority in support of it. In fact, 'sufficiently wide' *has* appeared in a small number of cases, but apparently only to indicate sufficiency of numbers.[130] The Tribunal was right to point out that the factors of numerical neglibility and personal nexus need not be exhaustive,[131] but if this interpretation was the one intended, its departure from case law should have been acknowledged and explained.

(3) A Trust which Excludes the Poor Cannot be a Charity

Having established that no case actually decided the point,[132] the Tribunal declared that it was 'right in principle' that a trust which excludes the poor cannot be a

[122] *National Anti-Vivisection Society v IRC* [1948] AC 31 (HL).
[123] [107].
[124] [96], [108].
[125] [109].
[126] [108].
[127] [89]; see also [111].
[128] See ch 2, part III, Test 2.
[129] [52], [83].
[130] eg, *Re Compton* [1944] Ch 378 (CA) 387; *Gibson v South American Stores* [1949] Ch 572 (CA) 580; *Re Coulthurst* [1951] Ch 193 (Ch) 196 (counsel for the AG); *Incorporated Council of Law Reporting for England and Wales v AG* [1972] Ch 73 (CA) 95, where a section of the public comprising judges and other legal professionals was described as 'sufficiently wide' (*and* 'sufficiently large'). (If this had been in consideration of class and wealth rather than numbers, the conclusion that the class was sufficient would seem questionable.)
[131] [141], the Tribunal concluding that it could not be said that a numerous class with no personal nexus *was* charitable (based on its analysis of *Compton* (n 130) and *Oppenheim v Tobacco Securities Trust Co Ltd* [1951] AC 297 (HL)).
[132] [178]; see also [89].

charity.[133] This was attributed to the 'underlying concept of charity from early times', but that concept was not explained.[134] It is assumed that it alludes to the significance of the relief of poverty, but whether all charity should, therefore, involve relief of poverty is itself the critical question and worthy of far greater investigation than this proposition implies.[135] It was also said to accord with judicial dicta to that effect, although, as noted above, the Tribunal had already acknowledged that the 'principal (if not exclusive) focus' of those dicta was on the *express* exclusion of the poor.[136] The Tribunal did add 'and, possibly as a matter of the policies adopted', but any such possibility was neither supported by authority nor posited with any apparent conviction.[137]

It has already been suggested that it might be legitimate to deny charitable status on the grounds of public policy where the constitution expressly excludes the poor and that is the case whatever the level of fees charged, or indeed whether fees are charged at all.[138] The Tribunal, however, applied this principle (that a trust which excludes the poor cannot be charitable) where there was no express exclusion and, like the Commission, also appeared to equate an obligation *not to exclude* the poor with a positive obligation *to include* the poor,[139] despite its acknowledgement that there is no authority even for the first proposition.[140] For reasons already explained, this is not a legitimate way of expressing the negative obligation.[141] And even if, in the absence of authority to the contrary, it were morally or logically legitimate to extend a principle that the poor should not be excluded expressly to one that the poor should not be excluded impliedly, it was not legitimate to do so, as a matter of law, without some clear legal rationale where there *was* judicial authority which affirmed charitable status notwithstanding implied exclusions on the terms and in practice.

Rich and Poor

The Tribunal defined 'rich' and 'poor' in two potentially conflicting ways: first, by reference to affordability and second, by reference to degrees of wealth. Thus, the 'rich' were defined as those who can afford the fees charged, although the position of people who make 'considerable sacrifices' in order to do so was not clear.[142] The 'poor' were defined as those who cannot *reasonably* do so, but there

133 [178].

134 ibid.

135 See also the 2 December decision (n 22) [4].

136 [162] (and its review of authorities appears to be limited in this way). As suggested in ch 4, however, the dicta appear to be *solely* limited to express exclusions.

137 ibid; and should be limited, in the writer's view, to deliberate policies to exclude the poor and not applied to policies based on financial imperative; see too [187].

138 See ch 4, p 98.

139 [112].

140 [89].

141 See ch 5, part III (first para).

142 [40].

was no indication of how reasonableness was to be measured in this context.[143] The Tribunal placed reliance on a 'well-established principle' that 'poor' does not mean destitute '*even in* the context of a trust for the relief of poverty' (emphasis added),[144] but failed to acknowledge that it is *only* where purposes comprise the relief of poverty, or where the terms specify a level of wealth,[145] that the courts have been concerned with the precise level of the intended beneficiaries' wealth and whether that level represents a state of poverty.[146]

At the same time, the Tribunal engaged in a different, and more complex, formulation of 'rich' and 'poor', based on descriptions of wealth rather than the affordability of the fees charged. Clearly influenced by cases concerning relief of poverty, where trusts for beneficiaries who are not poor in the normal sense have been held to be charitable, the Tribunal explained that 'the poor' may include persons of 'modest means',[147] those of 'some means',[148] or even persons who are 'quite well-off'.[149] On the other hand, the 'not-so-well-off', who are unable to afford the *complete* fees, appeared not to be 'poor',[150] although someone who could afford 25 per cent of a £12,500 per annum fee might be 'poor'.[151] It was also noted (in parenthesis and without further explanation) that the meaning of 'the poor' may vary across the different heads of charity.[152]

The two approaches do not appear to be entirely compatible. The first is simpler to apply, but means that someone able to afford £90,000 of a £100,000 fee would not be 'rich' but 'poor', assuming he could not reasonably be expected to afford more. The second offers more subtle usage, but is more difficult to interpret and to apply with any degree of consistency.[153] The Tribunal recognised 'the problem', but was never going to remove or solve it by providing an additional, and contradictory, way of defining 'rich' and 'poor' in an attempt to clarify 'the subgroup of those who are unable to pay fees', to whom it believed the Commission had intended to refer.[154] The consequence of the courts' expansive interpretation

[143] ibid (although the decision is not always consistent: see, eg, [233] where it is said that bursaries may be given to persons 'who are not poor but are unable to pay fees' (if the intention was to use the word colloquially, this should have been spelt out perhaps)).

[144] [40].

[145] eg, *Re Clarke* [1923] 2 Ch 407 (Ch) (care for persons 'of moderate means such as clerks, governesses and others', reviewed by the Tribunal, but without consideration of how 'well-off' clerks and governesses were [132]).

[146] See text to nn 14–17, ch 4.

[147] [179]; a reference to *Clarke* (n 145) (although it should be noted that the term 'moderate means' was express in that case).

[148] Referring to *Resch* (n 76), 528, 544.

[149] [179]; a reference to *Joseph Rowntree* (n 100), although the Tribunal did not consider (and neither did the Court in that case) quite how wealthy that made the beneficiaries; see also [173].

[150] [217].

[151] [255].

[152] [40].

[153] Unlikely to be called someone of 'modest means', he might, of course, be considered to be 'quite well off' and, therefore 'poor' (n 149), but is there not a danger that the word begins to lose all sensible meaning (*cf* [14])?

[154] [229].

of 'the poor' in cases on the relief of poverty was to enlarge the scope of charity. Adopting that same expansive interpretation in defining those who cannot be excluded, however, has the opposite effect.

(4) Trustees Owe a Duty to Carry Out the Purposes in a Way which is for the Public Benefit

The Tribunal concluded that trustees' duties were not changed by the 2006 Act[155] and that a charity had always been obliged to operate 'in accordance with its objects and subject to the constraints of charity law'.[156] Undoubtedly so. The Tribunal's further conclusion, however, that these obligations included a duty to 'operate in a way which was for the public benefit' (the Duty),[157] meaning to make 'adequate provision other than the provision of education to fee-paying students',[158] is doubtful. Despite the Duty's alleged longevity, the Tribunal cited no relevant legal authority in support of this view. And although not explicitly stated, it seems that the Duty may not apply unless the fees are 'high' or affordable only by those who are wealthier than the 'quite well-off'.

Standard of the Duty: Adequate Provision

Putting the absence of judicial authority to one side, one is left with the difficulty of understanding what is 'adequate' for these purposes. The Tribunal seemed to have the same difficulty as the Commission in providing any meaningful guidance to trustees of fee-charging charities as to how they should make adequate provision in discharge of their Duty, but the Tribunal's answers to the Attorney-General's questions (posed in the Reference) make some attempt.[159]

An endowed school 'might be expected to provide more', for example, but it cannot be said how much more, nor how much, is 'enough' and providing expensive services for as low a cost as possible would seem to be inadequate.[160] A specialist music school might have a lower threshold, apparently on the basis that it is more expensive to run and because it fulfils a need not generally met by the state,[161] but a school providing 'luxury education' has a greater burden of demonstrating a 'real' level of public benefit.[162] By somewhat circular argument, the saving to the

155 [191].

156 [194].

157 ibid (presumably part of acting in accordance with its objects, ie, an implicit term of its objects, rather than a constraint of charity law).

158 [214].

159 [237]–[258].

160 [254].

161 [258].

162 [219] ('real' here appearing to mean 'significant' or 'greater', rather than 'genuine'). Presumably the rationale is that a luxury education might tend to give a private benefit which is more than incidental to the individual scholars, but it is not entirely clear and the legal basis for requiring 'a stringent examination of how' such education is provided is not explained.

public purse was said to be of 'very little weight', the benefit being 'speculative', because it could not be known how many schools might pass the public benefit test if this wider benefit were to be allowed to require a lesser provision of public benefit.[163] And notwithstanding their apparent insignificance in *Resch*,[164] the focus was to be on direct benefits,[165] principally scholarships and bursaries, but might, depending on the constitution, include sharing teaching and facilities with local state schools.[166]

Whilst there is no categorical statement that trustees must provide means-tested bursaries to those unable to afford the fees, this would not be an unfair interpretation of the judgment, except that sponsorship of an academy school might be a sufficient alternative.[167] This option was given in respect of one of the hypothetical schools in the Reference, but even here the provision of £1m over five years was said 'probably' to mean that the school would be operating for the public benefit and, although its objects *might* have been sufficiently wide (and the Tribunal did not decide the point), sponsorship of an academy could constitute a breach of trust in the case of a school with less widely drawn objects.[168] Acknowledging that it cannot be assumed that pupils in state schools are unable to afford the fees,[169] the implication was that sharing teaching or facilities with such pupils (even if 'direct') might not satisfy the requirement for adequate provision to the poor.[170] Indeed, such activities were described as 'a start to the provision of public benefit' but insufficient on their own.[171] Similarly, subsidies to those unable to afford the full fees were 'for the public benefit' but probably insufficient on their own,[172] unless the recipients were unable to afford a sufficient proportion of the fees,[173] and an institution which includes 'a not insignificant number of persons whose fees are funded from other charitable sources' *might* be charitable.[174] Charity trustees are likely to continue to struggle to know what it is they must do.

[163] [207], [231].

[164] *Resch* (n 76). The Tribunal may have reached a conclusion that direct financial assistance was more than negligible, or 'by no means rare', but did not appear to suggest that it was a significant element in the Court's reasoning.

[165] [201].

[166] [197]; Garton also draws attention to the Tribunal's confused use of the terms 'direct', 'indirect' and 'wider' benefit: J Garton, *Public Benefit in Charity Law* (Oxford, Oxford University Press, 2013) 91–92.

[167] [247]; see too Luxton, 'Opening Pandora's Box' (n 12) 49, who notes the Government's policy of encouraging the founding of academies.

[168] The significance of the amount in the context of the school's overall financial position appears to be a consideration [246c].

[169] [246].

[170] Which depends on the constitution [197]. It is thought that this will be a question of whether a constitution provides specifically for such objects, so that the state school pupils are direct beneficiaries (although, perhaps questionably, the inclusion of the words 'for the public benefit' appear to suffice: [189]).

[171] [246b], [247].

[172] [217].

[173] [255] (which suggests that 75% bursaries to those able to afford only 25% of a £12,500 pa fee might be sufficient).

[174] [237].

Performance of the Duty: Discretionary but Proper

It would be tempting to conclude that the adequacy or inadequacy of the level of provision was of academic interest only, since the extent and nature of it was said to be entirely a matter for the trustees' judgement and discretion,[175] provided only that it exceeded a *de minimis* or token benefit.[176] If the threshold was so low and the discretion so autonomous, did trustees need to worry too much? Arguably yes, because the discretion was subject to 'acting within the range within which trustees can properly act',[177] inevitably raising questions of how that range is to be identified and implying scrutiny of the trustees' discretion.[178] Would the Commission not be the arbiters after all, albeit in fewer instances than suggested in the Commission's 2008 guidance? In fact, the range of 'proper' actions appeared to be the range of acceptable levels of provision,[179] and so it was unclear how far the Commission's test of reasonableness had actually been removed, and with what it was being replaced.[180]

Furthermore, the criteria to be applied in determining whether or not the public benefit requirement has been satisfied seemed to be subject to objective assessment: these were (i) what a trustee, acting in the interests of the community as a whole, would do; and (ii) what provision should be made once the threshold is met.[181] Other expressions of the Duty are open to a similar interpretation. Thus, there are benefits 'below which no reasonable trustees would go' and 'a limit outside which they must not step'.[182] Similarly, meeting the threshold is 'not necessarily enough'[183] and benefits must equal or exceed the minimum which 'any reasonable trustee could be expected to provide'.[184] Provision must also be 'adequate' and hardship awards may constitute benefit for the poor 'in the right circumstances'.[185]

Essentially, the requirement to act 'properly' appears to be determined according to the level of provision, rather than by reference to honesty or good faith as the word might suggest. For example, conferring a 'quite modest benefit' over and above the threshold might be 'acting properly' in some circumstances,[186] whereas (in the context of an endowed school) providing only one scholarship, even to a poor person, would not be 'enough' and the trustees would not be 'acting

[175] [220].

[176] Described as a 'low threshold' [229].

[177] ibid.

[178] One is reminded of OSCR's simple statement that it is for the trustees to avoid conditions being unduly restrictive but it is for OSCR to decide on whether public benefit is delivered (*Meeting the Charity Test: Guidance for Applicants and for Existing Charities* (OSCR, August 2011) 7.6(d)).

[179] [255].

[180] The Tribunal rejected the test of reasonableness which 'runs throughout' the Commission's guidance: [229].

[181] [215b], [216] (the criteria effectively, it seems, also defining the scope of the trustees' discretion).

[182] [220].

[183] [244].

[184] ibid.

[185] [217].

[186] [229].

properly'.[187] It is not clear how the requirement for trustees to act 'properly' is affected by geographical location and size of endowments[188] or circumstances such as class sizes, staff salaries and the school's business plan,[189] unless it is on the basis that such factors may account for varying levels of provision being considered appropriate.

The Commission's focus on activities and the exclusion of the poor in practice was said to be wrong, but, to all intents and purposes, appears to have been replicated by the Tribunal's deliberations and its responses to the hypothetical scenarios posed by the Attorney-General's Reference.[190] And its stipulation that policies should be agreed by trustees to be 'rational and justifiable *in the promotion of the public interest*' (emphasis added) appears rather obscure in this context, but may well go beyond the accepted duty to act in order to further the charity's purposes.[191] How the public interest should be promoted should, perhaps, have been outlined.

Breach of the Duty

Despite the lack of clarity surrounding the scope and standard of the Duty, which inevitably leads to uncertainty as to whether the Duty has been complied with in any given situation, the Tribunal outlines significant consequences which are likely to flow from a breach of that Duty. Thus, trustees might be 'brought to account' and 'compelled to act' for the public benefit and the school's assets might be reallocated under a cy-près scheme.[192] The first two are consequences properly associated with breach of trust, but the third pertains to charitable status and so the distinction between charitable status and trustees' duties, which appeared to have been carefully and properly drawn, called for closer attention.

Regrettably the Tribunal failed to clarify on which ground cy-près would arise, choosing to 'say nothing about that aspect',[193] but it does suggest that the Tribunal was envisaging the situation where a school had once been charitable but was no longer charitable due to inadequate social benefit being provided. The Tribunal went on to say that the need to apply for such a scheme may be suspended where there is a temporary inability to make adequate provision, the test being 'whether the original character of the institution has been "blotted out"'.[194] This test was

[187] [251].

[188] [243].

[189] [242].

[190] [228]; 2 December decision (n 22) [3].

[191] [218]; similarly [195], which refers to a charitable school operating 'in accordance with the public interest' and [215b], which refers to 'acting in the interests of the community as a whole' (neither expression being explained). On the other hand, the expressions might be seen as a reflection of the view that purposes are charitable because they are for the benefit of the public as a whole [111].

[192] [194].

[193] ibid.

[194] ibid; *cf* [241], which suggests that a temporary exclusion of the poor must be 'because of special circumstances'. The difficult question of entitlement to tax reliefs during such a period of uncertainty was not addressed.

based on *Cawse v Nottingham Lunatic Hospital Committee*, where it was held that an institution satisfied the definition of 'hospital' within tax exemption legislation, even though patients' fees had exceeded the costs of providing the services for a three-year period.[195] The decision in that case was reached, not on the basis that the hospital still received a sufficient number of the poor patients for whom it had originally been established, but because the income available to the trustees included charitable income, from endowments and annual subscriptions, and not just fees (which would fluctuate from year to year in any event). The case, therefore, would appear to indicate a need to consider the nature and source of a school's income, rather than the length of time during which fee reductions might be withheld or insufficient.[196]

V. Application of the Four Elements: Charitable Status

The Tribunal explained that charitable status was to be established by each 'alleged charity',[197] based on 'what it was established to do and not on what it does',[198] 'established' meaning 'set up' for these purposes[199] and an institution's objects being identified from its constitution.[200] In the absence of any written constitution, an institution's purposes would be identified by considering its activities, but otherwise, the Tribunal explained, charitable status did not depend on an institution's operations 'any more than it did before [the 2006 Act]'.[201] This appears to be somewhat at odds, however, with the Tribunal's conclusions of cy-près being applicable where trustees fail to provide adequate provision for the poor, something which necessarily depends on the charity's modus operandi.

(1) Where the Constitution Excludes the Poor

The Tribunal considered a hypothetical school's governing instrument, which provided that the school's purpose was to provide education to pupils whose families

[195] *Cawse v Nottingham Lunatic Hospital Committee* [1891] 1 QB 585 (QB) 591.

[196] And might, presumably, offer little assistance in the case of a school which was not originally established for poor pupils.

[197] [110]. Case law consistently describes charitable status as a question of law and it is assumed that the Tribunal intended no deviation from this; the 2 December decision emphasised that it was for the court or tribunal to decide whether a class of beneficiaries, defined in a constitution, was a section of the public ((n 22) [9]).

[198] [191].

[199] [188].

[200] [116].

[201] [193]. Note that consideration of charging and benefits provided to the community in *Resch* (n 76) was for the purposes of addressing public benefit in the second sense, rather than with a view to identifying the purposes (*cf* [193]).

could afford fees representing the cost of their education.[202] Whilst noting that such a provision would be very unlikely to exist in a school's constitution, it concluded that such a school could not be charitable, on the basis that its purposes 'fail to satisfy the public benefit test under the 2006 Act'[203] by excluding the poor.[204]

Somewhat surprisingly, however, it seems that this may have rested on the level and affordability of the fees, or their relation to cost, rather than any offensiveness in expressly excluding those unable to afford them. Hence the conclusion was 'all the stronger' if fees significantly exceeded costs in order to fund future development,[205] for example, and if the 'not very well off' were able to afford the full fees, the school might nonetheless be charitable, apparently notwithstanding the express exclusion of people unable to afford them.[206] Annual fees of £12,000, therefore, would mean that the poor are excluded, whereas fees of £2,000 per annum might not.[207] And since the poor might include the 'quite well off', is an institution which charges fees within the reach of the 'quite well off' also charitable? Do fees of, say, £5,795 per annum exclude the poor?[208]

(2) Where the Constitution is Silent

Since charitable status is determined by the constitution, the Tribunal concluded that a school whose governing instrument is silent as to its pupils' ability to pay fees, and is thus 'open to all', was 'generally speaking' established for charitable purposes only.[209] Less reservedly, the Tribunal also stated that a charitable institution 'which in practice excludes poor people *remains a charity*' (emphasis added),[210] although it is difficult to reconcile this with the above-mentioned consequences of cy-près where trustees fail to offer adequate provision.[211] On further analysis, it does seem that the threat to charitable status has not been removed. Critically, the effect of the decision is to make charitable status dependent on a constitutional provision that the school will carry out its purposes 'in a way which is for the public benefit', ie, that it will carry out the Duty, and that provision might be express

[202] [177]; this is the illustrative wording which appears in the Attorney-General's Reference; although inclusive rather than exclusive, it seems reasonable to treat it as an express exclusion of the poor. Luxton wonders whether the use of the word 'purpose' in this example led the Tribunal to treat fee-charging as relevant to charitable status and public benefit: P Luxton, '*Dingle v Turner* Forty Years On' (2013–14) 16 *Charity Law & Practice Review* 43, 50.

[203] [177].

[204] [208].

[205] [177]. Or is it the relation of fees to cost which is most significant (eg, School A might charge fees so as to provide a substantial reserve, but they might still be less than those charged by School B, which has only a limited reserve)?

[206] [179]; this qualification was mentioned within the context of considering an express exclusion ([177]–[186]): the judgment went on to consider a silent constitution from [187] onwards.

[207] [180] (and the school would not be charitable).

[208] Fees of £5,795 pa were charged by Highfield Priory (see ch 6).

[209] [189] (and so within the definition of charity contained in the 2011 Act, s 1).

[210] [228].

[211] See text to nn 192–94 above.

or implied. The effect appears to be that if that provision is absent, the school will not be charitable and, furthermore, the Tribunal notes that a subsequent inability to 'operate for the public benefit' may prove 'fatal'.[212] The suggestion that trustees are arbiters of the social benefit to be provided cannot be taken too far, therefore, if they are not also to be the arbiters of charitable status.

In the case of a new application for registration of a school with charitable status, it was said that this provision may be explicit but, even if 'foolishly' omitted, 'will often be implicit', except if it were apparent from all the circumstances that the school could never hope to operate for the public benefit (in this sense).[213] The only example given was where the school could only operate by charging full fees for all students.[214] In such circumstances, the school would not be charitable. It is not clear how such an assessment should be made, nor whether the Commission (if required) would have the necessary expertise to make it, and the ability of trustees to increase fees for some in order to subsidise others, and to raise funds by other means, may mean that such a conclusion is unlikely.[215] The term 'full fees' is not defined, however, and questions are likely to abound as to whether 'full fees' are charged where the school is in receipt of charitable income (other than fees) and regarding the impact of property endowments (which allow the school to operate without rent or property acquisition costs) and restricted funds.[216] If the settlor has 'resolved to settle a competent revenue' to cover some or all of the staff salaries, for example, does that remove the problem altogether, since the fees no longer represent the full cost of providing the education?[217]

In the case of existing charities, the Tribunal took the view that it was 'an almost inevitable conclusion' that this implicit provision existed.[218] Otherwise, it said, such a school might be entitled to apply its funds in a non-charitable way as a matter of its constitution, even if it provided a 'large amount of public benefit' by way of many generous scholarships for the poor.[219] This reasoning, however, appears to blur the distinction between charitable status and trustees' duties in a way not reflected in case law and also not to sit entirely comfortably with the courts' readiness to assume that trustees will act appropriately and lawfully.[220] Furthermore, might the 'almost inevitable conclusion' not be inevitable in some

[212] [194] (suggesting a fatality to the school's charitable status and not to the trustees); *cf* [228].

[213] [189]; the indication that it is sufficient to state expressly that the purpose is the advancement of education 'in a way which is for the public benefit' appears weak.

[214] ibid.

[215] The Commission's expectation that schools would find ways of funding bursaries was demonstrated in ch 6. (The acceptability of a temporary period of nil or inadequate provision also makes such an assessment more complex.)

[216] eg, a legacy for the construction of facilities which, otherwise, would be paid for by fees.

[217] [118], [114a]; see too [118].

[218] [190].

[219] ibid.

[220] See text to n 142, ch 2; similarly the possibility that an unincorporated association might reassociate itself for another purpose was considered irrelevant in *IRC v Yorkshire Agricultural Society* [1928] 1 KB 611 (CA) 633.

cases?[221] Indeed, might a school proffer its own inability (from the outset) to operate without charging full fees, or otherwise to provide sufficient public benefit, in a bid to retain control of its assets?[222]

VI. The Theoretical Basis of the Decision

The Tribunal's judgment is the most striking instance of judicial creativity in the history of the law of charities; and that such a judgment should have been handed down, not by the Supreme Court, nor even by the Court of Appeal, but by a tribunal is remarkable. Until the issues in this case are considered by our highest domestic court, they cannot be regarded as settled.

Peter Luxton[223]

This was not a case where the task of statutory interpretation invited a consideration of what Parliament had *intended* to say, because the 2006 Act clearly defined 'public benefit' by reference to case law alone. Indeed, the Tribunal ruled the parliamentary debates inadmissible[224] and concluded that the statute made 'little, if any, difference' to the legal position of independent schools.[225] In particular, the Tribunal concluded that there was no 'presumption of public benefit' prior to the 2006 Act and, therefore, no removal of any presumption.[226] No doubt this startled many who had seen the no-presumption provision in the 2006 Act as heralding a new regime, where schools would only have charitable status if they widened their access. They might also have been reassured, however, by the Tribunal's assurances that the Duty is imposed by law and that serious consequences might accompany its non-performance, including the reallocation of a school's assets.

Whilst acknowledging that the judicial dicta which support the principle that the poor should not be excluded were mainly, if not exclusively, restricted to express exclusions, the Tribunal did not restrict its application of the principle to that context and seemed to reject any such restriction altogether where fees were sufficiently low. It also chose to confine the relevance of judicial precedent to express exclusions of the poor and to disregard the significance of those cases which might have challenged the basis of its decision in relation to circumstances where the poor were, or might have been, excluded in practice. And notwithstanding its acknowledgement that there was no direct authority for the proposition that the poor must be included, it seemed content to assert that the need to include

[221] eg, where a school might have been considered to be able to operate only by charging full fees, had such an enquiry been made at the time of its registration (especially, but not necessarily, if it has charged full fees since then).

[222] On the basis that it was never subject to the Commission's jurisdiction (see ch 2, part III, Rule 3).

[223] Luxton, 'Opening Pandora's Box' (n 12) 52.

[224] [17]; also suggesting, however, that assistance was unlikely to be derived from the parliamentary debates regarding what was intended by the no-presumption provision.

[225] [88].

[226] [67], [68], [71], [83], [88].

the poor was part of the public benefit requirement, whether located within the second sense of public benefit or otherwise,[227] and/or that it was inherent in a duty which had always existed.[228]

These were legal proceedings which did not require the Tribunal to mediate between the parties, but to decide whether the Commission's guidance was correct in law and to offer clarification on the Attorney-General's hypothetical scenarios. In order to do that, its task was to decide what the law *was*, both as a matter of proper statutory interpretation of the 2006 Act and, in order to discover the meaning of 'public benefit', by an analysis of case law.[229]

Like the Commission, the Tribunal hinted that case law was inadequate to explain the requirement, since it gave no definition but only 'examples of when the public benefit requirement is or is not satisfied'.[230] Nonetheless, it went on to state a number of legal principles, including that the poor should be included, and to suggest that a new interpretation (or 'separate element') of public benefit was justified on the basis of either the 'focus' on public benefit which came from its express inclusion in the 2006 Act,[231] or the outdatedness of the Preamble,[232] or the fact that charitable purposes might be seen as for the public benefit in one age but not another.[233] These potential rationales are vaguely drawn, however, and none justifies a new interpretation of the public benefit requirement.

The proper performance of the Duty appears to have been based more on the belief that schools 'must be seen to be doing enough',[234] than on the fiduciary nature of a trustee's office, and the statement that the fiscal privileges afforded to charities 'underline the need for genuine public benefit' also makes it difficult to avoid the conclusion that the Tribunal has ventured into the realm of policy rather than law.[235] It is, no doubt, 'right in principle' that an institution should not, either expressly or by an operational policy to that effect, exclude pupils whose families cannot pay the full fees (but who could potentially be funded by another

[227] [112]: the Tribunal acknowledged that the need could be seen as separate from the first and second senses, but considered that the point did not need to be resolved.

[228] [194].

[229] It is worth remembering (as the Tribunal acknowledged [82]) that the statute, and the 'public benefit requirement' in case law, is concerned with charitable status (rather than trustees' duties (although it is accepted that if the test of charitable status *did* require a constitutional provision that a certain duty must be performed, then some explanation of that duty would become necessary)).

[230] [46]; see too [80].

[231] [88] (although it has been seen that charitable status was commonly explained by reference to 'public benefit' long before the 2006 Act).

[232] The Tribunal suggested that a court in recent times would not have based its reasoning on the test of satisfying the Preamble and that the 'conditions of the past' were 'transformed into the requirement to show a separate element of public benefit' [86]. It should be noted, however, that a test based on the Preamble was used as recently as 1994 (*Peggs v Lamb* [1994] Ch 172 (Ch)) and no 'transformation' is described which would justify any third sense of public benefit; see also *Hanchett-Stamford v AG* [2008] EWHC 330 (Ch), [2009] Ch 173.

[233] [23] (the proper meaning of which is contained in Lord Simonds' passage, set out in [101]).

[234] [213].

[235] [176] (whilst also commenting that tax relief for charities is properly a matter for Parliament (see n 18)).

source).[236] Whether it is 'right in principle' that the poor should be *included*, and what constitutes the 'public interest' in which trustees are required to act, however, are 'inherently political issues' which require political, and not judicial, resolution.[237]

In a neat, but essentially circular, rationale, it appears that the existence of the Duty rests on a provision in a constitution which itself is implicit because the Duty exists. Quite apart from the Tribunal's failure to cite academic and judicial authority threatening the intellectual integrity of the decision, as Hubert Picarda suggests,[238] the absence of any previous exposition of this rationale in case law casts serious doubt upon its legal justification. The decision might have its admirers for its creativity and perhaps its courage in taking a fresh approach to fee-charging charities: the judiciary has a role to play, after all, to ensure that the law develops, at least where it has the freedom and authority to do so alongside, or in place of, legislation. Others might feel, however, that the Tribunal overstepped its remit as a court of first instance, or that a greater level of clarity, and/or a closer degree of legal analysis, would have lent significantly more authority to its judgment. It seems hard to believe that the decision would receive the wholehearted approval of a higher court.

[236] Also acknowledged to be unlikely: any exclusion in practice is more likely to be because a school 'cannot afford not to choose such students' [210].

[237] See J Sumption: 'Judicial and Political Decision-making, the Uncertain Boundary' (FA Mann lecture November 2011) which concludes that 'judicial resolution of inherently political issues is difficult to defend'; *cf* S Sedley, 'Judicial Politics' (2012) 34(4) *London Review of Books* 15.

[238] See the opening quote from Picarda, '*Thornton v Howe*' (text to n 1).

9

More Recent Developments

I. Introduction

Charity law has continued to see developments since the Commission's public benefit assessment programme and the Tribunal's ruling in *R (Independent Schools Council) v Charity Commission*.[1] The 2006 Act and the Commission were each subject to formal review and the Commission replaced completely its general guidance on the public benefit requirement, together with its guidance for fee-charging charities and its legal analysis. At the same time, other common law jurisdictions were also carrying out their own charity law reforms.

The operation and effectiveness of the 2006 Act were reviewed first by Lord Hodgson,[2] and later by the Public Administration Select Committee (PASC),[3] the findings and recommendations of the two reviews differing in several respects. These will be considered below. The Commission was also subject to scrutiny by the Public Accounts Committee,[4] whose chair publicly denounced the Commission as 'not fit for purpose'.[5] The Committee was 'dismayed' at the Commission's slow and ineffective performance,[6] and its reactive (not proactive) approach,[7] and was also critical of its weak leadership and lack of coherent strategy.[8] The National Audit Office added its verdict that the Commission was not regulating charities effectively and not delivering value for money.[9] The Law Commission also commenced a review of charity law in March 2013, although its terms of reference were very specific and did not include broader considerations such as

[1] *R (Independent Schools Council) v Charity Commission* [2011] UKUT 421 (TCC), [2012] Ch 214.

[2] *Trusted and Independent: Giving charity back to charities* (TSO, July 2012).

[3] *The role of the Charity Commission and 'public benefit': Post-legislative Scrutiny of the Charities Act 2006*, Third Report of Session 2013–14 (TSO, June 2013).

[4] *The Charity Commission*, Forty-second report of Session 2013–14, HC 792 (TSO, February 2014).

[5] Margaret Hodge MP (5 February 2014): www.parliament.uk/business/committees/committees-a-z/commons-select/public-accounts-committee/news/publication-of-report-tax-reliefs-on-charitable-donations.

[6] *Charity Commission* (n 4) para 12.

[7] ibid, para 3 (echoed by the National Audit Office report (n 9 below) para 1.28).

[8] *Charity Commission* (n 4) paras 2, 6.

[9] *The regulatory effectiveness of the Charity Commission*, HC 813, 2013-14 (TSO, December 2013) para 24.

the definition of charity, as might once have been expected.[10] At the same time, further budgets saw the Commission's budget cut by almost 50 per cent in real terms since the Commission was established.[11]

II. Lord Hodgson's Review

The 2006 Act provided that the Minister for the Cabinet Office should appoint someone to carry out a review of the Act within five years of its being passed.[12] Lord Hodgson, a Conservative life peer who had led for the Conservatives during the passing of the 2006 Act, was duly appointed in November 2011 and his report, *Trusted and Independent: Giving charity back to charities*, was published in July 2012.[13] The terms of reference explained that the aim of the review was to report on the operation and effectiveness of the legislation and to consider whether further changes could be made to improve the legal and regulatory framework for charities. Lord Hodgson was also to examine the success of the Tribunal and the extent of its jurisdiction, the desirability of a UK-wide definition of charity and the objectives, functions and structure of the Commission. The review was to 'take a broad approach' but certain areas were to be given particular attention, including the definition of charity and 'the changes made by the 2006 Act in relation to the public benefit requirement', although these 'changes' were not spelt out.[14]

The review acknowledged the 'technical debate' and, in particular, the 'highly controversial' definition of 'public benefit', but recommended that the term should remain undefined in statute.[15] Expressing a preference for the 'flexibility of case law', Lord Hodgson considered it sensible to see how the recent developments of the Tribunal's ruling on the meaning of public benefit and the Commission's new guidance 'played out'.[16] The report did recommend, however, that the Government should stimulate a widespread sector and public debate about 'what constitutes a charity' in 'practical as opposed to historical-legal terms',[17] and that this debate should take into account matters such as volunteering, state funding and

[10] Areas for review included social investment by charities (which was given priority), constitutional amendments to charities created by Royal Charter or statute, charity mergers and incorporations, and the powers of the Commission and the Tribunal (including in relation to References).

[11] See text to nn 110–12, ch 1.

[12] 2006 Act, s 73. Lord Hodgson described the automatic review procedure as the first of its kind (*Trusted and Independent* (n 2) Foreword).

[13] *Trusted and Independent* (n 2). References in this part II are to this Report unless otherwise stated.

[14] ibid, App C, p 149(a). Other areas were considered under the 'broad approach', such as the controversial issue of trustees' remuneration and the merits of introducing a Charity Ombudsman.

[15] paras 4.7, 4.13.

[16] ibid; the guidance was in consultation form at that stage. It seems that Lord Hodgson had in mind only *ISC* (n 1) and not also *AG v Charity Commission* [2012] UKUT 420 (TCC), [2012] WTLR 977 (see too para 4.3, *cf* 4.14).

[17] p 42, no 5.

fee-charging.[18] Lord Hodgson showed a distinct lack of appetite for improving the lot of cross-border charities, however. Whilst he clearly saw a UK-wide definition of charity as 'desirable' as a matter of logic, and noted that 'many' charities would welcome it, he pointed to 'the significant minority' who saw the burdens for cross-border charities as a 'small price to pay' and concluded that the status quo was 'the least worst option … at least for the time being'.[19] Recognising that 'much could be done to streamline the existing dual regulation', which he described as a 'needless waste of resources', his conclusion that it would be better to do this at the same time as enacting a UK-wide definition seemed similarly lacklustre.[20]

Lord Hodgson considered that no change should be made to the Commission's status or to its statutory objectives, although his report recommended a re-prioritisation of its functions.[21] The Commission was also urged to simplify its guidance and to consider (presumably meaning to 'improve') its quality.[22] With regard to the Charity Tribunal, Lord Hodgson noted that the schedule which set out the Tribunal's jurisdiction was viewed as 'over-complicated and too narrowly drawn' by the vast majority of contributors to the review and the fact that the Tribunal had struck out a 'large number' of cases for want of jurisdiction was said to raise questions.[23] It was recommended that the schedule should be repealed and that the Tribunal should have jurisdiction to hear appeals against all legal decisions and to review other decisions of the Commission.[24]

Lord Hodgson registered a plea for the Tribunal to make its judgments 'clear to all', suggesting that a 'short, plain English summary' should be included and that it should reconsider the 'structure, length and language of some of its judgments!'.[25] The report also recommended that the Commission should be given the power to make references to the Tribunal without needing to obtain the Attorney-General's consent, a development which would be particularly welcome in light of the Attorney-General's apparent opposition to a Reference being made in the case of the Preston Down Trust.[26]

More generally, the report identified problems which it saw in the clarification and development of case law, namely that the Tribunal (being a court) was bound by the rules of precedent and was, therefore, obliged to 'look backwards', whereas the Commission had often adopted a 'purposive approach' in applying the law

[18] para 4.20.

[19] paras 4.17, 4.18.

[20] paras 5.35, 5.36.

[21] p 58, no 2; para 5.9. Lord Hodgson also suggested that the Commission be renamed 'Charity Authority' to reflect more closely its regulatory role (para 5.23).

[22] See, eg, paras 3.20 and 6.34, adding '"[l]ess" may often be "more"' (para 3.18); the need to distinguish between legal requirements and 'best practice' was also emphasised (paras 4.13 and 5.10).

[23] para 7.16 (referring to 2011 Act, sch 6).

[24] p 85, no 3; *cf* para 7.19. McKenna notes concerns over Lord Hodgson's proposals: A McKenna, 'Applications to First-Tier Tribunal (Charity) by Persons Affected' (2013–14) 16 *Charity Law & Practice Review* 147.

[25] para 7.28.

[26] para 7.30; see also text to nn 20–28, ch 2 and n 80 below.

and was, therefore, able to allow the law to evolve to reflect social and economic circumstances.[27] It went on to urge the Government to consider whether the Tribunal could be 'empowered to take changing social and economic circumstances into account in addition to legal precedent',[28] and recommended formally that the Tribunal's attention should be drawn to 'the important role it has to play in ensuring case law precedents reflect emerging social mores'.[29] Whilst Lord Hodgson might call himself 'unequivocally not a lawyer',[30] this approach does seem somewhat startling. One of the difficulties may be the obscurity in the term 'social and economic circumstances', but unless it is intended to have some exceptional meaning, it seems possibly misguided: it is hard to imagine the courts ignoring such circumstances, at least where they would impact on a determination of charitable status, and it is the courts' responsiveness which has underpinned the flexibility of case law much favoured by Lord Hodgson and others.[31] At the same time, the Commission does not have law-making powers and, in so far as it exercises a quasi-judicial function, it is required to act (and indeed holds itself out as acting) in the same way as the courts, and this includes following precedent. The 'social policy role' played by the Charity Commissioners during the nineteenth century may rightly be applauded by the report,[32] but the 'parallel jurisdiction' which the Commission shares with the courts does not, and should not, legitimise an approach to defining charitable status which is based on social policy considerations to the exclusion of legal precedent.[33] It is not just 'in an ideal world' that their approaches should be united.[34]

The language of the report is also telling. There is a marked contrast between the positive language used to describe the purposive and facilitative approach of the 'well-respected' and 'largely effective' Commission,[35] and the less positive portrayal of the Tribunal's backward-looking approach and emphasis on the status quo.[36] Charitable status is also repeatedly described as a 'privilege not a right', where it seems the accompanying tax reliefs and funding need to be earned by discharging a moral responsibility to pursue the organisation's objectives 'to the best use that is

[27] paras 4.14, 7.27.

[28] para 7.27. It might be noted that Francesca Quint, in evidence to the PASC, considered that it would be 'helpful' if the Commission, courts and tribunals could be 'not bound by precedent in the sense that they can take account of social and economic circumstances' ((n 3) Q148). Such a suggestion would need to be implemented with the greatest of care.

[29] p 41, no 2.

[30] para 7.28.

[31] para 7.27.

[32] paras 1.5–1.7.

[33] Luxton accuses the Commission of 'cherry-picking *Re Resch*' and playing 'fast and loose' with case law: P Luxton, 'Making Law? Parliament v The Charity Commission' (Politeia, 2009) 22, 28; see also *Trusted and Independent* (n 2) para 5.3. The Commission does share some parallel powers, such as the directing of administration and cy-près schemes, but it is essentially an administrative body which forms part of the executive, not the judiciary.

[34] para 7.27.

[35] paras 5.1 and 5.25 respectively.

[36] para 4.14.

reasonably possible rather than settling for minimum compliance'.[37] This appears reminiscent of the Commission's tendency to confuse matters of law with matters of morality or social policy and the better view may be that charitable status is, in fact, a right and not a privilege.[38]

III. The Report of the Public Administration Select Committee[39]

The PASC then took up the reins, conducting a post-legislative scrutiny inquiry which was designed to build on Lord Hodgson's Review and also to respond to other developments, including the further reductions in the Commission's budget, the *ISC* case,[40] and the Commission's refusal to register the Preston Down Trust.[41] Publishing its report in June 2013, the PASC's views differed from those of Lord Hodgson in several respects,[42] and generally took a harder line, most notably berating the 2006 Act as 'critically flawed' and in need of clarification by Parliament.[43]

Sharing the view that the Commission's core role must be the regulation of the charity sector, the PASC was more critical of the regulator's statutory objectives, which it described as 'too vague and aspirational',[44] recommending in particular that the Commission's statutory objective of raising awareness and understanding of the public benefit requirement be repealed.[45] Noting that such a framework was 'an all too frequent shortcoming of modern legislative drafting',[46] it concluded that the 2006 Act 'represented an ambition which the Commission could never fulfil, even before the budget cuts were initiated'.[47] Although it endorsed Lord Hodgson's recommendation that the Commission's advisory role was better undertaken by

[37] para 3.12 (see also paras 3.11, 3.13, 4.6).

[38] See text to nn 7–9, ch 3. Lord Hodgson also refers to charities' failure to report on 'how' their actions have benefited people (paras 4.8, 4.9), although it will be remembered that the regulations require charities to provide a summary of their (main) activities and achievements and not 'to report on the public benefit delivered' (para 4.8 (see ch 3, part II (iii)); see also text to nn 176–78 below.

[39] *Post-legislative Scrutiny* (n 3). References in this part III are to this Report unless otherwise stated.

[40] *ISC* (n 1).

[41] para 6 (and see text to nn 20–28, ch 2).

[42] eg, not supporting Lord Hodgson's recommendations for the introduction of charges (para 32), or increasing the compulsory registration threshold (para 49) or his 'deregulatory' proposal which would facilitate remuneration of trustees of large charities (para 129). It did, however, support the proposal to rationalise the duplication of reporting requirements to Companies House and the Commission (para 51).

[43] paras 92, 163.

[44] para 22; see also para 24.

[45] There may be much to commend this and, of course, its removal would not prevent the Commission from issuing guidance.

[46] para 22.

[47] ibid.

the sector's umbrella bodies, it did note the concern expressed by many of them that they too lacked the necessary resources to perform the role adequately.[48] It also wanted more for cross-border charities, urging the Commission, OSCR, ministers and others to develop a passporting system in order to lessen the regulatory burden which currently falls on them.[49]

In its straight talking style, the PASC called it 'an injustice' that the legal disputes between the Commission, on the one hand, and the ISC and Preston Down Trust on the other, had imposed 'a considerable financial burden' on the charities concerned, as well as the Commission.[50] Pointing out that the Commission is a branch of the executive and not the appropriate body for resolving issues of public benefit and charitable status,[51] it spoke of the 'vacuum of definition in the [2006] Act'[52] and called it an 'administrative and financial disaster' which had absorbed vast amounts of energy and money.[53] Parliament, it said, should be 'under no illusion' about the scale of the task it had set the Commission, when it failed to define public benefit and involved the Commission in the party political controversy over independent schools.[54] Whilst this came close to an expression of sympathy for the Commission, the PASC made no attempt to conceal that it was 'far from happy' with the way the Commission had 'conducted policy concerning public benefit',[55] and equally dissatisfied with its 'disruptive' interpretation of public benefit.[56]

On the question of the definition of charity, the PASC took the opposite view from Lord Hodgson. As far as it was concerned, Parliament 'must legislate' to clarify the position of charitable status and public benefit.[57] It also recommended that the 'removal of the presumption' be repealed.[58] Leaving aside the argument that no such presumption existed, it seems to be the case that the PASC's intention was to silence those who argued that the provision had brought about a change in the law but who, at the same time, had failed to make clear what that change was. This is to be applauded but more may be needed. Removing a provision which states that *x* must not be presumed is not to say that *x* must henceforth be presumed, but it might be tempting for some to draw that conclusion.

[48] para 18. Dunn explores the shift towards the sector's self-regulation and suggests that it might not have been thought through adequately: A Dunn, 'Regulatory Shifts: Developing Sector Participation in Regulation for Charities in England and Wales' [2014] *Legal Studies* 1.

[49] para 52.

[50] para 59.

[51] para 86.

[52] para 92

[53] para 86.

[54] para 85.

[55] para 87 (reflecting the Committee's view of the Commission's handling of the Preston Down Trust matter in particular).

[56] para 162.

[57] para 163.

[58] para 93 (referring to the no-presumption provision in the 2011 Act, s 4(2)).

IV. The Government's Response

A few months later, in September 2013, the Government published its combined response to the sometimes conflicting recommendations in Lord Hodgson's Review and the PASC Report.[59] The overriding impression is that the Government favoured the status quo: it rejected proposals to introduce charges,[60] to raise thresholds for registration[61] and to allow greater remuneration for charity trustees,[62] and it also joined with Lord Hodgson and the PASC in rejecting calls for a Charity Ombudsman.[63] On the other hand, it showed support for some proposals which might be considered and explored over time, and which had the backing of both Lord Hodgson and the PASC, such as the introduction of voluntary registration,[64] fines for late filing of returns[65] and ending the need to file accounts with both Companies House and the Commission.[66]

With regard to the definition of charity, the Government was not persuaded by the PASC's forceful criticisms, but favoured Lord Hodgson's approach, satisfied that the case law 'definition of public benefit' had 'served us well for over 400 years'.[67] In view of the Tribunal's confirmation that no presumption of public benefit had existed in case law, it also rejected the restoration of a public benefit presumption as impossible, apparently assuming (without question) that this would be the effect of the PASC's proposal to repeal the no-presumption provision.[68]

Confident that a 'widespread debate' about what it means to be a charity had already begun,[69] the Government chose to reject a statutory definition of 'public benefit' at this stage, on the basis that it would be 'inflexible and risk ossifying the law' and be just as likely to result in legal challenges.[70] It appeared to be satisfied that the law on public benefit and education and poverty had now been 'clarified',[71] although it did accept that there had been a lack of certainty in relation

[59] *Government Responses* (Cm 8700, 2013). References in this part IV are to this Response unless otherwise stated.

[60] pp 9, 33 (proposed by Lord Hodgson).

[61] pp 9, 27 (proposed by Lord Hodgson).

[62] pp 17, 23 (proposed by Lord Hodgson).

[63] pp 15, 47.

[64] pp 10, 28.

[65] pp 9, 33.

[66] pp 10, 29.

[67] p 13; see also p 21. (One normally sees reference to a centuries-old definition of 'charity', rather than 'public benefit', but it is assumed that the terms were regarded as synonymous.)

[68] p 14 (whilst apparently still entertaining doubts ('a presumption … that may never have existed')); also signalling its (separate) conclusion that to introduce a presumption in respect of particular types of charity would not be supported by most charities.

[69] p 22; see text to nn 17–18 above.

[70] p 13.

[71] pp 12, 13.

to religious charities.[72] It also based its rejection of legislative reform on the premise that because the Commission had had difficulty in issuing guidance on public benefit, charity law was, therefore, too complex to encapsulate in a simple statutory definition.[73] Undoubtedly the Commission had found the task difficult, and a 'simple statutory definition' may be both unachievable and undesirable, but a simple statutory definition is not the only possibility and it is surely worth noting that neither the Scottish Act nor OSCR's guidance has been subject to legal challenge. The inclusion of relevant criteria, such as fee-charging, in a statutory definition could at least avoid the conflict with case law on this significant point.[74] As if extending an olive branch, however, or perhaps anticipating further legal challenge, the Government also signalled that a change of position on legislative reform should 'not be completely ruled out'.[75]

The 'injustice' and 'disaster' which the PASC had attributed to the legal challenges to date was brushed aside by the Government, which regarded them as 'almost inevitable', particularly in the fields of education, poverty and religion, where a presumption had been 'widely considered' to exist.[76] It is disappointing that the Government should have regarded such extensive challenges as 'almost inevitable', especially having regard to how soon after the 2006 Act those challenges were made. It also took the view that the 'clearly worrying issues' raised were only relevant to a small proportion of charities and it held the parties responsible for the high legal costs they had incurred, apparently firm in the belief that the Tribunal provided a low-cost avenue of redress which could be approached without legal representation, or certainly with *less* legal representation.[77] Lord Hodgson's recommendations for reform of the Tribunal's appellate jurisdiction were, however, supported in principle, although the Government was clearly wary of increasing the Tribunal's workload or exposing the Commission to challenges for non-intervention, in circumstances where such non-intervention was consistent with the Commission's risk and proportionality framework.[78] It was recognised that any reform would require primary legislation, but the Government did undertake to explore the possible options and likely impact.[79] Lord Hodgson's recommendation that the Commission should be enabled to make references to the Tribunal without the Attorney-General's consent was referred to the Law

[72] ibid, 11. The Government supported the PASC's position that it would be reasonable to consider the ministerial intent behind the statute by consulting the Official Report, although the purpose of doing so is not clear (p 11).

[73] p 13.

[74] The question of removal of charitable status and its consequences would still need to be addressed.

[75] p 21; see also p 13.

[76] p 12.

[77] pp 12, 14; noting that Parliament intended the Charity Tribunal to be 'a lower cost route than the High Court'. It seems unrealistic to believe that the ISC could have mounted its legal challenge without legal representation and equally ambitious to think that the Commission's legal staff could have defended it alone.

[78] p 34.

[79] ibid; undertaking to work with the Commission, Ministry of Justice and HM Courts and Tribunals Service.

Commission.[80] The further recommendation that the Tribunal should consider including 'a plain English summary' in its judgments was passed on to the Senior President of Tribunals, although the Government's indication that the current practice was to publish summaries of the Upper Tribunal may have missed the point.[81]

It is some comfort that the Government did not endorse Lord Hodgson's suggestion that the Tribunal should be empowered to take account of changing social and economic circumstances in reaching its decisions, in addition to legal precedent.[82] The Government did not understand 'the extent of what it means' and pointed out that the law has flexibility already, for example, by recognising new charitable purposes by analogy to existing charitable purposes.[83] Nonetheless, it spoke of this as a 'change', but rejected it because of the legal uncertainty and significant problems which it, whatever it was, would create.[84]

As for the difficulties caused by the different approaches across the UK, the Government undertook to 'work proactively' with the devolved administrations in seeking to minimise regulatory burdens, 'while respecting the UK's different charity jurisdictions'.[85] More detail is needed to understand how feasible this can be and the Government made no express reference to the PASC's support for a passporting system.[86] Nor did it offer any more to Lord Hodgson, who had considered harmonisation of the definition of charity across the UK as 'desirable in the longer term'.[87]

The Government ruled out any legislative change to the Commission's statutory objectives,[88] but it joined with Lord Hodgson and the PASC in signalling that the Commission should prioritise its regulatory functions and focus its efforts and resources carefully.[89] It did indicate, however, that the Cabinet Office would work with the Commission to investigate the options for removing or reducing statutory functions that are resource intensive but which add little value to charity regulation.[90] It will be interesting to see how this project progresses.[91]

[80] p 36.

[81] ibid.

[82] See text to nn 27–34 above.

[83] p 36.

[84] ibid. It did, however, note that it had written to the President of the Lower-tier Tribunal (General Regulatory Chamber) to draw attention to Lord Hodgson's recommendation that the Tribunal should be made aware of its important role in ensuring that case law precedents reflect emerging social mores (p 21).

[85] p 10 (also agreeing to keep PASC informed of progress).

[86] pp 10, 46.

[87] p 46. The Calman Report (see ch 7, n 191) appears to have fallen on deaf ears.

[88] p 7 (its expression of support for the PASC's conclusions clearly excluding the Committee's conclusions that the statutory objectives were flawed).

[89] pp 7, 25, 26, 46. The Government made a particular note that the Commission's public benefit objective should 'not be such a significant focus' compared with its other core regulatory objectives (p 13).

[90] p 7 (recommended by the PASC).

[91] The Government also notes that the Law Commission will consider the transfer of powers from the Commission to charity trustees, with appropriate safeguards (pp 7, 27).

Perhaps not surprisingly, the Government signalled no prospect of increasing the Commission's resources, which it considered 'sufficient',[92] although it was willing to accept that the Commission's 'limited resources' inevitably meant a limited regulatory role.[93] The challenge for the Commission, it said, was to ensure that it put those limited resources to maximum effect.[94]

V. The Commission's Revised 2013 Guidance and Legal Analysis

In the same month, September 2013, the Commission's revised guidance was finally published.[95] Rather than simply revising those parts which the Tribunal had threatened to quash, the Commission produced a completely overhauled set of guidance. Whilst this presented an opportunity for a complete 'fresh start' and followed extensive public consultation,[96] it also resulted in over one hundred more pages for lawyers and charity trustees to read.[97]

This time, the guidance was contained in three separate web-based publications, each of which made reference to a myriad of further publications, although these are clearly flagged as not part of the public benefit guidance to which charity trustees are obliged by statute to have regard.[98] The first of the three publications, for example, directs readers to no fewer than 13 other publications. On the face of it, this strategy might be applauded for reducing the burden on charity trustees (by reducing the amount of guidance to which they must have regard), but the level of guidance one receives *without* recourse to the extra materials is extremely limited. There is no guidance, for example, on political purposes.[99] The end result is an extensive duplication of material, both in terms of numerous repeated introductory pages and also in the range of additional documents. The reader is led through a maze of interconnected links, constantly referring him or her to another section or annex, or often another publication altogether, for information which, in most cases, could just as easily have been provided in the principal document. Following frustrated cries on the Commission's blog, which it had set up for the purposes of the consultation, PDF files were also made available, but the navigational challenges remain and they are hardly less irritating for those who choose

[92] p 26 (but note n 112, ch 1).

[93] p 8.

[94] ibid.

[95] See text to n 100 below. It was originally intended to be published in March 2012.

[96] Presumably also taking into account the reports of Lord Hodgson and the PASC.

[97] Of course the guidance has an unlimited audience.

[98] 2011 Act, s 17(5).

[99] Any guidance is tucked away in Annex B of *What makes a charity* (Commission, September 2013) which directs the reader further to *Speaking Out: Campaigning and Political Activities by Charities* (Commission, March 2008).

instead to print the guidance in all its various forms. The contrast with the Scottish guidance remains stark indeed.

As mentioned, the 'public benefit guidance' is now separated into three 'guides': *Public benefit: the public benefit requirement* (PB1); *Public benefit: running a charity* (PB2); and *Public benefit: reporting* (PB3).[100] The rationale given for producing three documents is that a clearer separation is needed between public benefit in its 'three different contexts', namely: (i) being a charity; (ii) operating as a charity; and (iii) reporting on a charity's work.[101] Strictly speaking, however, it is only in respect of (i) that the Commission is obliged to publish guidance in pursuance of its public benefit objective, since the public benefit requirement pertains to charitable status.[102]

The Commission does acknowledge this point, but justifies the second and third guides on the basis that the legislation requires trustees to have regard to the Commission's guidance 'when exercising any powers or duties to which the guidance is relevant'.[103] The Commission's logic is that this statutory provision demonstrates that Parliament clearly intended the Commission's public benefit objective to extend to publishing guidance on both the trustees' duty to further the purposes for the public benefit and trustees' reporting obligations.[104] Guidance which explained only the requirement for purposes to *be* for the public benefit, it said, would have 'little relevance' to the trustees' powers and duties once the charity was established.[105] Whether or not it reflects the view of many in Parliament, however, this appears to rewrite the statute where there is no ambiguity on the face of it. It is entirely appropriate that regard should be had to guidance on the public benefit requirement (as defined and relating to charitable status) in respect of several powers and duties. A power to alter an institution's purposes, for example, should be exercised so as to ensure that the amended purposes are also 'for the public benefit' and the duties to exercise powers for their proper purposes and to apply for a cy-près scheme where charitable purposes can no longer be carried out also need to be considered in light of the public benefit requirement.

The Commission's efforts to distinguish more clearly between charitable status and trustees' duties are to be welcomed and it is, of course, entitled to issue guidance on any matters it considers appropriate. This attempt to embrace the second and third guides within the guidance to which trustees are obliged by statute to have regard, however, relies on a logic which is no less dubious than that which

[100] The Commission refers to the guides as PB1, PB2 and PB3.

[101] *Public benefit guidance: Table of changes* (Commission, September 2013); see too *Analysis of the law relating to public benefit* (Commission, September 2013) (2013 Analysis) para 30.

[102] 2011 Act, s 1, s 17(1).

[103] 2013 Analysis (n 101) para 30; 2011 Act, s 17(5). Relating this duty to when the *guidance* is relevant (rather than when the public benefit requirement is relevant) has already been noted to be questionable (see ch 3, part II (ii)).

[104] 2011 Act, s 14; 2013 Analysis (n 101) para 30.

[105] 2013 Analysis (n 101) para 30.

takes a duty to further purposes which are described as 'for the public benefit' and transform it into a duty to deliver social benefit.[106]

A 'Table of changes' was published which signposted where parts of the old guidance were now to be found, whether in the new guidance or elsewhere, and where they had been removed altogether.[107] It also noted a few differences in terminology, for example that 'principles' have been replaced by 'aspects' and 'private benefit' by 'personal benefit'. A document which signposted more significant or substantive changes would have been considerably more useful, however.

The New Legal Analysis

The Commission also produced a new legal analysis, *Analysis of the Law relating to Public Benefit* (2013 Analysis), which replaced the older version and presented 'a statement of the law'.[108] The new document is striking in two respects. First, it is less than half the length of the original and, second, it relies heavily on the *ISC* judgment to support its interpretation regarding fee-charging charities,[109] in place of the pre-2006 case law which it had cited previously. Gone is the suggestion that the Commission's task is to deal with unclear areas of the law by applying its own interpretation, or to 'shape the legal understanding of what is charitable',[110] and the standard of its legal analysis is significantly higher, judicial dicta now being placed in context and with relevant commentary. It is clear that the Commission took notice of the objections made to the length (and perhaps the standard) of its 2008 publications, but one suspects that the reduced length and substance might also have been motivated by a wish to reduce the risk of further criticism and legal challenge.

It is worth noting, in particular, that the confident reference to the removal of a presumption of public benefit has been replaced by a statement that a presumption was 'widely considered' to exist,[111] but that none actually existed, or rather that no purposes had been recognised as charitable by virtue of the operation of any presumption.[112] It also makes clear that the decisions of the courts prior to 2006 'continue to be relevant',[113] although the doubts and qualifications which it expressed in refusing to register the Preston Down Trust were not entirely removed by its eventual decision to register it, a decision which post-dated the 2013 guidance by several months.[114]

[106] Arguably the different meaning of 'public benefit' in this respect is highlighted by the newly separated guidance, where fee-charging is dealt with in PB2 (but see text to n 165 below).

[107] *Table of changes* (n 101).

[108] 2013 Analysis (n 101) para 3.

[109] *ISC* (n 1).

[110] *Analysis of the law underpinning Charities and Public Benefit* (Commission, December 2008) (2008 Analysis) 1.10.

[111] 2013 Analysis (n 101) para 12 (also acknowledging that view on the nature and effect of any such presumption differed).

[112] ibid, para 26 (relying on *ISC* (n 1) [88]).

[113] ibid, para 24.

[114] Decision of the Charity Commission in the Application for Registration by the Preston Down Trust (3 January 2014).

Like its predecessor, the 2013 Analysis acknowledges that purposes and activities are distinct, and that the legal concept of charity does not depend on the popular meaning of the word, but the content on poverty and fee-charging charities is difficult to reconcile with this.[115] Notably, there is still no attempt to distinguish between express exclusions and implied exclusions in practice. The notion of charity law changing with changing social perceptions is still to be found, although it receives less attention,[116] and references to the Commission conducting public benefit assessments of existing charities no longer appear.[117]

Status of the Current Guidance

The new guidance no longer purports to set out the key principles distilled from case law, but does purport still to explain 'what the law says' on public benefit and how the Commission interprets and applies that law.[118] It acknowledges that the guidance is not 'the law' and that it cannot cover all the complexities of the relevant law, but describes it as 'high level general guidance', although 'high level' is neither defined nor explained.[119] The statement that the Commission makes decisions based on the law and not on its guidance may be a response to the criticism which it received, not only in respect of its public benefit assessment programme, but also individual decisions on applications for registration; but the claim is untested as yet.[120]

Charitable Status: Principle 1 and the 'Benefit Aspect'

The old Principles 1a and 1b have been simplified and, in many places, the focus on the noun 'benefit' has been replaced by a focus on the adjective 'beneficial'.[121] The 'benefit aspect' of 'public benefit' is explained as a requirement that the purpose is beneficial in a way that is 'identifiable' and capable of being described, although it need not be quantified or measured.[122] Like its predecessor, the 2013 guidance explains that evidence might be needed where the beneficial nature of a purpose is 'not clear', although this time it gives no indication of what form

[115] 2013 Analysis (n 101) para 24; *cf* PB2, Annex C.

[116] 2013 Analysis (n 101) para 31.

[117] See text to nn 163–68 below.

[118] PB1, 3; *cf Charities and Public Benefit* (Commission, January 2008) (2008 Guidance) Foreword.

[119] Whether it alludes to the guidance emanating from the statutory regulator or indicates that the generality stems from a high level of abstraction is not clear.

[120] PB1, 3; P Luxton and N Evans, 'Cogent and Cohesive? Two Recent Charity Commission Decisions on the Advancement of Religion' (2011) 75 *Conveyancer and Property Lawyer* 144.

[121] But not all: see, eg, paras 46 and 48.

[122] Somewhat confusingly, the point is made in the new guidance under the sub-heading 'measuring what is beneficial' (PB1, 7); also somewhat curious is the bald statement that the court can have regard to the consequences of pursuing a charitable purpose in order to determine charitable status (para 47; *cf* text to n 156, ch 2 and n 77, ch 3).

that evidence might take.[123] The 2013 Analysis offers little more, stating that the 'quality of evidence' will depend on the circumstances.[124]

Nor does the revised guidance offer any more clarification as to when there might be no need for evidence, simply repeating the example of an organisation which provides emergency aid to victims of a natural disaster.[125] Such an example is, of course, 'obvious', and a less obvious example might have been more useful. The obviously beneficial nature of a mainstream education could have been included, for example, and an attempt to offer guidance on whether the advancement of religion qualifies as obviously beneficial would clearly have been valuable.[126] The Commission could have, and arguably should have, taken this opportunity to set out its position more specifically on the continued relevance of case law, in relation to religion in particular, and also to affirm the courts' refusal to examine a religion's internal practices. This might have gone some way to avoiding the many problems otherwise faced by the Commission's approach in the case of the Preston Down Trust, which now look set to be repeated.

The requirement for a purpose to be 'beneficial' is nonetheless clearly seen as an additional requirement to appearing in the statutory list of purposes, implying that purposes appearing on that list must also be separately assessed as beneficial. In itself, this is not objectionable, perhaps, but their inclusion on the list should be understood to signify that they are considered prima facie beneficial, so that satisfying the benefit aspect requires consideration of possible disqualifying factors, rather than separate evidence of benefit.[127] If a purpose which appears on the list is *not* charitable, therefore, it will be because it is against the law or contrary to public policy in some way (for the advancement of a banned religion, for example, or a school of pickpockets) or simply not public (such as a cloistered religious community). The removal of Principle 1b, which had required that the 'benefits must be related to the aims', is to be welcomed since its value was questionable. Together with the reduced focus on actual benefits, it also suggests that any future assessment of public benefit, if indeed any were to be carried out, would not replicate the extensive listing of individual relevant and irrelevant benefits that appeared in the public benefit assessment reports.[128] An assessment of an independent school should, therefore, be entirely straightforward in respect of the benefit aspect.

Principle 1c is not significantly changed, although greatly reduced in length, which is to be welcomed. Previously expressed as a principle that benefits must be balanced against any detriment or harm, this part of the 'benefit aspect' now

[123] The possibility of corroborative evidence being required has (more happily) been removed (see n 41, ch 3).

[124] 2013 Analysis (n 101) para 50.

[125] PB1, 3.

[126] The suggestion that evidence is required to prove both educational value and public benefit has (happily) been omitted, however (see text to n 70, ch 3).

[127] The Commission said that it would have regard to legislation in deciding benefit (eg, 2013 Analysis (n 101) para 48).

[128] See ch 6; the 2013 Analysis, however, may suggest otherwise ((n 101) para 99f, citing *ISC* (n 1) [203] (not [204] as stated)).

explains that a purpose cannot be charitable 'where any detriment or harm resulting from it outweighs the benefit'.[129] Such detriment or harm is to be taken into account where it is 'reasonable to expect' that it will result from the purposes, based on evidence and not on personal views.[130] The rather unenlightening examples and illustrations which appeared in the 2008 guidance, such as the provision of motorised transport for the disabled (despite its polluting effects), have not been improved upon but simply removed and not replaced.[131] The only other piece of guidance is that if the purpose's benefit is 'obvious and commonly recognised', the need for evidence of detriment to be 'clear and substantial' is 'even greater', although it is not immediately obvious why the basis on which the beneficial nature of the purpose is decided (namely being obvious rather than proved by judicial evidence) should have such a consequence.[132]

Charitable Status: Principle 2 and the 'Public Aspect'

Principles 2a, 2b and 2c have also been simplified and 2d only slightly changed. The 'public aspect' of public benefit requires that the purpose 'must benefit the public in general or a sufficient section of the public' and not give rise to more than 'incidental personal benefit', and the stipulation that any restrictions must be reasonable has been removed.[133]

The original principle that beneficiaries should be 'appropriate to the aims' seems to have taken on a slightly different meaning, the stipulation now being that the section of the public must be 'appropriate (or "sufficient") in relation to the specific purpose', suggesting that 'sufficient', the normal word used in case law, means 'appropriate', but not offering any explanation of what is appropriate.[134] Adding that a sufficient section is called 'a public class', and that what is sufficient for one purpose might not be sufficient for another, tells us little and the 2013 Analysis offers no greater clarity.[135] In fact, the tendency of the Commission to clothe ideas in vague language persists: a section of the public defined by a geographical location, for example, is sufficient 'in most cases', a section defined by a particular charitable need is 'often' sufficient and a section defined by reference to an occupation or profession 'can' be sufficient 'depending on the circumstances'.[136]

[129] PB1, 8. This echoes the explanation offered in the previous guidance, which referred to a 'net benefit'.

[130] The insistence on 'real evidence' has been removed.

[131] 2008 Guidance (n 118) E4.

[132] PB1, 8.

[133] PB1, 5.

[134] PB1, 9; *cf* Principle 2a of the 2008 Guidance (n 118). The possibility of a class of potential beneficiaries being defined in a capricious manner appears in the 2013 Analysis (n 101) para 69.

[135] ibid; 2013 Analysis (n 101) paras 58–65 (although the removal of the suggestion that the differences depend in part on social and economic conditions (2008 Analysis (n 110) 3.9) is welcomed).

[136] PB1, 9, 10 (although an example is given of this last category ('former and retired teachers and their dependents [sic]'), a contrasting example would better have illustrated the qualification 'depending on the circumstances').

Similarly, defining a section by reference to a personal or contractual nexus means that the section is not sufficient 'in general' and whether it is sufficient to define a section by other sorts of personal characteristic 'depends on the purpose … and the specific circumstances'.[137]

Of course, beyond the reasonably well articulated principle that a personal nexus is not permitted save in cases for the relief of poverty, case law might suggest that the 'public aspect' is not much clearer than being a question of the purposes feeling broadly public or private,[138] but the value of guidance in such vague terms as these has to be questioned. The rather obscure indication that a personal nexus will not disqualify purposes for the prevention of poverty 'in some cases' may be understandable (even if it is unsatisfactory) in light of *Attorney-General v Charity Commission*,[139] but some attempt could have been made to explain the qualification. No attempt is made to define 'numerically negligible' as a disqualifying factor and the seemingly sensible qualification contained in the 2008 guidance, that the number might legitimately be small provided that anyone who qualifies as a beneficiary is eligible to be considered, no longer appears, although the 2013 Analysis continues to lend support to this view.[140]

Fee-Charging Charities

If the part of Principle 2b which dealt with fees and Principle 2c were given less prominence than one might have expected in the 2008 guidance, they have been given less again in 2013. The only mention of fee-charging and poverty in PB1 (concerned with *being* a charity) is that a charity's purposes should not be defined so as to exclude the poor, 'the poor' being a relative term which depends on the circumstances but which 'can include' people of modest means (which itself is not defined).[141] More accurately, the guidance states: 'Charities must not *define their beneficiaries* in the following ways as these will not benefit a sufficient section of the public' and includes in the list which follows: '*a purpose which* excludes the poor from benefiting' (emphases added).[142] The wording is not without ambiguity. The prohibition is linked to the way the beneficiaries are defined, which might suggest that it is only intended to target express exclusions of the poor (and nothing else in this publication suggests that any exclusion of the poor which results from fee-charging in practice should affect charitable status), but the wording

[137] PB1, 11.

[138] *Dingle v Turner* [1972] AC 426, 449 (where Lord Cross called it a 'question of degree').

[139] *AG v Charity Commission* (n 16) [69]–[82]. The example of a care home which caters for only a small number of persons has been removed, perhaps as a result of *Re Duffy* [2013] EWHC 2395 (Ch), although the decision in that case may be questionable as a matter of principle and authority (see ch 2, part III, Principle H).

[140] PB1, 12; 2013 Analysis (n 101) para 62.

[141] PB1, 12; 2013 Analysis (n 101) para 80 (where the footnote citation of cases (without comment) fails to acknowledge those concerned with the relief of poverty (see text to nn 14–17, ch 4)).

[142] PB1, 12.

is sufficiently ambiguous to embrace implied exclusions in practice. In view of the scope for charitable status to be affected, both in the *ISC* judgment and the Commission's other publications, this must be a possibility.[143] The 2013 Analysis also fails to distinguish between express and implied exclusions, simply stating that 'it is not possible to create a charitable purpose whose potential beneficiaries exclude the poor'.[144]

The current guidance for fee-charging charities is principally to be found in Annex C of PB2 and is significantly shorter than that to be found in both the general guidance of 2008 and the separate publication, *Public Benefit and Fee-charging*, which was withdrawn in its entirety.[145] Some parts of the 2008 guidance have been removed, including the specification that charges should be 'reasonable and necessary', but although much of the tautologous content has been reduced, the essence of the original guidance remains.

PB2 states that trustees may focus on certain beneficiaries provided they 'do not exclude the poor from benefit'[146] and that, where fees are charged which are more than the poor can afford, they must 'run the charity in a way that does not exclude those who are poor'.[147] The obligation is also expressed more positively, in that trustees 'must ensure that the poor can benefit'.[148] Again, the meaning of 'the poor' is said to depend on the circumstances, but may include people of modest means (which is not defined), and that, 'in general', what the poor cannot afford is what someone of modest means 'will not find readily affordable'.[149] Explaining one term by reference to something equally vague can hardly be described as helpful, however. And although 'high fees' and 'low fees' are no longer classed as 'technical terms', the rather unhelpful examples which appeared in the 2008 guidance are repeated, so that charges which the poor can 'usually afford' are said to include membership for 'a few pounds', 'small entry fees', 'low' prices and 'small' subscriptions.[150]

Clearly independent school fees fall outside this range and must, therefore, ensure that the poor can benefit. Here, the guidance amounts to directing that the provision for the poor should be 'more than minimal or token', clearly reflecting the Tribunal's choice of words, and it is said that this may be achieved by including 'a reduction in charges … *or* … supporting the delivery of similar services by a state-run organisation' (emphasis added).[151] Although it stands out more in the

[143] *ISC* (n 1); and see below.

[144] 2013 Analysis (n 101) para 79. If the intention had been to refer only to express exclusions, it is regrettable that it was not made clearer.

[145] *Public Benefit and Fee-charging* (Commission, December 2008), which does not look set to be replaced, unlike the supplementary guidance for the individual purposes of relieving poverty, advancing education and advancing religion (according to notes on the contents page of each, as amended November 2011 (available on the Commission's website)).

[146] PB2, 9.

[147] ibid, 10.

[148] ibid, 17.

[149] ibid, 16.

[150] ibid, 16–17.

[151] ibid, 17.

much abbreviated guidance, we should not attach too much weight to the word 'or' here. The suggestion that an independent school might satisfy the public benefit requirement (in this sense) without needing to provide means-tested bursaries was also present in the 2008 guidance, and yet the Commission's approach in practice was clearly focused on such financial assistance. Despite the much reduced prospect of further public benefit assessments, this is likely to remain a concern for some high fee-charging charities.[152]

Trustees continue to be told that there are 'no objective benchmarks', but that they must make decisions within the range of decisions which trustees could properly make in those circumstances.[153] The reader is directed to an additional publication, *It's your decision: charity trustees and decision making*, but whilst this explains that neither the Commission nor the court can judge whether the trustees have made the 'right' decision, or even the 'best' decision, it offers little more guidance than an explanation that trustees should follow proper processes in considering matters adequately and recording their decisions.[154] There seems to be little to help trustees decide what type of provision for the poor they must make, or how much.

Perhaps most unhelpfully, the guidance directs the reader to the Tribunal decision in *ISC*,[155] suggesting that trustees of independent schools may 'find it helpful' to review the Tribunal's answers to the Attorney-General's hypothetical questions and even to view the full judgment in order to understand these answers in context.[156] Of course, the Tribunal itself was 'sad' that it was 'simply not possible' to state the legal requirements clearly in the case of schools and it must be doubtful whether this suggestion of the Commission would prove helpful at all.[157] The revised guidance specifies some factors to be taken into account (arising from the *ISC* judgment), but again the level of assistance given is questionable: it is hard to imagine trustees *not* having regard to the level of fees charged, for example, or the facilities the school provides, the availability of endowment funds or its financial position.[158] Neither is it clear what it means to take into account 'how the charity operates on the ground', nor how the level of qualification required by the school's staff would affect such decisions.[159]

Significantly, the Commission has chosen to rely on the *ISC* decision to such an extent that the 2013 Analysis no longer relies on *Re Resch* and the accompanying

[152] Considered below.

[153] PB2, 17; see also 2013 Analysis (n 101) para 99e.

[154] *It's your decision: charity trustees and decision making* (Commission, May 2013). It is suggested that compliance with this publication (which is not part of the public benefit guidance) may demonstrate decision-making within the proper range (PB2, 17) but trustees are also advised that some decisions may be made only 'provided that' they are made in accordance with it (PB2, 9), which would seem to require the trustees to have regard to guidance which is said not to be guidance to which they must have regard.

[155] *ISC* (n 1).

[156] PB2, 18.

[157] *ISC* (n 1) [224]: 'we have explained the principles as best we can'.

[158] PB2, 17–18; see also 2013 Analysis (n 101) para 99.

[159] PB2, 17. The wording is taken from *ISC* (n 1) [242].

cases previously relied on in connection with excluding the poor and charging fees.[160] This avoids the very questionable analysis of 2008, but to put forward only one recent and much criticised first instance decision in place of more established and higher precedent is most regrettable.

Principle 2d has been little changed in substance, but again reduced in length. 'Private benefits' are now called 'personal benefits' and they must still be 'incidental', but the stipulation that the benefit should be 'reasonable' has been removed. No explanation for the change is given, but the explanation of 'incidental' is narrower than before and possibly more accurate: incidental benefits are those which are 'a necessary result or by-product of carrying out the purpose' and no longer include the alternative of benefits which 'directly contribute towards achieving the charity's aims'.[161] In keeping with much of the legal reasoning behind the new documents, the 2013 Analysis states simply that whether a benefit is incidental 'is a question of degree'.[162]

Assessment of Public Benefit and Loss of Charitable Status

Separating the public benefit requirement (in PB1) from the operational duty to carry out the purposes for the public benefit (in PB2), is useful in some respects. In connection with charitable status, the Commission simply says that it will consider each of an organisation's purposes and decide, on the basis of the facts in each case, whether or not they are for the public benefit.[163] If it decides that they are not, an application for registration will be refused or, in the case of an existing charity, the trustees should either change the organisation's purposes or the institution would be removed from the Register.[164] There is nothing to explain, however, in what circumstances, or on what basis, the purposes of an existing charity would fall to be considered in this way by the Commission. Although the practice of charging fees and providing opportunities for the poor is dealt with as a matter of trustees' duties in PB2, the scope of the principle (in PB1) that the poor must not be excluded, together with the ambiguity in the Tribunal's ruling in *ISC*, could lead to a challenge to charitable status based on inadequate provision of social benefit being made.[165] It is not inconceivable, perhaps prompted by complaints from the public, that the Commission might seek to challenge a high fee-charging independent school which offers no means-tested bursaries and limited (even if 'more than minimal') alternative provision. At the Commission's public meeting in 2010, and recognising its limited ability to review the entire number of charities on the Register, the Commission invited members of the public to contact the Commission if they suspected charities of failing the public benefit requirement

[160] *ISC* (n 1); *Re Resch* [1969] 1 AC 514 (PC); and see ch 5, part II.
[161] PB2, 11; *cf* 2008 Guidance (n 118) F12.
[162] 2013 Analysis (n 101) para 86.
[163] PB1, 6, 12.
[164] ibid, 6.
[165] See text to nn 141–44 above; see too ch 8, part V.

(in this sense) and, although any such communication would fall to be considered according to the Commission's risk strategy, the prospect of the Commission ignoring a blatant case of limited social benefit may be doubtful.[166]

Even in connection with the alleged duty to carry out the purposes for the public benefit, there is no explanation, or even mention, of the Commission assessing the adequacy of opportunities provided to the poor or determining what is necessary and appropriate in individual cases, since the provision of social benefit is now described as a matter for the trustees and not the Commission.[167] The prospect of a detailed assessment of an individual charity or its trustees, therefore, appears to have disappeared, but it should be noted that the Commission's aims include ensuring that charity trustees 'carry out their duties and responsibilities as required by law', which would presumably include the duty described in PB2.[168] Trustees are likely to wonder, therefore, what the consequences would be if their decisions were not considered to fall within the range that trustees can properly make. First, the Commission states that it would consider whether it might allow trustees time to 'make any necessary changes' and whether it would take any regulatory action (without giving further details).[169] Second, if it is 'no longer, or never was' possible for the purposes to be carried out for the public benefit (in this sense), the Commission's view is that this would suggest that the purposes themselves were not for the public benefit and if the purpose could not be redefined, or the difficulties 'put right', the organisation would not be a charity.[170] It follows that removal from the Register is not limited to cases of rectification of mistakes and that charitable status could be lost if inadequate provision is made, but the consequences of removing a charity from the Register remain unclear. The reader is directed to PB1 but, in fact, this tells him little more (except to confirm that an institution could be removed from the Register where its purposes cannot be changed) and the reader is redirected to *Maintenance of an Accurate Register of Charities*.[171]

The Commission is more explicit in a separate publication, *It's your decision: charity trustees and decision making*.[172] Here, trustees are informed that failing to make decisions in the proper range would be breach of trust, to which would attach a personal liability and that this could result in trustees having to repay the charity themselves.[173] Trustees would be forgiven, however, for having little idea how this liability would be calculated in the case of an independent school which provides 'inadequate' social benefit, and the warning that the consequences could

[166] Public Meeting, 29 September 2010, London (attended by the author).

[167] PB2, 17.

[168] *The Risk Framework* (Commission, June 2012).

[169] PB2, 12 (considering its options in light of the *Risk Framework* (ibid)).

[170] ibid.

[171] *Maintenance of an Accurate Register of Charities* (Commission, December 2012) which does not form part of the public benefit guidance. This publication was considered in ch 3.

[172] *It's your decision* (n 154), referred to in PB2, but not specifically with regard to the consequences of a breach of the duty described therein. This is said not to be public benefit guidance to which trustees must have regard.

[173] ibid, 13.

be 'serious', particularly where there is 'uncertainty about whether a decision is valid or not' (because of a risk of litigation),[174] could cause concern for trustees, especially in view of the uncertainty which pervades the guidance and even the Tribunal's decision. It should also be noted that the courts' jurisdiction to excuse trustees' liability is based not just on the honesty and reasonableness of a trustee's actions, as suggested here, but also on a more wide-ranging consideration of whether he or she 'ought fairly to be excused'.[175]

Reporting

The language of PB3 is reminiscent of the 2008 guidance, in referring to the duty to report 'on public benefit' and on 'how' the charity has carried out the purposes for the public benefit,[176] but some of the misleading comments have been removed and the guidance is significantly shorter in length.[177] Although Part 2 of PB3 may be misleading in omitting some detail (for example, that smaller charities must also list their main achievements), helpfully this revised guidance does include a relevant extract from the reporting regulations in an annex.[178] Beyond this, however, the level of guidance contained in PB3 is extremely limited and the reader is directed to three further publications which do not form part of the public benefit guidance.

Considering the revised publications as a whole, undoubtedly there are improvements in both the guidance and legal analysis of 2013, but problems do remain. The guidance, in particular, is seriously undermined by vague and over-generalised language. One continues to feel sympathy for the trustees of an independent school (or other fee-charging charity): the questions which they had before, and which were hardly answered with any clarity in the 2008 guidance or *ISC*,[179] remain unanswered. *Must* they provide means-tested bursaries? *Will* their liaison with the local state school be sufficient? And if it is all a matter for their discretion, is the 2013 guidance really necessary?

Although the presentation of the 2013 Analysis is an improvement on its predecessor, the tendency to extrapolate principles which are broader than the cited authority justifies has not been eradicated,[180] nor the willingness to state a proposition with no authority at all,[181] and there is no attempt made to explain why

[174] ibid.

[175] ibid; *cf* Trustee Act 1925, s 61; *Re Pauling's Settlement Trusts* [1964] Ch 303 (CA).

[176] PB3, 5.

[177] eg, the statement that regard should be had to the guidance 'in deciding what activities the charity should undertake' (2008 Guidance (n 118) G3).

[178] Charities (Accounts and Reports) Regulations 2008, SI 2008/629 (although only Regulation 40 (which relates to non-parent charities) is set out).

[179] *ISC* (n 1).

[180] 2013 Analysis (n 101) para 93, citing *IRC v Educational Grants Association Ltd* [1967] Ch 993 as authority for the proposition that the trustees must consider the whole class of potential beneficiaries, before choosing those actually to benefit.

[181] eg, [81], [94].

pre-2006 case law fails to illustrate the 'social benefit' meaning which the Commission attaches to the duty to operate for the public benefit in the context of fee-charging charities.[182] Apart from pointing to the Reporting Regulations and *ISC*,[183] the Commission cites *Inland Revenue Commissioners v Educational Grants Association* but, as mentioned previously, it was the relationship of employment amongst the recipients of the grants which prevented entitlement to the tax exemption in this case.[184] And although the prospect of public benefit assessments has been reduced, there are hints that the Commission's approach to assessing the performance of the trustees' duty, or perhaps even the charitable status of the school, might not have changed: the Analysis, for example, states that the use of a school's facilities for adult education in the evenings would 'not contribute significantly to the discharge of the trustees' duty to further the purposes of the charity for the public benefit'.[185]

VI. Developments in Other Jurisdictions

England and Wales, and Scotland, are not alone in having introduced legislation in recent years which has sought to define charity and it may be worth mentioning, very briefly, some of the developments which have taken place elsewhere during this period.

Northern Ireland, the remaining UK jurisdiction, had two bites at the cherry. The Charities Act (Northern Ireland) 2008 had emerged with a hybrid test of charitable status: the purposes having to be 'for the public benefit', as in England and Wales, but regard being had, as in Scotland, to unduly restrictive conditions in determining whether a body 'provides or intends to provide' public benefit.[186] The two limbs of the test were incompatible and so the Charities Act (Northern Ireland) 2013 was passed. This adopted the 'more straightforward' English test, even though it seems that the 'more robust' Scottish test had been preferred but later abandoned.[187] The definition of 'public benefit' by reference to case law of Northern Ireland means that the term will bear similar, but not identical, meanings in the two jurisdictions, the difference being more pronounced in relation to religious purposes, where the case law includes pre-partition cases which applied a subjective test and gave rise to a broader legal interpretation than English cases.[188]

[182] *Harries v Church Commissioners* [1992] 1 WLR 1241 is cited as authority for a duty to further the purposes of the trust and to exercise powers properly in so doing, but it does not provide authority for the duty described by the Commission (2013 Analysis (n 101) para 89).

[183] See nn 1 and 178 above; neither of which provides authority for this interpretation.

[184] *Educational Grants* (n 180); 2013 Analysis (n 101) para 93.

[185] 2013 Analysis (n 101) para 92; see also para 99f. In fact, this should constitute merely an incidental benefit, irrelevant to whether the purposes are for the public benefit or are being properly carried out.

[186] Charities Act (Northern Ireland) 2008, s 3 (as originally enacted).

[187] For an account of the legislative amendment process, see F Marshall, 'The Charities Act (Northern Ireland) 2008 – Cause for Concern?' (2013) 15 *Charity Law & Practice Review* 75, 82–85.

[188] eg, *O'Hanlon v Logue* [1906] IR 247; Charities Act (Northern Ireland) 2008, s 3(3) as amended.

Revised guidance following the 2013 Act also echoed the rather minimalist approach of the Commission's 2013 guidance.[189]

The Republic of Ireland's Charities Act 2009 requires purposes to be 'of public benefit' and there is special provision for the amount of any charge, and its likely effect on the number or class of potential beneficiaries, to be taken into account.[190] The statute further provides that a gift for the advancement of religion shall be presumed to be of public benefit unless the contrary is proved,[191] and that any such gift shall be construed and take effect in accordance with the 'laws, canons, ordinances and tenets of the religion concerned'.[192] If the gift is for the benefit of an organisation or cult which 'employs oppressive psychological manipulation of its followers or for the purpose of gaining new followers', it will not be charitable.[193]

Australia's new Charities Act 2013 requires that charitable purposes should be 'for the public benefit', and defines this to mean that achievement of the purpose should be 'of public benefit' and that the purpose should be directed to a benefit which is available to the members of the general public or a sufficient section of the general public.[194] Regard is to be had to all relevant matters, including identifiable benefits (tangible or intangible), possible identifiable detriment, personal benefits, the relationships between potential beneficiaries and the numerical size of the section to whom the purpose is relevant.[195] There is no mention of fees and charges, but a charity must be a 'not-for-profit' entity.[196] If there are any 'disqualifying purposes', the entity cannot be a charity.[197] These are purposes of engaging in, or promoting, unlawful activities or activities that are contrary to public policy and also purposes of promoting or opposing a political party or candidate for political office.[198] Like Scotland, the restriction on political purposes is thus much narrower than in England and Wales.[199] Australia's legislation also provides that certain purposes are presumed to be for the public benefit, including the advancement of education and (like Ireland) the advancement of religion,[200] and closed religious orders are not subject to the public benefit requirement, provided they regularly undertake prayerful intervention at the request of members of the general public.[201]

189 *The Public Benefit Requirement* (Charity Commission for Northern Ireland, December 2013).

190 Charities Act 2009, s 3(7)(b) (although there is no 'unduly restrictive' (or similar) test imposed).

191 ibid, s 3(4) (and the Attorney-General's consent is required to any determination that such a gift is *not* of public benefit (s 3(5)).

192 ibid, s 3(6).

193 ibid, s 3(10). The statute contains no prohibition of political purposes.

194 Charities Act 2013, s 6(1).

195 ibid, s 6(2)(3)(4).

196 ibid, s 5(1)(a). Charities and not-for-profit entities are regulated together: Australian Charities and Not-for-profits Commission Act 2012.

197 ibid, s 5(c).

198 ibid, s 11.

199 And reflects the decision of the High Court of Australia in *Aid/Watch Incorporated v Commissioner for Taxation* (2010) 241 CLR 539 (HCt Australia); see ch 2, part III, Principle C.

200 Charities Act (Australia) (n 194) ss 7(1)(b), 7(1)(e). Other purposes presumed to be for the public benefit are the prevention and relief of sickness, disease or human suffering, the relief of poverty, distress or disadvantage of individuals or families, the caring for and support of the aged or disabled (s 7(1)).

201 ibid, s 10(2) (which is not a new provision: Extension of Charitable Purposes Act 2004, s 5); see also s 10(1) regarding self-help organisations.

In December 2013, the Law Reform Commission of Hong Kong published a report on charity law reform which recommended a statutory definition of charity.[202] The report rejected the approach of Australia and Ireland in setting out presumptions of public benefit and concluded that all charitable purposes should be required to be for the public benefit, although the difficulties of defining public benefit were not resolved.[203] Acknowledging, too, the political dimension to the consideration of public benefit,[204] it noted arguments that the Commission's guidance in England and Wales had generated 'a lot of confusion and misunderstanding'.[205]

Jersey also passed new legislation in 2014, which provides for the appointment of a single Charity Commissioner and requires charities to 'provide public benefit to a reasonable degree', taking into account (inter alia) whether any fees charged are unduly restrictive.[206]

Stepping outside the common law jurisdictions for a moment, it might also be interesting to note that the European Commission published a proposal in 2012 for a new European Foundation Statute.[207] This would introduce a new entity which would be optional and additional to Member States' existing arrangements. Essentially a foundation for public benefit purposes, this would have separate legal personality and limited liability and its main advantage would be to facilitate cross-border investment across Member States without the difficulties currently faced because of the multiplicity of regulatory and tax regimes. Interestingly, 'public benefit purposes' are defined in a list which is closed and does not allow for extension by analogy, and which includes purposes for education and training, but not purposes for advancing religion. Amendments were proposed to the original draft which would import a test similar to the Scottish test regarding fee-charging charities, but the proposal has not found its way into the draft currently under consideration.[208]

From this very brief consideration of other jurisdictions it is evident that some legislative authorities have sought to provide some clarity on several of the issues where clarity has been lacking in England and Wales, including that some purposes shall be presumed (effectively) to be charitable, that charging fees for services clearly can affect charitable status (with the obvious implication that regard must be had to the less well-off in society) and that whilst party political purposes will not be acceptable, other notionally 'political' purposes might be.

[202] Charities (Hong Kong Law Reform Commission) Report (6 December 2013) available at: www.hkreform.gov.hk.

[203] ibid, paras 2.208, 2.209 and 2.219.

[204] ibid, para 2.218(3).

[205] ibid, para 2.204; also noting how *ISC* (n 1) had highlighted the controversial issues surrounding the public benefit requirement which might arise (para 2.218).

[206] Charities (Jersey) Law 2014.

[207] Proposal for a Council Regulation on the Statute for a European Foundation (European Commission, February 2012) (COM (2012) 35 final).

[208] Opinion of the European Economic and Social Committee, Mall Hellam (18 September 2012).

10

Conclusions

It will not do to pass an Act that is clearly uncertain in the present law, half-deal with it, and leave it to the Charity Commission.

Lord Wedderburn[1]

The preceding chapters have told a sorry tale of development in charity law. The playing out of social, educational and fiscal policy in the charitable status arena has ensured—as Lord Campbell-Savours foresaw in 2005—that charity law has been made 'an absolute nonsense of'.[2] The foregoing chapters have described 'tests', 'principles', 'senses' and 'aspects' pertaining to charitable status and public benefit, which appear similar but actually reveal significant discrepancies in legal interpretation between the author, the Commission and the Tribunal. In the case of fee-charging independent schools, where the purpose of providing an education is unquestionably charitable in nature, their charitable status has come under threat and now appears to depend, at least in part, on the extent of benefits offered to people who cannot afford their fees. At the same time, the schools' trustees are facing potential liability for breach of trust where they do not act properly in offering enough. For charities which charge high fees, it seems that the term 'public benefit' has indeed been replaced by 'social benefit'.

This chapter will draw conclusions regarding the original plan, the extent to which it succeeded or failed, and how, even after a challenge in the courts[3] and the statutory five-year review,[4] unpredictability and confusion continue to surround the legal obligations and liabilities of trustees and the potential for charitable status to be removed.

The Plan and Its Promising Start

Part of making the charity sector 'a more active partner with government in shaping policy and delivery'[5] was the widening of access to the education and facilities offered by independent schools, for the benefit of those in the state sector.

[1] HL Deb 9 February 2005, vol 669, col GC91 (in the context of amateur sport, but the message has a broader relevance).

[2] ibid, col GC69 (see p xiii).

[3] *R (Independent Schools Council) v Charity Commission* [2011] UKUT 421 (TCC), [2012] Ch 214.

[4] *Trusted and Independent: Giving charity back to charities* (TSO, July 2012).

[5] *Private Action, Public Benefit: A Review of Charities and the Wider Not-For-Profit Sector* (Cabinet Office, September 2002) (Strategy Unit Report) 7.

Suzi Leather, former chair of the Commission spoke frankly at a conference in 2008: 'This is about ensuring that as many of our children as possible benefit from the opportunities to learn which charitable independent schools have offered for so long'.[6] The political desire for greater partnership might not have been new, but the plan to link widened access to continued charitable status, making it a matter of legal obligation and consequence, was new. Fiscal policy considerations might have been prominent in driving reform, but social and education policy considerations also played a role.

It is not intended to speculate here as to whether the long-term intention was to force the closure of independent schools, or simply to remove their charitable status, either in relation to the sector as a whole or otherwise. But the assertion that the Commission would be 'robust', and remove charitable status where organisations failed to meet 'the new public benefit test',[7] was not borne out either by the tenor of the Commission's publications or its failure to remove from the Register those schools which it 'failed'. In both respects, the indications are that the plan, at least initially, was limited to achieving greater social benefit by *threatening* charities with a loss of charitable status (and tax privileges), a threat which might also have adverse consequences for the continued control and ownership of their assets. (And the additional threat to trustees, of liability for breach of trust, assumed a greater significance as events unfolded.) If the purpose had in fact been to remove charitable status in response to a lack of adequate social benefit, the Commission could have achieved it and set an example in respect of the two 'failed' schools, albeit at the risk of legal challenge.[8] But removing an organisation's charitable status, apart from possibly threatening its future viability or even its existence, would also remove it from the Commission's jurisdiction and, therefore, remove from it any continuing obligation to provide social benefit. The real purpose would be denied. It does not seem to be an overstatement to describe an approach which relies on such threats as a bullying one.[9]

On one level, the plan was a clever one: it was effective, even in its early stages, as 'that slight frisson of worry' prompted schools to do more.[10] Schools understood the message, even if the detail was muddled: they could survive as charities, and avoid unwelcome publicity, but only if they could make clear that they

[6] Suzi Leather, Brighton College conference speech (8 May 2008): apps.charitycommission.gov.uk/Charity_requirements_guidance/Charity_essentials/Public_benefit/bccspeech.aspx.

[7] Geraldine Peacock, chair of the Commission, quoted in Parliament: HL Deb 20 January 2005, vol 668, col 948 (Baroness Pitkeathley).

[8] It will be remembered that it was the risk of judicial review which appeared to cause OSCR to change its mind and pass the High School of Dundee (see text to nn 137–39, ch 7).

[9] Although not the prime architects of this approach, it might be noted that the charge of bullying has been made previously against the Commission: Public Administration Committee, Minutes of Evidence (10 December 2009, Q67); the First-tier Tribunal (Charity) also expressed concern at the Commission's approach in putting pressure on appellants to withdraw their appeal: *Morris and Mason v Charity Commission*, CA/2010/0001 (26 March 2010).

[10] HL Deb 28 June 2005, vol 673, col 165 (Earl of Onslow).

were providing an acceptable level of social benefit. And so schools were seen to replace scholarships with means-tested bursaries,[11] and to provide more facilitated access and other opportunities.[12] The impact of the Commission's interpretation (or misrepresentation) of the public benefit requirement was extensive. It had already appeared in official publications,[13] but it also entered the public consciousness by appearing in the press and sector press and it provided a new focal point for trustees' annual reports.[14] 'Public benefit' had become synonymous with 'social benefit', and the term's legal or technical meaning was in danger of being lost altogether.

On another level, however, the plan was less clever: a threat which turns out to be an empty threat risks becoming useless. On a practical level, and to be effective, any threat should carry with it sanctions which are capable of being clearly understood and which might, realistically, be enforced from time to time. Equally, the ways of avoiding those sanctions should be both readily understood and feasible. On a theoretical level, the entire plan should be legally justified.

Flawed in Its Inception

> *A changing view of whether purposes are charitable 'does not provide an unfettered discretion to extend or overturn the law'.*
>
> The Commission[15]

The plan was flawed at its inception, however: the law did not require charity trustees to provide social benefit, nor did it punish breach of trust by removing charitable status. The 2006 Act should have laid the necessary legal foundations for the plan's success, but it did not. So far as charitable status was concerned, the statute was not so much a compromise as a failure.[16] So far as 'the law' was concerned, it changed nothing.

[11] Arguably a good outcome, if one takes the view that applying charitable funds to scholarships does not necessarily 'advance education' so much as reduce the cost of that education (which is not charitable unless the recipient is poor).

[12] The trend may have gathered momentum following the 2006 Act, fuelled, at least in part, by 'fear and anxiety': *The Impact of the Public Benefit Requirement in the Charities Act 2006: Perceptions, Knowledge and Experience* (Sheffield Hallam University, June 2012) 3.

[13] eg, Strategy Unit Report (n 5); House of Commons Memorandum SN/HA/5222, *Charitable Status and Independent Schools* (Home Affairs Section, July 2010); Explanatory Notes to 2006 Act, para 25; see too ch 3, part II(iii).

[14] Academic publications also demonstrated agreement with aspects of the Commission's interpretation, in varying degrees (most notably in connection with the alleged presumption of public benefit). Some have been referred to during the course of this work but there are many others, eg, N Hancox, 'An Education in Charity' (2008) 158 *New Law Journal* 113; D Morris: 'Fee-Paying Hospitals and Charitable Status: A New Dawn or Lost Opportunities?' (2007) 18 *King's College Law Journal* 455, 458.

[15] *Analysis of the law underpinning Charities and Public Benefit* (Commission, December 2008) (2008 Analysis) 1.3.

[16] The 2006 Act was said to have achieved 'a delicate balance as regards the public benefit issue': HL Deb (n 10) col 154 (Lord Hodgson) and the Tribunal described it as 'something of a compromise': *ISC* (n 3) [18].

The 'New' Definition of Charity

The law may not have been entirely straightforward, but it was clear enough. It determined charitable status according to an institution's constitutional purposes at the time it was established and not according to how those purposes were carried out thereafter, or what benefits were delivered. It had its own definition of charity, which encompassed the relief of needs far broader than the relief of poverty 'in its limited sense of the lack of money',[17] and, recognising that some services are expensive to provide, upheld charitable status when fees were charged (provided there was no intention to make private gain), despite the inevitable consequence that some, perhaps many, would be excluded as a result. It also recognised that a charity's financial position was fickle and neither made demands for a minimum size gift nor imposed conditions relating to continuing sources of income.[18] It determined charitable status according to the giving and not the receiving. A settlor was free to choose, therefore, to dedicate his property to relieving poverty or to providing an expensive education, and he could dictate that a potential beneficiary should make a contribution if he so wished. The giving had to be altruistic and public, as opposed to private, but he could also select his beneficiaries, whether clerks and governesses, nobility and the gentry, or the down-and-outs.

It is worth adding that many of the complexities for which charity law is known did not feature where purposes were for the advancement of education, and certainly not in the context of a school education. Rightly or wrongly, the Preamble's indiscriminatory inclusion of all schools of learning provided the defining test for charitable status. Thus, all schools, for rich or poor, gentry or peasants, fee-paying or not, were regarded as charitable unless either the students were joined by a personal nexus, or the school was a cloistered or profit-making establishment, or in the unlikely event that the settlor stipulated that the poor should be excluded.[19] Whether the trust was public or private depended 'not upon the scholars … but upon the terms on which, and the circumstances in which education [was] given'.[20] Perhaps because education was regarded as so fundamentally beneficial to the community, the benefit to individual scholars and the saving to the public purse were no more than additional, but incidental, benefits.

One might well take the view that the law had 'got it wrong' somewhere along the line. Perhaps the courts were wrong to adopt the categorisation of the four heads of charity and to attach such great significance to a preamble of an Elizabethan statute which had not even sought to define charity. Arguably, the effect was that the courts were not required at all to ask whether something *was* charitable, or deserving of charitable status, but only whether it qualified for a certain

[17] *Special Commissioners of Income Tax v Pemsel* [1891] AC 531 (HL) 571 (Lord Herschell).

[18] *Hall v Urban Sanitary Authority* (1885–86) LR 16 QBD 163 (QB) 171, which concerned the interpretation of 'public charity' in rates legislation, but the principle is sound (see *Girls Public Day Trust Ltd v Ereaut* [1931] AC 12 (HL) regarding charitable status in the educational context).

[19] Arguably a school with 'numerically negligible' student numbers might have presented difficulties.

[20] *Dilworth v Commissioners of Stamps* [1899] AC 99 (PC) 108 (Lord Watson).

nomenclature.[21] Or one might argue that the majority of the House of Lords was quite wrong to endorse this approach in dealing with exemptions from taxation.[22] Or that the courts should have developed a different approach in respect of fee-charging charities, or schools in particular, especially once an alternative state education had become available and/or once additional taxes were introduced or tax rates increased. And certainly Parliament could have been bolder.

But however attractive the proposition might be that a failure to include the poor or to provide social benefit should be an additional disqualifying factor, it is not to be found in case law. If case law had required some pupils to be poor or unable to afford the fees, or if schools had been required to extend their facilities to others outside the school, one might have expected a number of cases to have reached the courts, whether for breach of trust or determination of charitable status or otherwise, and particularly in a fiscal context. Perhaps then, the proposition might have become a legal principle.

If the law was to be changed, it was a job for Parliament. The Commission was not likely to be given law-making powers and the prospects of a case reaching the Supreme Court were negligible.[23] But by tying the definition of public benefit and, therefore, the test of charitable status to case law, Parliament missed an opportunity to make considerations of poverty and social benefit an integral and defining characteristic of charity. It also deprived the Commission of the freedom which it might have thought had been given to it and, instead, ensured that both the Commission and the judiciary would continue to be bound by established legal principles. The new Scottish Parliament, on the other hand, seized the opportunities available to it. It left no room for doubt that the charging of fees could legitimately result in charitable status being denied or removed and it gave OSCR both discretion and authority to establish and police the boundaries of charitable status.

Westminster was warned that, as drafted (and as passed), the intended outcome would not be achieved by the Bill,[24] so why did it not follow Scotland's example and allow the Commission some freedom to shape the public benefit requirement beyond the confines of existing legal precedent? Did it not understand the warning, or did it choose to ignore it, at least in respect of independent schools, because it was afraid of 'arousing the middle classes'?[25] It seems possible that it was simply seen as irrelevant: if there was any concern that the new Act would fail to achieve the plan in legal terms, there may also have been a confidence that the perceived weight of public opinion and principle on the Government's side would ensure

[21] *Morice v Bishop of Durham* (1805) 10 Ves Jr 522, 541; 32 ER 947, 955 ('not because they can with propriety be called charitable, but as that denomination is by the Statute given' (Lord Eldon)). Romilly had based the four categories on 'philology not law' (ibid, 528/950).

[22] *Pemsel* (n 17).

[23] And even there, the scope for a change in the law would be limited (see text to n 55 below).

[24] See n 44, ch 2.

[25] HL Deb (n 7) col 907 (Lord Phillips).

that no challenge was successful, or even likely. Either way, the understanding of many, both inside and outside the Houses of Parliament, appears to have been that the new statute *was* changing the law: that it *would* require independent schools to demonstrate social benefit and that it *would* enable the Commission to set out the basis on which charitable status was to be granted or denied. Perhaps the will of Parliament was discernible in the comment of Lord Hodgson: 'we have made the Charity Commission responsible for the public benefit definition … we should adopt a hands-off policy and pass it over … uncomplicated as possible'.[26]

The Sanctions for Failure

The plan was also flawed because the proposed sanctions were not provided for in law. Charitable status could be lost, but only in very limited circumstances and certainly not as freely as suggested (but never adequately explained) by the Commission.

Again, the 2006 Act failed to bring clarity or authority to the plan. Parliament was warned that the muddled position on removal of charitable status was 'considerably more serious than the Government are [*sic*] prepared to recognise',[27] but the warning went unheeded. Whereas Scottish law allowed a charitable trust to lose charitable status without risking becoming void as a result,[28] English law would present enormous difficulties. It might be regretted that neither of the 'failed' schools refused to submit plans for increasing their social benefit provision. Such a refusal might have provided a useful test of the Commission's resolve and the lawfulness of its approach.[29]

Nor did the 2006 Act require the regulator of charities to conduct a review of existing charities, unlike the Scottish Act. Of course, one might argue that the act of assessing charities' compliance with the public benefit requirement was all part of ensuring that the Register was 'accurate', but specific provision, as in the Scottish Act, would have been a better basis for requiring existing charities to 'manifestly demonstrate' their charitable status or their provision of social benefit. The Commission had already mapped out the path it planned to follow, long before the 2006 Act,[30] and it seems it was this, and not any reversal of a non-existent presumption or new statutory objective, which directed its steps.

Taking the only course available in order to avoid one sanction should not lead to the risk of another sanction being imposed. And yet requiring trustees to

[26] HL Deb (n 10) col 168 (or at least a parliamentary consensus, even if some of its members were more enthusiastic than others).

[27] HL Deb 3 February 2005, vol 669, col GC10 (Lord Goodhart).

[28] Assuming that its purposes were sufficiently public to continue as a public trust.

[29] Although it is not suggested that the outcome would have been materially different.

[30] eg, *The Review of the Register of Charities* (Commission, October 2001); J Burchfield, 'Private Action, Public Benefit' (2003) 2 *Private Client Business* 110, 113 (where the author describes the Commission's practice of 'rigorously [testing]' all applications for registration 'to establish the degree of public benefit which they provide').

concern themselves with the relative poverty or wealth of potential beneficiaries (both users of the school's facilities and recipients of financial assistance and other benefits) in order to meet their legal obligations, was not only a difficult and unfair burden, but arguably one which also distracted them from the task in hand. They are, after all, charged by the settlor with 'advancing education' and not relieving poverty. If the only way in which a school can provide sufficient social benefit is by actively seeking donations and legacies, and conducting other trading and fundraising activities, it may be that it is being asked to do something which goes beyond its trustees' recognised duties of care and investment. And whilst raising fees in order to offer subsidies to a few will clearly benefit those few potential beneficiaries, the likely effect will be to exclude more than can be included and might be said not to represent the best means of achieving the charity's purposes with the resources available to it.

A Fiscal Flaw

It follows from the above, with the threat of a loss of charitable status being neither lawful nor real, that if any part of the plan *had* been to remove fiscal privileges from some or all independent schools, it was never going to be achieved. Parliament failed to heed this warning too and the long-criticised failure to separate questions of charitable status and fiscal privileges, described as 'the root of the problems',[31] remained.

Flawed in Its Exposition and Defence

> *It is important that the law adapts to life's experience when it should, but it is every bit as important that the law remains true to its fundamental principles and that it avoids unnecessary change. If it does not, its intellectual and moral authority and coherence are lost, and its rules become uncertain and confused, so that people do not know where they stand in the eyes of the law.*
>
> Lord Neuberger MR[32]

The Commission undoubtedly raised awareness of the public benefit requirement, but did little to promote understanding of it. Essentially, it changed a test which applied legal principles to an organisation's purposes into a test which required a charity 'to operate for the public benefit', as was the case in Scotland. But it failed to answer the questions which school governors and bursars needed to have answered, principally to what extent must they provide means-tested bursaries and to what extent would their existing resources be taken into account? And by framing the public benefit requirement in such a way that every case had to be assessed individually, taking into account unlimited circumstances in the

[31] HL Deb 7 June 2005, vol 672, col 822 (Lord Wedderburn), several months after posing the question set out on p xiii (HL Deb (n 1) col GC68).

[32] Lord Neuberger MR, 'The Life of the Law: the Logic of Experience', Lionel Cohen lecture (Jerusalem, 2010) para 38.

most general terms, the Commission awarded itself an excessive and unauthorised discretion which would make greater uncertainty unavoidable. It also failed to explain adequately the consequences for an institution's continued existence, its assets and its trustees, in the event of it failing to satisfy the Commission's principles or otherwise becoming non-charitable. This was a matter of law and of critical importance to charities, not something to be worked out by the Commission at a later date.

Of course, extrapolating legal principles from centuries of case law was never going to be an easy task and it is entirely understandable that the Commission's legal staff found it difficult.[33] Surely it would have been better, then, for consultation on the meaning of public benefit to have been had with legal experts and not the public, and also for the guidance to have been written by legal experts and not by staff whose expertise was policy and not law. To make the subject 'as correct and as clear as it can be' was a worthy and proper objective,[34] but it was not achieved.

Good legal analysis stems from an understanding and application of precedent, construction and legal principle, but the Commission plucked dicta from cases and presented them as authority for its guidance with no proper analysis, thereby giving the impression that the process of legal analysis was secondary, both in time and importance. With scant regard for its statutory powers and obligations, and perceiving its role as being 'to shape the legal understanding',[35] the Commission played 'fast and loose' with case law,[36] at the same time using the term 'public benefit' (or lack of it) as something of a catch-all phrase which risked diluting and distorting its meaning in law. It also laid claim to a flexibility in interpreting the cases, partly on the basis that they were few in number and, more significantly, on the basis that charity law was inherently adaptable and responsive to changing social conditions. Neither premise justified its interpretation of the law.

The Commission's legal analysis was applicable, of course, to all fee-charging charities and not just independent schools, but the Commission's worthy note of caution, that principles should not be transferred from one head of charity to another, was conveniently forgotten as it attached an unprecedented and unwarranted significance to a hospital case with persuasive authority only.[37] Repeating arguments which had been explicitly rejected by the courts, in this case and others, the Commission also failed to explain how its interpretation could be reconciled with some prominent education cases, including the unquestioning description

[33] Especially in view of comments about the Commission's inability 'to attract sufficiently qualified staff, particularly on the legal side' (HL Deb (n 7) col 902 (Lord Sainsbury)); a concern echoed by Lord Hodgson (n 4) para 5.22.

[34] *Charities and Public Benefit* (Commission, January 2008) (2008 Guidance) Foreword.

[35] 2008 Analysis (n 15) 1.10.

[36] P Luxton, 'Making Law?: Parliament v The Charity Commission' (Politeia, 2009) 28.

[37] *Re Resch* [1969] 1 AC 514 (PC), described as no better than 'a straw lance' in a battle with a school wanting to offer nothing (HL Deb (n 1) col GC120 (Lord Phillips)). Morris points to the low threshold posed by the case: 'By this test, no fee-charging charity should ever fail the proposed public benefit test' ('Fee-Paying Hospitals' (n 14) 478).

of Brighton College (which charged substantial fees on commercial principles) as a charity,[38] the dismissal of the 'startling proposition' that a school could only be charitable if it provided education for nil or reduced fees[39] and the rejection of an argument that the students' means needed to be taken into account in ascertaining whether or not a college was charitable.[40] Such cases deserved careful analysis and received none. Without authority for many of its propositions, and with careless legal analysis, the Commission fashioned its own intentions and belief as to what the law *should* say and presented them as if they were the law itself.[41]

Flawed in Its Execution

The Commission's public benefit assessment programme was unnecessarily resource-intensive and its reports were significantly poorer in quality than those published by OSCR.[42] The Commission's focus on the details of a charity's operations and activities could hardly be described as taking 'the same approach as the courts',[43] and indications that the Commission might review trustees' fee-setting and fundraising decisions further risked meddling with trustees' discretionary powers and independence. If the Commission took into account a school's resources, or the cost of providing the education, it was not obvious how or to what extent it did so, and whether the persons to whom opportunities were offered were actually poor or able to afford any fees charged was often left to chance. Its actions in respect of the two 'failed' schools were inconsistent with its own conclusions, and its legal interpretation, and suggested a distinct lack of appetite for actually carrying out the threat on which the plan was based. At the same time, the fact that the schools were not entitled to challenge the Commission's conclusions only emphasised the bullying character of the plan.[44]

The Flaws Adjusted

> *It would not be appropriate for a public body to regulate and possibly prosecute on the basis of guidance which is manifestly wrong in law.*
>
> Goldring J[45]

[38] *Brighton College v Marriott* [1926] AC 192 (HL).

[39] *Abbey Malvern Wells Ltd v Ministry of Local Government and Planning* [1951] Ch 728 (Ch).

[40] *R v Special Commissioners of Income Tax ex p University College of North Wales* (1909) 78 LJKB 576 (CA).

[41] Or at least the Government's intentions: hindsight lends an extra dimension to the slip of the tongue by Lord Bassam, in referring to 'the guidance that *we* publish' (HL Deb (n 27) col GC6 (emphasis added)).

[42] Perhaps Lord Hodgson had this programme in mind when he was critical of 'expensive, administratively cumbersome and often ineffective box ticking': *Trusted and Independent* (n 4) para 3.8.

[43] 2008 Analysis (n 15) p 5. The courts were more concerned in the detail of a charity's operations in applications for schemes, but determining charitable status and directing a scheme should not be confused.

[44] See text to nn 229–33, ch 3 and note the contrast that now exists with Scotland (text to nn 133–34, ch 7).

[45] *Association of British Travel Agents Ltd v Civil Aviation Authority* [2006] EWHC 13 (admin), [2006] ACD 49 (QB) [80] (Goldring J).

The fact that newly published guidance was subject to an application for judicial review within only 14 months of its publication, notwithstanding recent parliamentary debate and extensive consultation, should be a cause for serious concern and not shrugged off as 'almost inevitable'.[46] Of course, those who expected substantial amounts of the guidance to be quashed, or who hoped for some of the burden and red tape imposed by the Commission's approach to be cut, were disappointed. But the complexity and ambiguity of the Tribunal's decisions will have disappointed many more.[47]

Although we might welcome the Tribunal's observation that little or nothing had changed for independent schools, on the basis that there was no presumption of public benefit to be removed,[48] this also left it with no choice but to conclude either that the obligation to provide social benefit did not exist, or that it had always existed. It chose the latter. And yet it was unable to cite a single case in which a court had found an organisation to be non-charitable, or the trustees to be in breach of trust, on the grounds that the organisation had failed to make adequate provision for the poor. Nor could it offer any authority in which the courts had suggested that the provision of social benefit was required as a matter of law. It has to be wondered why matters of charitable status or trustees' duties were not challenged or discussed more often, if the law had always been as outlined by the Tribunal.

The Tribunal was undoubtedly right not to base its judgment on a change of public policy, but its apparent wish to reach a decision which was acceptable both politically and to the parties may have forced it to construe the law in such an artificial and questionable way that, whilst some questionable aspects of the Commission's interpretation were improved, others remained and yet more were added. Keen to endorse the principle that the poor should be *included*, and not simply that they should not be excluded, for example, it engaged in linguistic gymnastics to redefine the 'poor' in a way that would reconcile *Re Resch*,[49] and other cases, with its conclusions. In doing so, its interpretation of poverty bore little relation to the common understanding, or the Commission's explanation of it, and it also ignored the very limited context in which the courts had construed the term.[50] Regrettably the Tribunal appeared not to share the view, recently expressed

46 See text to n 76, ch 9.

47 The Sheffield Hallam report describes the continuing debate about the 'precise legal impact of the changes as indicated by [the Tribunal]' ((n 12) 21) and the fact that the report still refers to the removal of a presumption of public benefit by the 2006 Act, when the Tribunal at least appeared clear on its non-existence, might be evidence of that ambiguity (but cp pp 1 and 22).

48 *ISC* (n 3) [88].

49 *Resch* (n 37).

50 Notwithstanding the description of the word as one of 'wide and indefinite import' (*Re Coulthurst* [1951] Ch 661 (CA) 666) and see text to nn 13–17, ch 4; the consequence of more people being labelled 'poor' is also unfortunate. (The way in which the term 'the poor' has been used in case law avoids the more uncomfortable use of it by the Commission and the Tribunal.)

by the Supreme Court, that 'clarity and simplicity are highly desirable qualities in the law' and that the 'simple answer' is to be preferred where there is 'no plainly right answer' or 'other good reason'.[51]

And whilst we might also welcome the emphasis on decisions about social benefit being in the trustees' hands, the extent to which a school's financial circumstances might affect its obligations and, therefore, its trustees' potential liability, was not adequately explored and the fact that an alleged breach of duty could be investigated by the Commission inevitably undermines any impression that the regulator was being taken out of the picture. Although it went some way towards untangling the confusion between charitable status and breach of trust which ran through the Commission's publications, the Tribunal left open the possibility of a school's charitable status being removed, but failed to offer an adequate explanation of the critical term 'full fees', or to clarify the consequences (either for the institution or its trustees) where those trustees, in choosing the level and type of social benefit to provide, failed to exercise their discretion within the range of decisions which reasonable trustees might make. The threat was not removed, merely reformulated.

The Tribunal's treatment of case law in the education context was disappointing. In particular, its dismissal of education cases on the grounds that they did not involve express exclusions of the poor appeared more convenient than sound. The Tribunal offered no explanation of why it was that the courts in those cases neither enquired into the schools' provision for people unable to afford their fees, nor ascertained whether 'full fees' were charged, nor stipulated any sort of qualification or proviso aimed at ensuring that sufficient provision would be made. *Attorney-General v Earl of Lonsdale*,[52] for example, was dismissed on the basis that it did not explicitly exclude the poor. But one wonders whether a school which expressly excludes the lower classes from a free education is not just as objectionable as one which expressly excludes the poor from a fee-paying education?[53]

It is undoubtedly correct that charity law is not static, but the scope for legal change needs to be understood. The Commission was never given law-making powers and, like the courts, is bound by legal precedent. And whilst Lord Neuberger may have spoken of the need for judges to develop the common law to reflect the changing needs and standards of society, including 'moving the law on when Parliament has not got the legislative time, or even sometimes the political

[51] *FHR European Ventures LLP v Cedar Capital Partners LLC* [2014] UKSC 45, [2014] 3 WLR 535 [35]. The authorities were somewhat more balanced on both sides of the debate in that case (concerning constructive trusts over bribes and secret commissions) than they are in respect of fee-charging charities (which, arguably, do provide a 'right answer').

[52] *AG v Earl of Lonsdale* (1827) 1 Sim 105, 57 ER 518.

[53] And might an over-subscribed and academically selective academy school in an affluent area give cause for concern?

will to do so',[54] he also marked out the boundaries of the courts' authority: the law must still be obeyed and judges 'cannot go against Parliament's will when it is expressed through a statute'.[55] In the present case, legislation has expressly endorsed and upheld case law. The Tribunal may have attempted to chart the 'very delicate waters indeed',[56] and to tackle some of the issues which Parliament had avoided, but this may have been to overstep the mark and to make the waters even more difficult to navigate in the future.

The Flaws Preserved

Despite strongly worded criticisms of the Commission and the 'critically flawed' legislation,[57] any hopes of prompt reform were dashed by the Government's response to the reports of Lord Hodgson and the Public Administration Select Committee. Even in respect of cross-border charities, where discontent was broadest, there is small hope of any improvement and yet no amount of collaboration between the separate regulators can overcome the differences which exist between the legal definitions of charity and regulatory frameworks in each of their jurisdictions. Those differences reflect a perfectly legitimate consequence of devolution and cannot be ignored. Here too, it seems, we must wait and see how things 'play out'.[58] The Commission's latest publications have also been reduced to such a degree that very little guidance is on offer at all. Scotland may not have everything right, but its southern neighbours must surely gaze with envy at the more robust and accomplished approach north of the border.

Flawed but Not a Failure

> *How are the authorities at Somerset House to determine what constitutes a trust for charitable purposes? The majority of the Court of Appeal tells them they must be guided by the popular meaning of 'charity' and that 'each individual case must be decided on its own facts'. There is certainly no indication in the Act that such a hopeless task as that was laid on the Special Commissioners.*
>
> Lord Macnaghten[59]

It would be wrong to conclude that the plan failed, however much the integrity of the law and the law-making process might appear to have been failed. It is

[54] 'Who are the Masters now?' (Second Lord Alexander of Weedon lecture, 6 April 2011) para 72; Lord Neuberger MR, 'Has Equity had its Day?' (Hong Kong University lecture, 2010); *Kernott v Jones* [2011] UKSC 53, [2012] 1 AC 776 [78] ('In the light of the continued failure of parliament … I warmly applaud [this] development of the law of equity' (Lord Wilson)).

[55] 'Who are the Masters now?' (ibid) para 73; Garton also concludes that the implication of *ISC* (n 3) was that the purpose of the Commission's statutory public benefit role was 'to clarify, rather than advance, the law in this area': J Garton, *Public Benefit in Charity Law* (Oxford, Oxford University Press, 2013) 27.

[56] HL Deb (n 1) col GC115 (Baroness Scotland).

[57] *The role of the Charity Commission and 'public benefit': Post-legislative Scrutiny of the Charities Act 2006*, Third Report of Session 2013–14 (TSO, June 2013) para 92.

[58] See text to n 16, ch 9.

[59] *Pemsel* (n 17) 587 (Lord Macnaghten).

tempting to suggest that the law cannot be changed by a misstatement of it in judicial review proceedings, any more than it can be changed by popular opinion or a widespread misunderstanding of it. That raises an interesting question, perhaps, but, rather like whether including or excluding the poor is located in the first or second sense of public benefit, it may also be a fruitless one.[60] The fact is that the Tribunal is a court of record and its decision constitutes a precedent which will bind the First-tier Tribunal and itself. In other words, rightly or wrongly, the decision will be taken to represent the law, unless and until it is corrected by a superior court or legislation.[61]

On that basis, it might be said that the plan has succeeded: trustees of fee-charging charities are now obliged, it seems, to consider the poor and to offer them opportunities to benefit from the services they provide. But serious flaws remain. Poverty, wealth and affordability are at the centre of the redefined 'public benefit', but they are relative and subjective concepts and their juxtaposition with a standard of performance, which depends on the subjective position of individual charities, risks making meaningful and consistent application of the test described virtually impossible. In Scotland, the same obligation is unequivocally a matter of charitable status and failure to discharge it impacts directly upon the organisation's status, resulting in its denial or loss. Here, the 2013 guidance and the decision in *Independent Schools Council v Charity Commission*[62] seem to prefer to suggest that the provision of opportunities is relevant only to trustees' duties, but public benefit has not been cut loose from charitable status altogether.[63] The charitable status of independent schools might be a politically sensitive issue, but it should not be allowed to come or go according to trustees' decisions about the use of facilities or fee-setting, or the availability of surpluses or third party funding from year to year, any more than it should depend on activities or the size or nature of the initial gift or how it is invested, or be influenced by the availability of tax privileges. Determining charitable status according to purposes offers this certainty; determining it according to their activities does not, and cannot.

Trustees, beneficiaries and donors are entitled to know that they are dealing with, or involved in, a charity, with all the legal and other consequences that follow. Trustees have been placed in an unenviable position, however. They may be confused about who is 'poor', unsure as to the nature and extent of opportunities to be provided, or struggle to fund those opportunities where resources are

[60] If the Court had said that any organisation with two or more trustees was a charity, would it have constituted the law?

[61] Moss concludes that the 'unclear and uncertain quandary … appears now to be the law': F Moss, 'New Ingredient' (2011) 155(40) *Solicitors' Journal* 10; *cf* n 67 below.

[62] *ISC* (n 3).

[63] If this was the intention, it should have been clearer, especially having regard to the stark contrast with Scotland which would result. The clear link between the public benefit requirement in statute and charitable status hardly makes this a feasible option, however.

limited. If they fail, are they to be held personally liable to account for opportunities not given? And, if charitable status is lost, might they also be liable for unpaid debts and redundancy costs? It seems that 'the hopeless task' may have been imposed after all: the essence of the popular meaning of charity has become part of the test of charitable status and trustees' duties, and a branch of the executive is to determine both on a case-by-case basis.[64]

The plan's future success may depend on the extent to which the Commission's guidance and Tribunal's judgment are applied and the duties enforced. Rules which are not enforced risk losing the respect of those they are intended to regulate, but the Tribunal's emphasis on trustees' discretion, together with the Commission's limited resources and withdrawal from public benefit assessments, all suggest that the regulator may be unlikely to challenge independent schools or their trustees in the future.[65] Only time will tell.

One is left wondering whether much expense, fear and antagonism might have been avoided, and possibly more achieved, by some sort of voluntary code. The practice of providing social benefit and the willingness of the sector to provide it were evident to Parliament, the Tribunal and the Commission, and there is great merit in the view that a relationship between state and independent sectors 'works best when it is voluntary … forced co-operation is likely to breed resentment and is unlikely to be particularly fruitful'.[66] The blank canvas which existed a decade or so ago is no longer there, however, and with the Commission taking a back seat, it will be interesting to see whether the trend of increased means-tested bursaries (and fundraising to support them) continues, or whether schools might be tempted to reconsider their positions and relax their efforts.[67]

Looking Forward

There are some obvious lessons to be learned. Where difficult legal concepts need to be explained to the public, legal expertise should be employed to analyse and present those concepts, so that the risk of legal challenge is reduced and so that practical guidance, which rightly draws on the expertise of the responsible body, has a sound legal basis. Recruiting trustees can be difficult, but it will not become any easier if the guidance offered to them fails to offer the help and clarity they need to perform their duties. The indications are that the Commission has little intention of assessing the level of social benefit provided by independent schools

[64] See text to n 59.

[65] Of course, the Commission may need to respond to a challenge brought by another party.

[66] D Laws, 'The Lib Dems' View on Independent Schools', *Funding for Independent Schools* (undated): www.fismagazine.co.uk/opinions/lib_dems.html.

[67] Of course, a change in government could well influence matters and it is interesting to note that Tristram Hunt MP, Shadow Education Secretary, recently cast doubt upon what had been achieved: 'When last in government, [Labour] … urged the Charity Commission to take a much closer look at the public benefit activities of private schools. Thanks to opposition from the Independent Schools Council, that strategy collapsed in the law courts' (*The Guardian*, 24 November 2014).

or other fee-charging charities. But where it chooses to, or is compelled to, it should be required to give clear reasons for any decision that an organisation has failed to satisfy any of the aspects of public benefit, also stating (if appropriate) what would be in its view a 'reasonable and appropriate' amount of social benefit.[68] More succinct judgments from the Tribunal would also be a positive step and it is to be hoped that any reform to its appellate jurisdiction will more closely reflect the original intention that there should be easy and affordable access to a tribunal. The Commission's assurance, that charities which are unhappy with its decisions should be able to challenge them, is to be applauded. Now it needs to be enacted.

It is not surprising, perhaps, that the Government has signalled such a lack of appetite for legislative reform, but the debate over the charitable status and fiscal advantages of independent schools seems likely to continue. It must be hoped, if a new momentum does gather, that the size and importance of the sector will merit specific consideration and that charitable status and fiscal treatment might finally be separated.[69] Broad considerations of policy should be properly informed, not simply by a calculation of what the sector provides in facilitated access or receives in tax allowances, but by a thorough analysis of the extent to which schools can feasibly be expected to provide more. This might well have appeared too politically inflammatory a decade ago, and the broad cross-charity approach certainly allowed some difficult issues to be sidestepped, but the irony of the social benefit test protecting the tax privileges of richly endowed schools, more than those unendowed schools which struggle to raise sufficient funds, will not have gone unnoticed. It is not obvious why schools which have been fortunate enough to receive substantial funds from wealthy benefactors should be treated more favourably than those which rely on fee-paying parents. Put simply, is education, or is it not, so fundamentally beneficial to society as a whole, that the application of funds to its advancement, regardless of the number or wealth of the few who benefit directly, should be regarded as charitable?

If the perceived mischief is the automatic entitlement of independent schools, and perhaps other charities, to fiscal privileges, adjustments to their fiscal status should be made in the fiscal arena and should not be confused with concepts of what constitutes a charity or the duties owed by charity trustees. If tax advantages were to continue to be available in some measure, entitlement to them could properly be made dependent on the way a charity operates or, more specifically,

[68] Suzi Leather, Chair of the Commission until July 2012, had signalled an unease with a practice which had grown up of favouring 'action plans' and informal regulatory 'investigations' rather than statutory inquiries, perhaps deliberately to limit the Commission's accountability: 'We also need to be more relaxed about challenge from the charity tribunal … frankly I don't think we should endlessly work in such a way that it's impossible for the decisions we've made to be challenged': 'Interview: Dame Suzi Leather' Third Sector, 21 February 2011, available at www.thirdsector.co.uk/interview-dame-suzi-leather/governance/article/1055835. A new trend towards using statutory inquiries has since been reported by the National Audit Office: *The regulatory effectiveness of the Charity Commission*, HC 813 2013–14 (4 December 2013) paras 3.8, 3.9.

[69] Trustees' duties might be seen as a third area which should also be kept separate.

how its funds are applied.[70] It is beyond the remit of this book, and the expertise of its author, to propose an appropriate test or formula, but it is doubted whether one could sensibly be drafted which would take into account the provision of other (non-financial) benefits, as opposed to simply the level of facilitated access.[71] The impact of any such proposal should be properly assessed and any test should be defined, and any discretion exercisable, only by reference to criteria which are both coherent and achievable.

There may be considerable appeal in a broadened definition of charity, which embraces all purposes for the public good. It would avoid much of the difficulty and expense of the present test and end the much-criticised rejection of (and the need for ways to circumvent) the law relating to non-charitable purpose trusts in England and Wales.[72] The availability of tax privileges would still require attention, however, perhaps even more so. If this seems a step too far, the uncertainty in the law surrounding loss of charitable status, including the artificial distinction which appears to divide charitable trusts and companies, needs to be resolved, not least before any proposal to remove charitable status, or to adopt the Scottish charity test, is pursued.

Final Comment

> *It is rather startling to find the established procedure of so many years suddenly set aside by an administrative department of their own motion.*
>
> Lord Macnaghten[73]

There are differences, of course, in the context between Lord Macnaghten's musings and the present situation, but perhaps the greatest is that, in this case, the established law seems to have been set aside not just by a part of the executive but also by a court of record. There is undoubtedly an attractive logic in the proposition that if express exclusions of the poor are wrong, then excluding the poor on the terms or in practice is also wrong and should not be countenanced. The propositions that independent schools should be required to offer their facilities to the community, or to provide financial assistance wherever possible, or both, might well be attractive to a significant proportion of the population.[74] The law, however,

[70] Note that previous discussions on the separation of fiscal privileges and charitable status have not always sought to exclude fee-charging schools, but have included education generally or the teaching of, or research in, selected subjects only: G Cross, 'Some Recent Developments in the Law of Charity' (1956) 72 *LQR* 187, 204 and 207.

[71] eg, The Higher Education Act 2004 prohibited universities from charging more than £6,000 pa unless they obtain approval, based on their measures to encourage poor students to apply.

[72] P Ford, 'Supervising Charities: A Scottish-civilian Alternative' (2006) 10 *Edinburgh Law Review* 352, 377, where the author concludes that the inevitable increase in charity registrations would better reflect a pluralistic society (which is unable to arrive at a consensus on which organisations should be charitable) and avoid the state being an inappropriate arbiter.

[73] *Pemsel* (n 17) 591 (Lord Macnaghten).

[74] It should be noted that the author has expressed no opinion on this: as a matter of policy, it is irrelevant to the question of law which has been the subject of this book.

has developed according to a technical meaning of charity, which supports neither proposition and which presents substantial and unresolved difficulties in their potential application. That law was unchanged by the 2006 Act: the statutory public benefit requirement was a modern restatement of old law, but the public benefit requirement which has evolved appears to be quite new.

This tale has indeed been a sorry one. An approach which relies on threats and bullying is a shameful approach to take, and one which should be neither perpetuated nor repeated. The public, and perhaps the charitable sector in particular, deserves to be treated fairly and honestly and charity trustees, the majority of whom give their time and expertise voluntarily, should know exactly what is expected of them.

The plan required legislation and Parliament failed. The issues which needed to be confronted have still to be confronted and resolved. The test of charitable status for fee-charging charities may appear transformed, and trustees' duties extended, but it seems far from certain that the Tribunal's decision would be upheld if it were ever to reach the Supreme Court. The title of this book asks whether the 'new' public benefit requirement has made sense of charity law and one wonders how Lord Macnaghten or Lord Simonds, for example, might have responded. Alert to public perceptions and political pressures, they might have felt some sympathy with the Commission or recognised the procreative tendencies of an equitable jurisdiction,[75] but one suspects that they would feel some dismay that a requirement, not unfamiliar to them, had been robbed of the sense which had once attached to it. In the Tribunal's place, or even in the highest court, it seems that their Lordships would have trodden a much more conservative path. With unswerving regard to legal precedent and established practice, one suspects that their conclusions might have been critical of the legislature's shortcomings, but at the same time resounded with echoes of the Preamble and *Pemsel*, rather than policy and compromise, satisfied that, in so doing, they were avoiding the uncertainty which otherwise would be bound to result and which now feels uncomfortably familiar.

[75] Lord Denning famously commented that 'Equity is not past the age of child bearing': *Eves v Eves* [1975] 1 WLR 1338.

BIBLIOGRAPHY

Albery, M, 'Trusts for the Benefit of the Inhabitants of a Locality' (1940) 56 *Law Quarterly Review* 49.

Atiyah, PS, 'Public Benefit in Charities' (1958) 21 *Modern Law Review* 138.

Bell, J and Engle, G (eds), *Cross on Statutory Interpretation*, 3rd edn (Oxford, Oxford University Press, 2005).

Breen, O, Ford, P and Morgan, G, 'Cross-border Issues in the Regulation of Charities: Experiences from the UK and Ireland' (2009) 11(3) *International Journal of Not-for-Profit Law* 5.

Bright, S, 'Charity and Trusts for the Public Benefit—Time for a Re-think' (1989) *Conveyancer and Property Lawyer* 28.

Brunyate, J, 'The Legal Definition of Charity' (1945) 61 *Law Quarterly Review* 268.

Buckley, C, 'The Charities Act 2006: Consolidation or Reform?' (2009) 11 *Charity Law & Practice Review* 1.

Burchfield, J, 'Private Action, Public Benefit' (2003) 2 *Private Client Business* 110.

Burkes, *Genealogical and Heraldic History of the Landed Gentry*, 18th edn (London, Burke's Peerage Ltd, 1964–72) Vol 3.

Claricoat, J, and Phillips, H, 'Removal from the Register' (1997/98) 5 *Charity Law & Practice Review* 13.

Clarke, P, 'The Charitable Status of Rifle Clubs: Out with a Bang?' (1992/93) 1 *Charity Law & Practice Review* 137.

—— 'The Charitable Status of Rifle Clubs: The Explosion Occurs' (1993/94) 2 *Charity Law & Practice Review* 97.

Cross, G, 'Some Recent Developments in the Law of Charity' (1956) 72 *Law Quarterly Review* 187.

Dawson, I and Alder, J, 'The Nature of the Proprietary Interest of a Charitable Company or a Community Interest Company in its Property' (2007) 21 *Trusts Law International* 3.

Dunn, A, '*McGovern v Attorney-General*' (2013–14) 16 *Charity Law & Practice Review* 105.

—— 'Regulatory Shifts: Developing Sector Participation in Regulation for Charities in England and Wales' [2014] *Legal Studies* 1.

Dutton, J, 'Charitable Companies Ceasing to be Charitable' (2000) 7 *Charity Law & Practice Review* 31.

Ford, P, 'The Scottish Charity Test: Do We Really Need It?' (2004) 8 *Edinburgh Law Review* 408.

—— 'Supervising Charities: A Scottish-civilian Alternative' (2006) 10 *Edinburgh Law Review* 352.

Garton, J, *Public Benefit in Charity Law* (Oxford, Oxford University Press, 2013).

—— '*Re Macduff* and the Charity of the Wise' (2013–14) 16 *Charity Law & Practice Review* 21.

Gousmett, M, *The Charitable Purposes Exemption from Income Tax: Pitt to Pemsel 1798–1891* (University of Canterbury New Zealand, 2009).

Gravells, N, 'Public Purpose Trusts' (1977) 40 *Modern Law Review* 397.

Hancox, N, 'An Education in Charity' (2008) 158 *New Law Journal* 113.

Harding, M, 'Trusts for Religious Purposes and the Question of Public Benefit' (2008) 71 *Modern Law Review* 159.

Hodgson, M and McNeely, A, 'Trusteeship and the Charitable Corporation'(1984) 4(2) *The Philanthropist* 26.

Holmes, R, 'Purposes, Descriptions of Purposes and Drafting an Objects Clause' [2009] *Private Client Business* 295.

Jaconelli, J, 'Independent Schools, Purpose Trusts and Human Rights' [1996] *Conveyancer and Property Lawyer* 24.

Jessel, C, 'Public Benefit Gifts by Trustees of Land' (1998) 72 *Conveyancer and Property Lawyer* 246.

Jones, G, *History of the Law of Charity 1532–1827* (Cambridge, Cambridge University Press, 1969).

—— 'Charitable Trusts: What is Public Benefit?' (1974) 33 *Cambridge Law Journal* 63.

Lejeune, A, in *Burke's Genealogical and Heraldic History of the Landed Gentry*, 18th edn (London, Burke's Peerage Ltd, 1964–72).

Luxton, P, *The Law of Charities* (Oxford, Oxford University Press, 2001).

—— 'Making Law? Parliament v The Charity Commission' (Politeia, 2009).

—— 'Opening Pandora's Box: The Upper Tribunal's Decision on Public Benefit and Independent Schools' (2012–13) 15 *Charity Law & Practice Review* 27.

—— '*Dingle v Turner* Forty Years On' (2013–14) 16 *Charity Law & Practice Review* 43.

Luxton, P and Evans, N, 'Cogent and Cohesive? Two Recent Charity Commission Decisions on the Advancement of Religion' (2011) 75 *Conveyancer and Property Lawyer* 144.

Marshall, F, 'The Charities Act (Northern Ireland) 2008—Cause for Concern?' (2013) 15 *Charity Law & Practice Review* 75.

McKenna, A, 'Applications to First-Tier Tribunal (Charity) by Persons Affected' (2013–14) 16 *Charity Law & Practice Review* 147.

Meakin, R, *The Law of Charitable Status: Maintenance and Removal* (Cambridge, Cambridge University Press, 2008).

Megarry, R, (1951) 67 *Law Quarterly Review* 164.

Morgan, G, 'Public Benefit and Charitable Status: Assessing a 20-year Process of Reforming the Primary Legal Framework for Voluntary Activity in the UK' (2012) 3 *Voluntary Sector Review* 67.

Morris, D, *Schools: An Education in Charity Law* (Aldershot, Dartmouth Publishing, 1996).

—— 'Fee-Paying Hospitals and Charitable Status: A New Dawn or Lost Opportunities?' (2007) 18 *King's College Law Journal* 455.

—— 'The First-tier Tribunal (Charity): Enhanced Access to Justice for Charities or a Case of David versus Goliath?' (2010) 29 *Civil Justice Quarterly* 491.

Moss, F, 'New Ingredient' (2011) 155(40) *Solicitors' Journal* 10.

Mummery, J, '*The Commissioners for Special Purposes of Income Tax v Pemsel*' (2013–14) 16 *Charity Law & Practice Review* 1.

Nobles, R, 'Selling Charity' (1983) 46 *Modern Law Review* 782.

Oosterhoff, AH and Gillese, EE, *Text, Commentary and Cases on Trusts*, 6th edn (Toronto, Carswell, 1998.

Owen, D, *English Philanthropy 1660–1960* (Massachusetts, Harvard University Press, 1964).

Palmer, H, 'Trustees' Responsibilities and the Public Benefit Requirement' [2008] *Private Client Business* 413.

Partington, M, *Introduction to the English Legal System 2014–15*, 9th edn (Oxford, Oxford University Press, 2014).

Pettit, P, *Equity and the Law of Trusts*, 12th edn (Oxford, Oxford University Press, 2012).

Picarda, H, 'Charity in Roman Law: Roots and Parallels' (1992/93) 1 *Charity Law & Practice Review* 9.

—— *The Law and Practice Relating to Charities*, 4th edn (Haywards Heath, Bloomsbury Professional, 2010) and First Supplement (Haywards Heath, Bloomsbury Professional 2014).

—— '*Thornton v Howe*: A Sound Principle or a Seminal Case Past its Best Buy Date?' (2013–14) 16 *Charity Law & Practice Review* 85.

Radan, P and Stewart, C, *Principles of Australian Equity and Trusts* (Chatswood NSW, LexisNexis Butterworth, 2009).

Raz, J, 'Legal Principles and the Limits of Law' (1972) 81 *Yale Law Journal* 823.

Rivington, S, *The History of Tonbridge School* (Rivingtons, 1869).

Sedley, S, 'Judicial Politics' (2010) 34(4) *London Review of Books* 15.

Smith, J, 'Notes on the Finance Acts: Section 30 of and Schedule 6 to the Finance Act 2010: Charity Re-defined' [2010] *British Tax Review* 415.

Swadling, W, 'Explaining Resulting Trusts' (2008) 124 *Law Quarterly Review* 72.

Synge, M, '*Independent Schools Council v Charity Commission*' (2012) 75 *Modern Law Review* 624.

Thayer, JB, *A Preliminary Treatise on Evidence* (Boston, Little, Brown, 1898).

Tyerman, C, *A History of Harrow School 1324–1991* (Oxford, Oxford University Press, 2000).

Virgo, G, *The Principles of Equity and Trusts* (Oxford, Oxford University Press, 2012).

Warburton, J, 'One Definition for all Purposes in the New Millennium' [2000] *British Tax Review* 144.

—— 'Charities and Public Benefit—From Confusion to Light?' (2008) 10 *Charity Law & Practice Review* 2.

Warburton, J, Morris, D, and Riddle, NF, (eds), *Tudor on Charities*, 9th edn (London, Sweet & Maxwell, 2003).

Wendell Holmes, O, 'The Path of the Law' (1997) 110 *Harvard Law Review* 991.

Williams, I, *The Alms Trade* (London, Unwin Hyman, 1989).

Wrangham, F, *The Works of the Rev Thomas Zouch … With a memoir of his life* (York, 1820).

INDEX

www.ingramcontent.com/pod-product-compliance
Lightning Source LLC
LaVergne TN
LVHW052301200926
848481LV00002B/428
9781509917730